Varanasi & Bodh Gaya

Shade of the Bodhi Tree

A Photographic Exploration

Scott Shaw

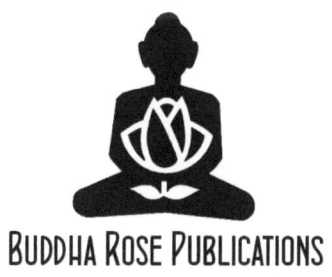

Buddha Rose Publications

Varanasi and Bodh Gaya: Shade of the Bodhi Tree
A Photographic Exploration
Copyright © 1985 & 2014 by Scott Shaw
www.scottshaw.com
All Rights Reserved

No part of this book may be reproduced in any manner
without the expressed written permission of the
author or the publishing company.

First Edition 2014

ISBN: 1-877792-79-9
ISBN 13: 978-1-877792-79-3

Printed in the United States of America
10 9 8 7 6 5 4 3 2 1

Varanasi & Bodh Gaya
Shade of the Bodhi Tree

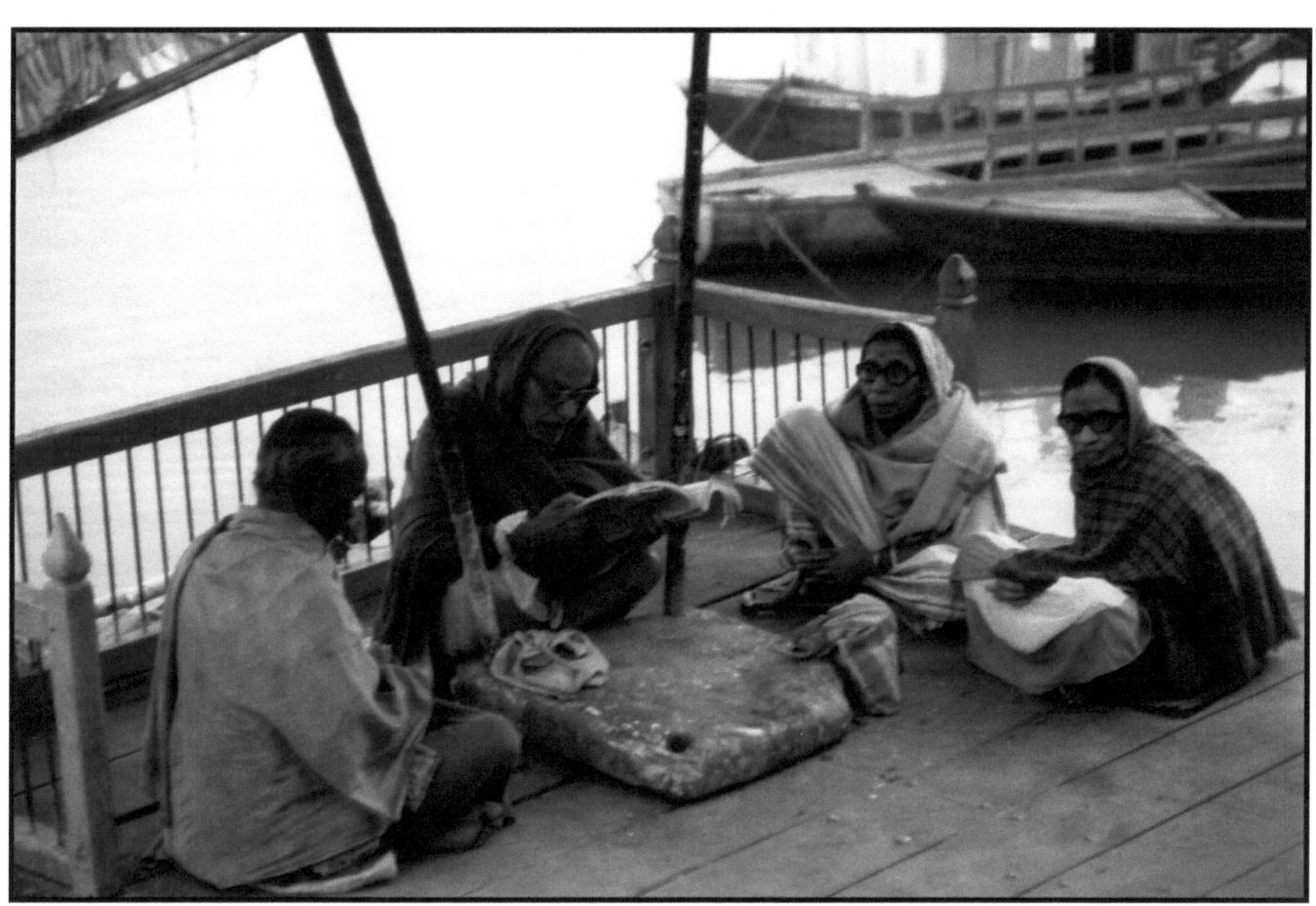

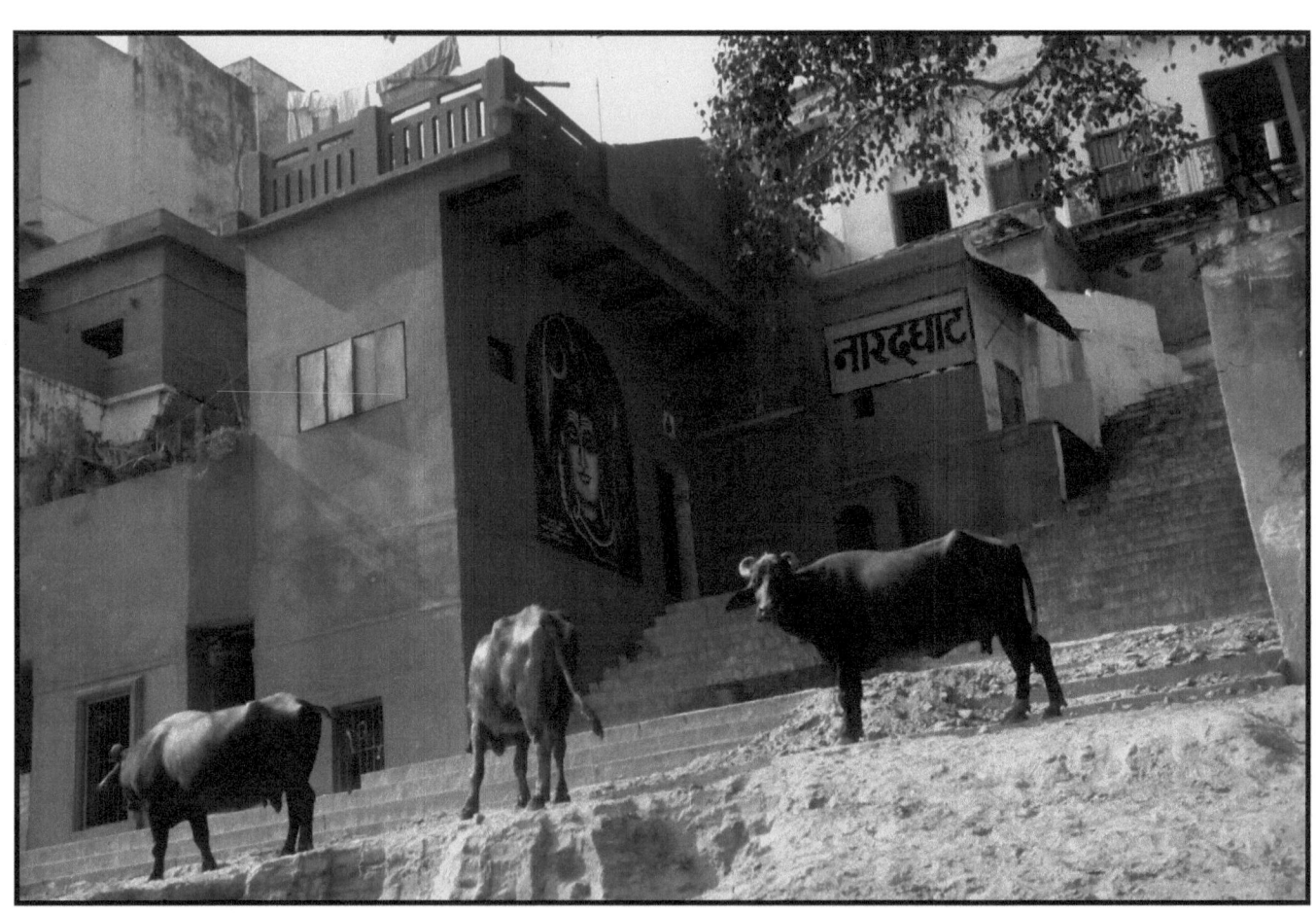

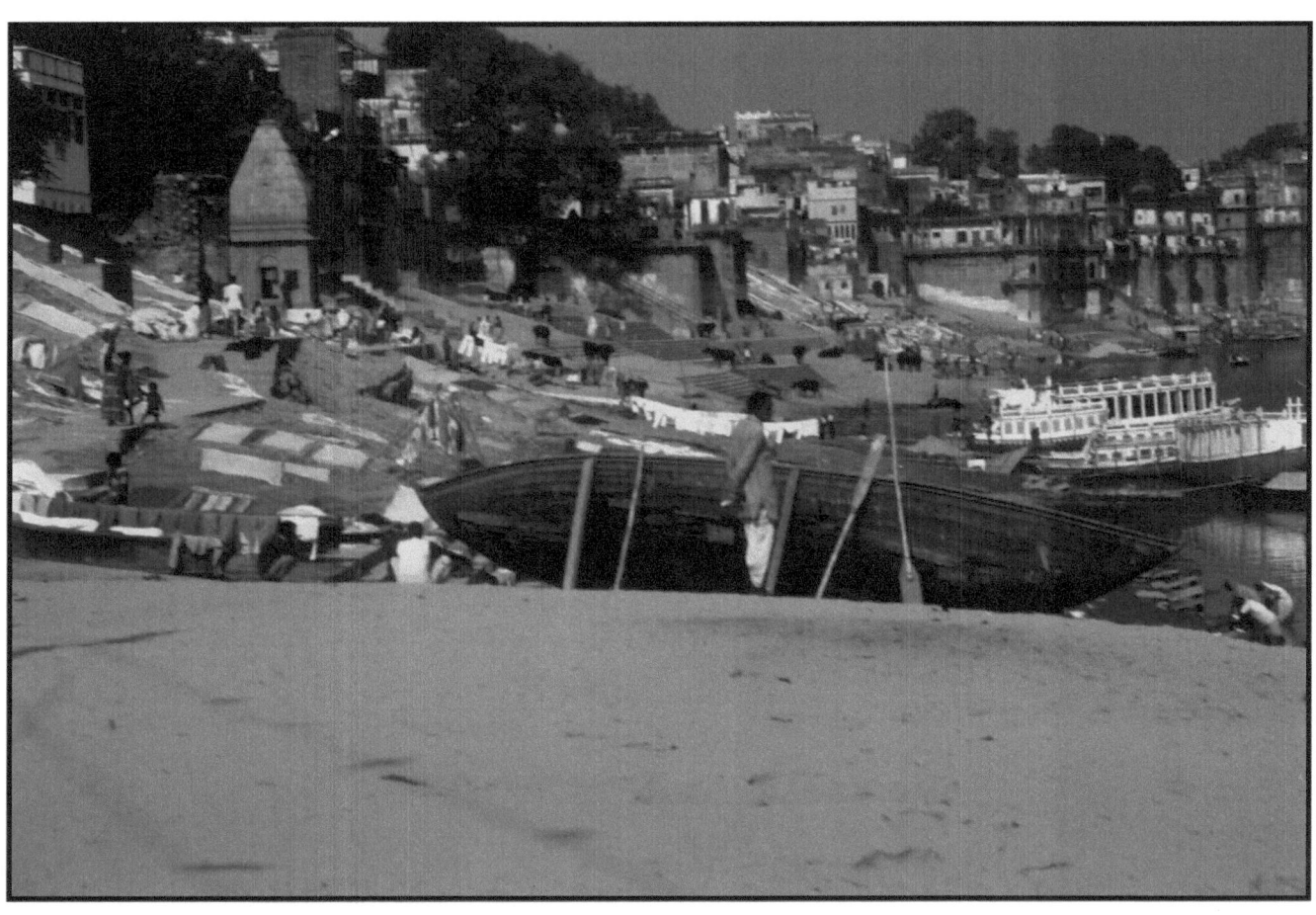

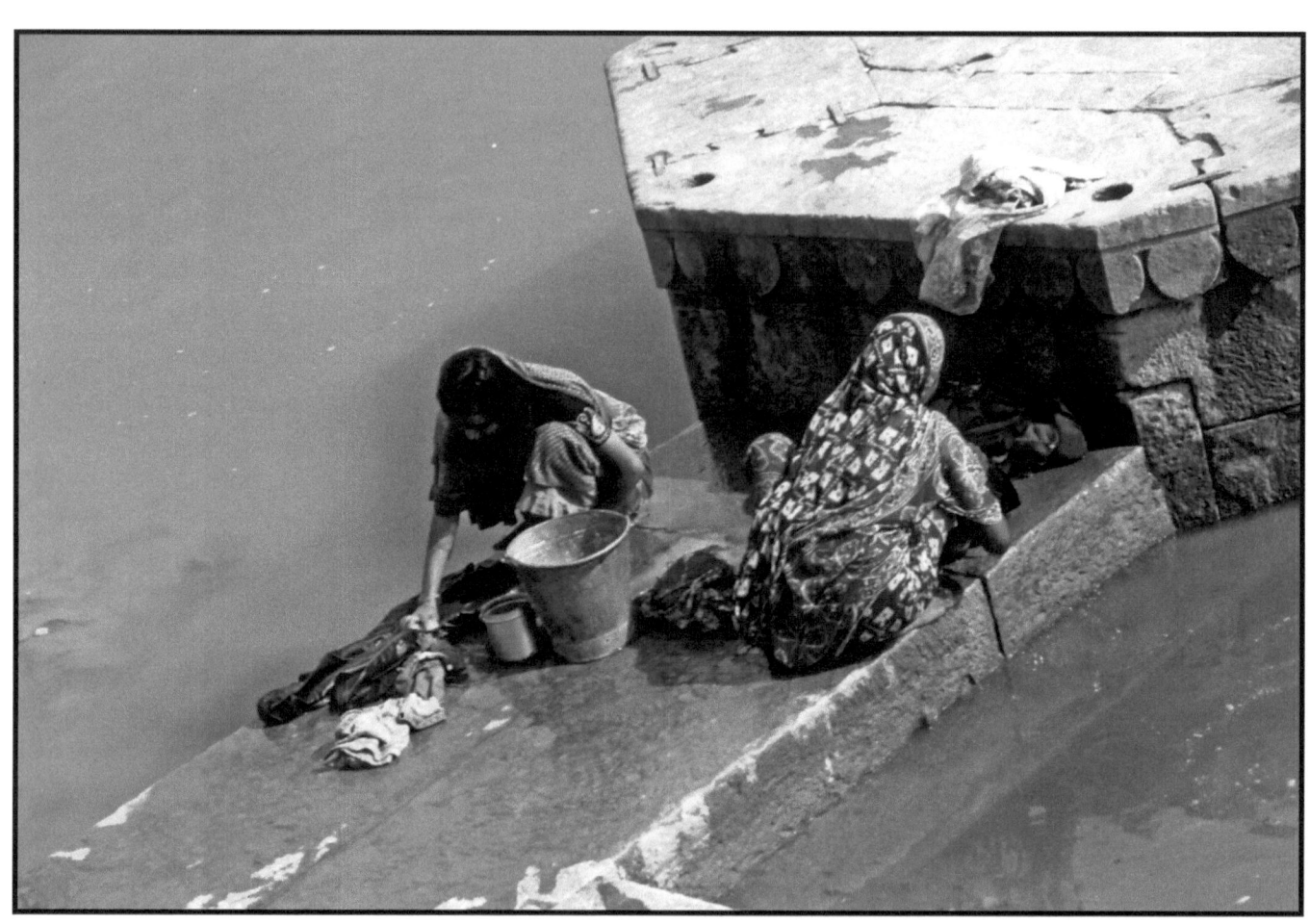

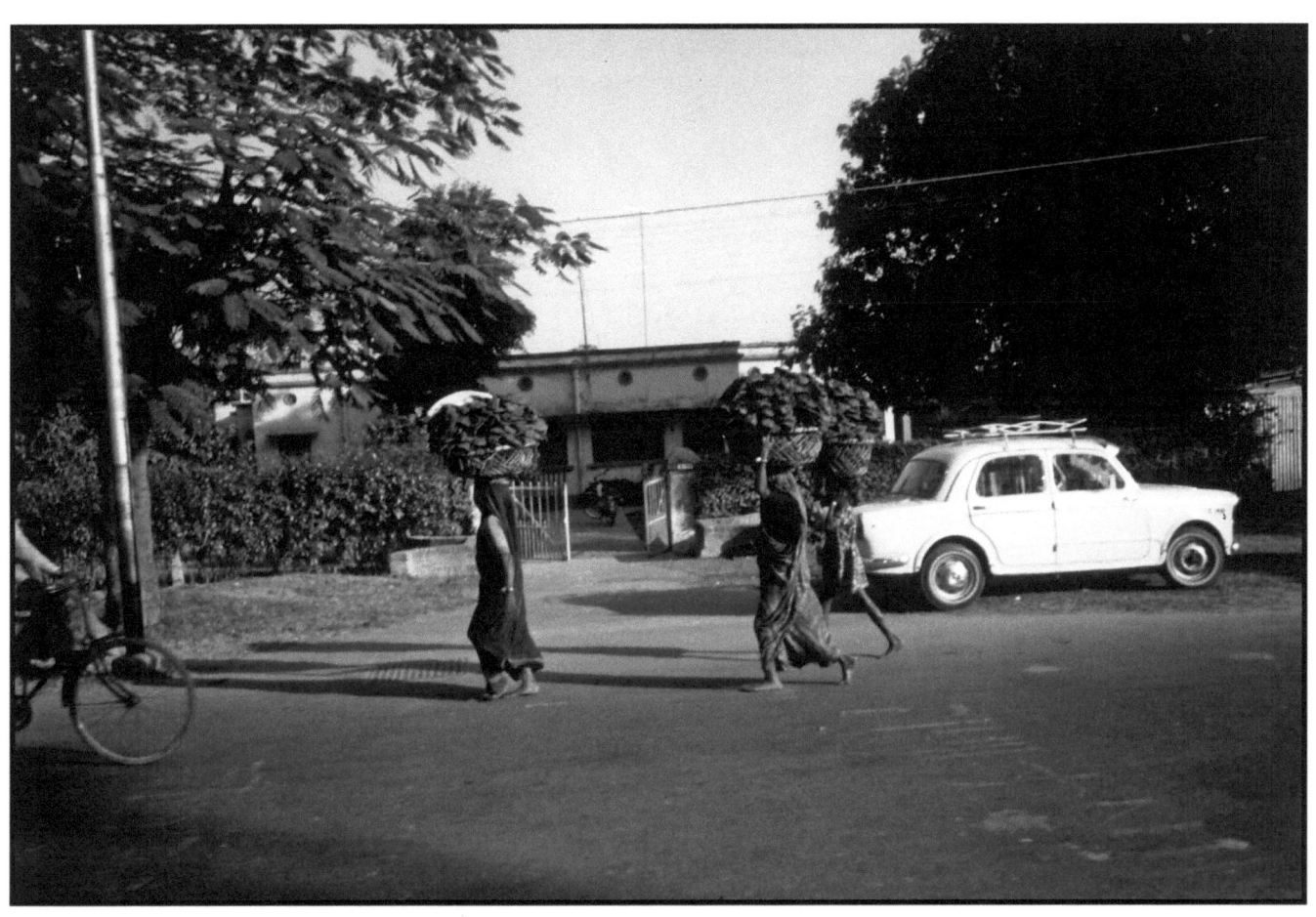

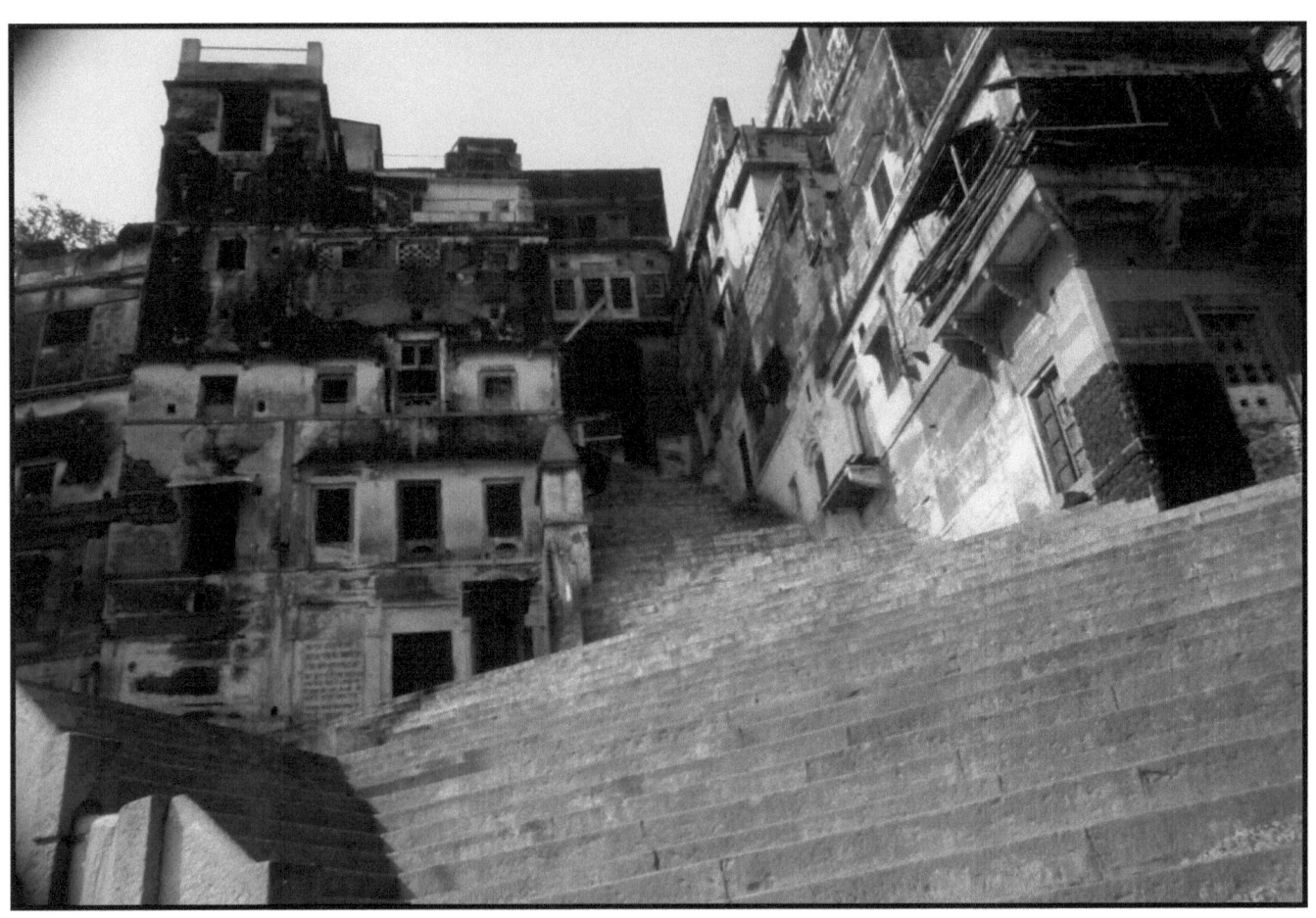

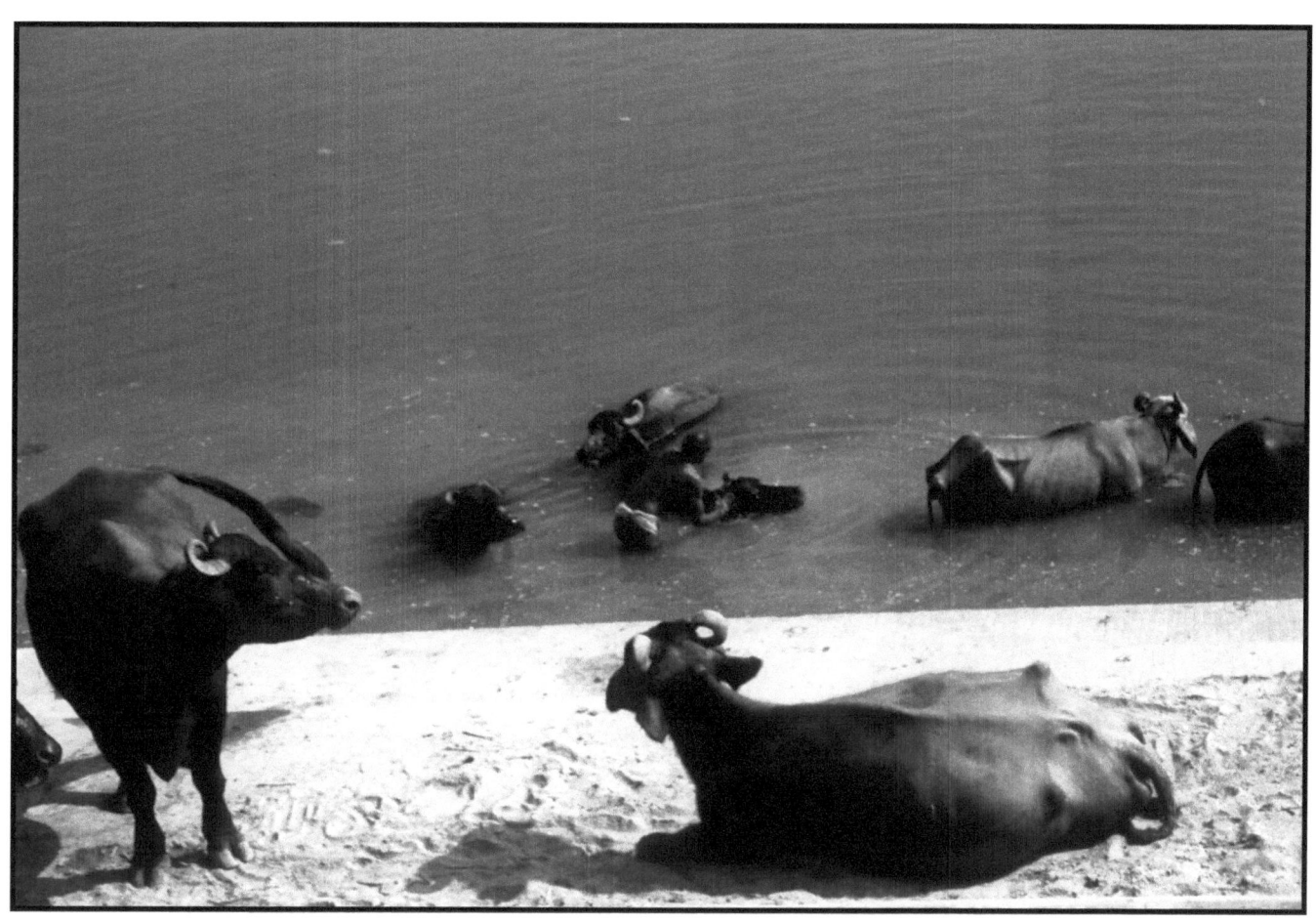

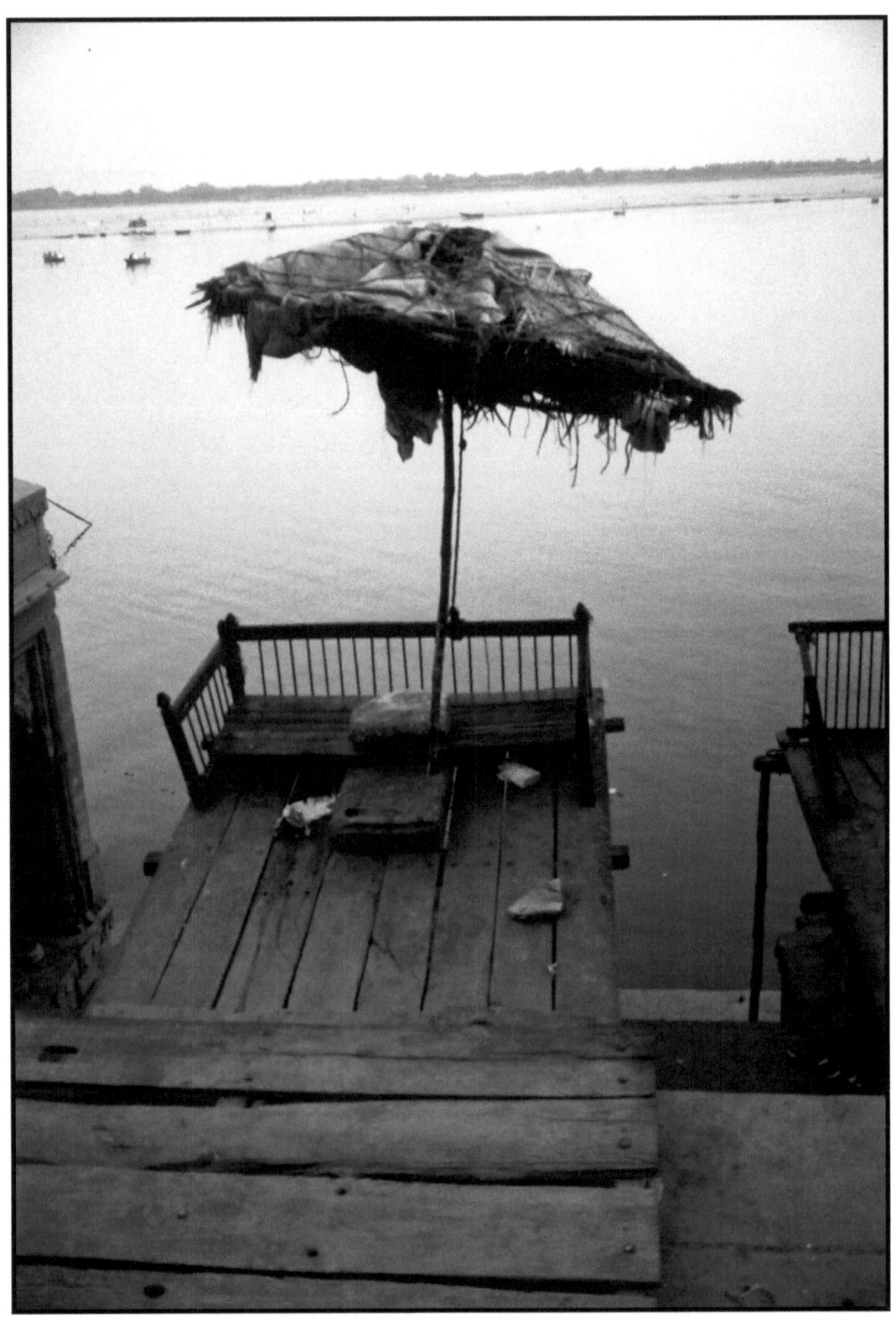

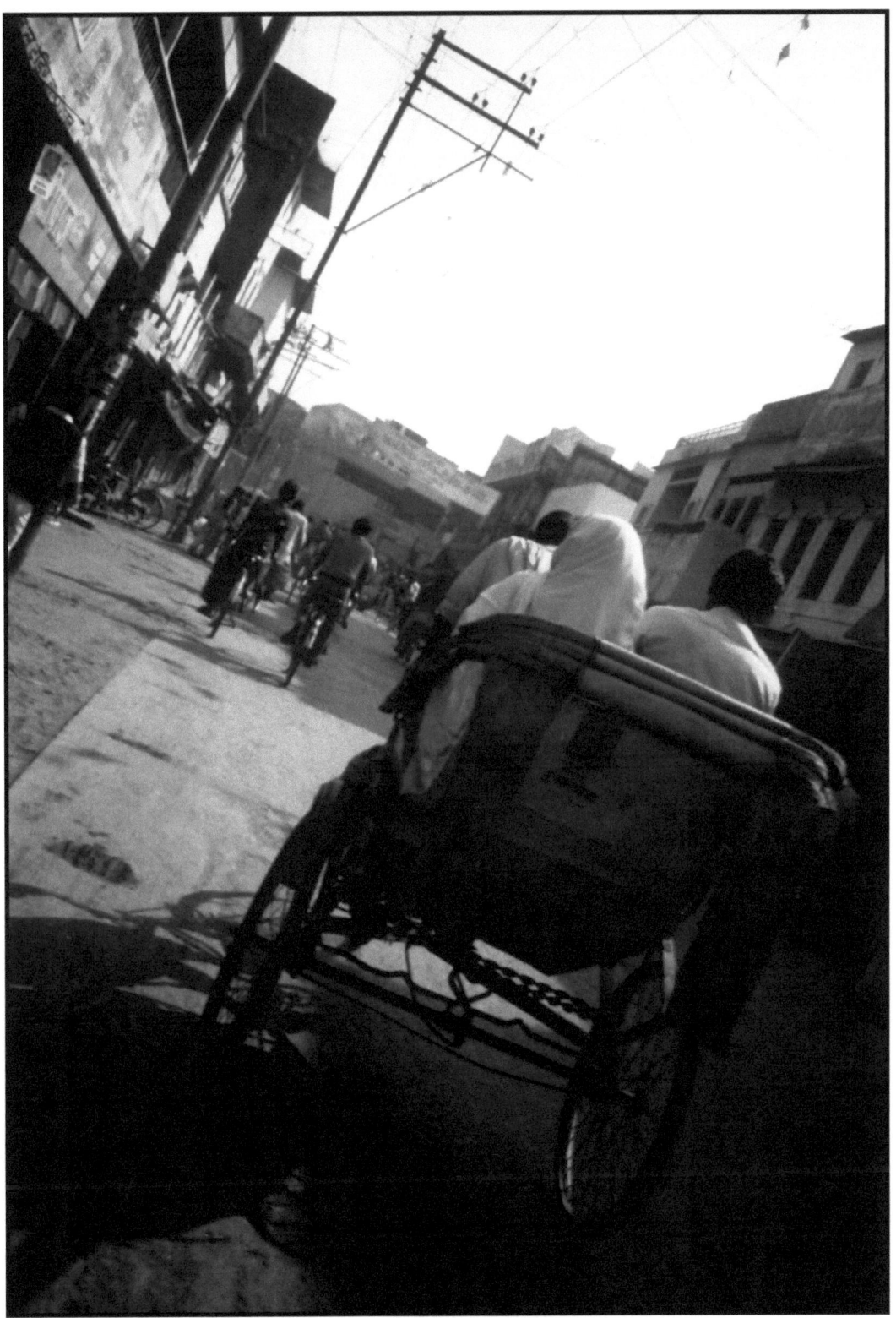

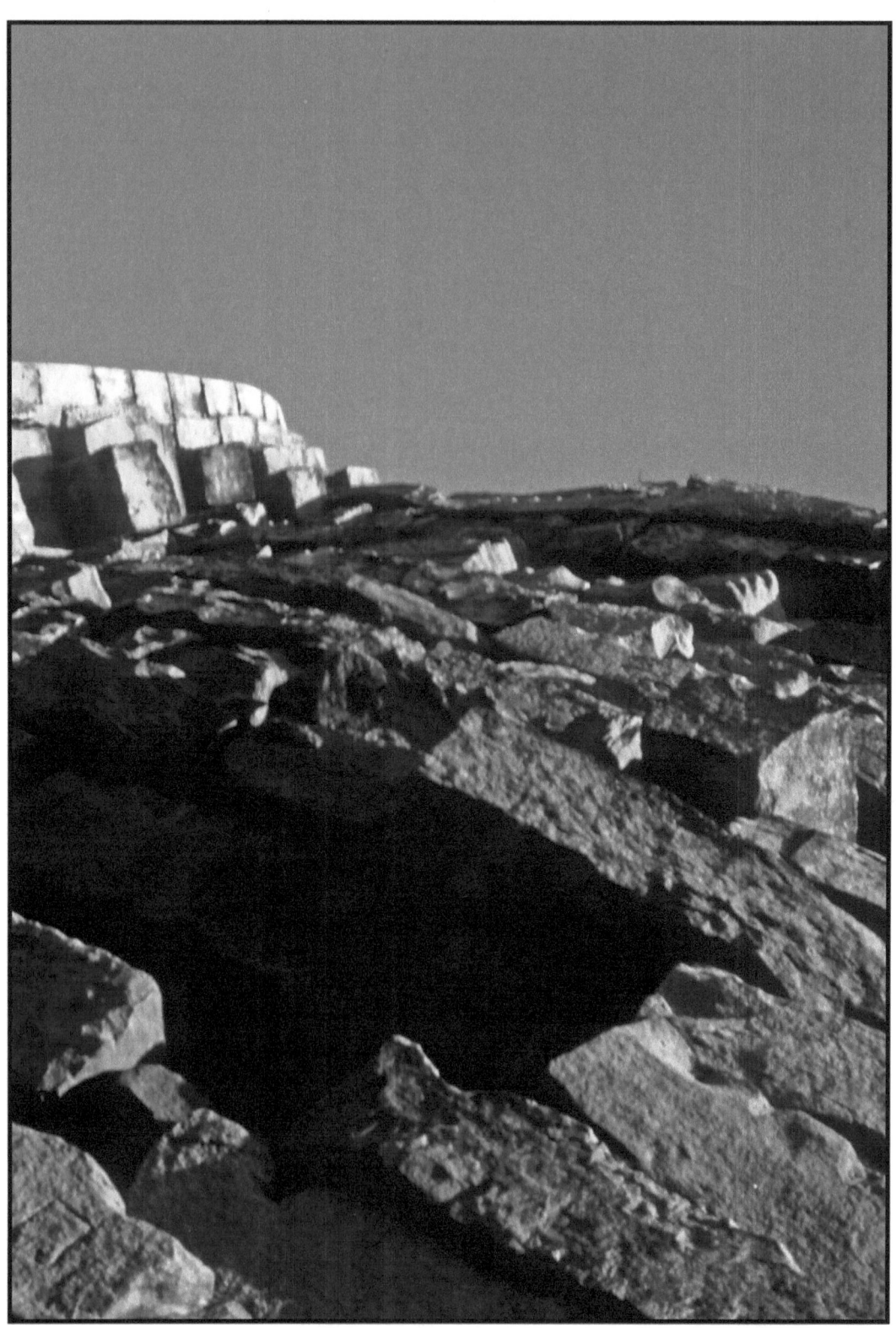

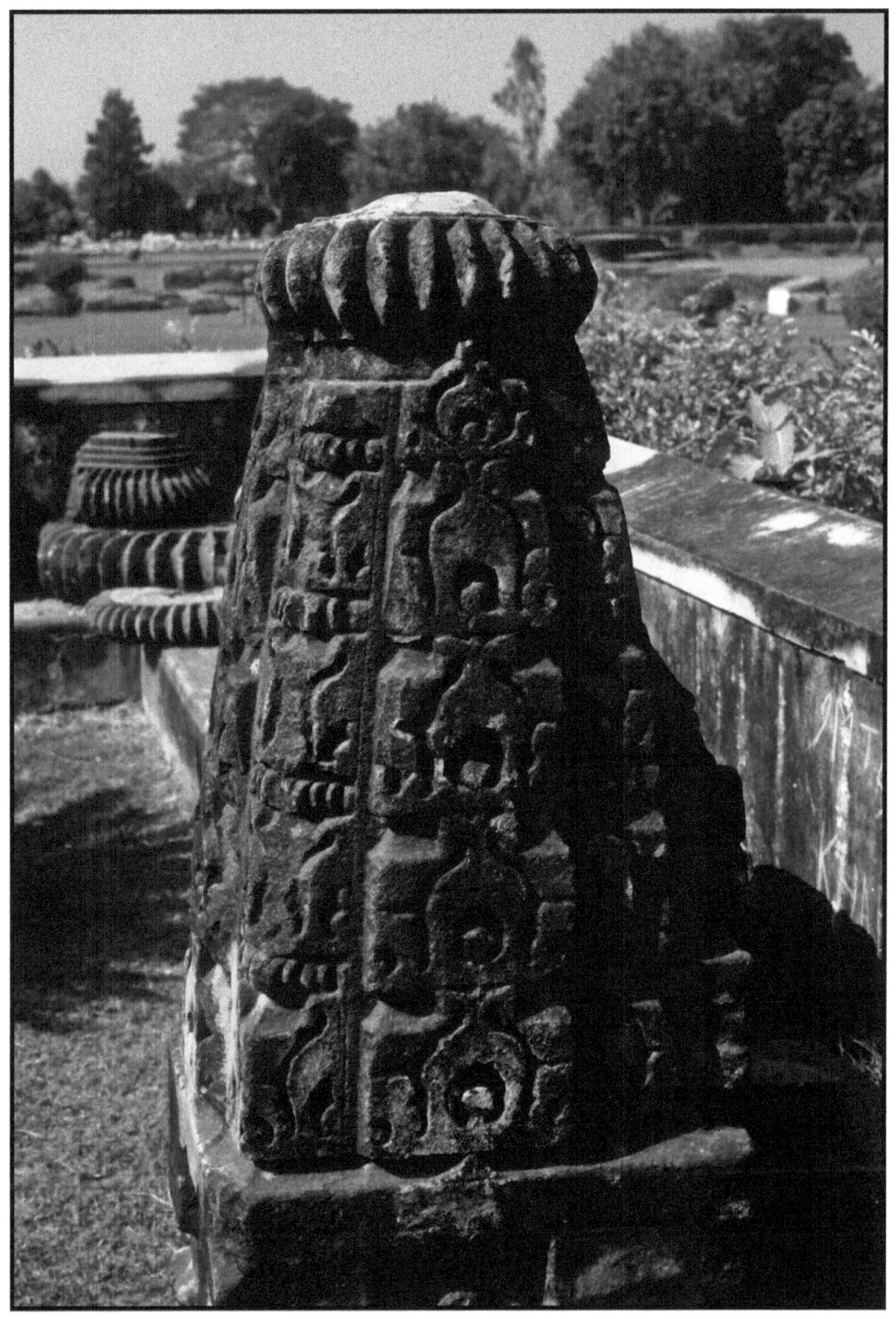

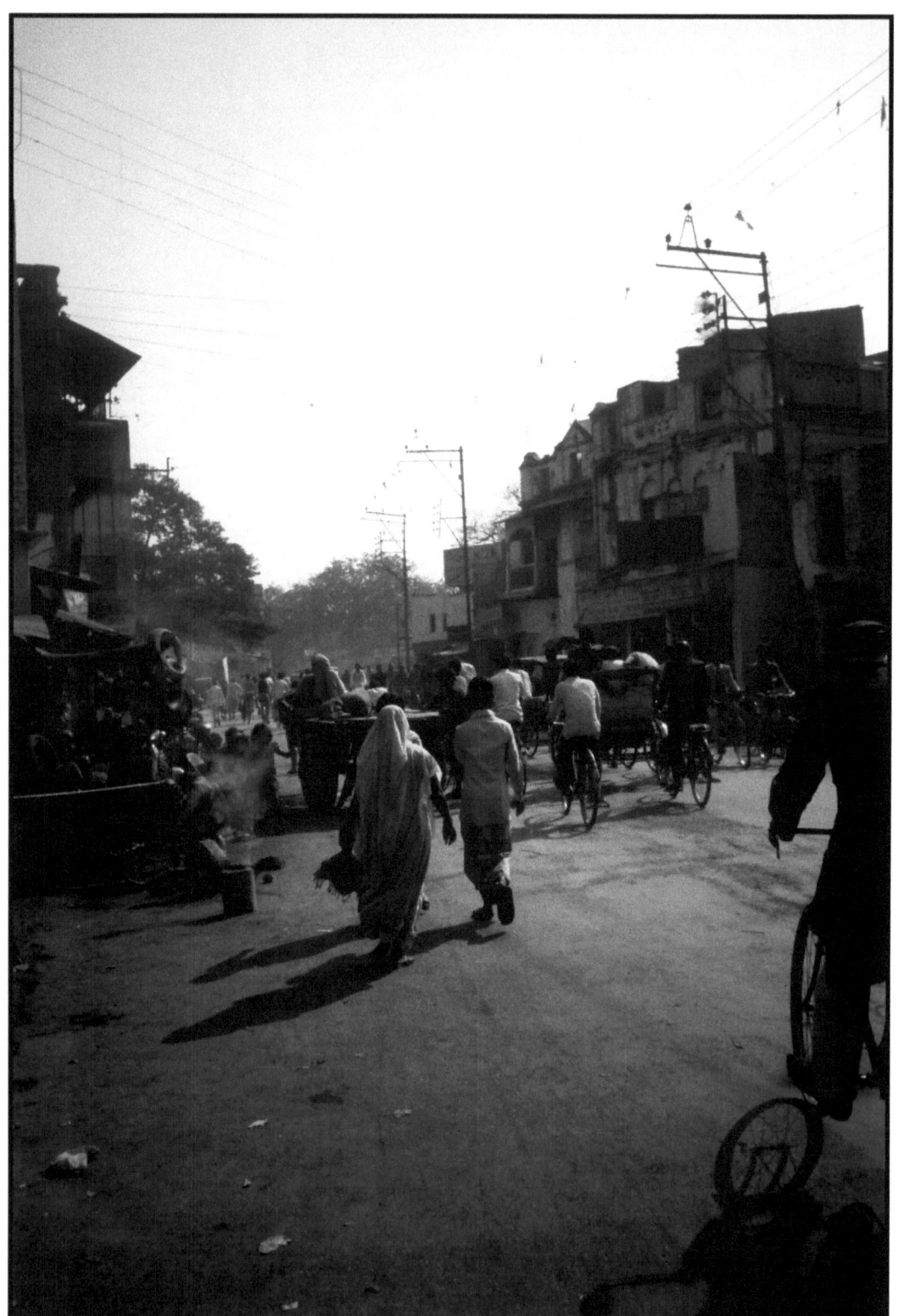

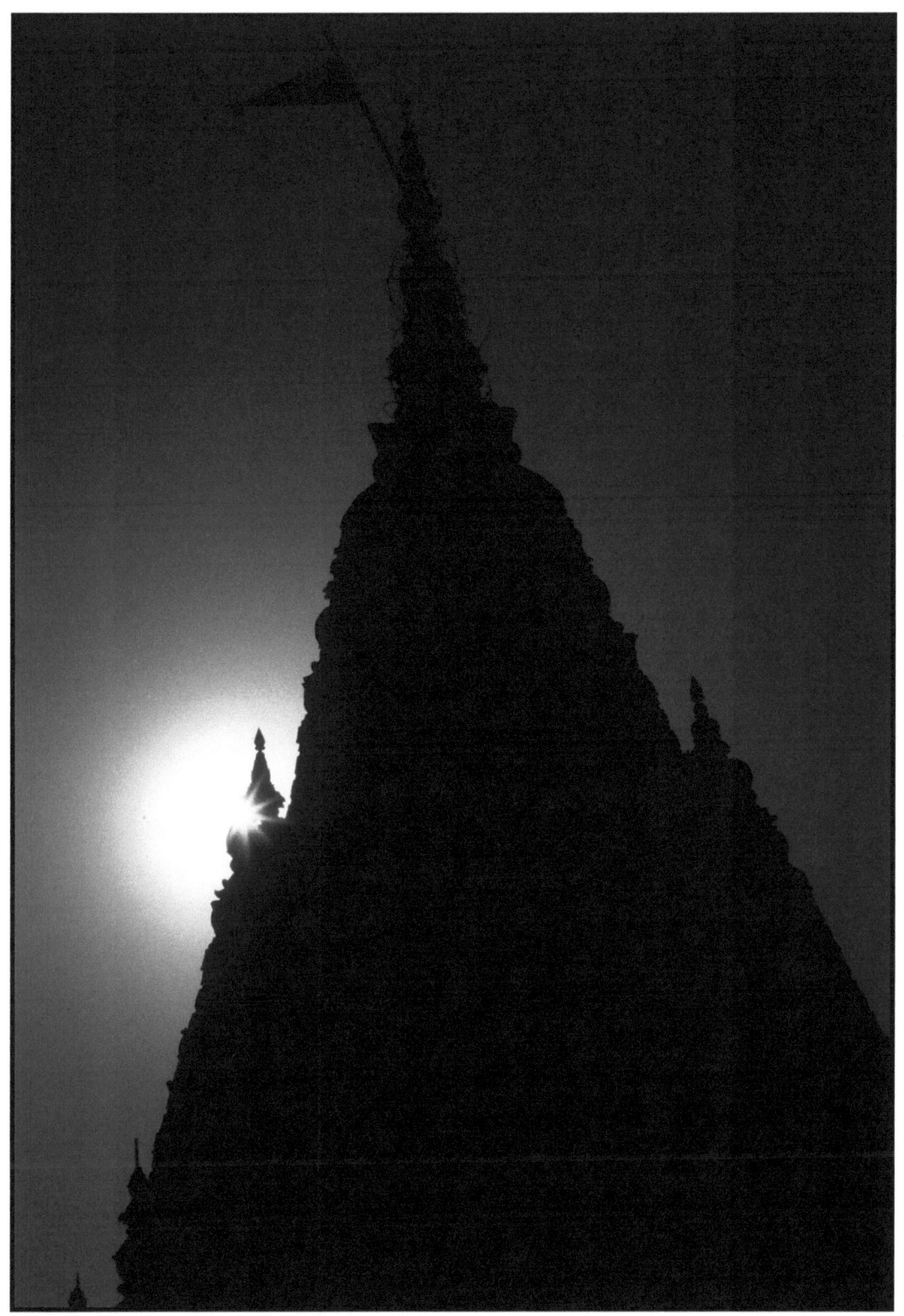

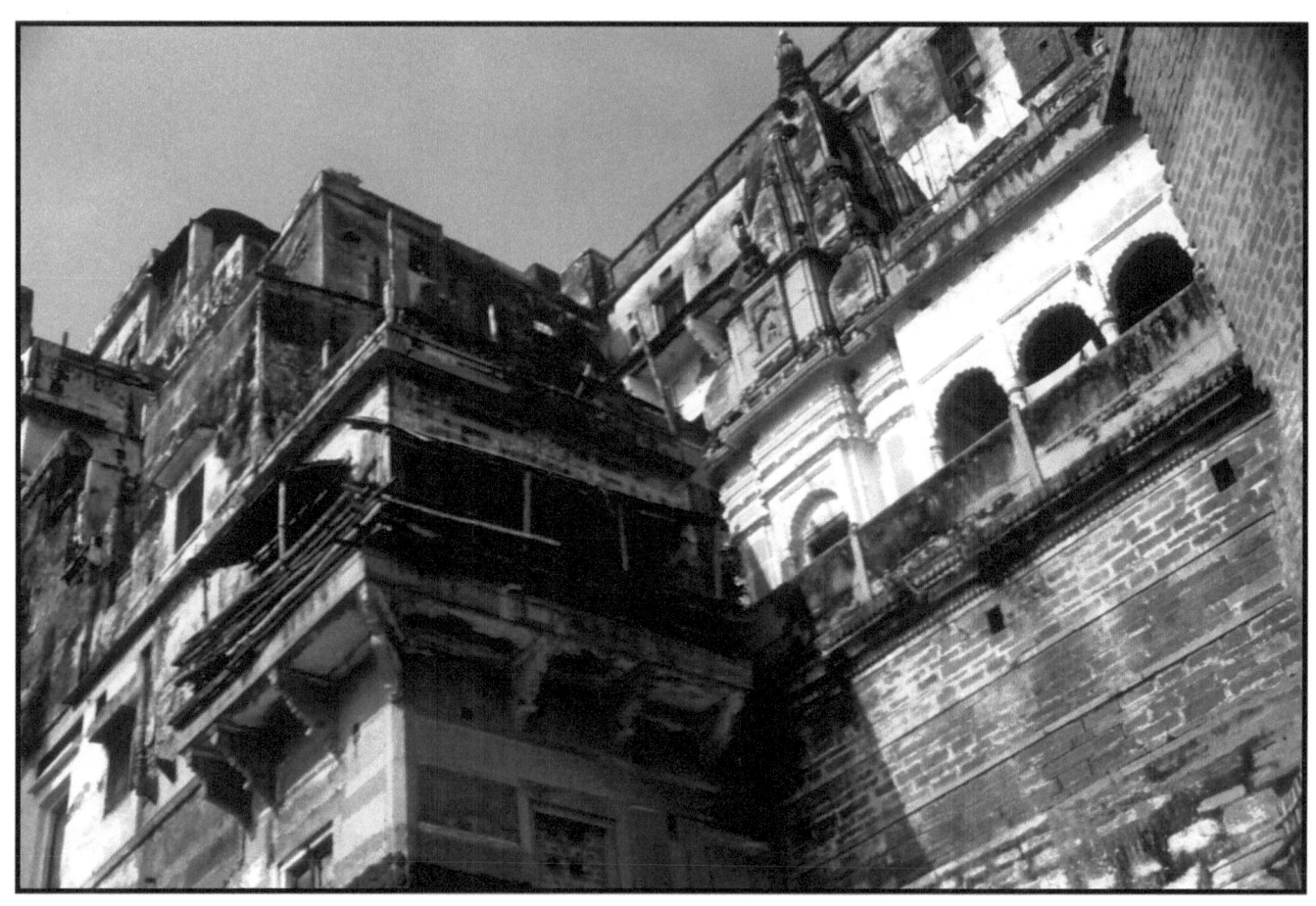

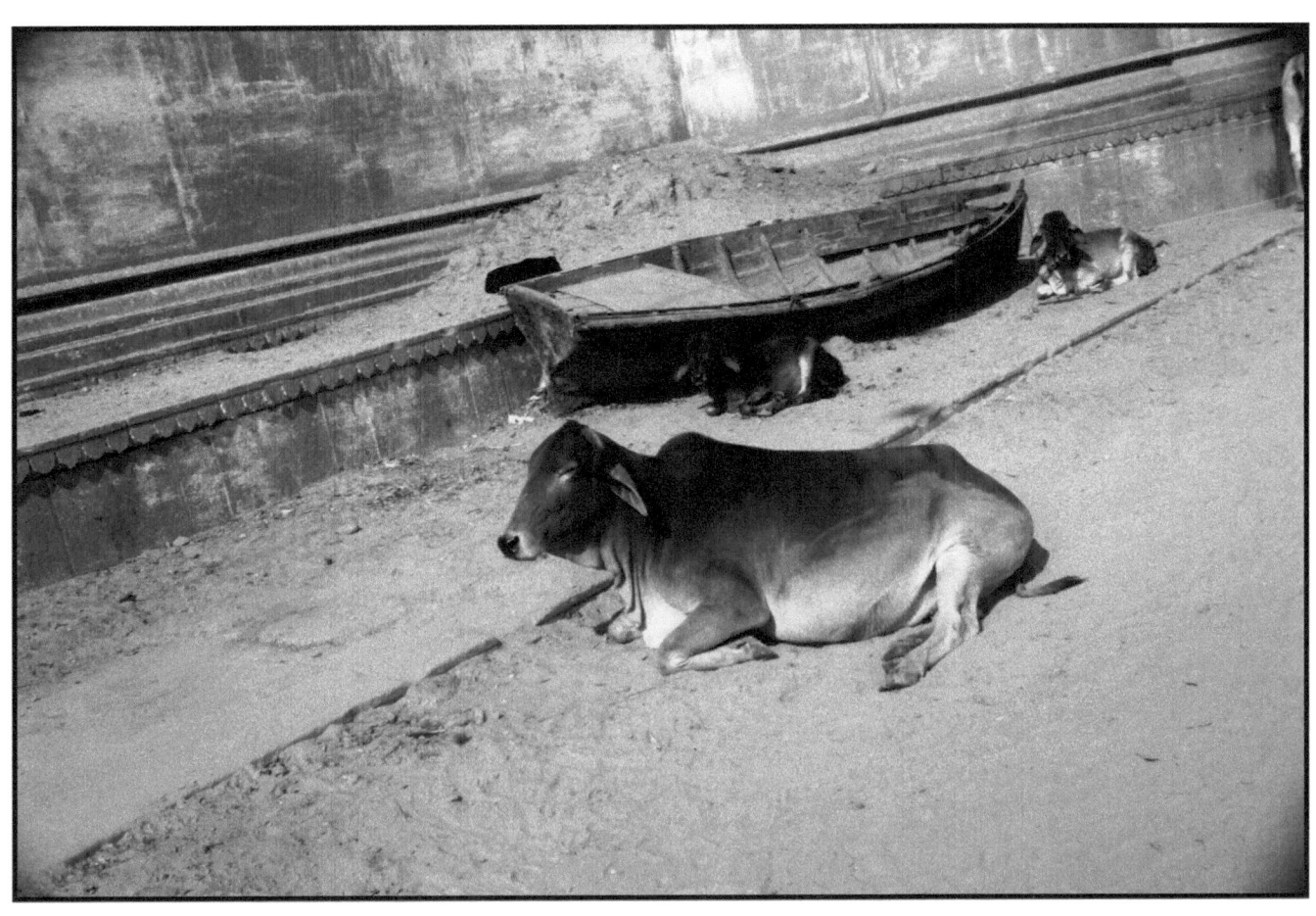

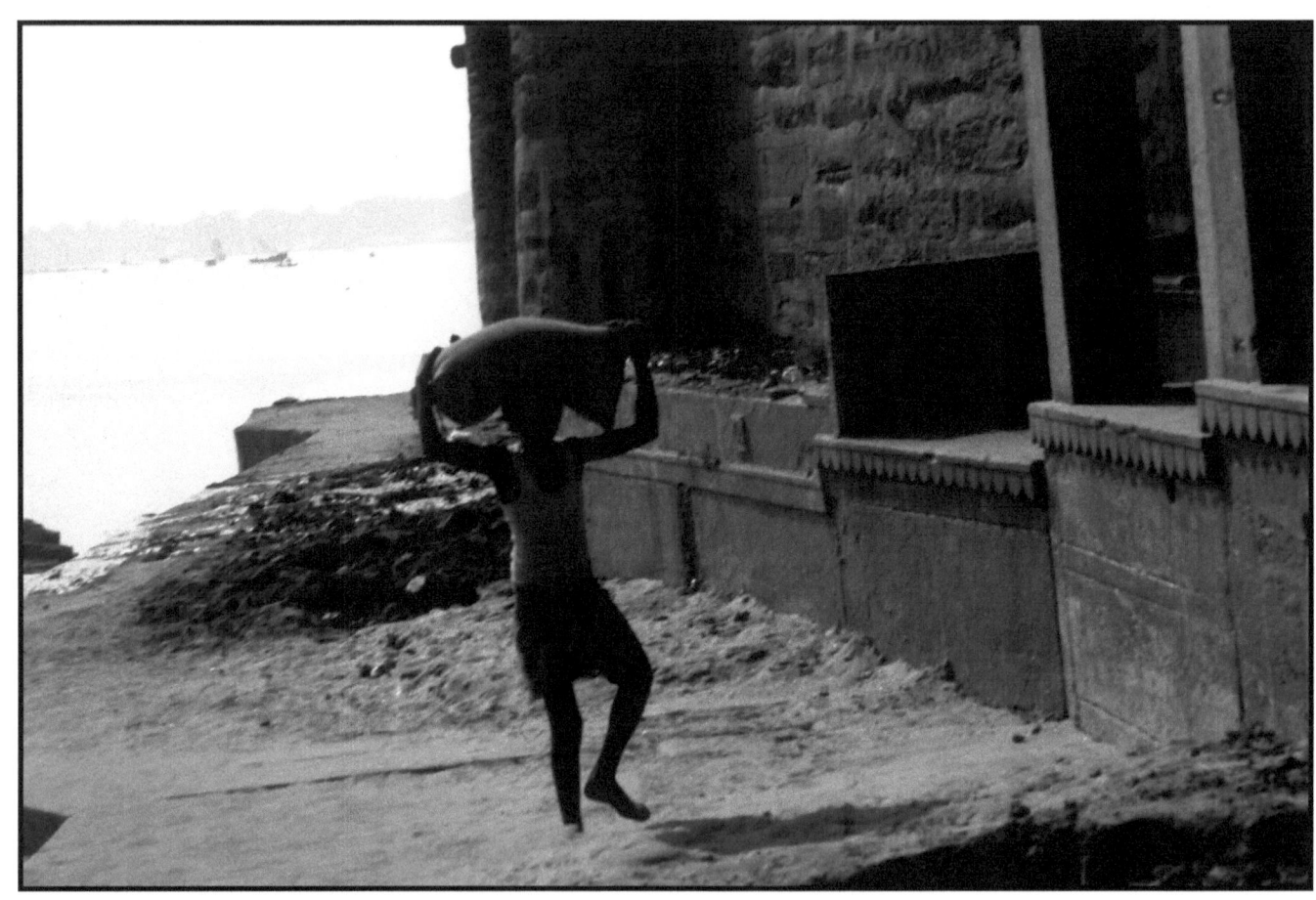

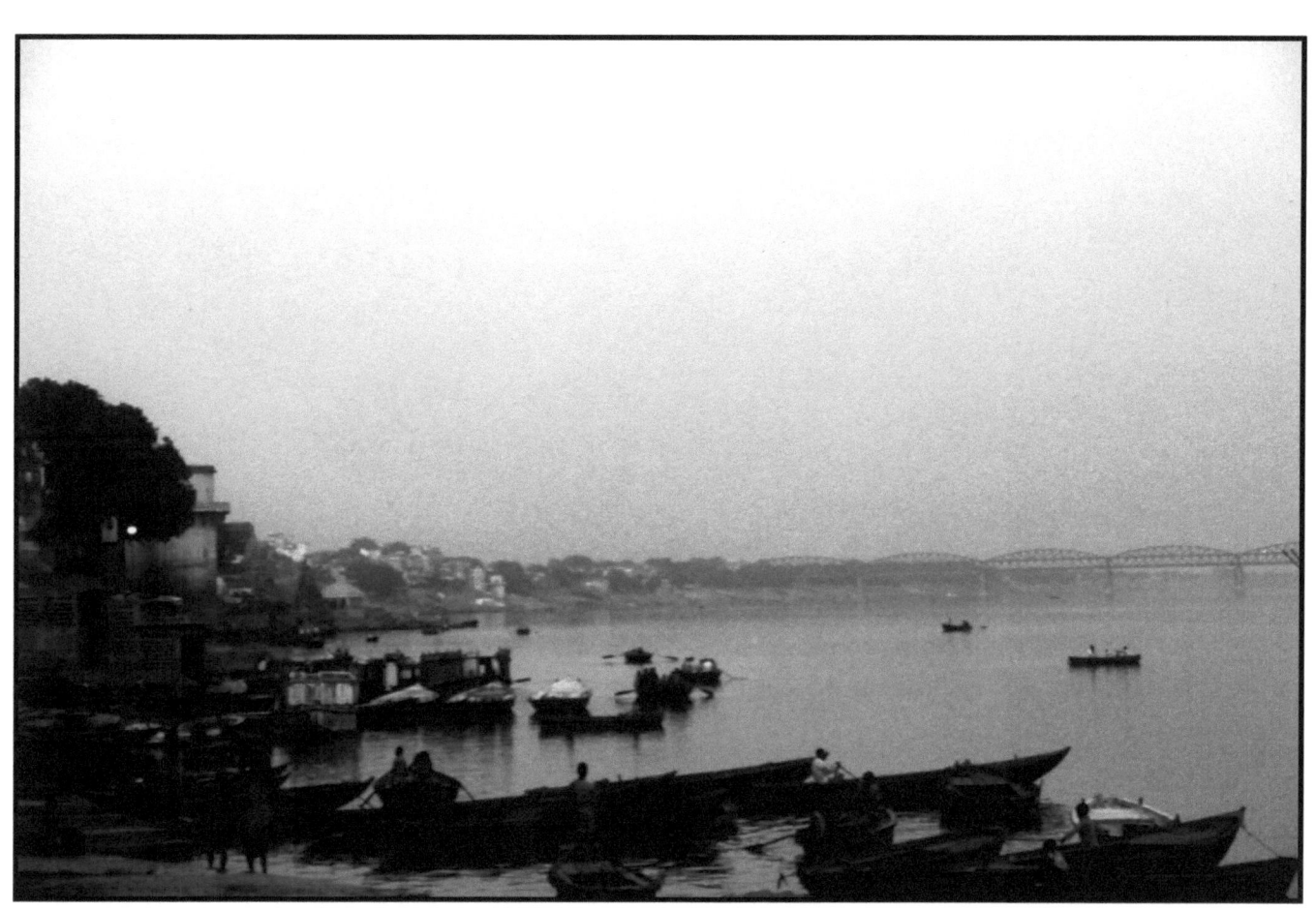

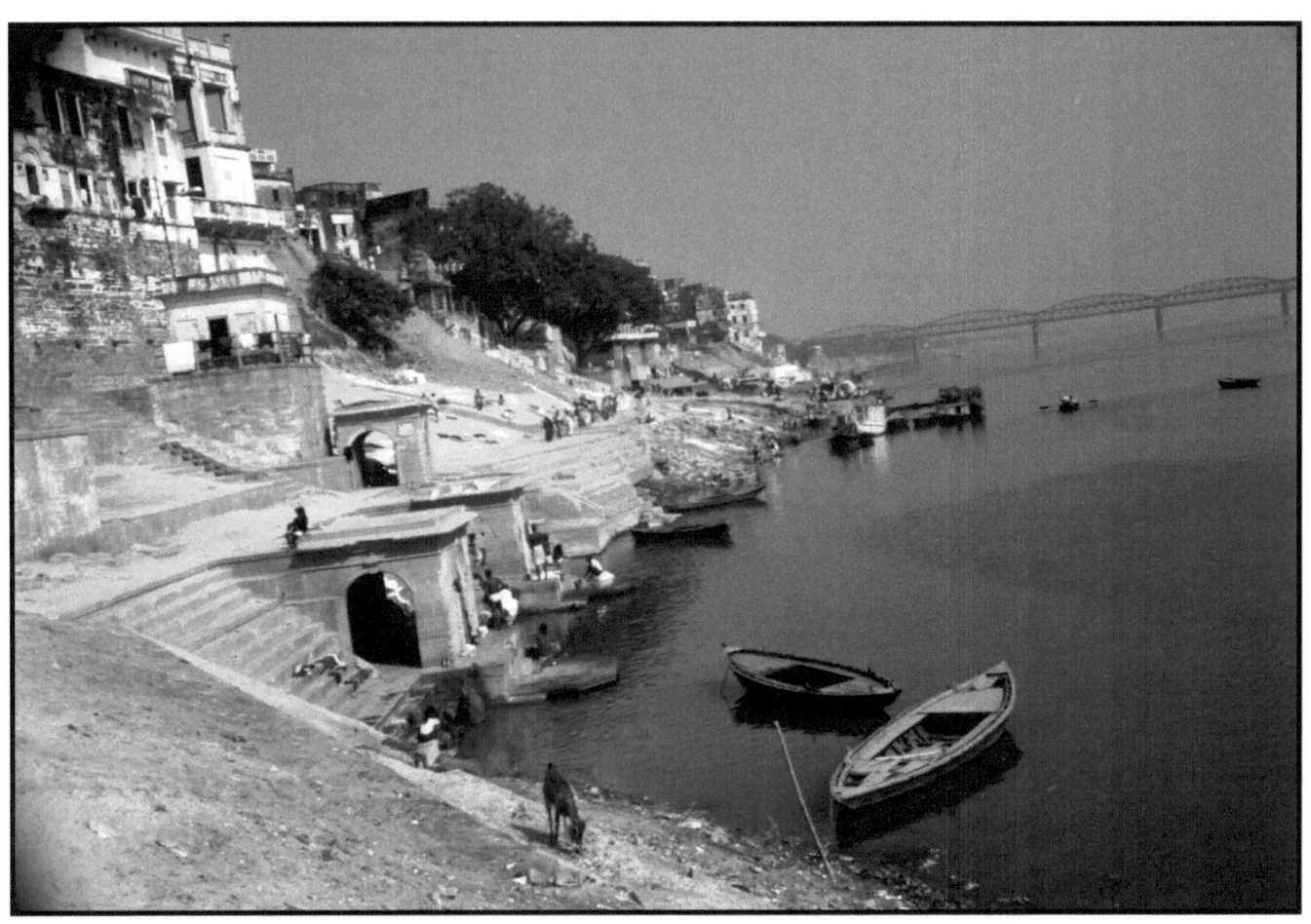

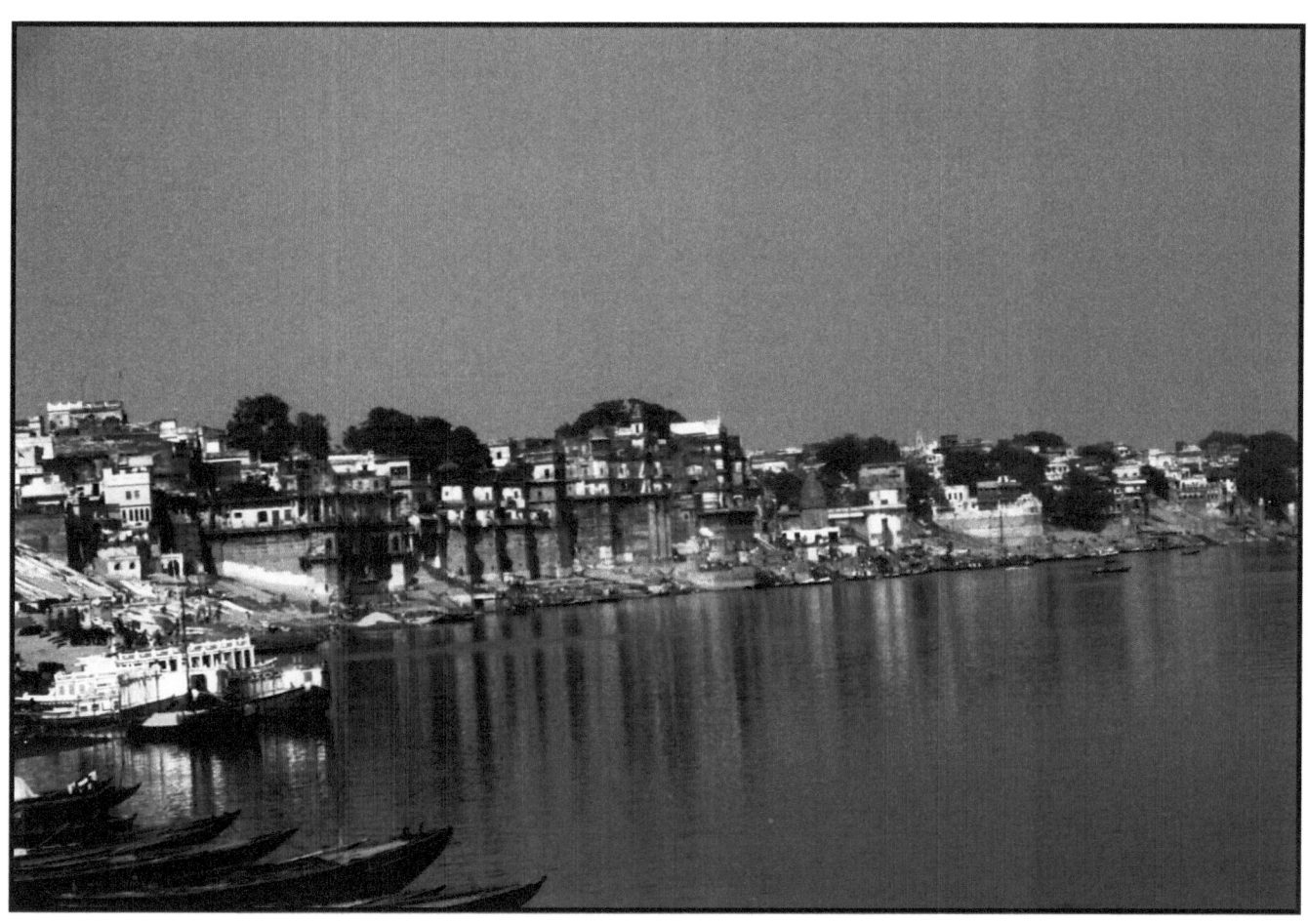

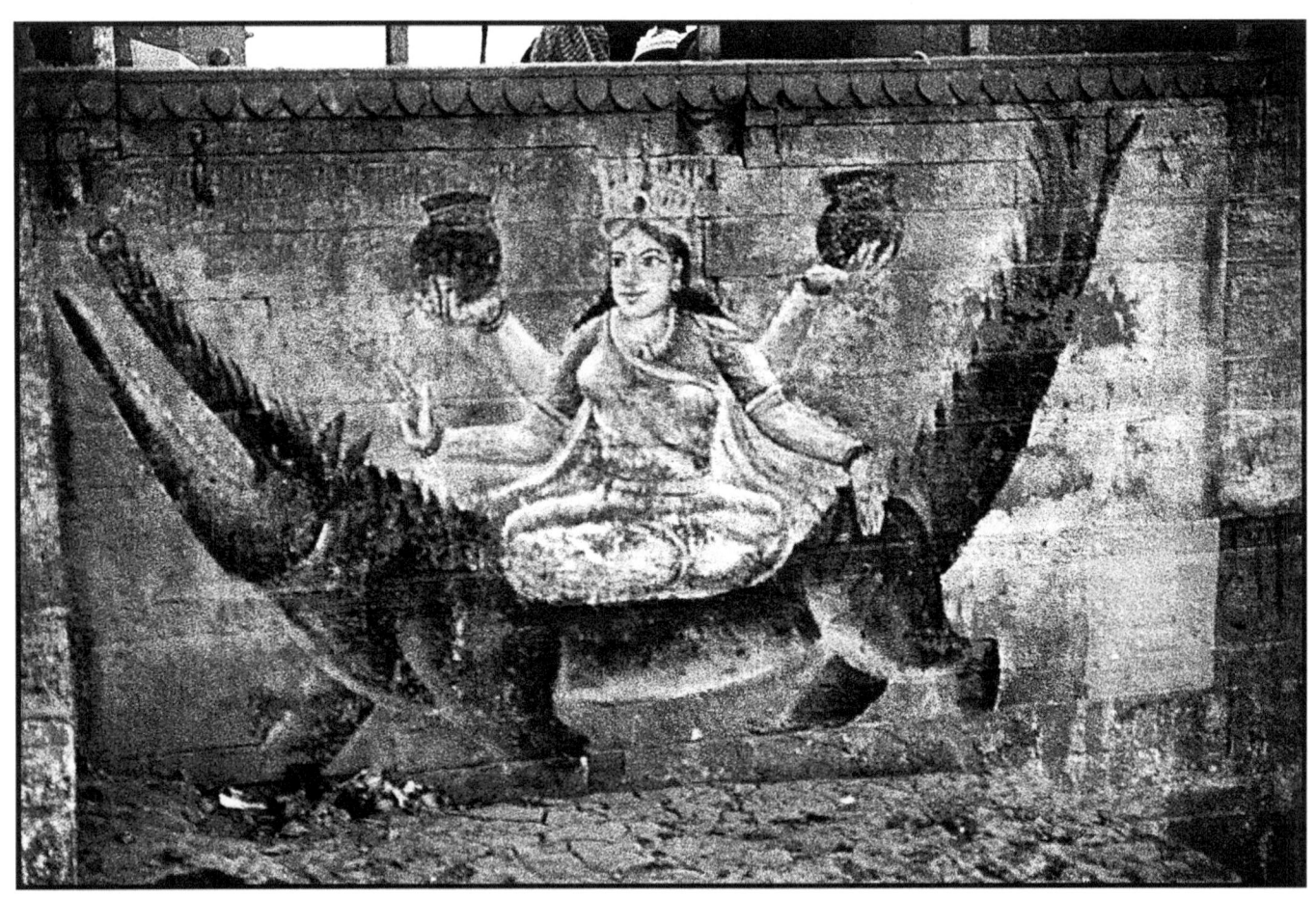

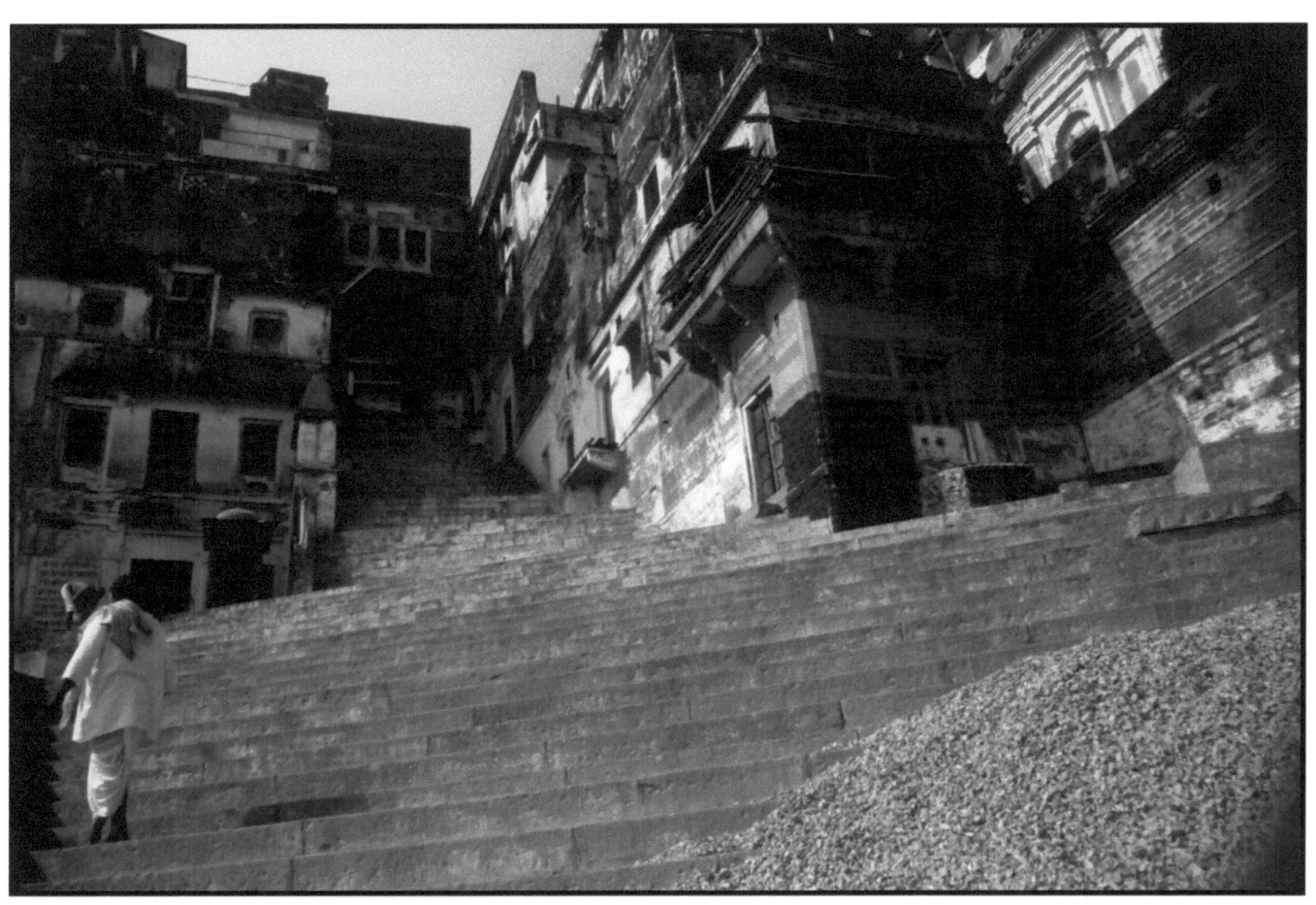

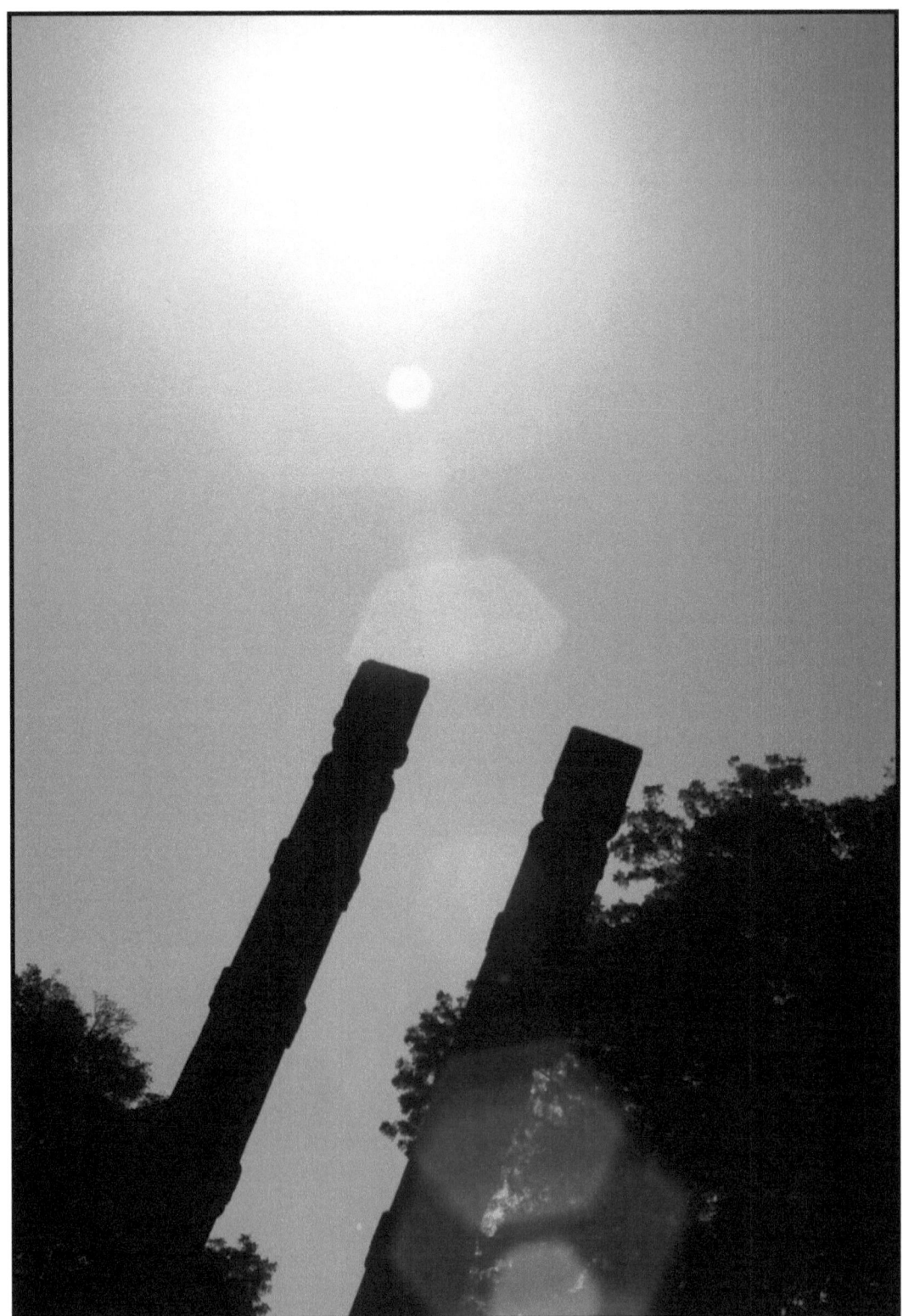

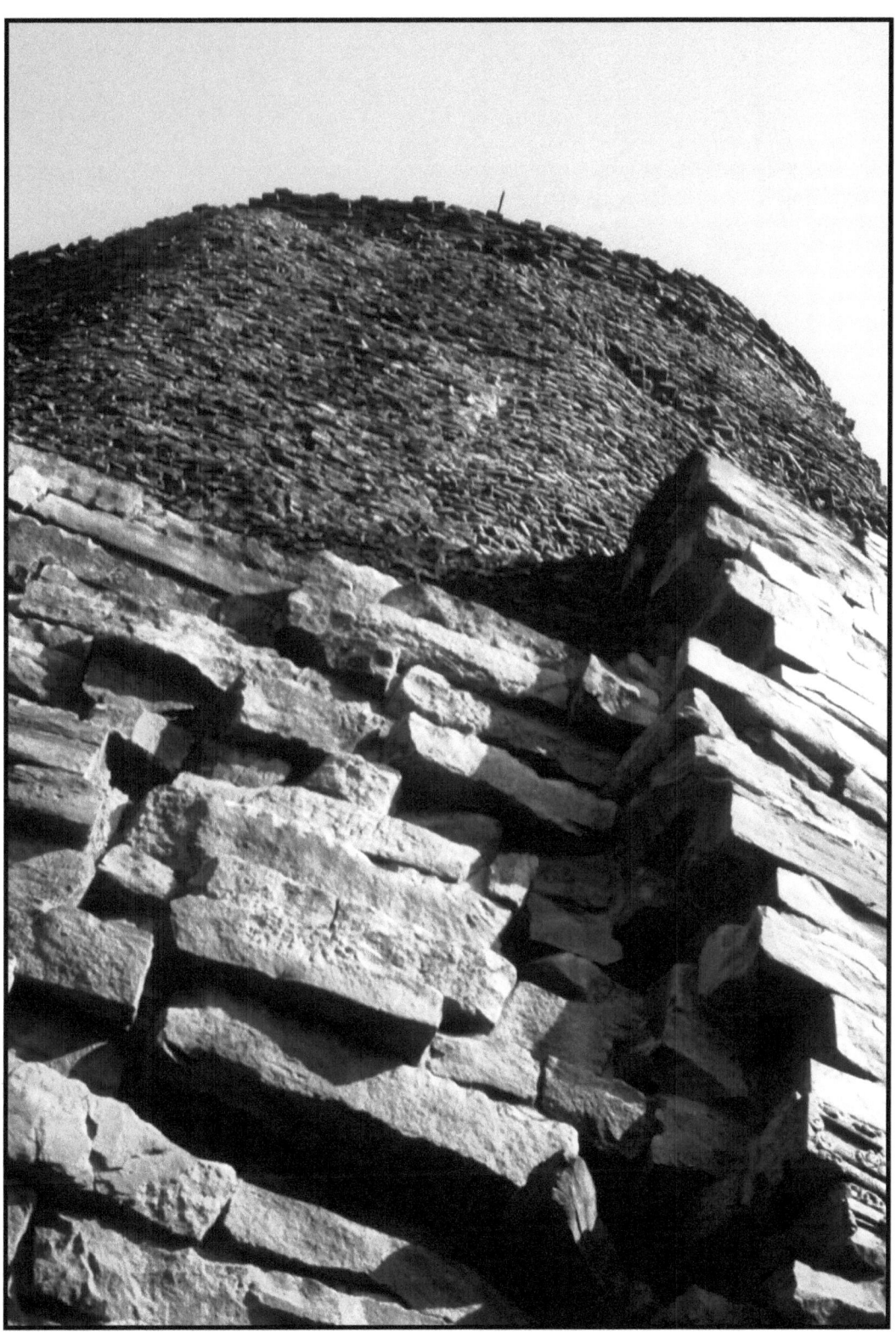

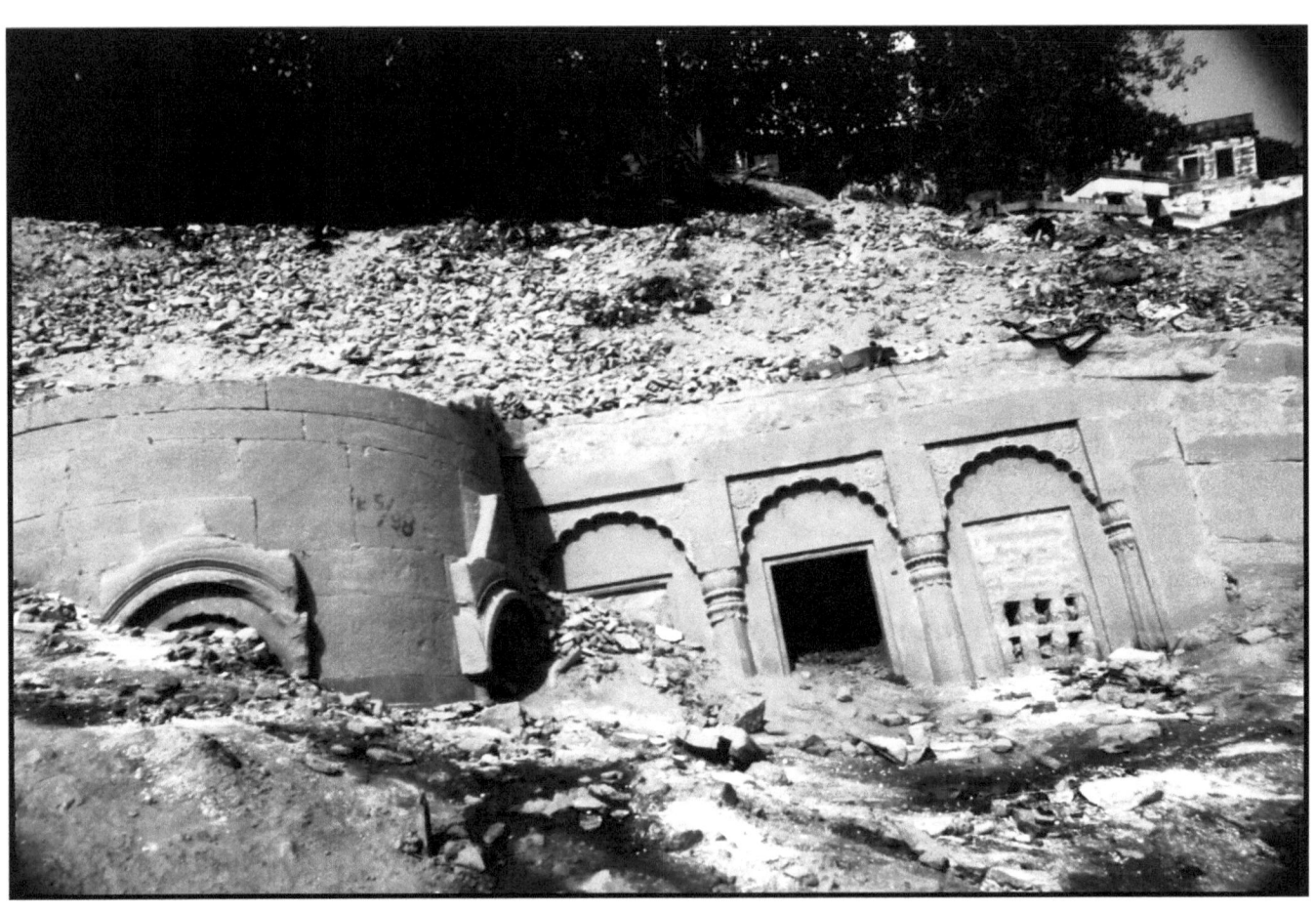

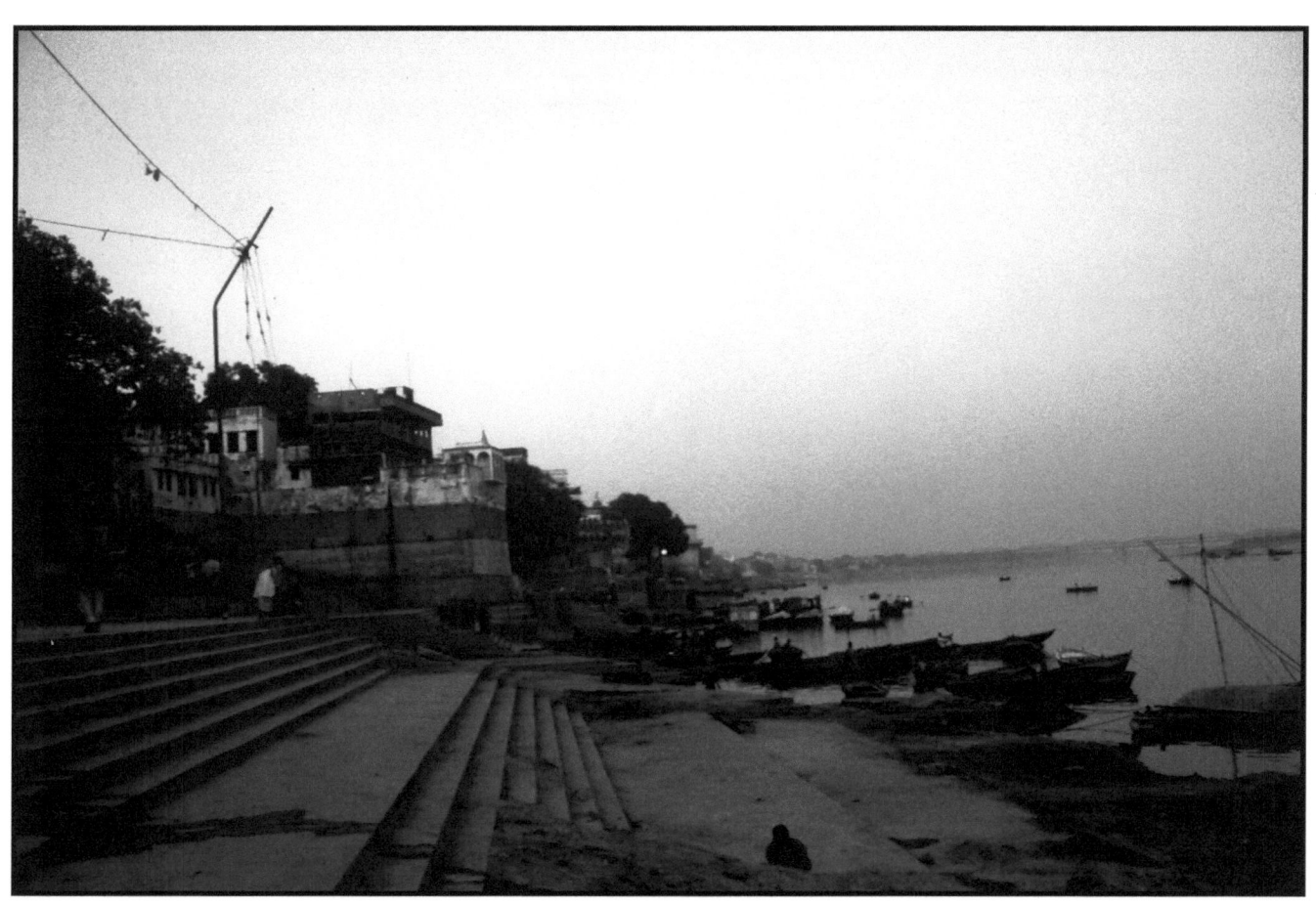

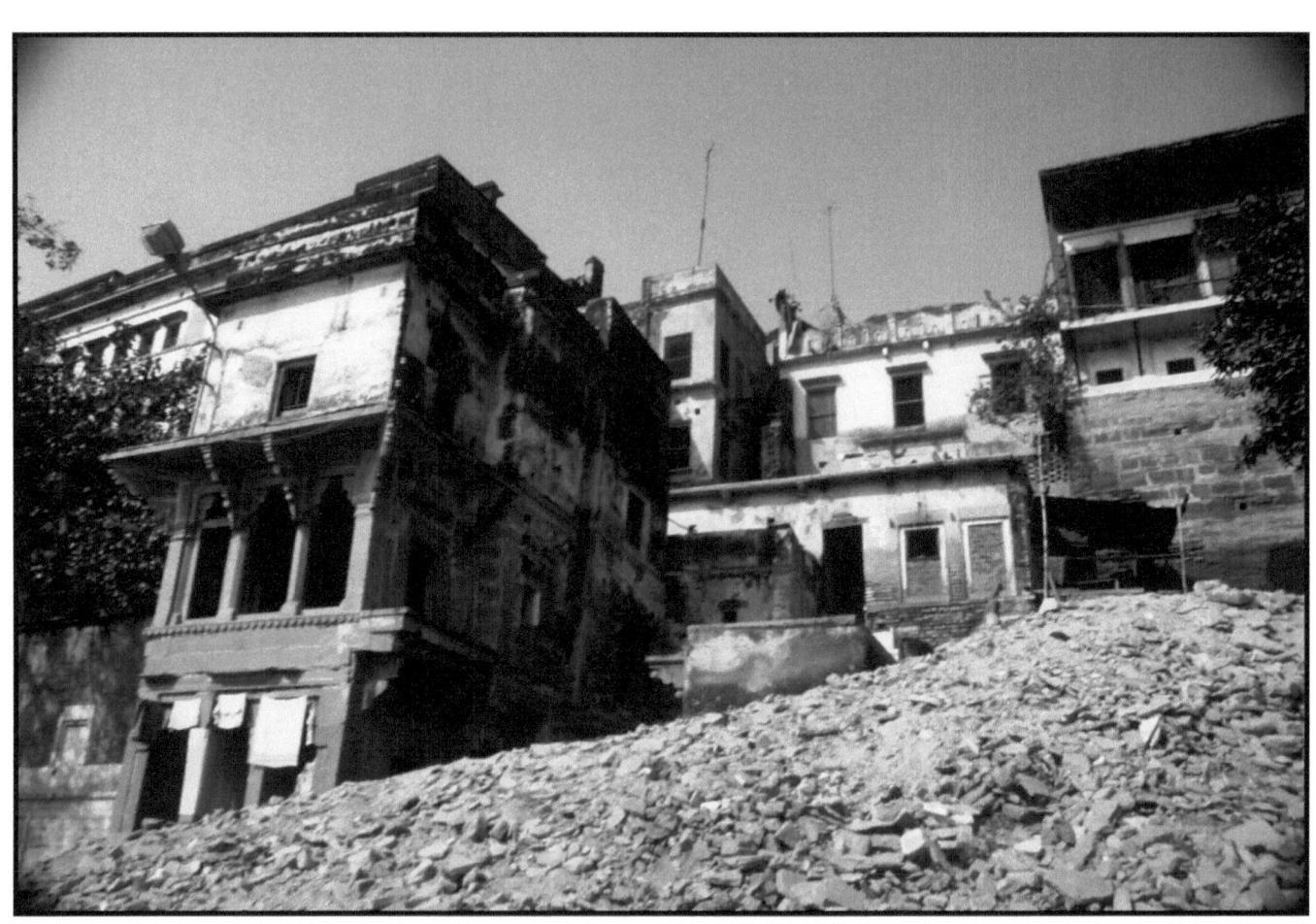

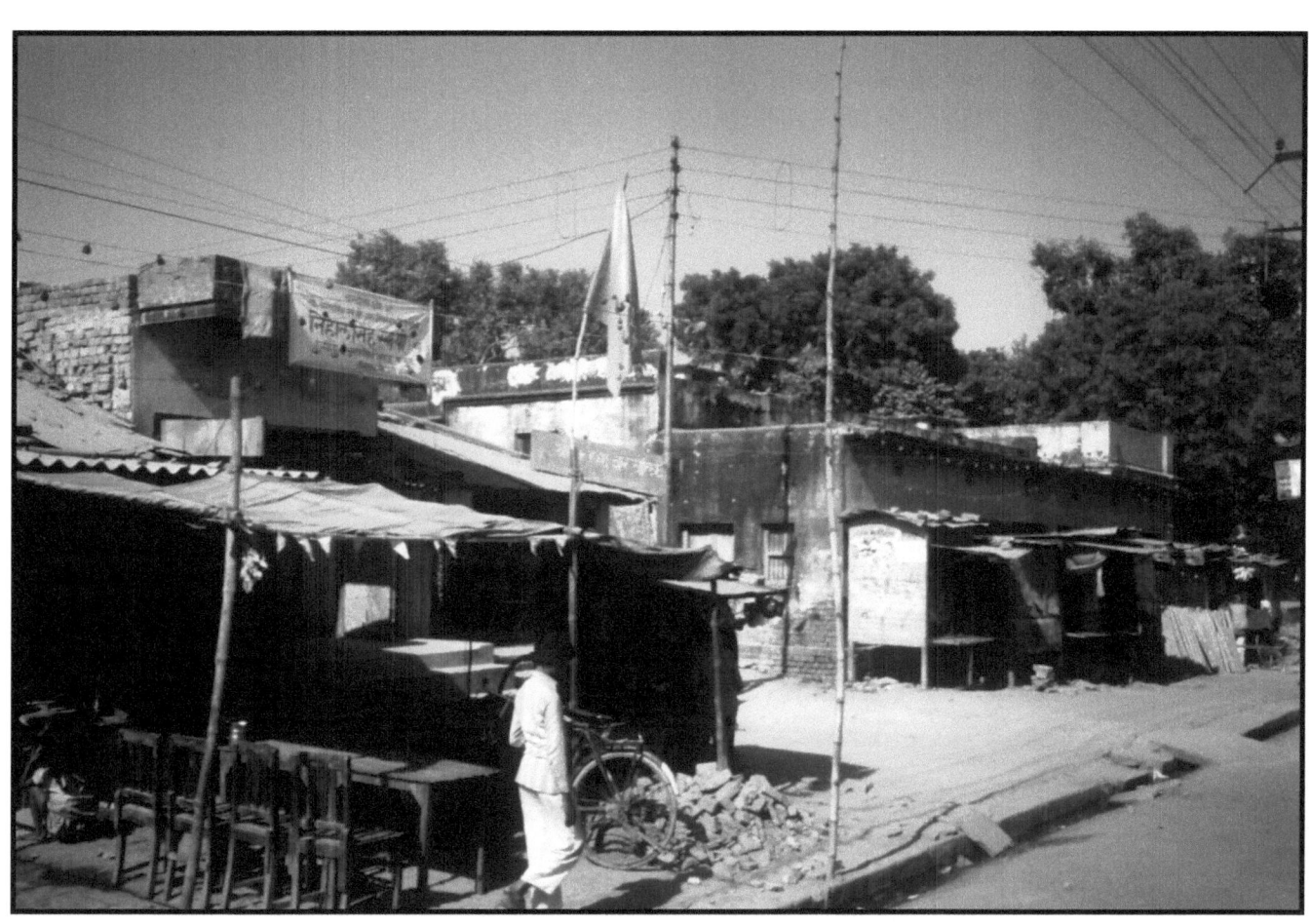

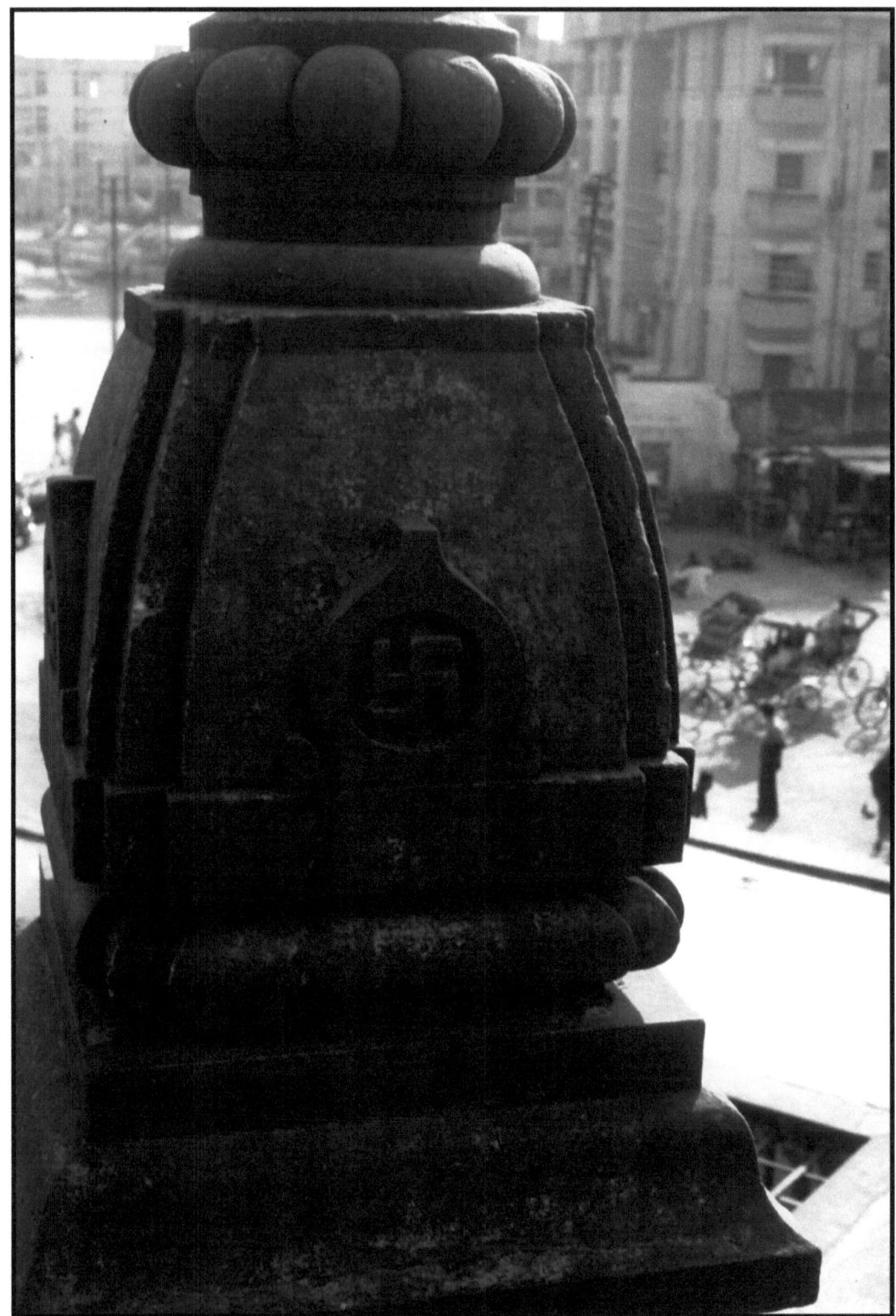

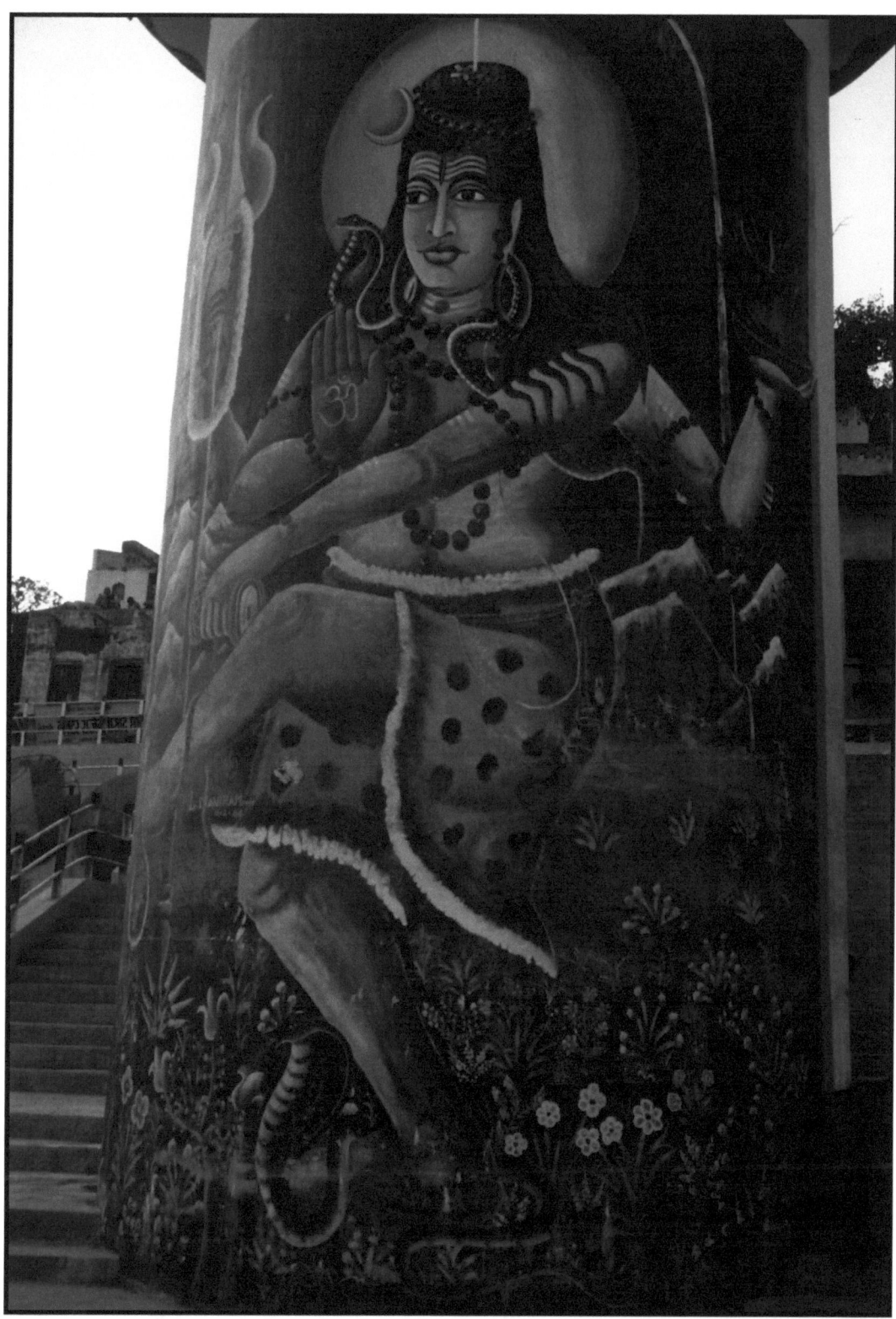

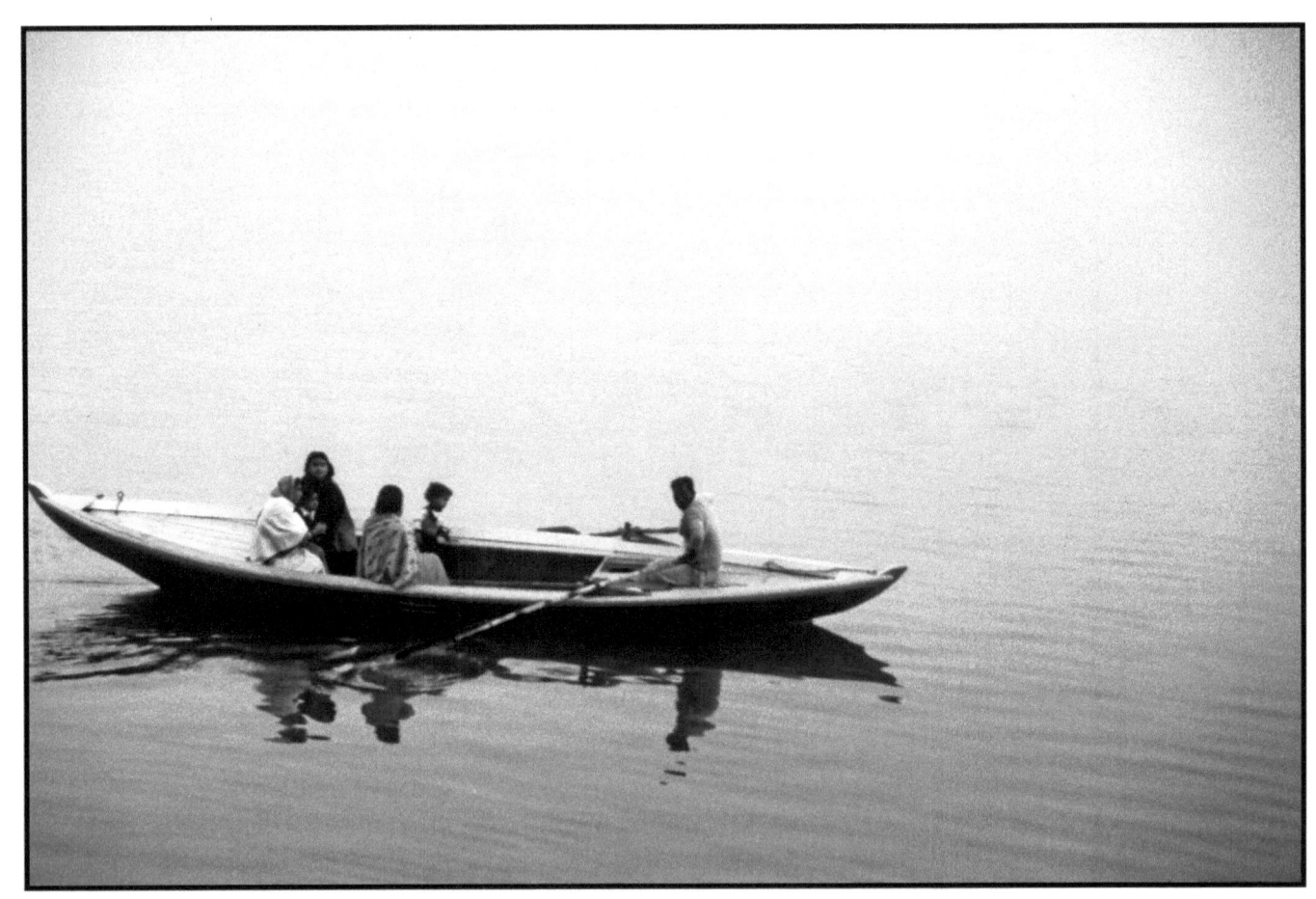

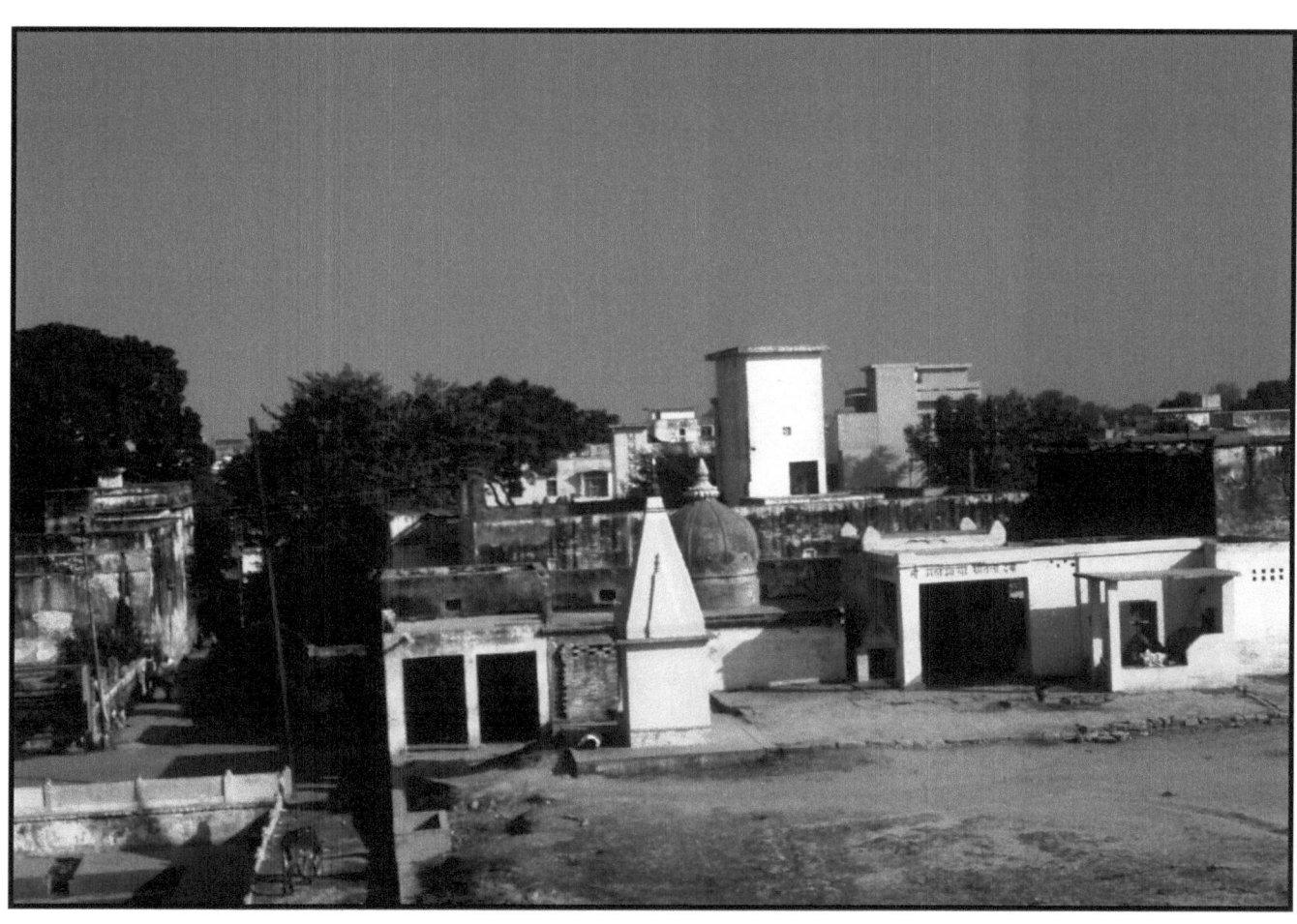

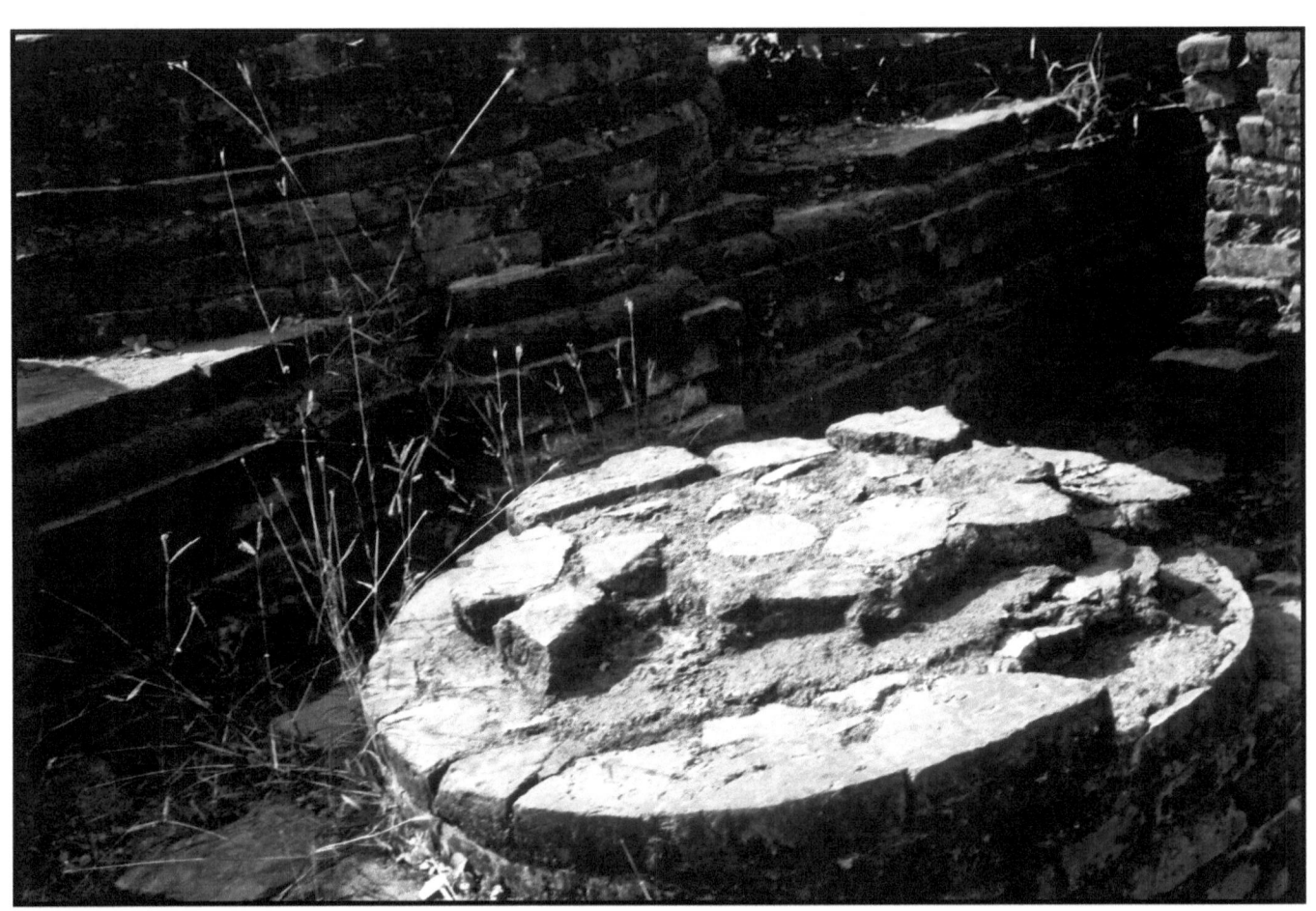

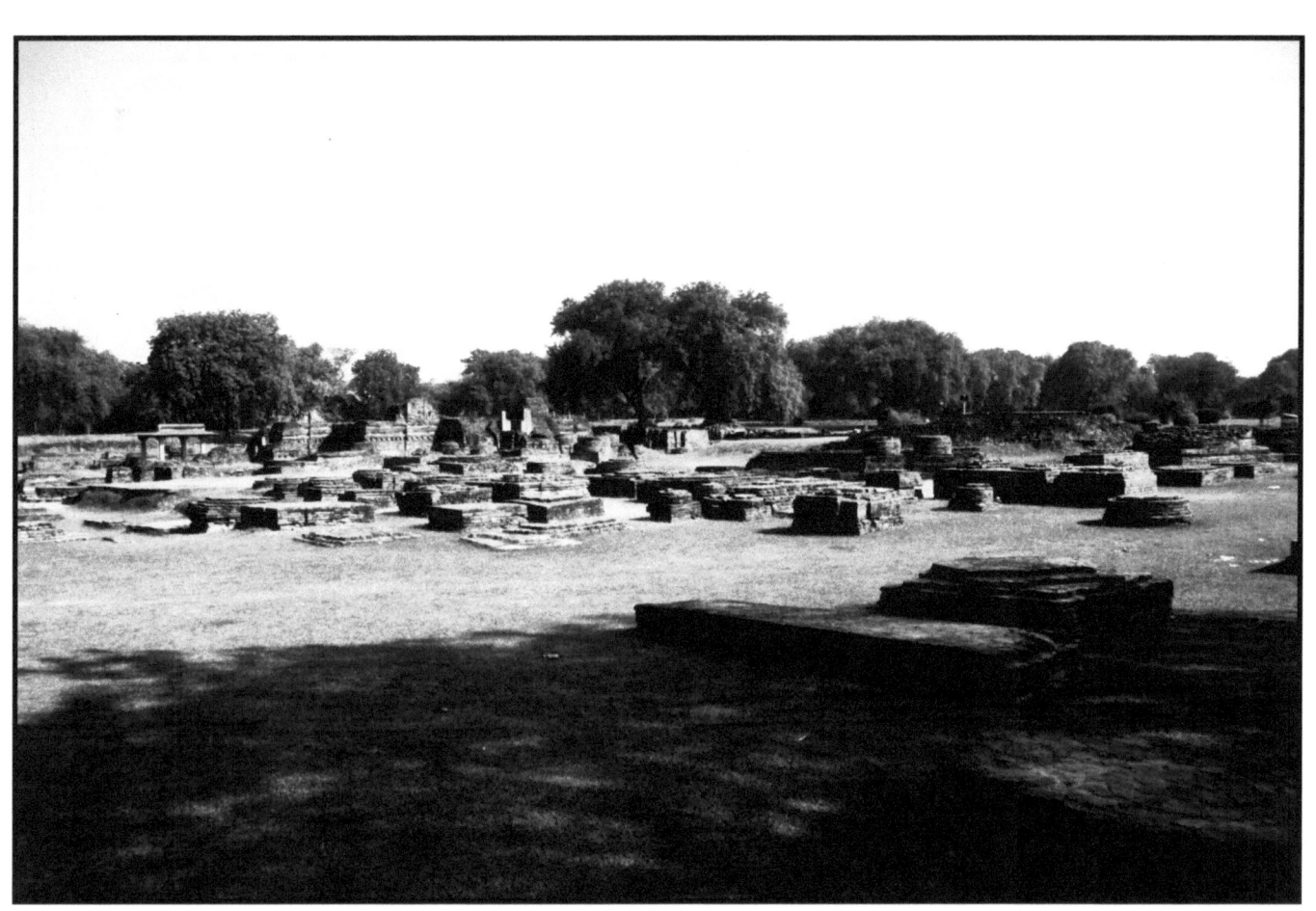

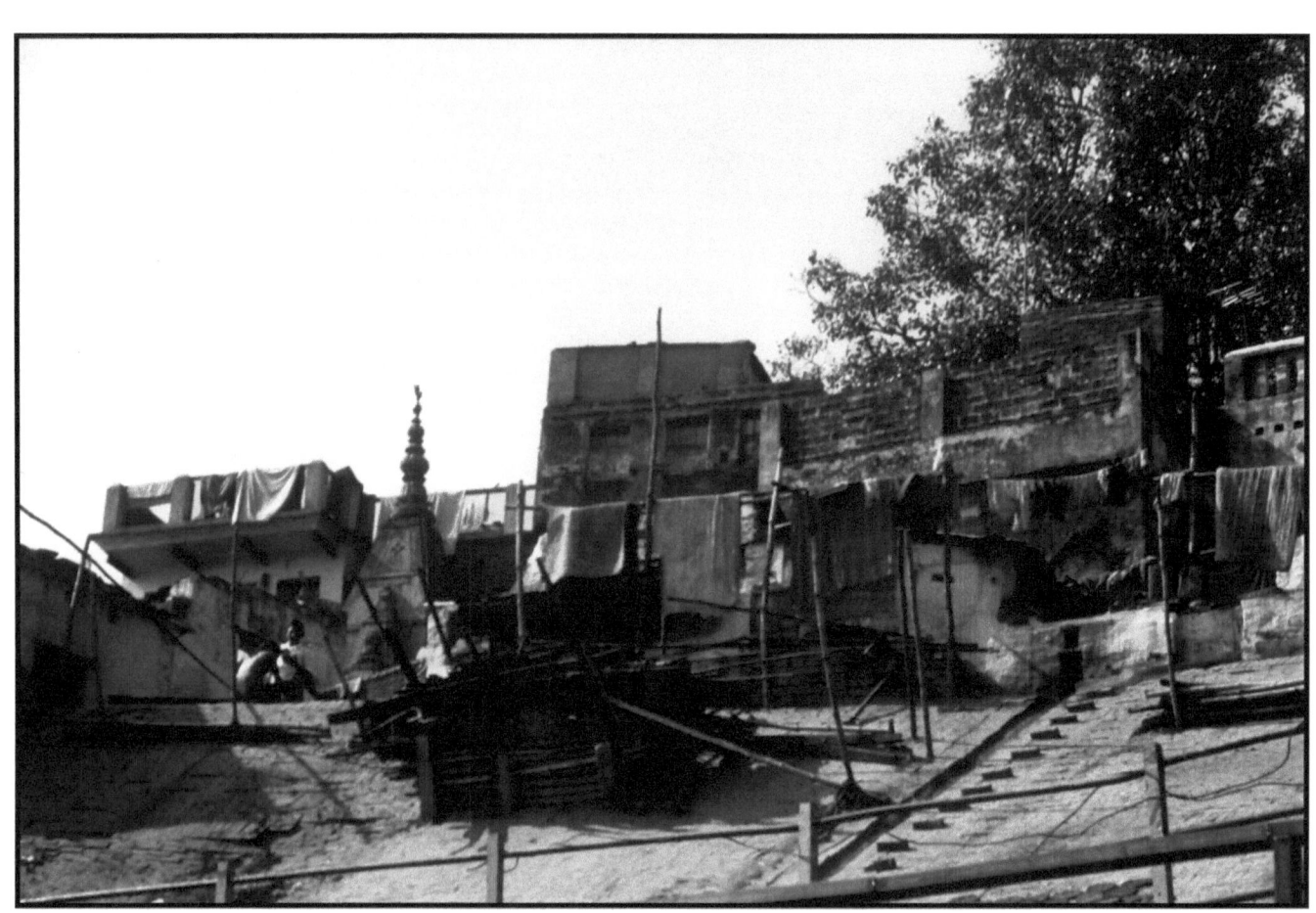

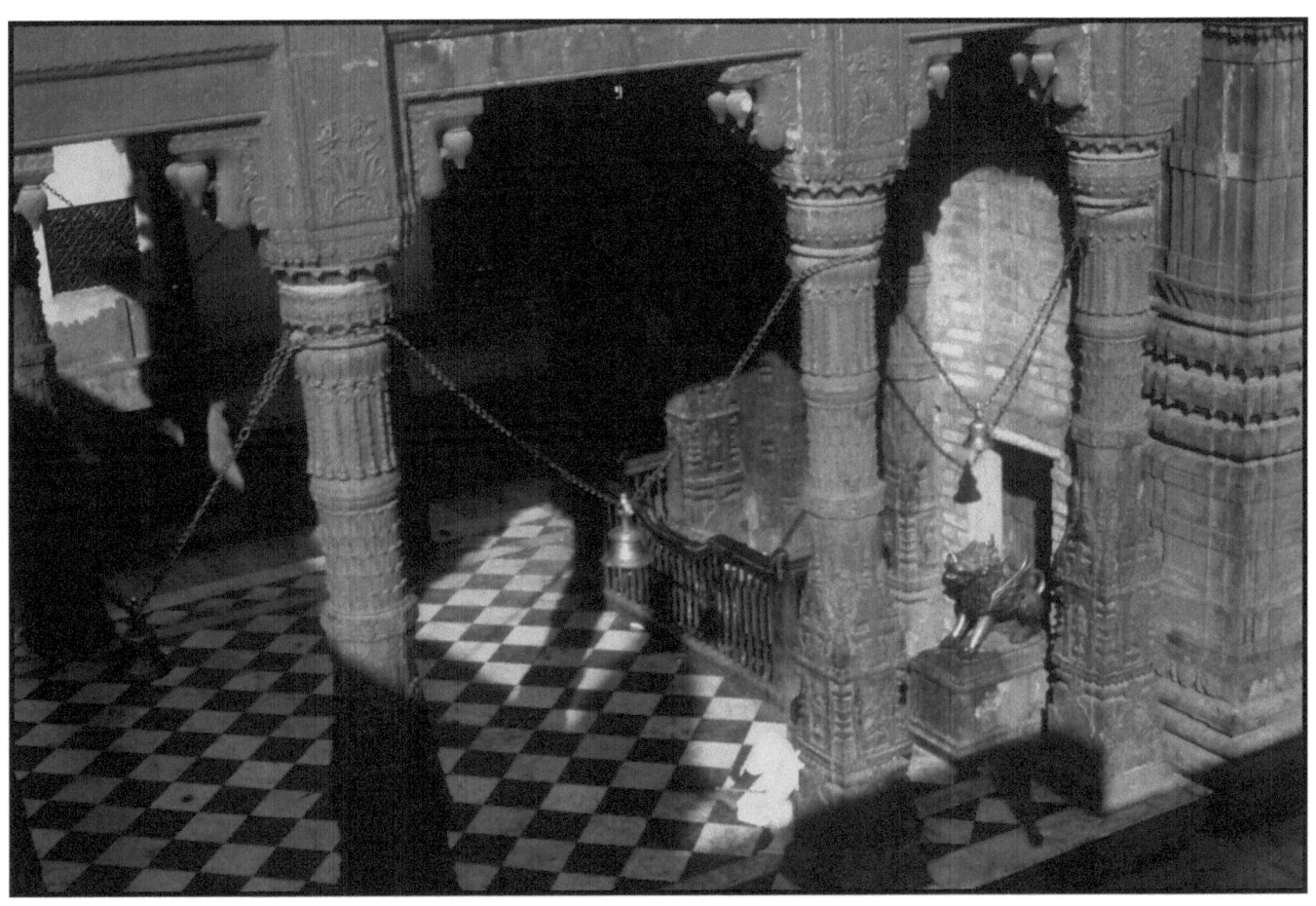

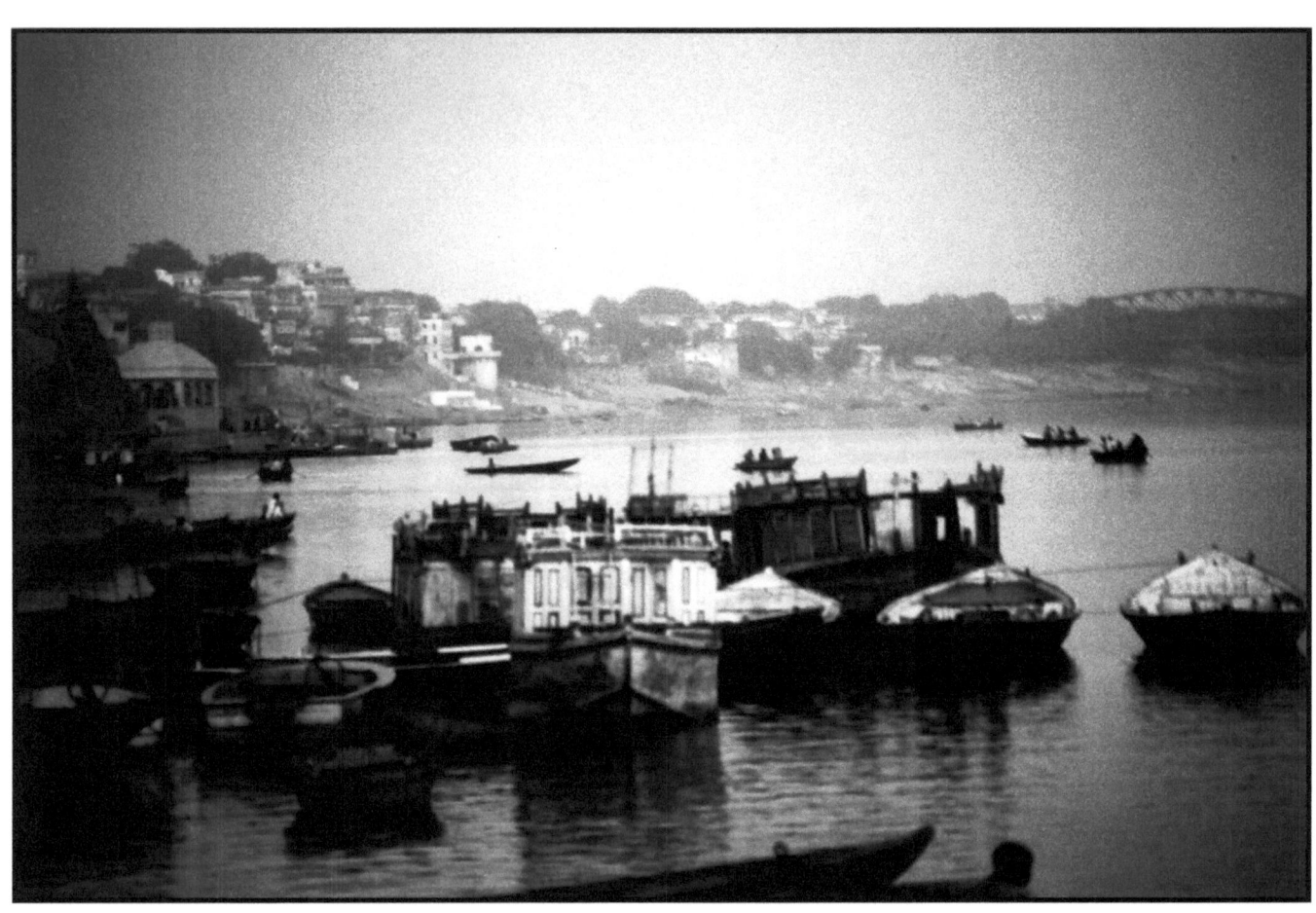

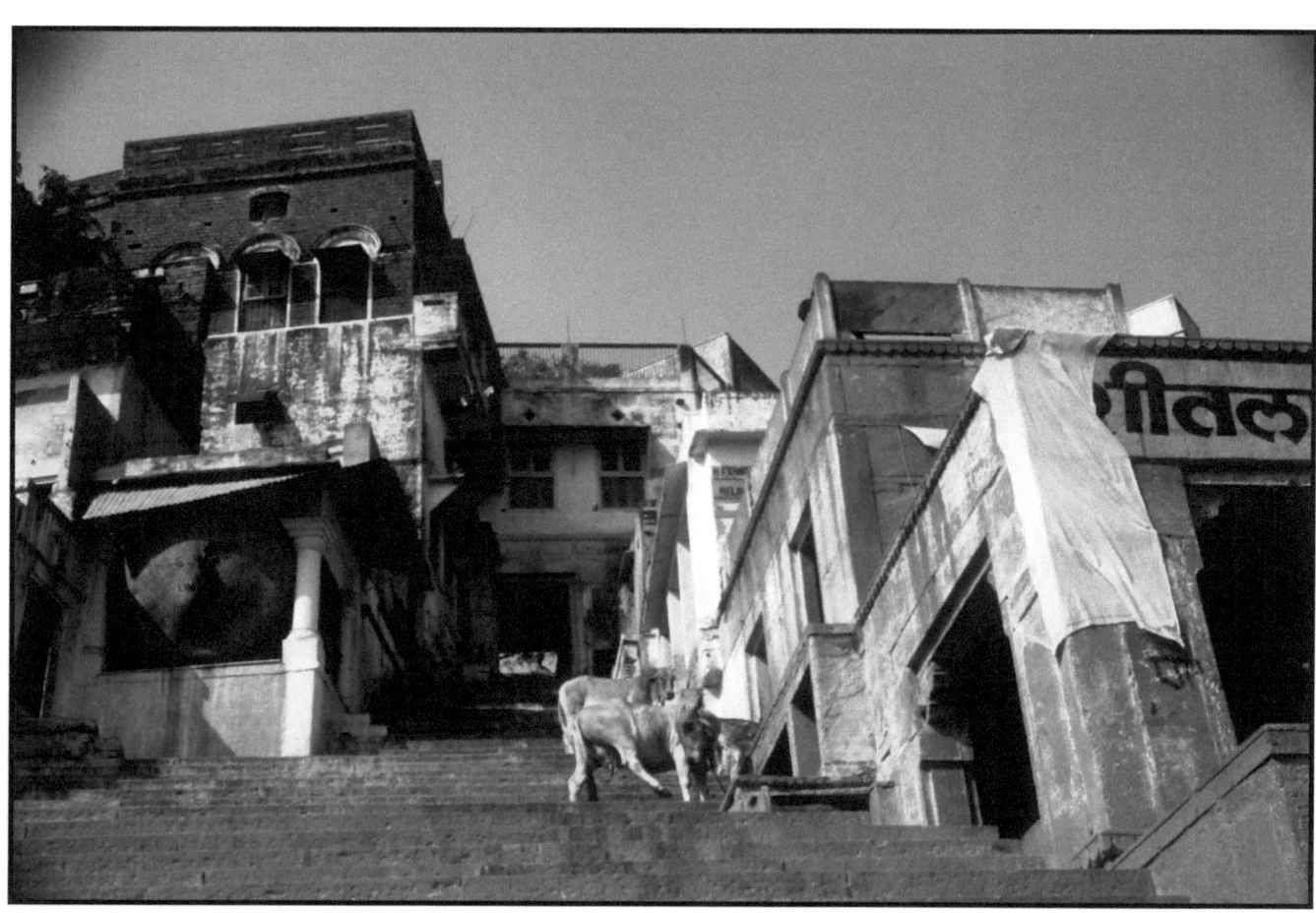

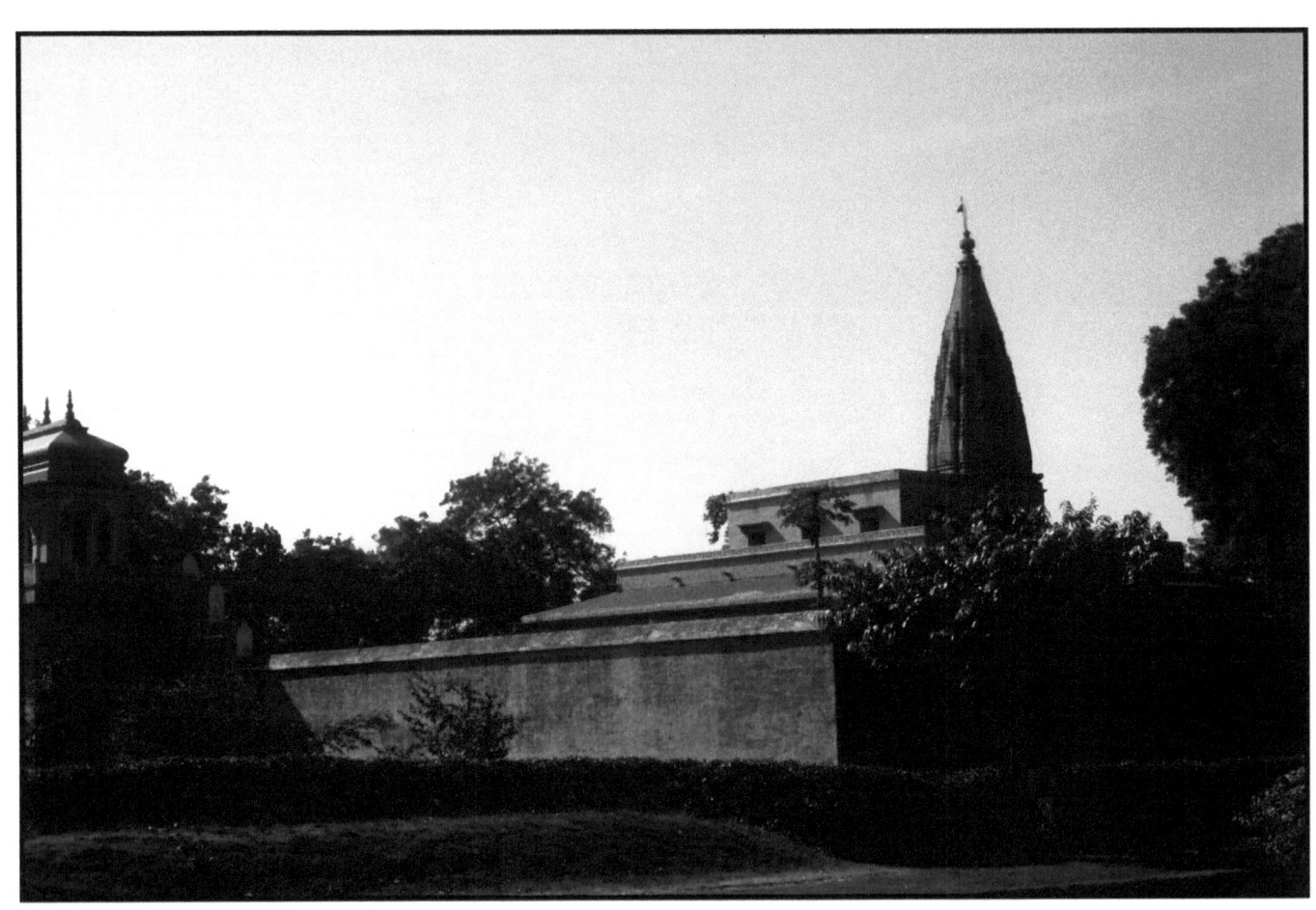

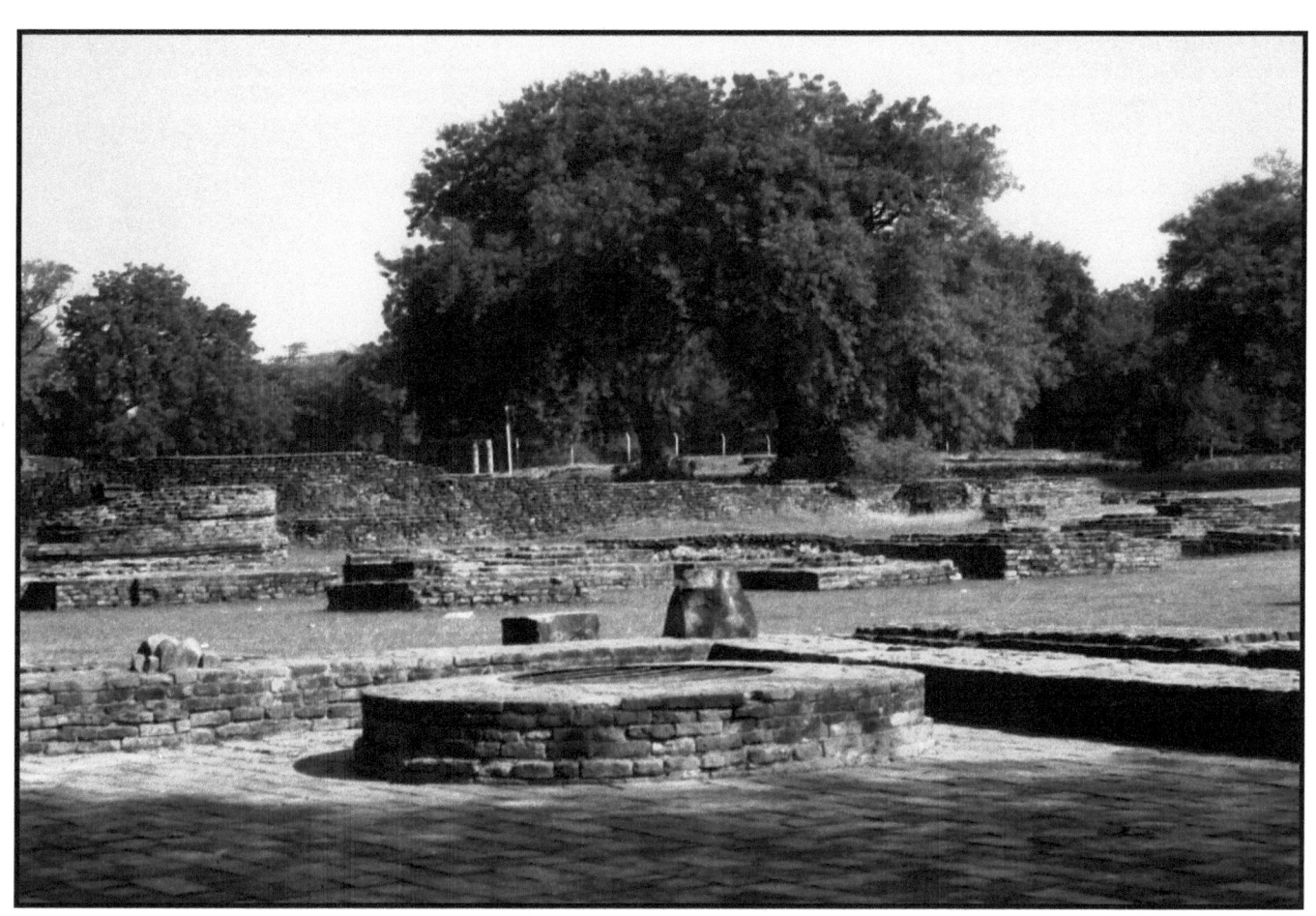

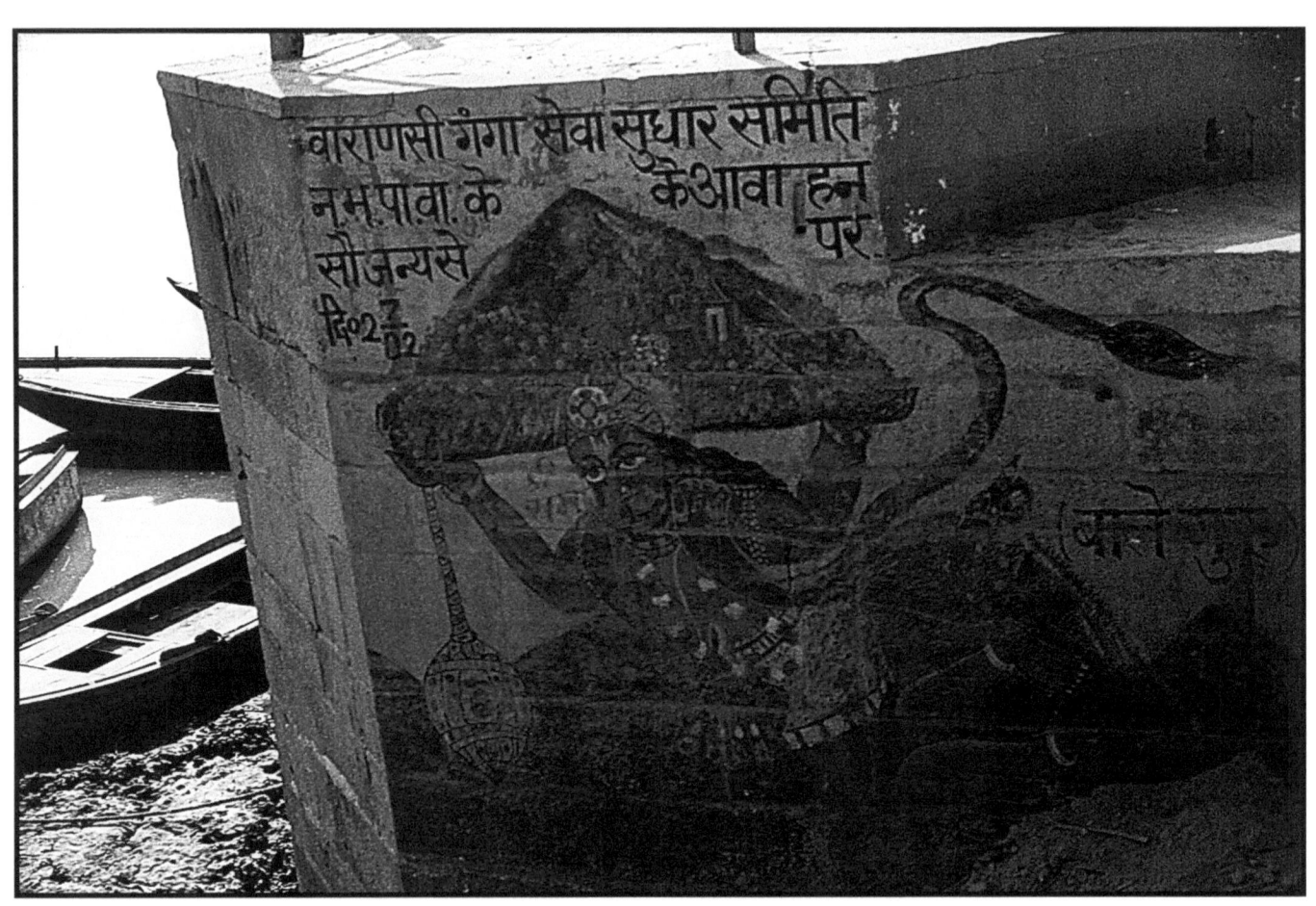

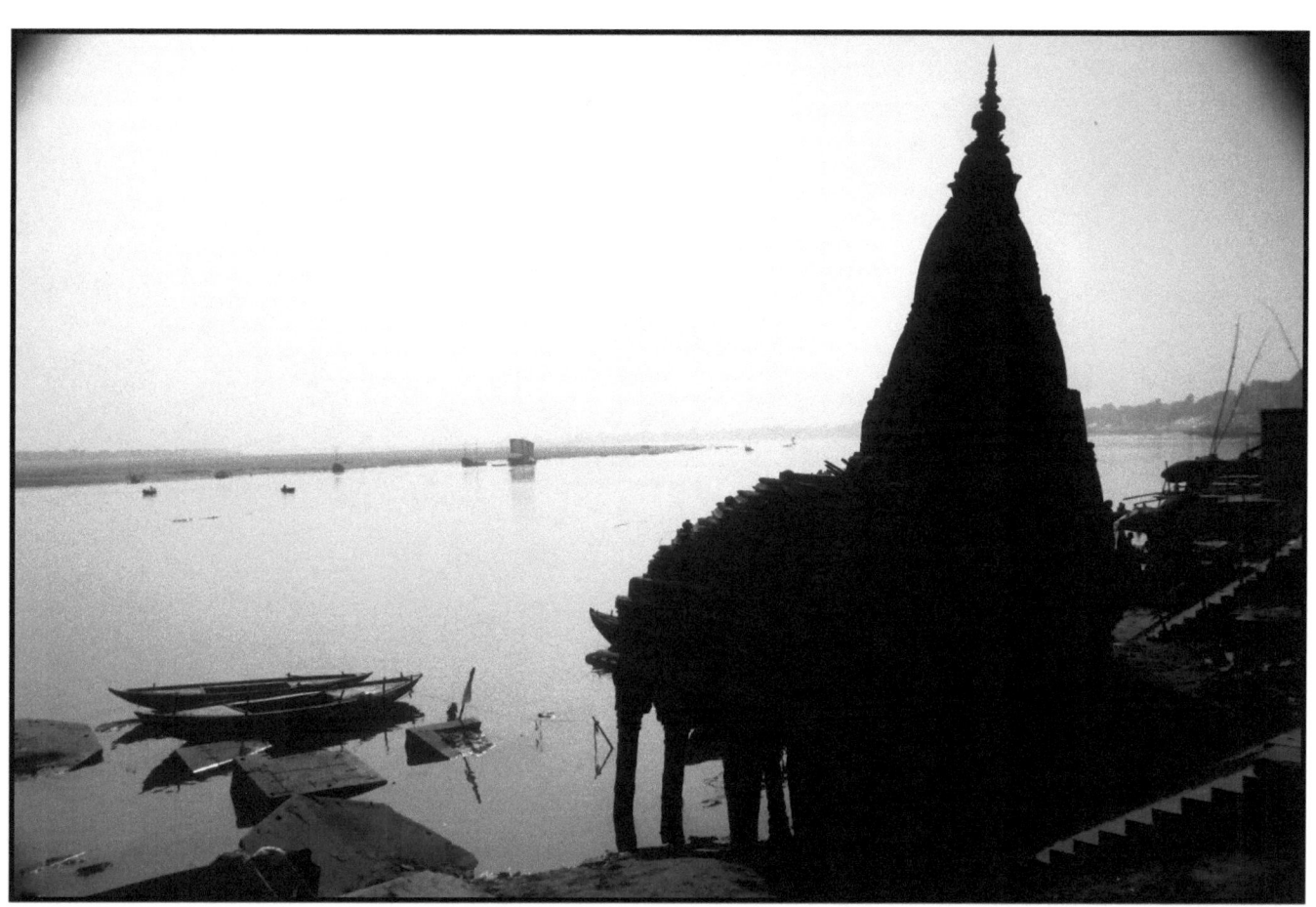

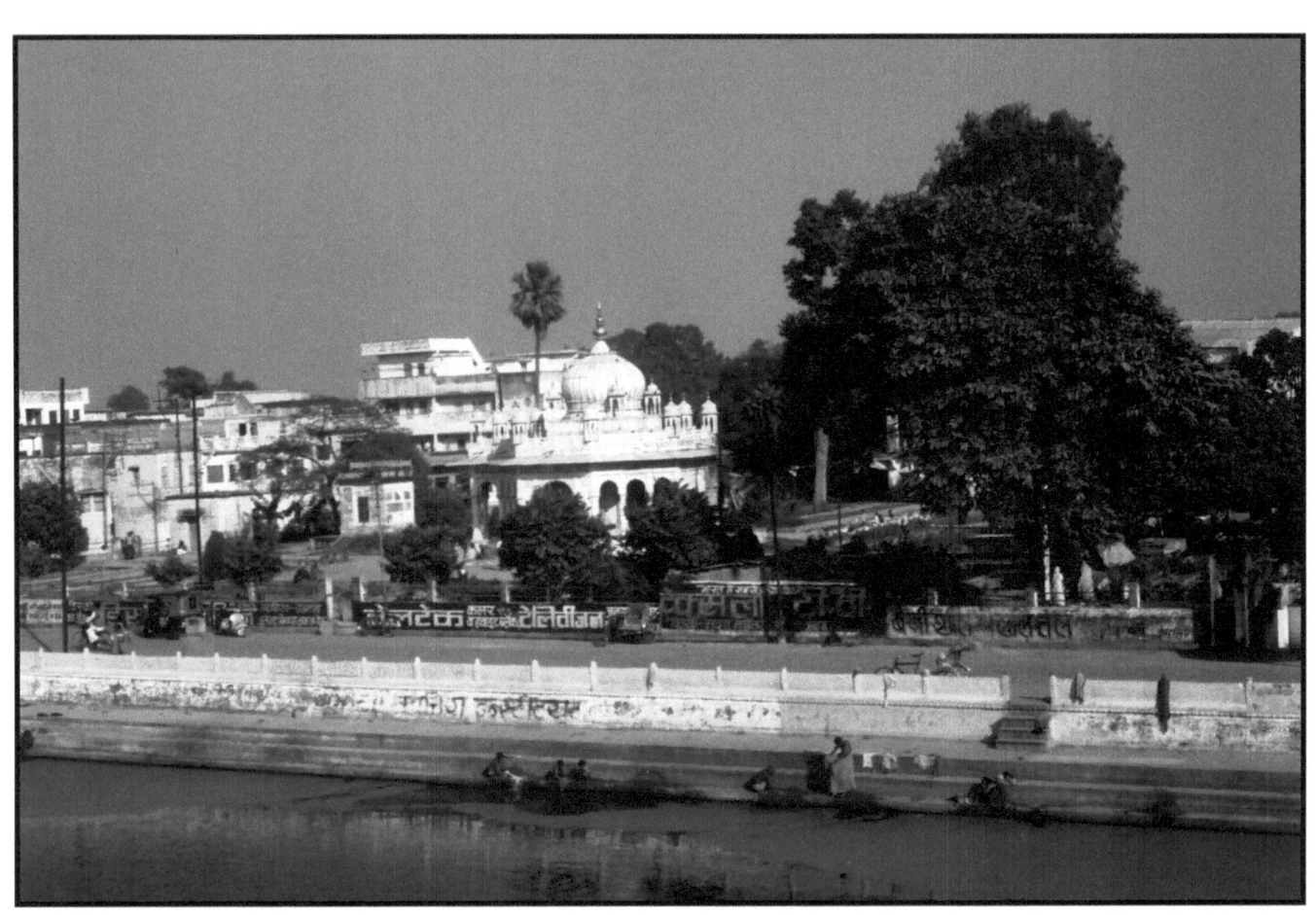

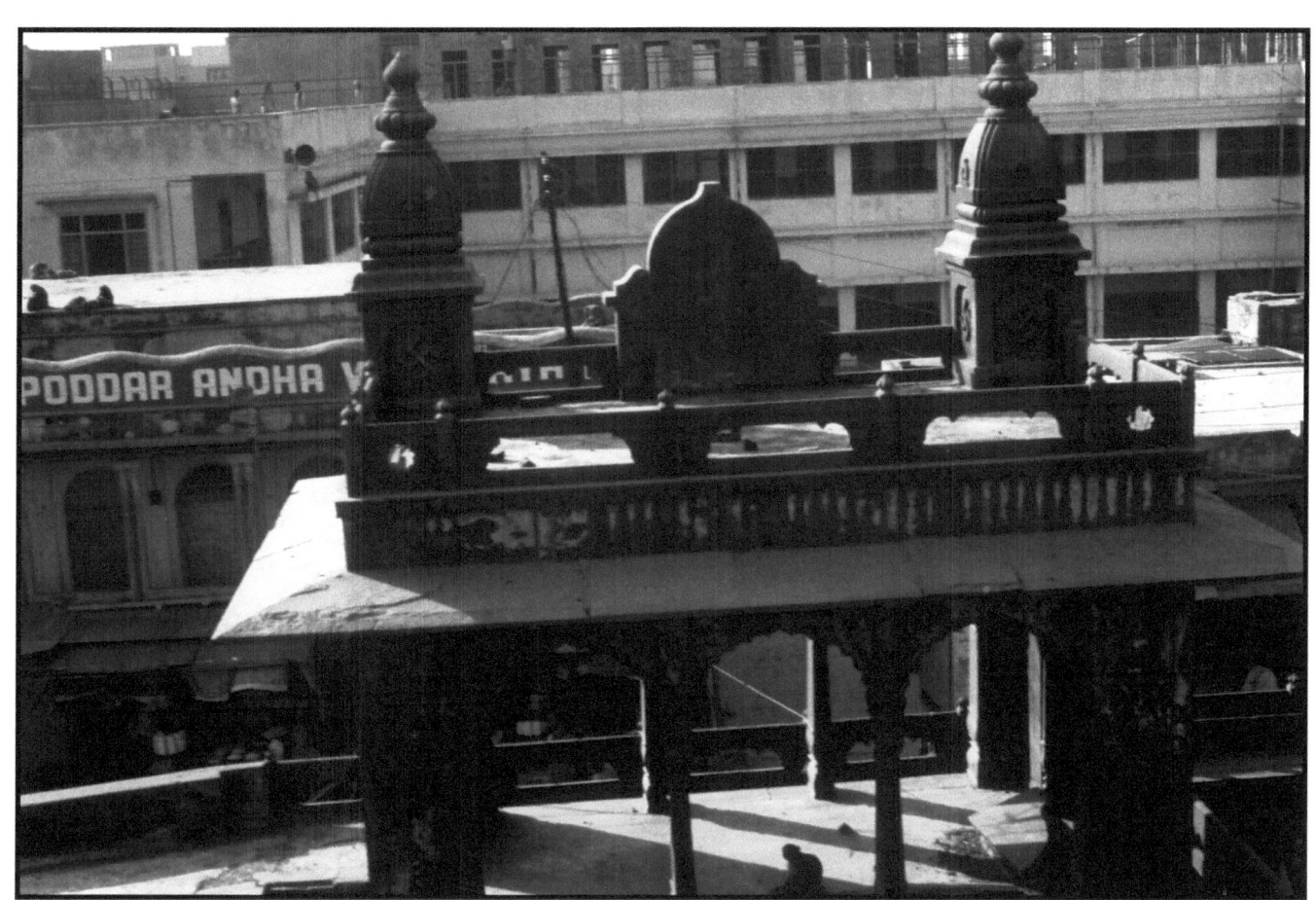

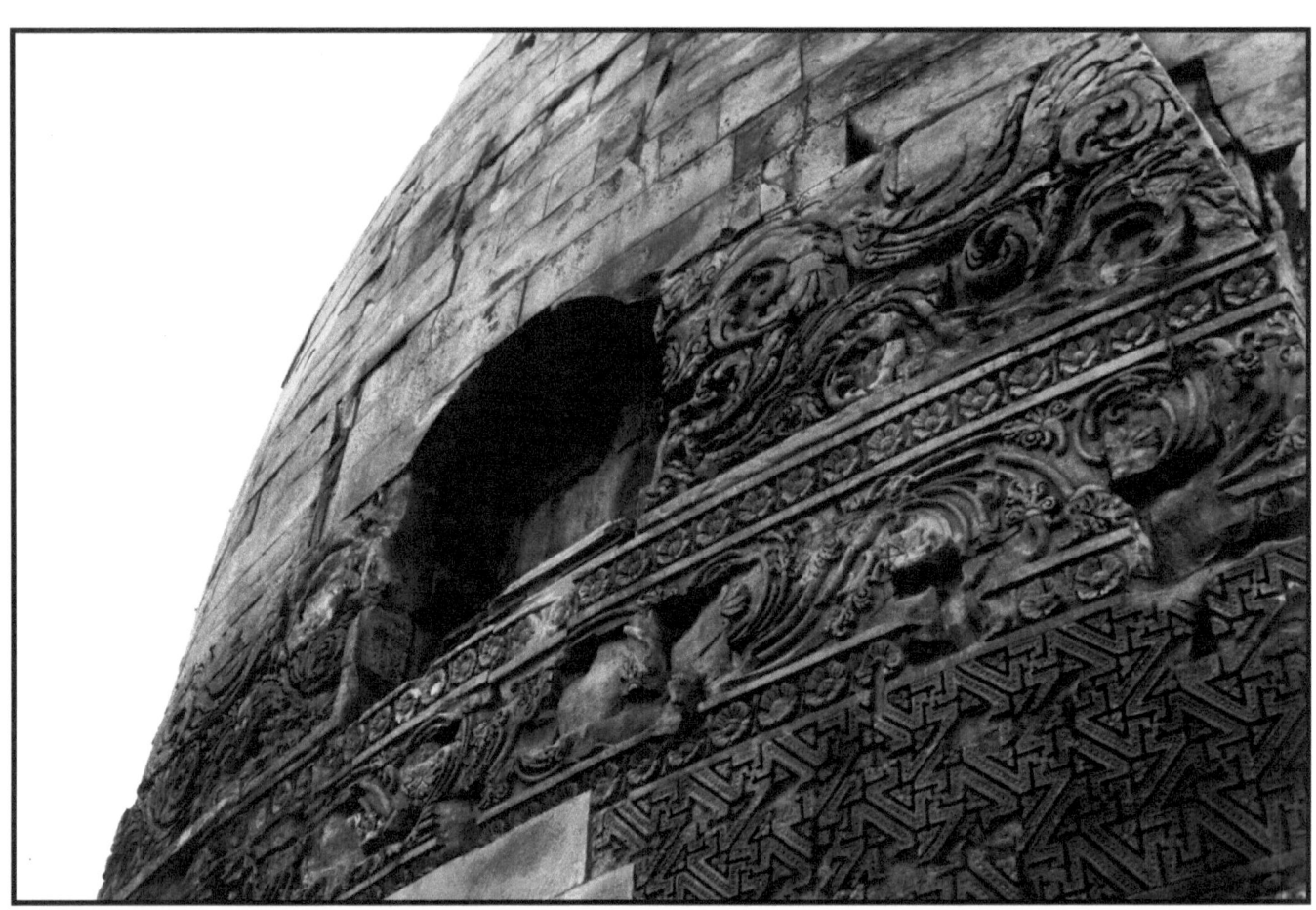

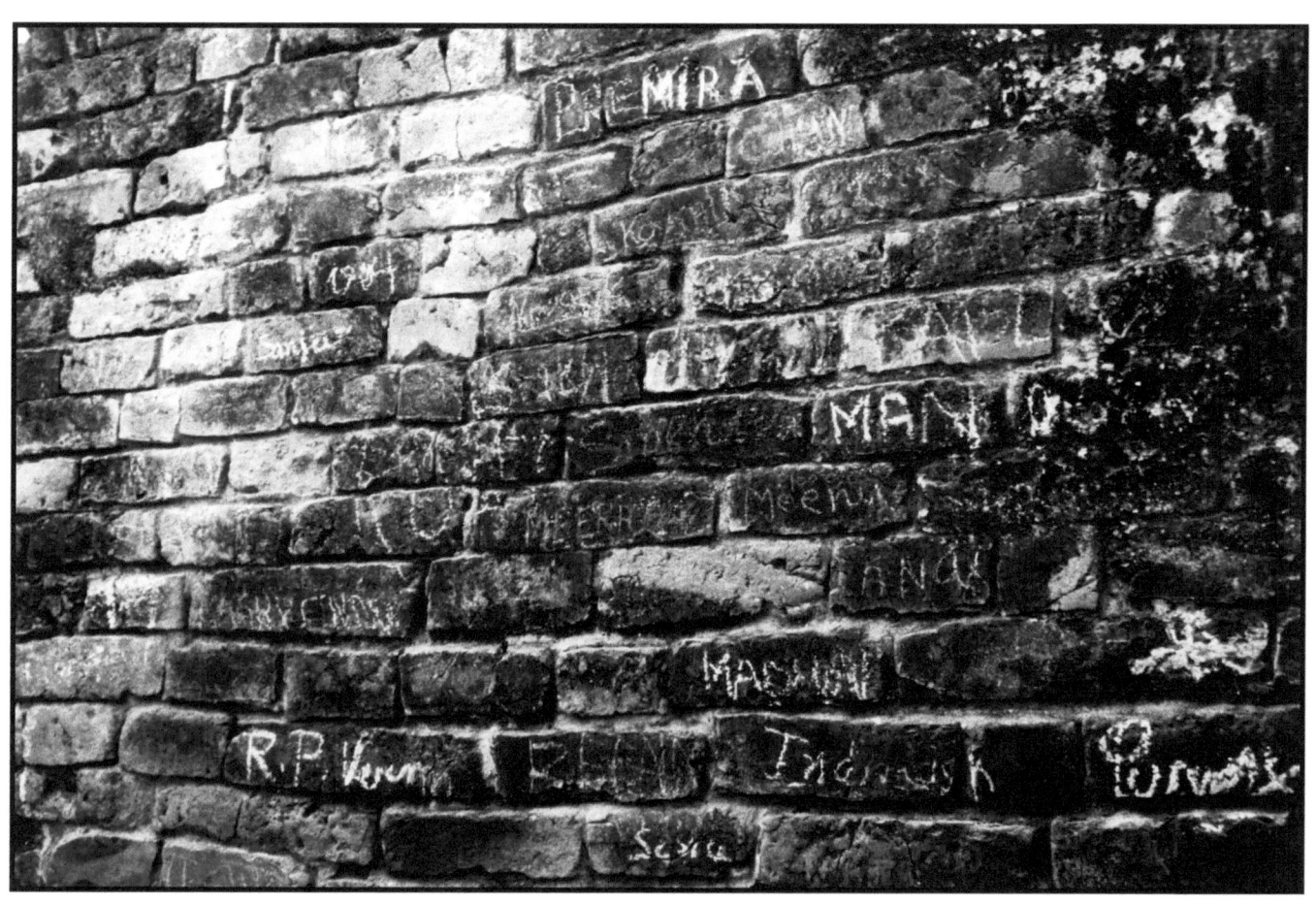

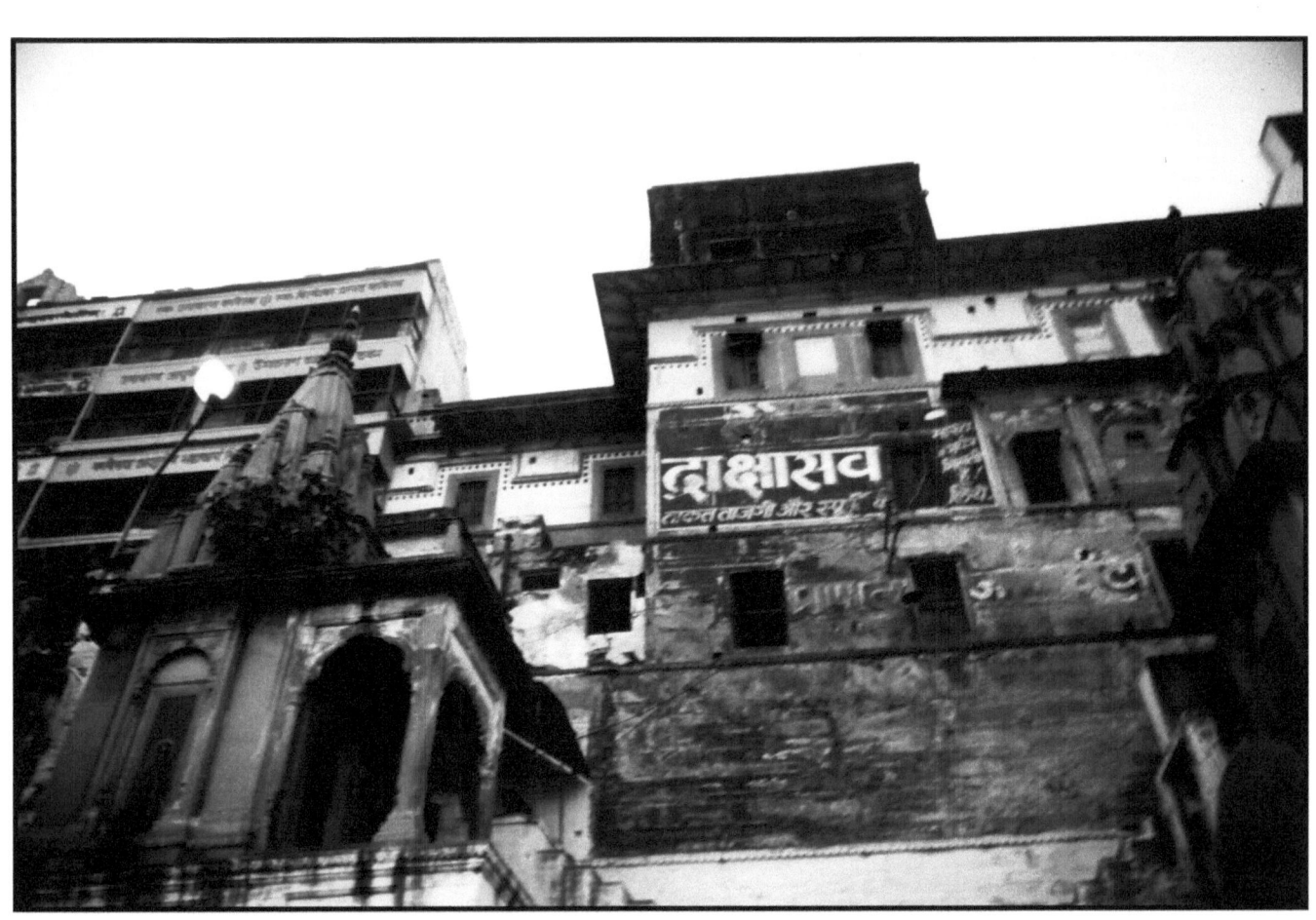

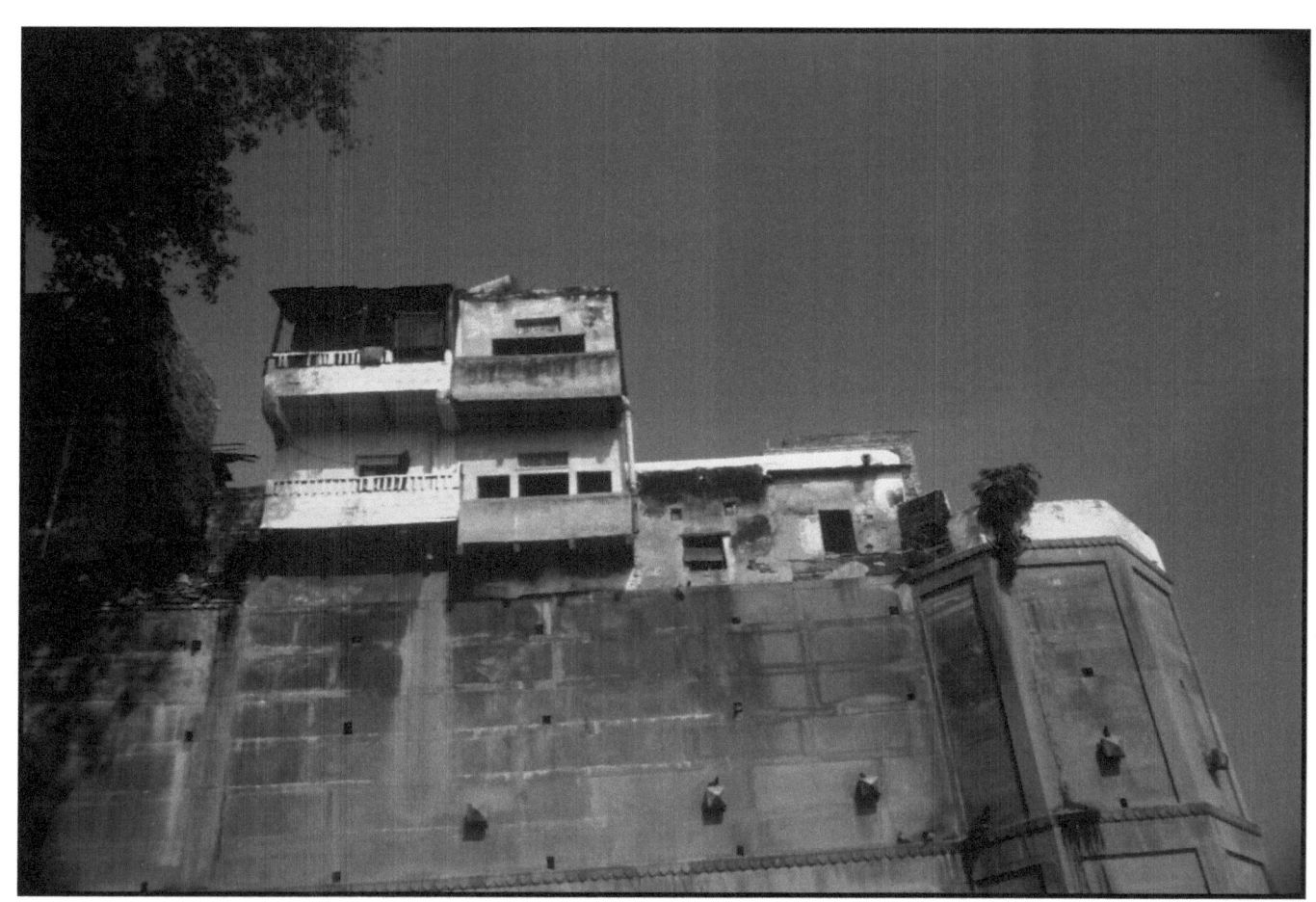

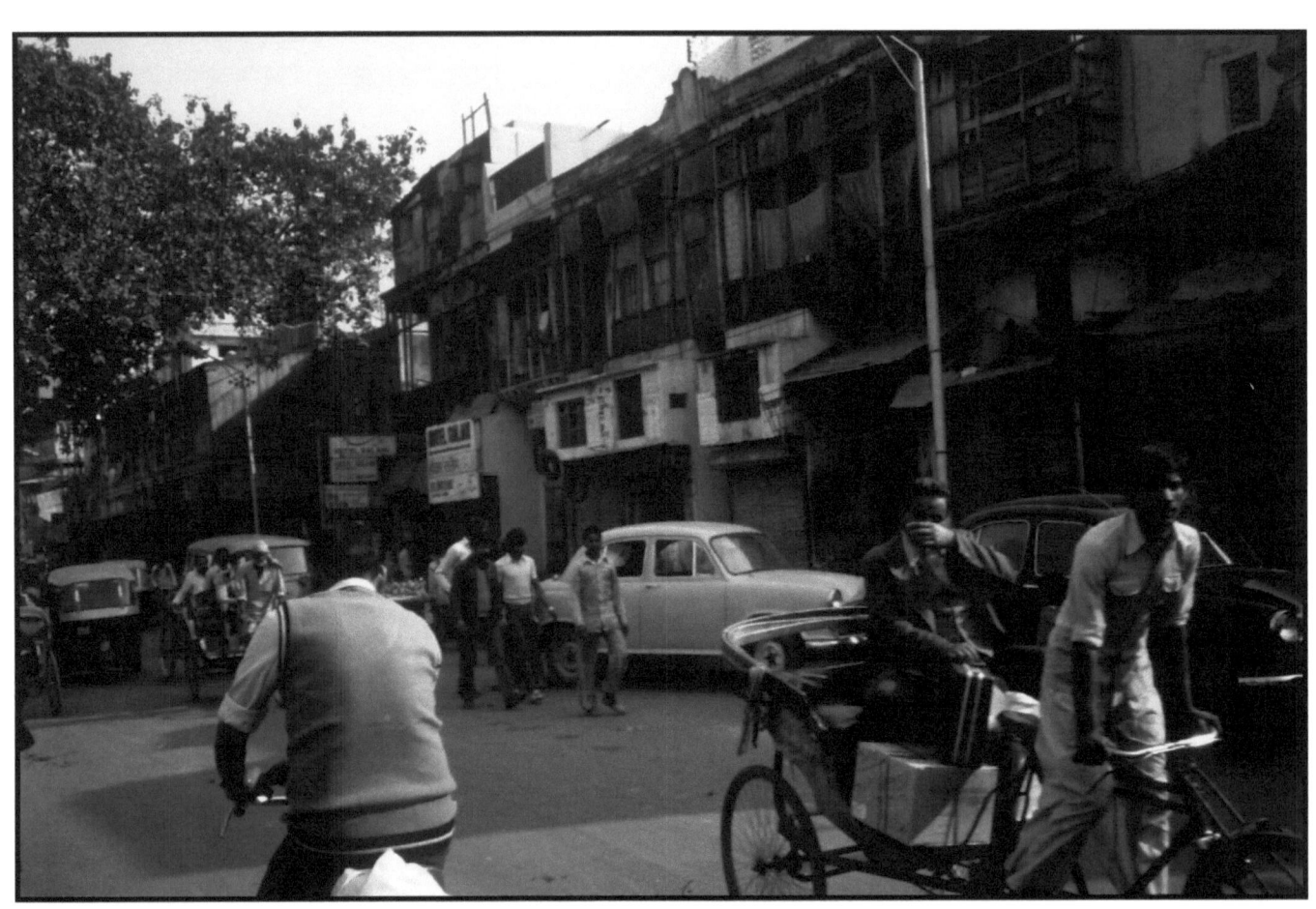

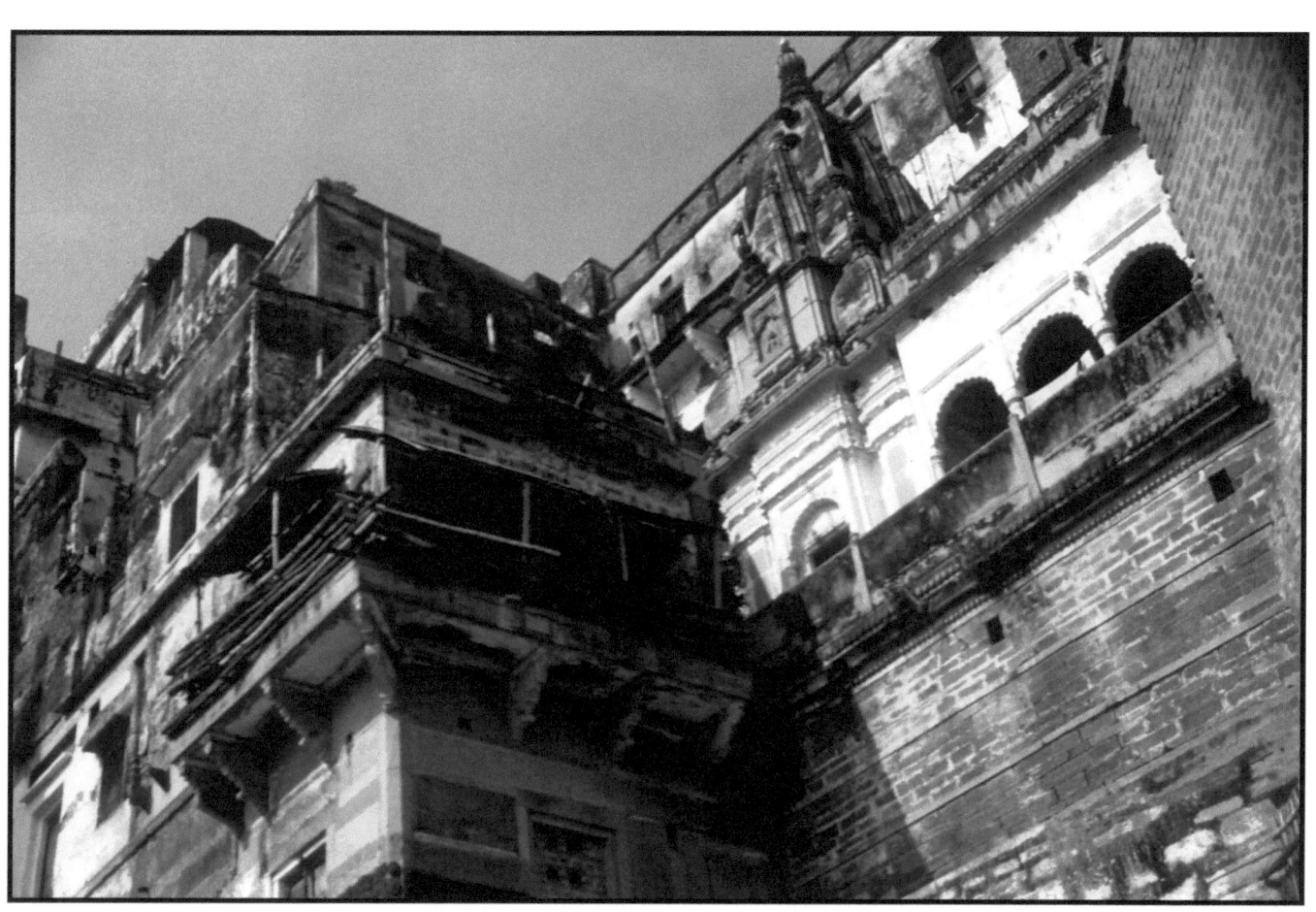

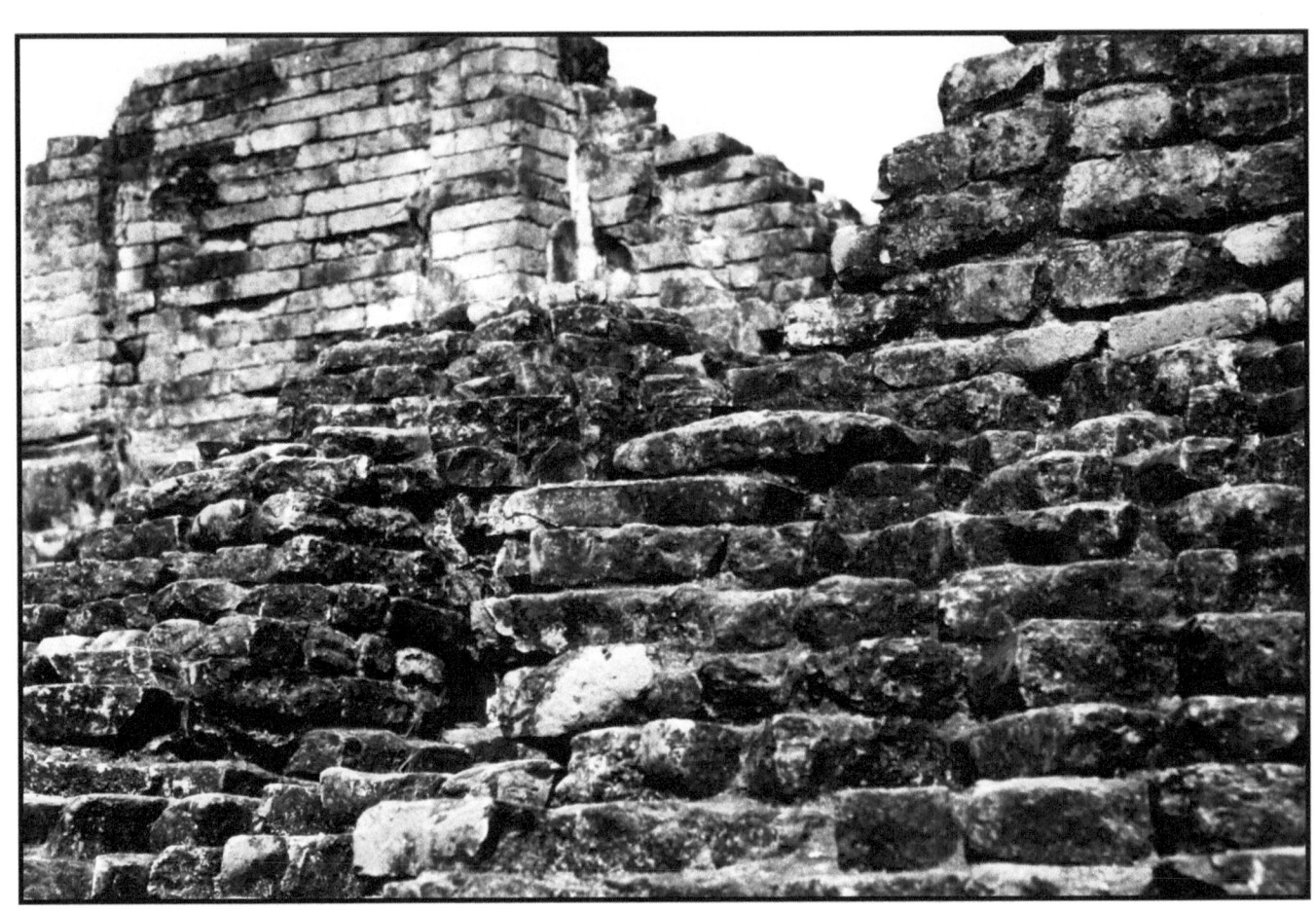

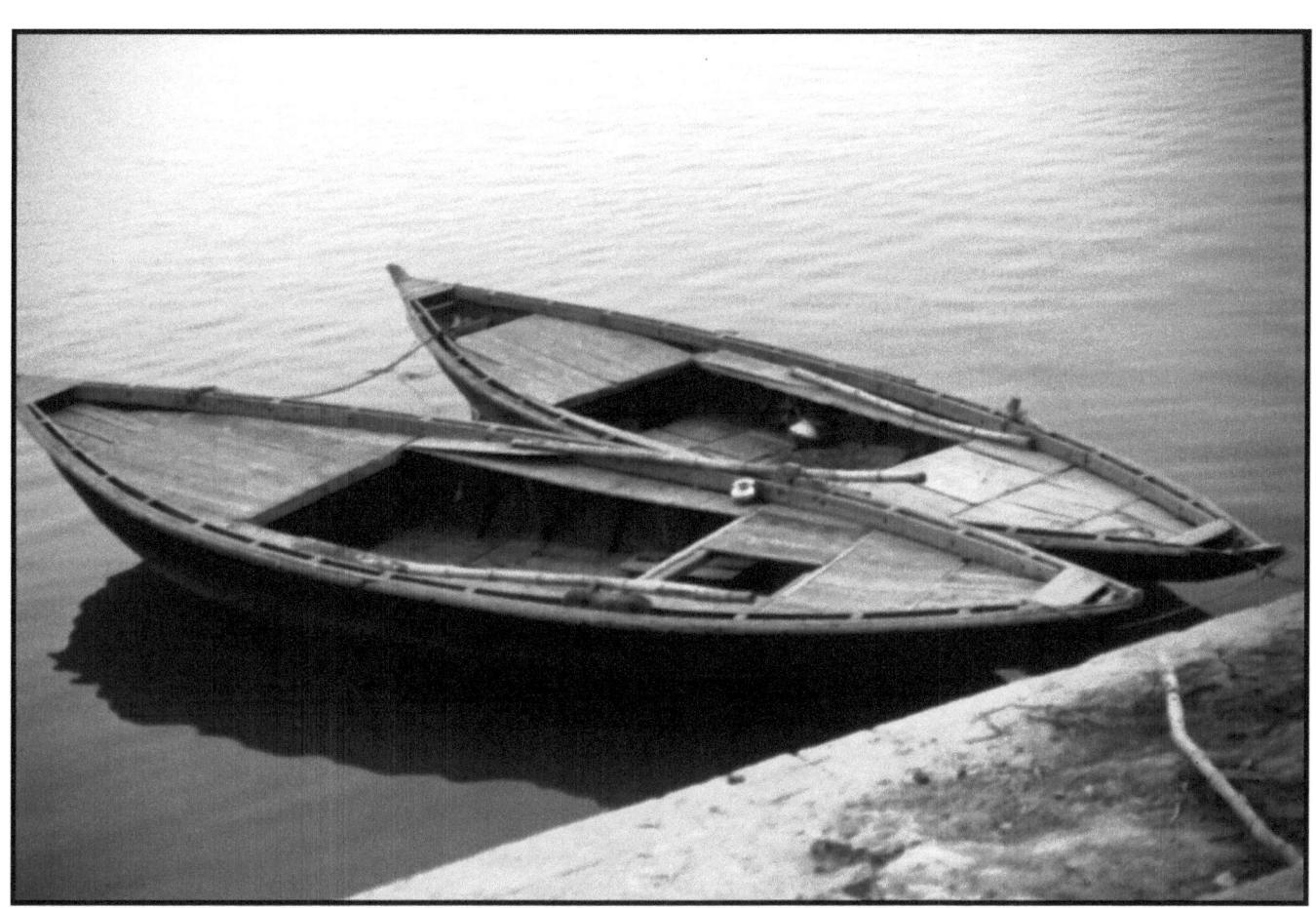

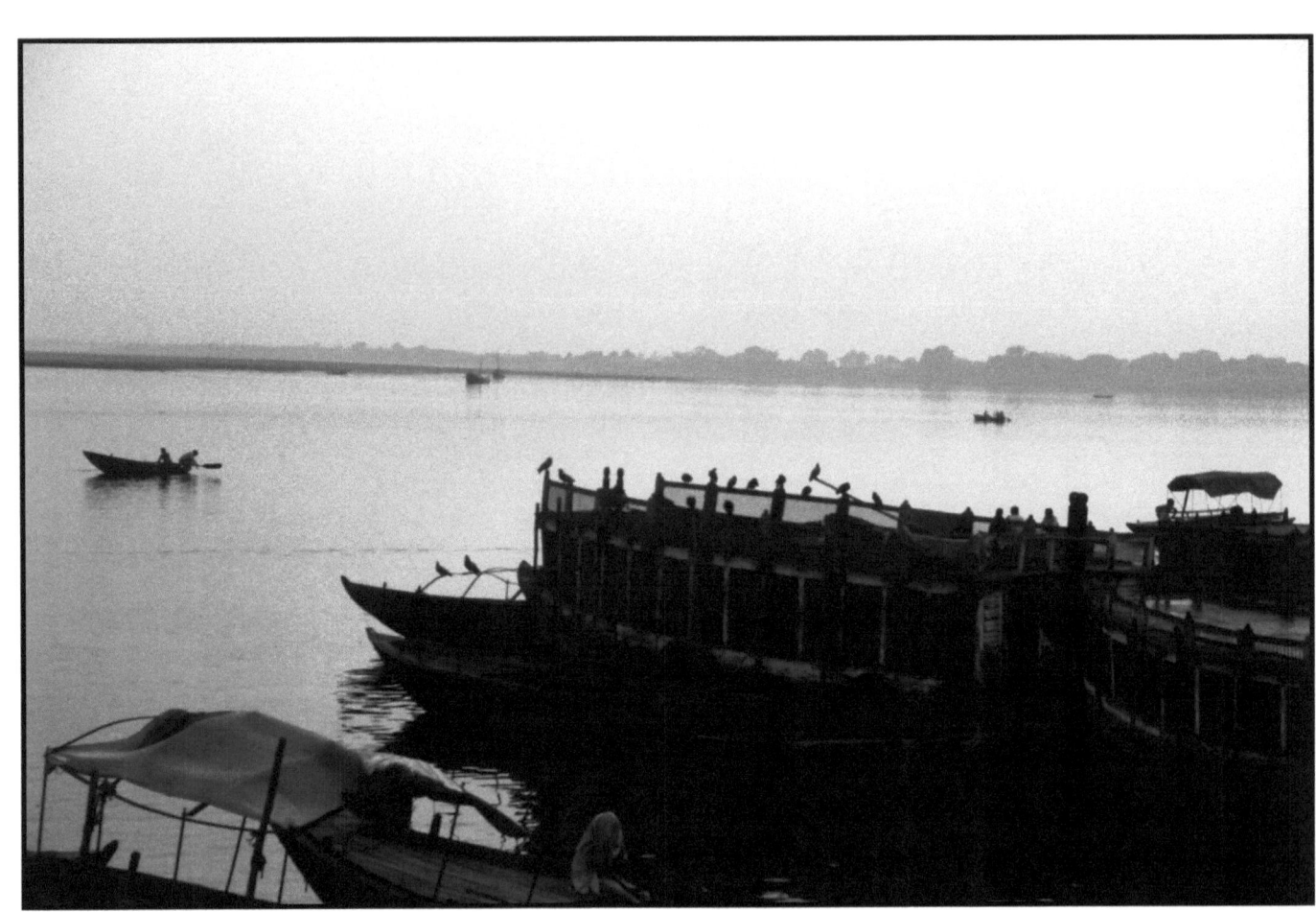

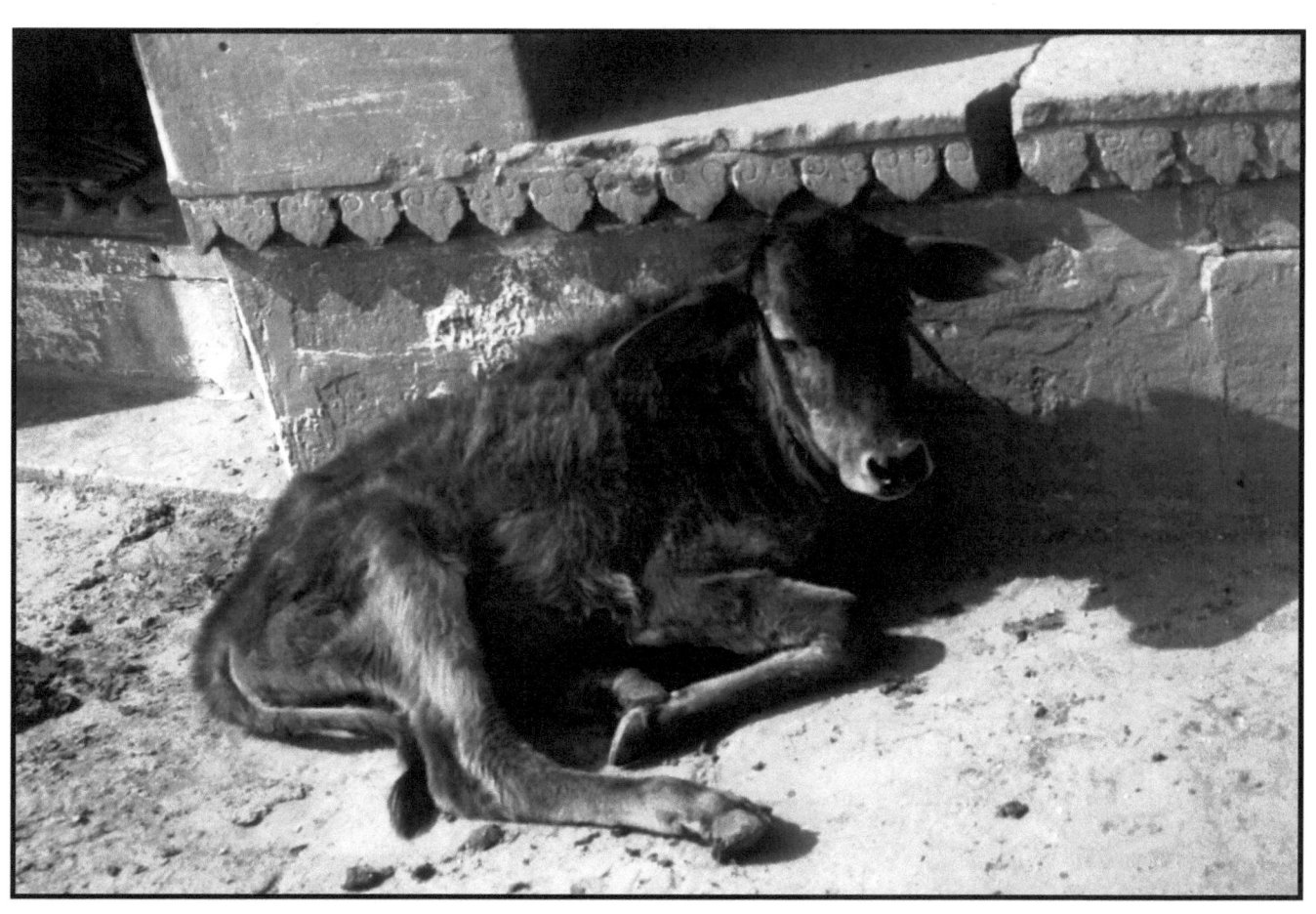

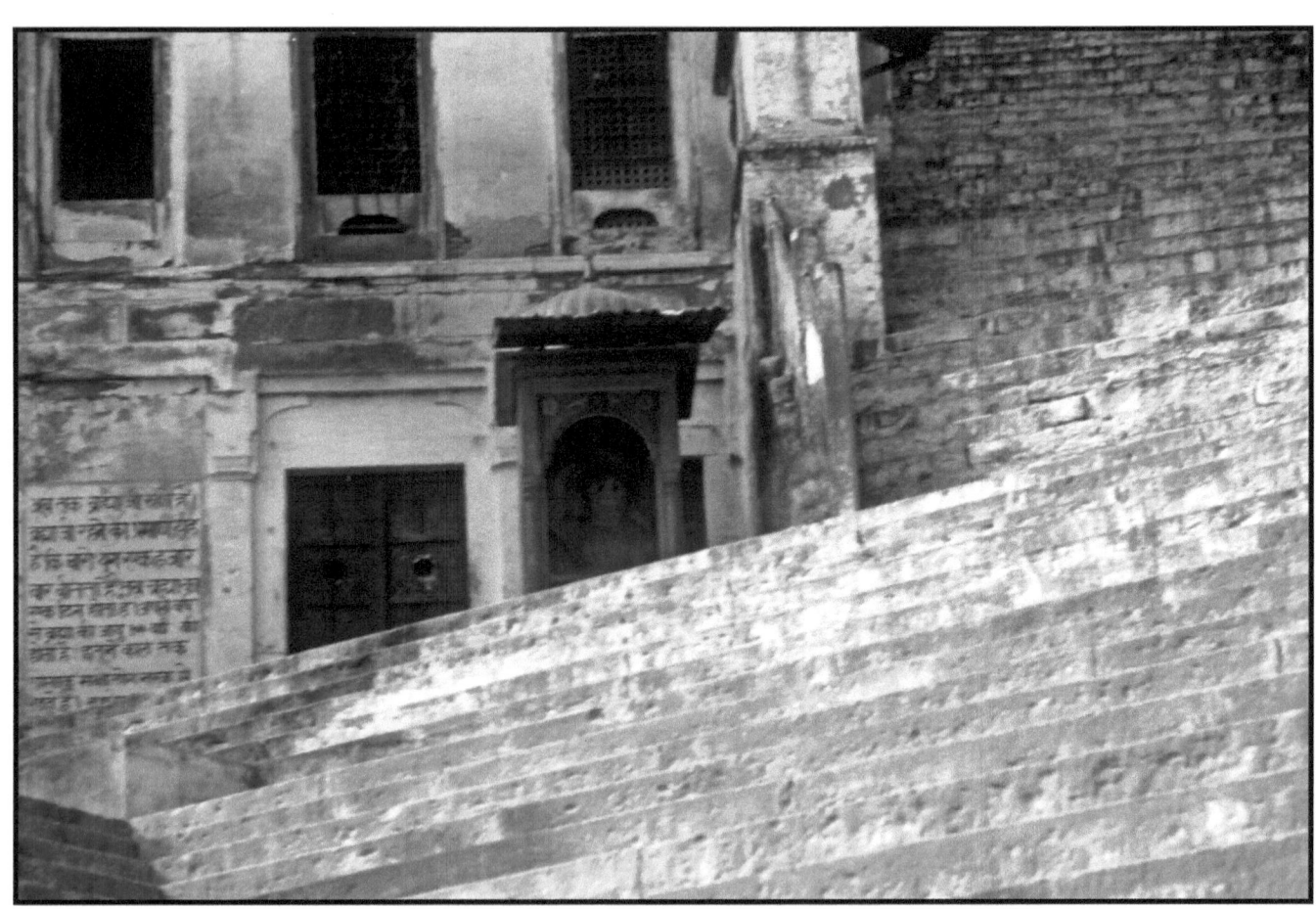

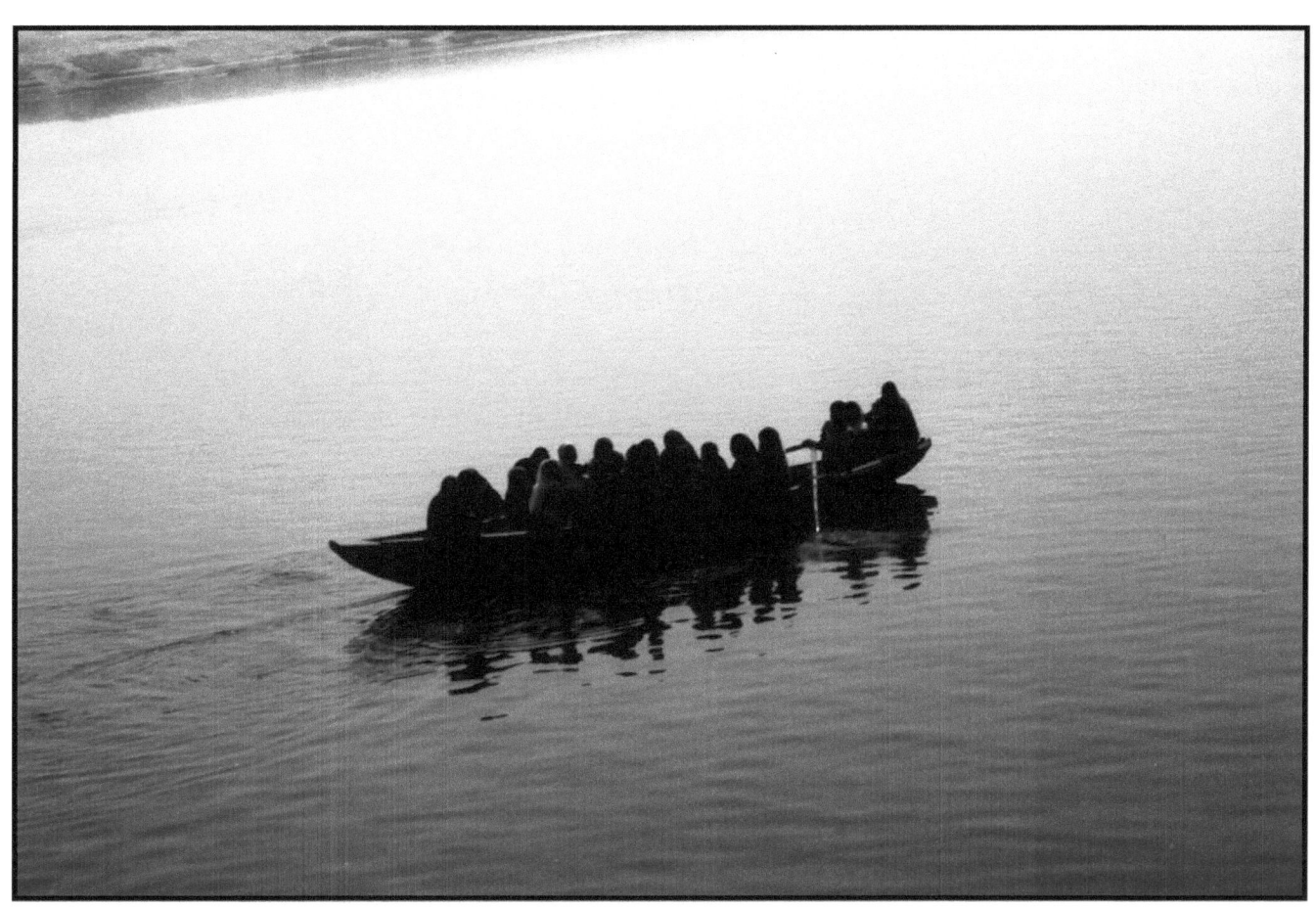

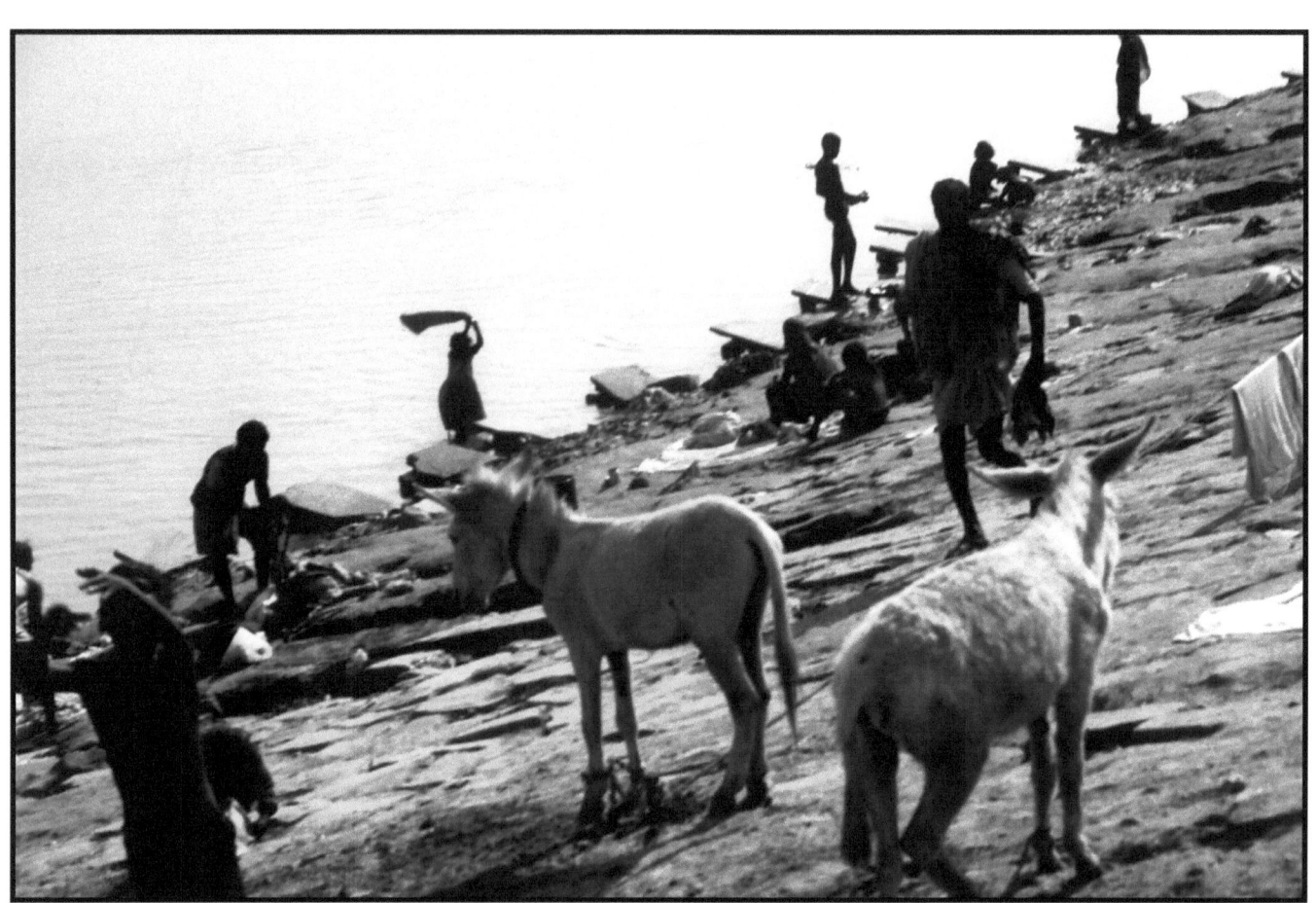

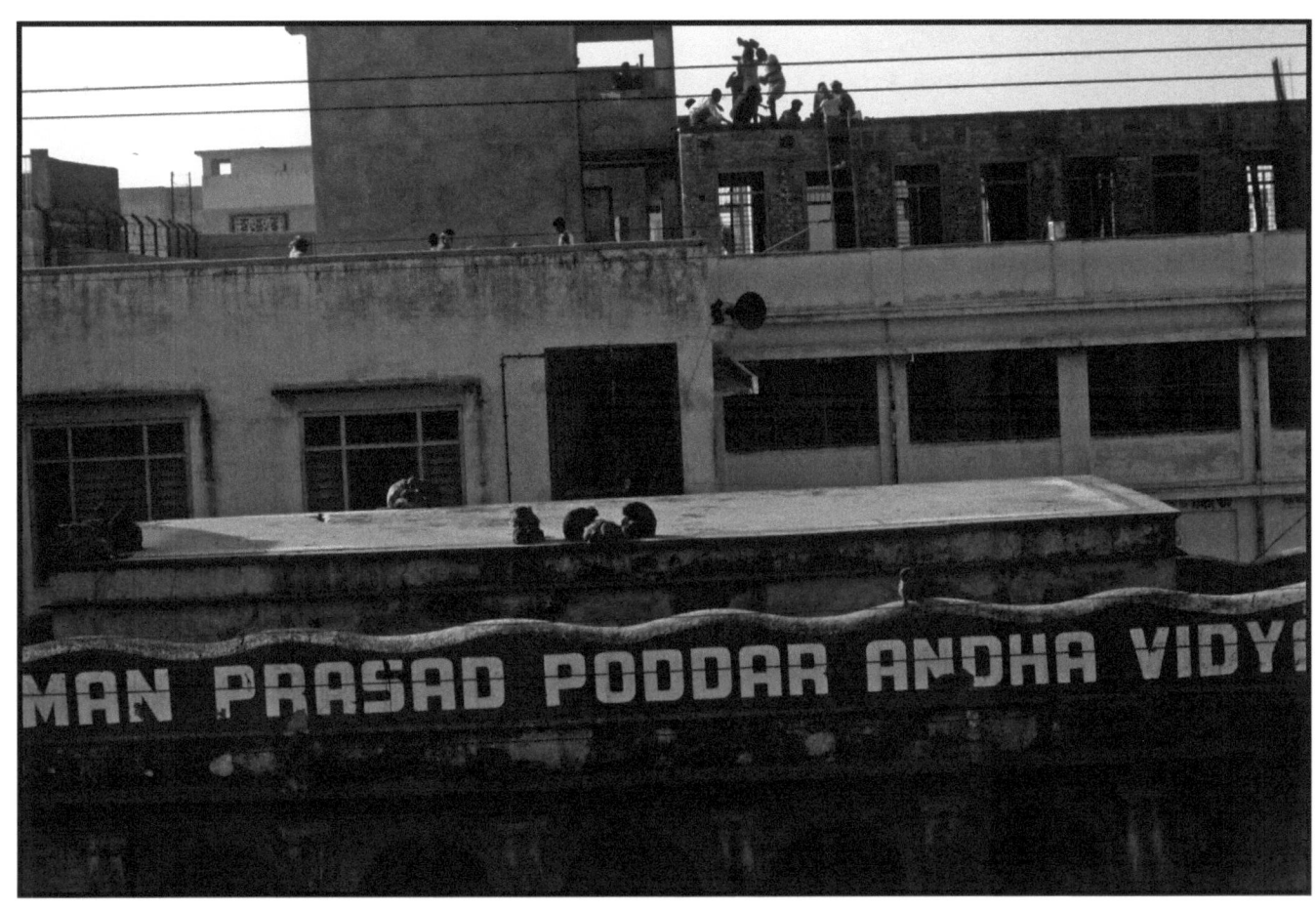

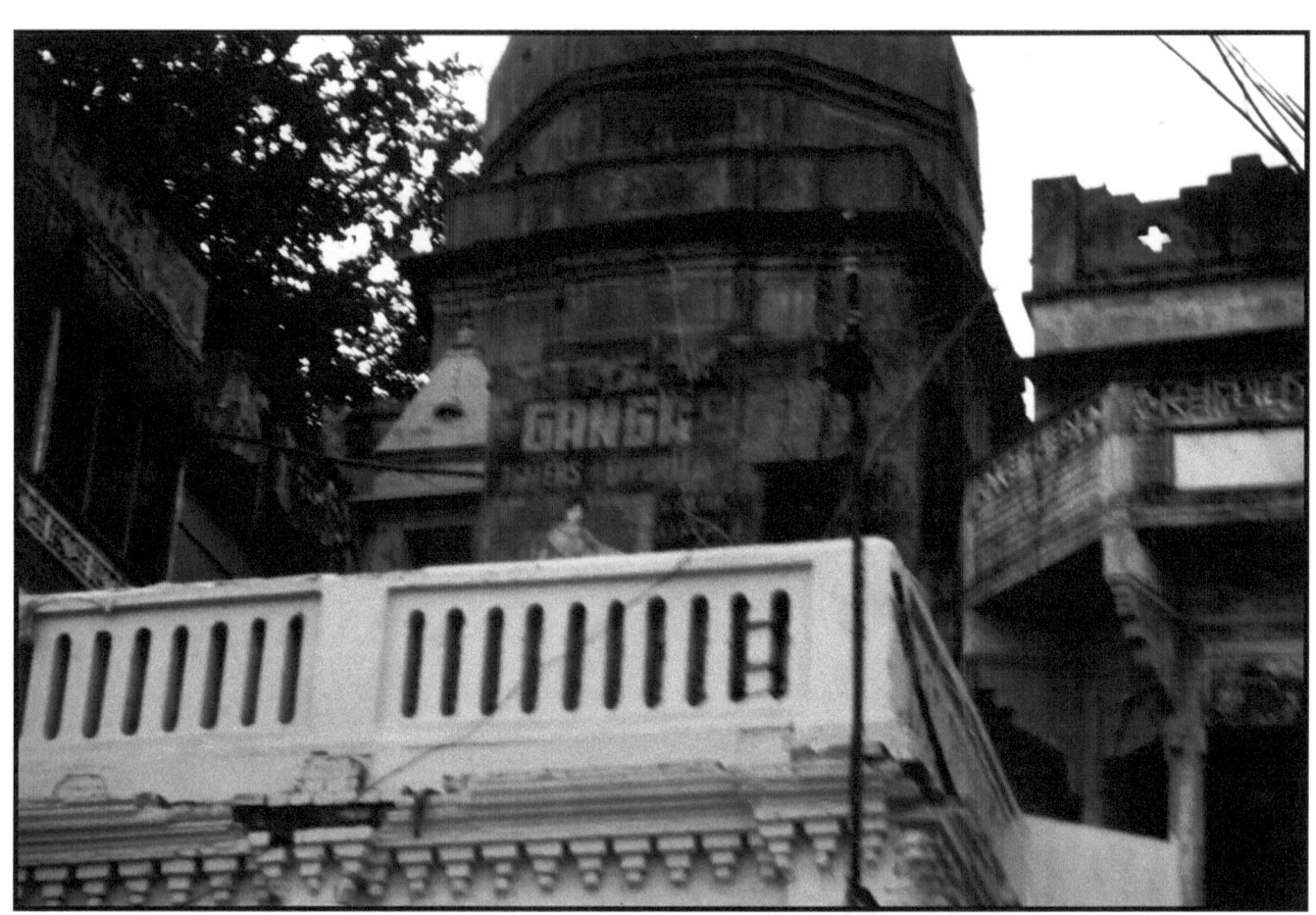

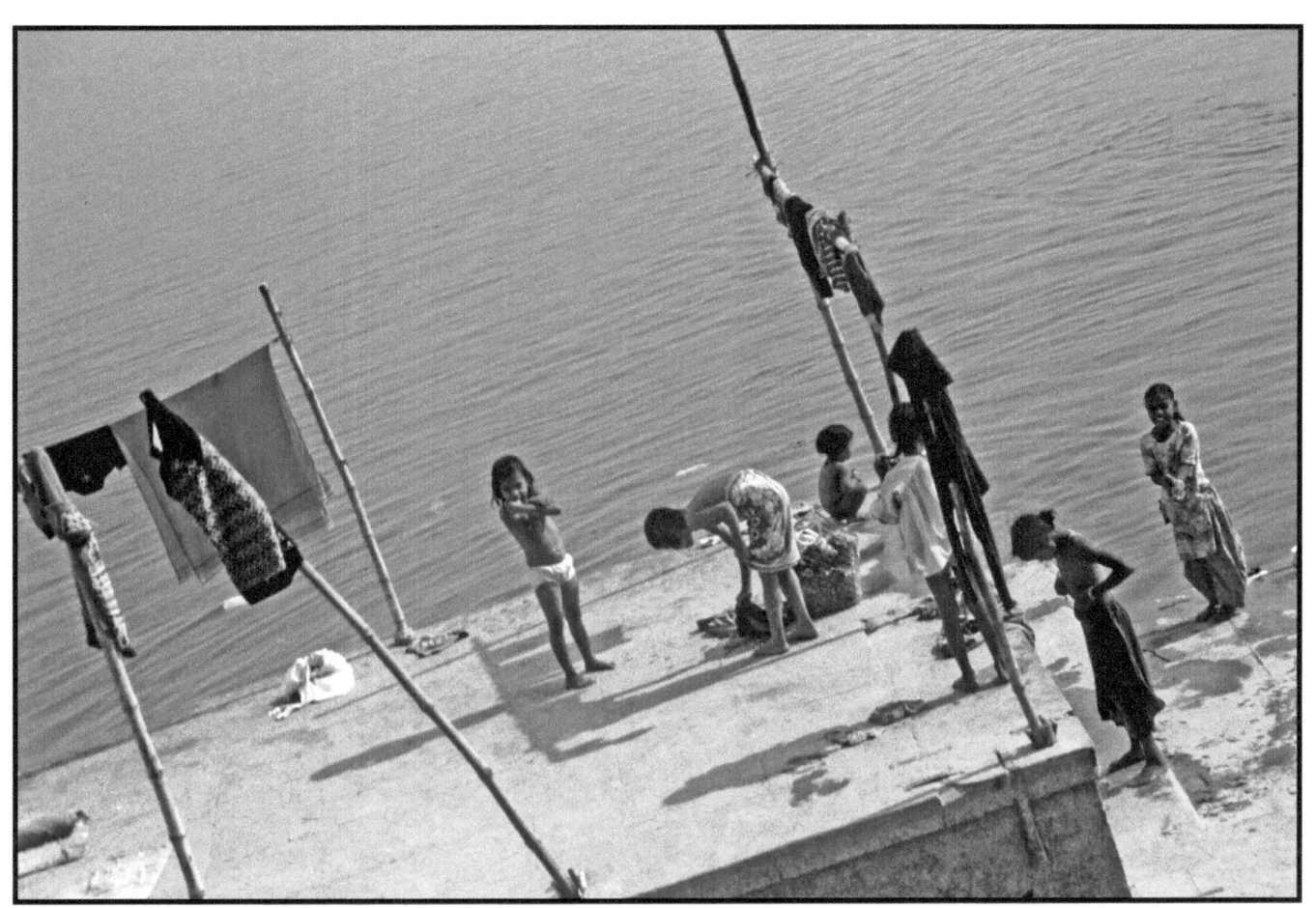

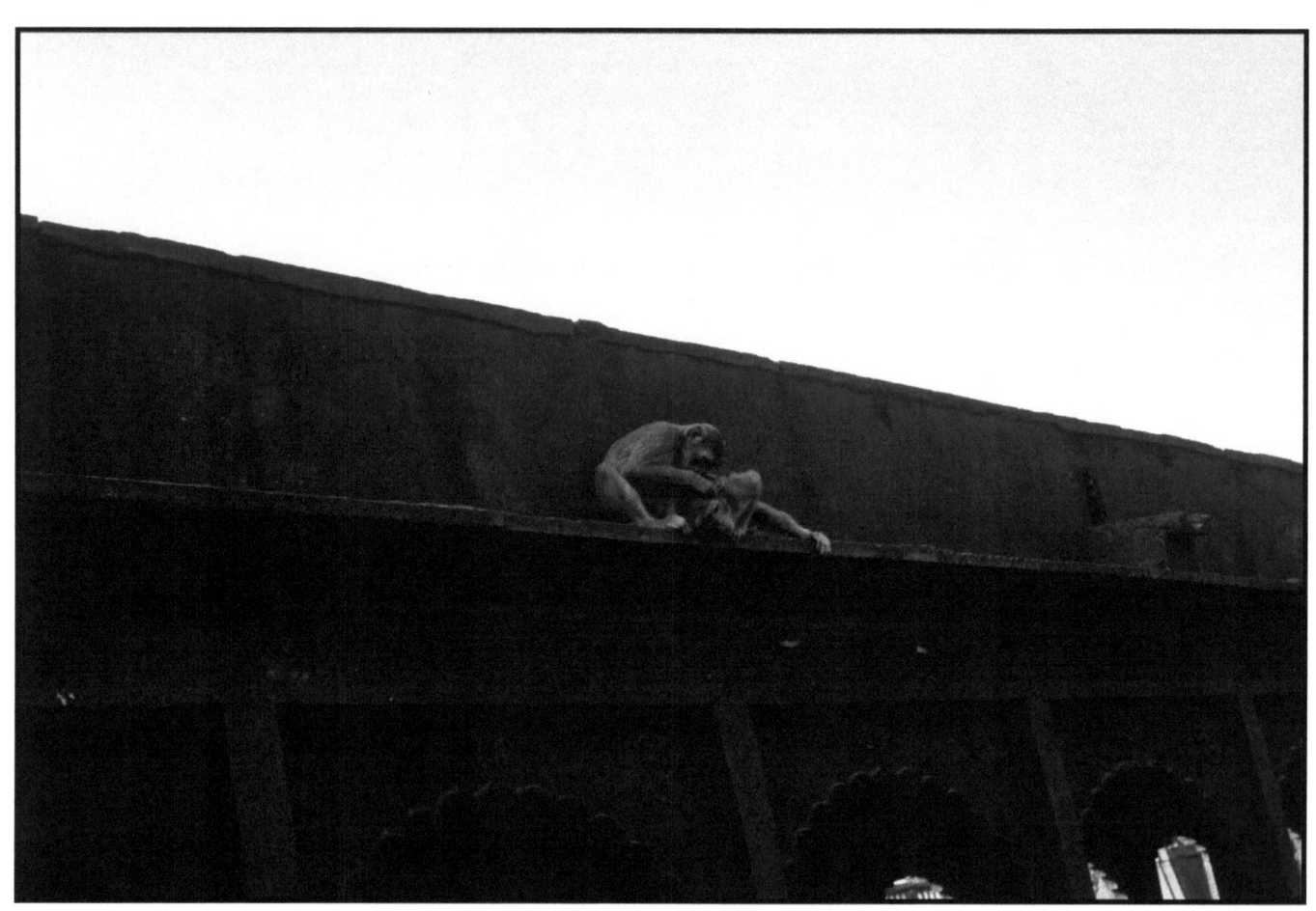

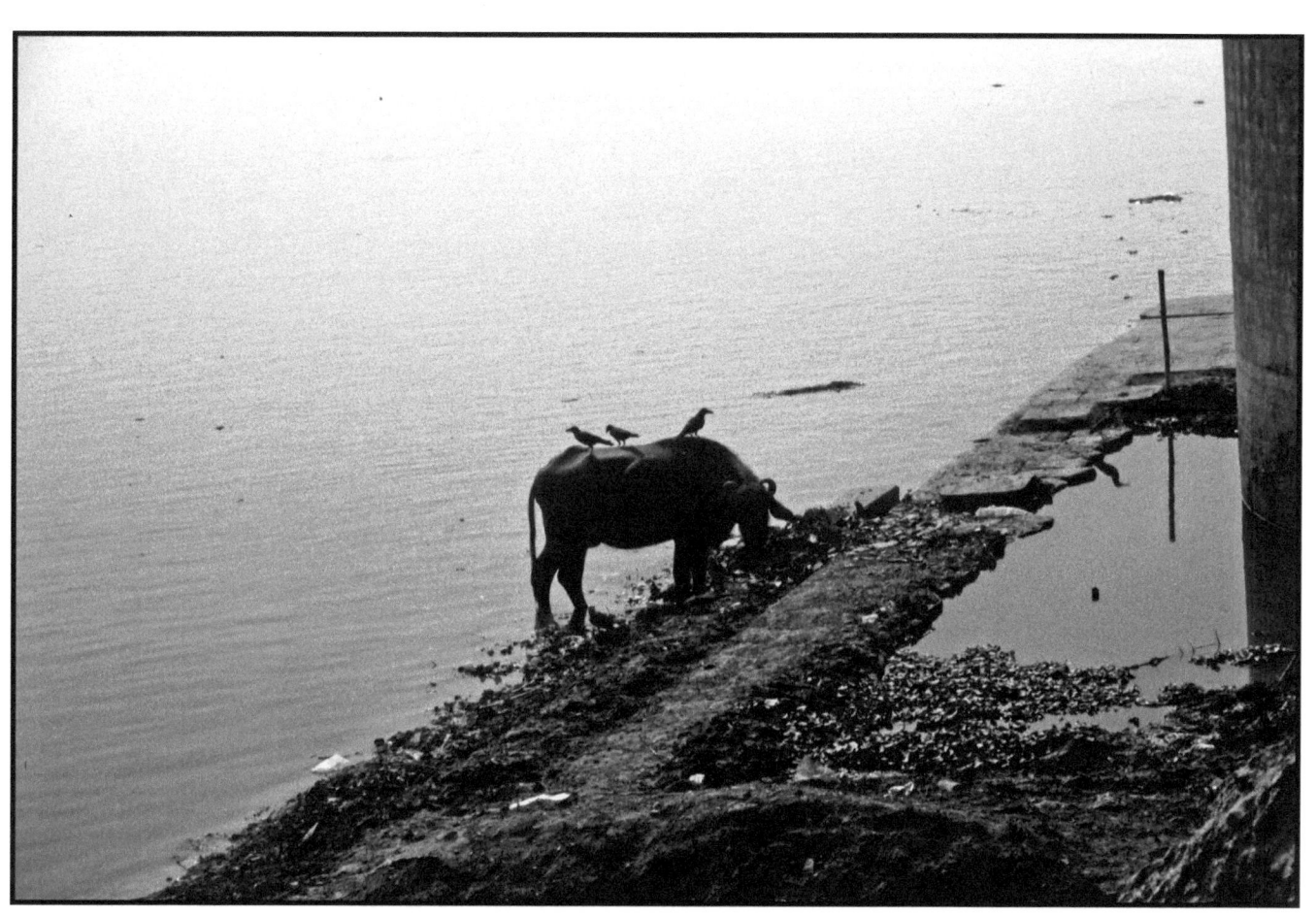

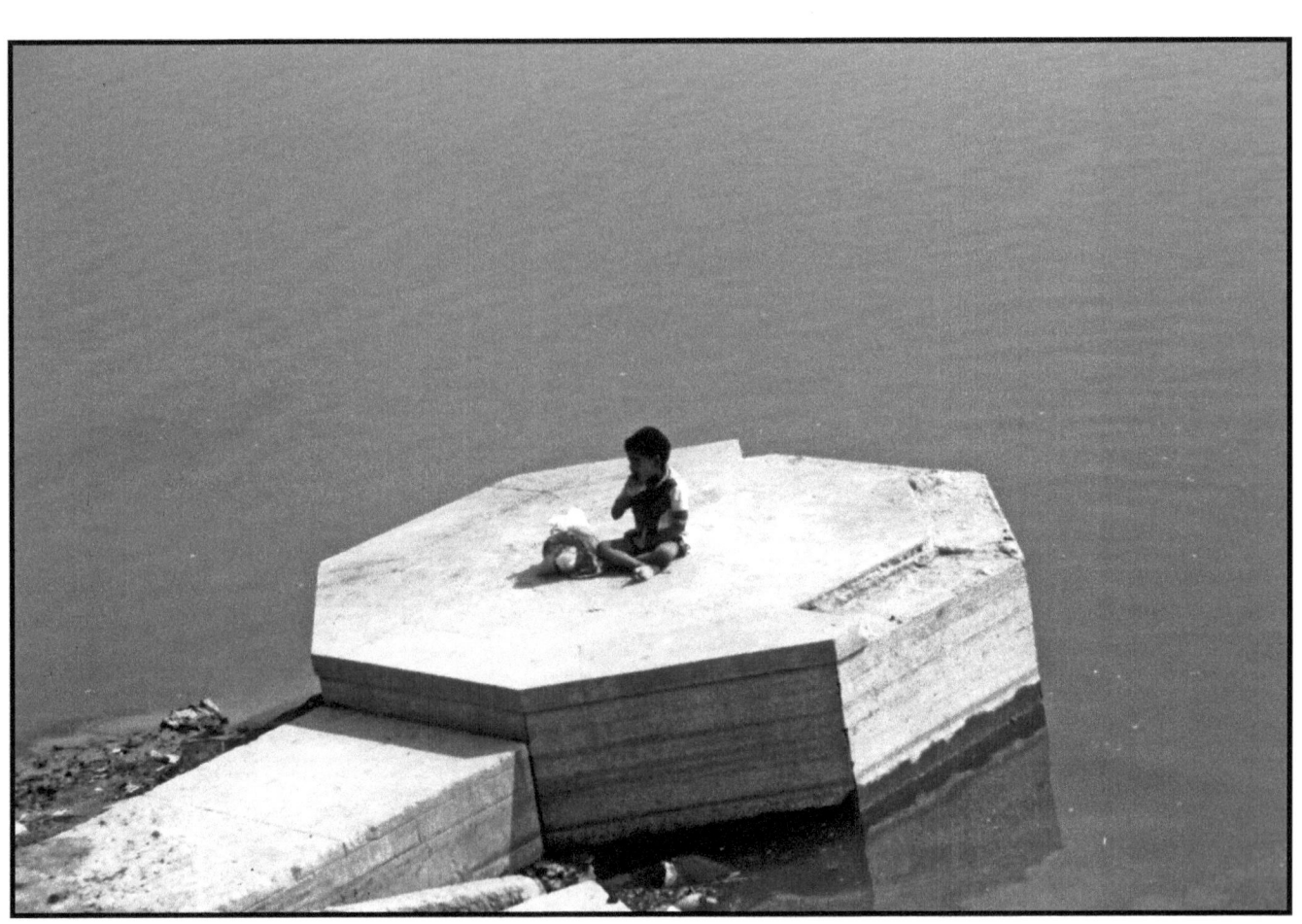

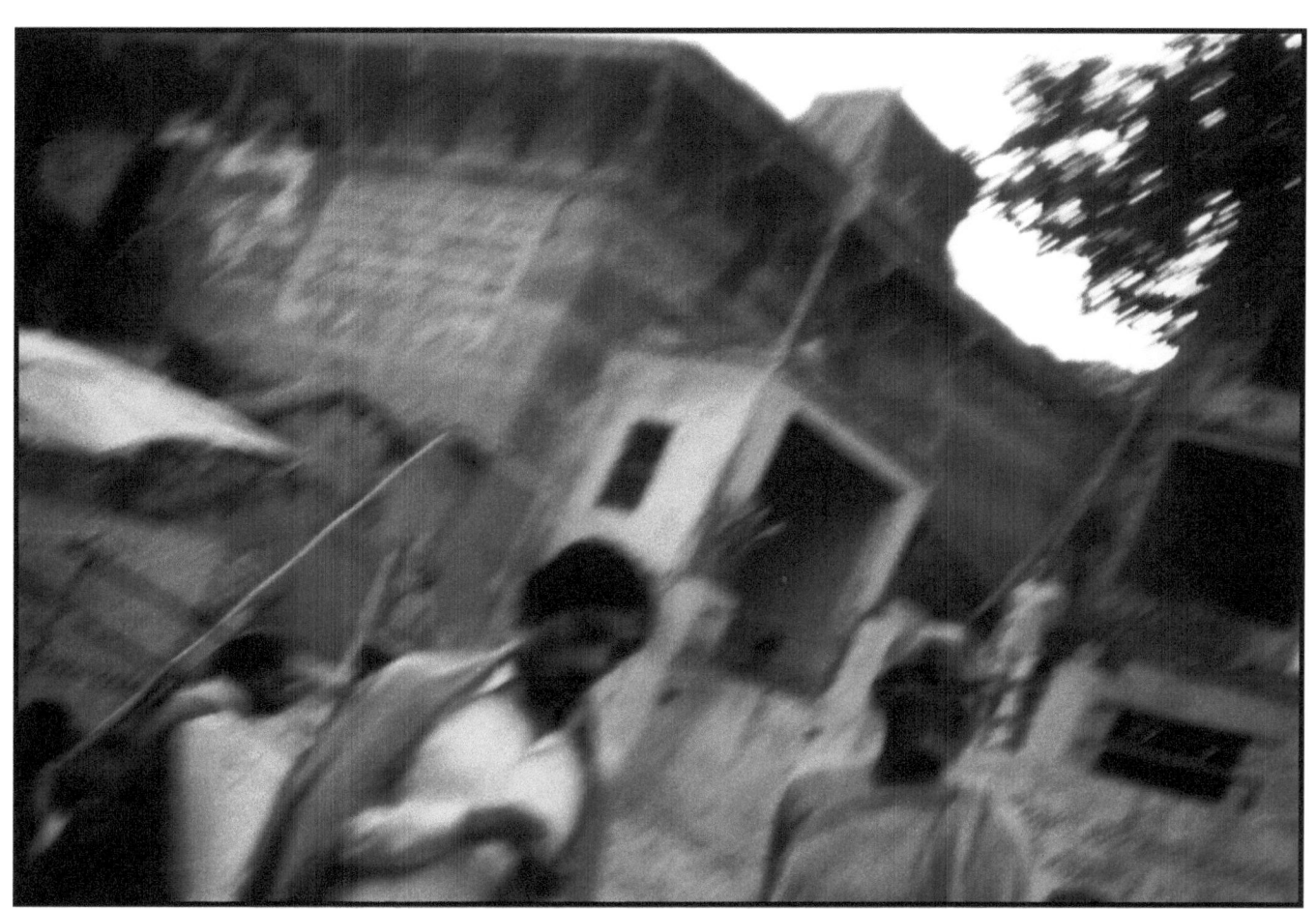

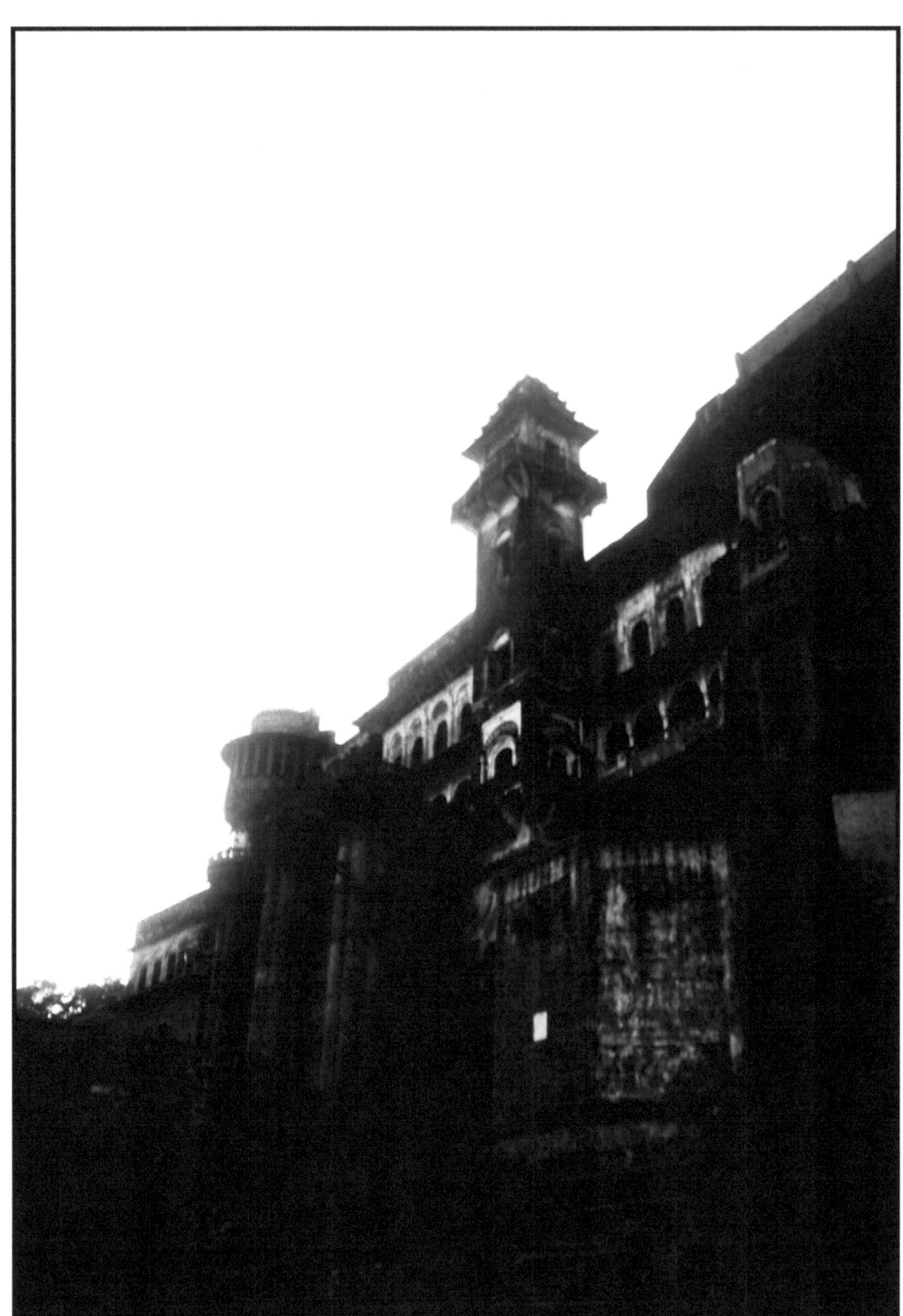

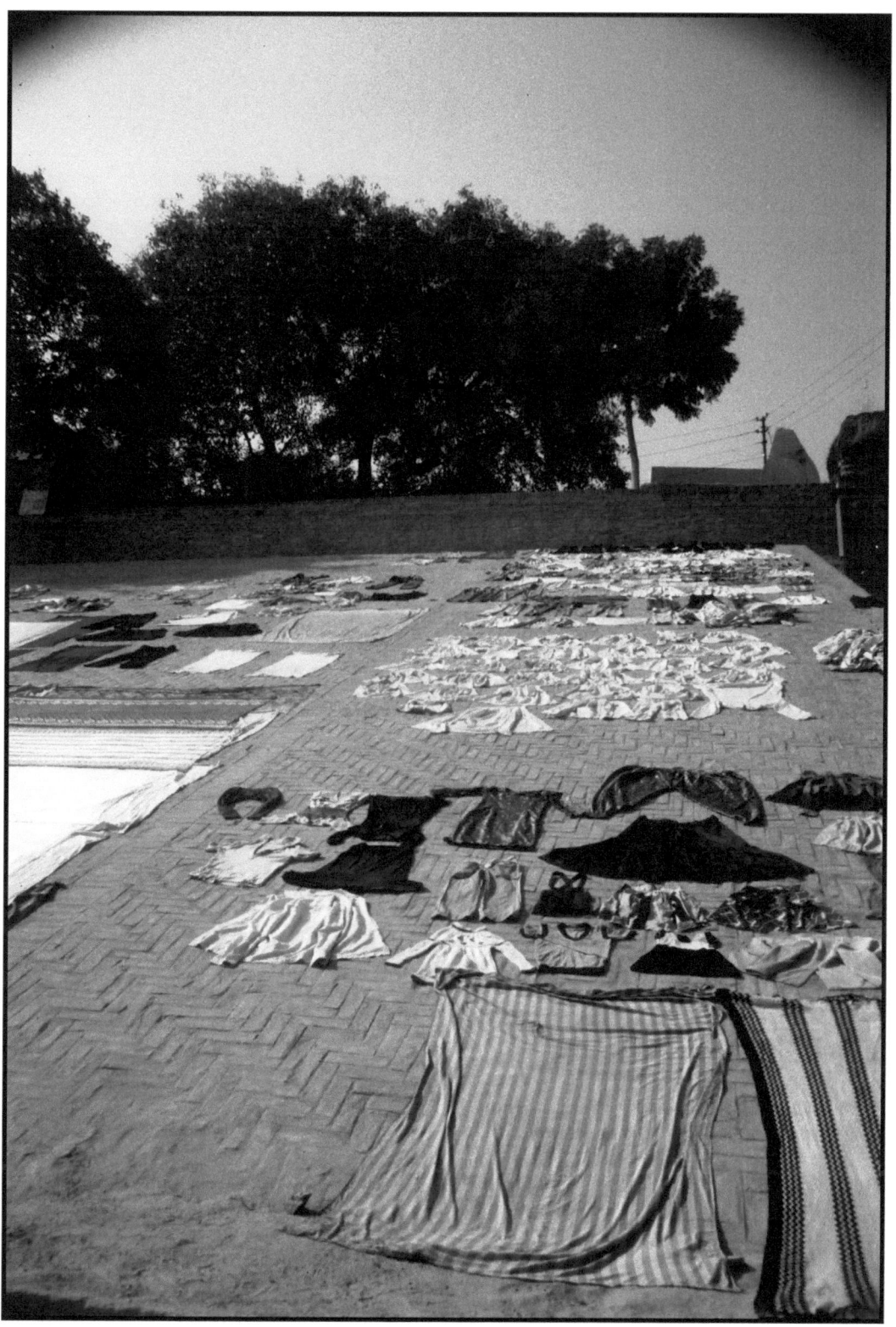

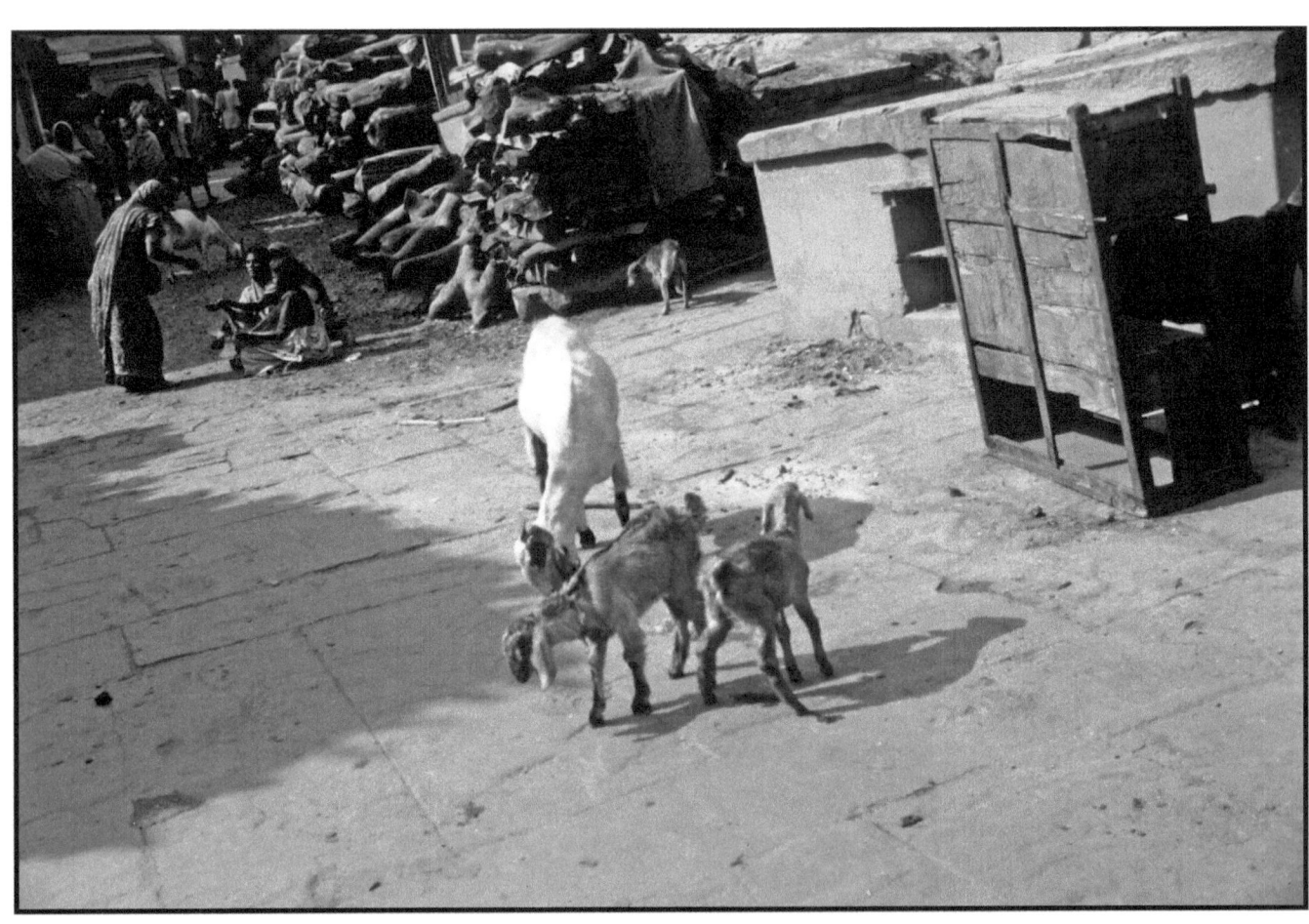

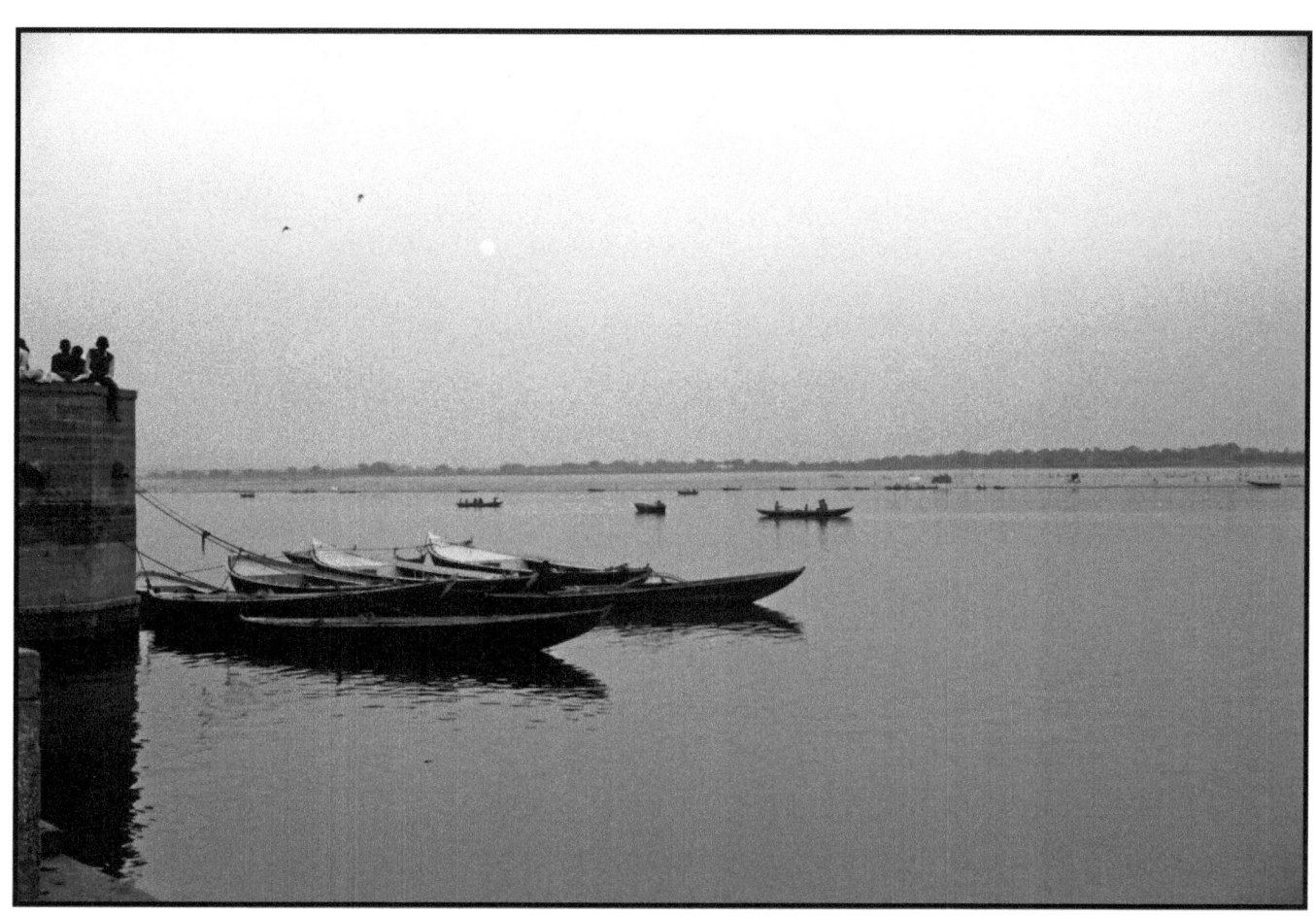

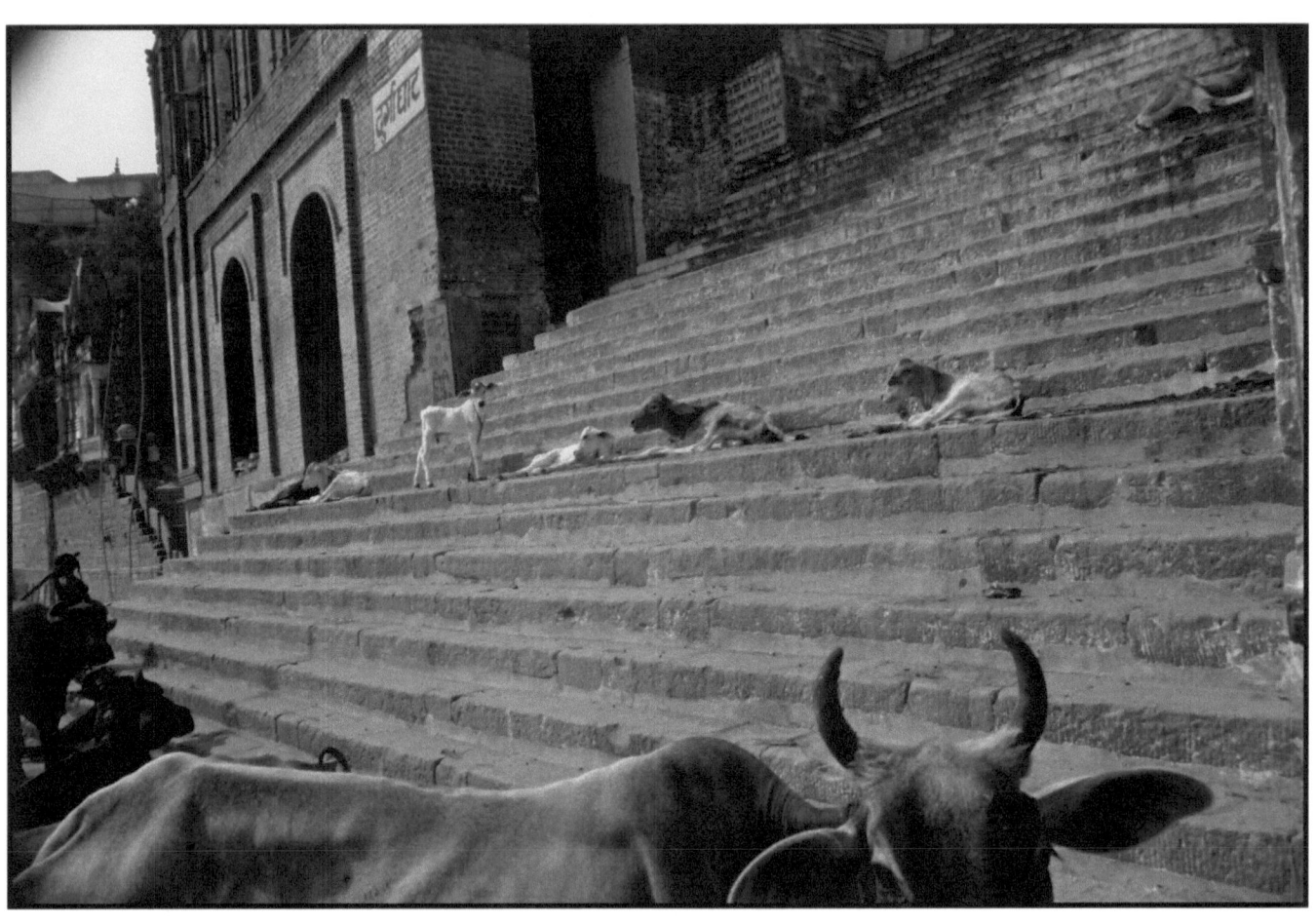

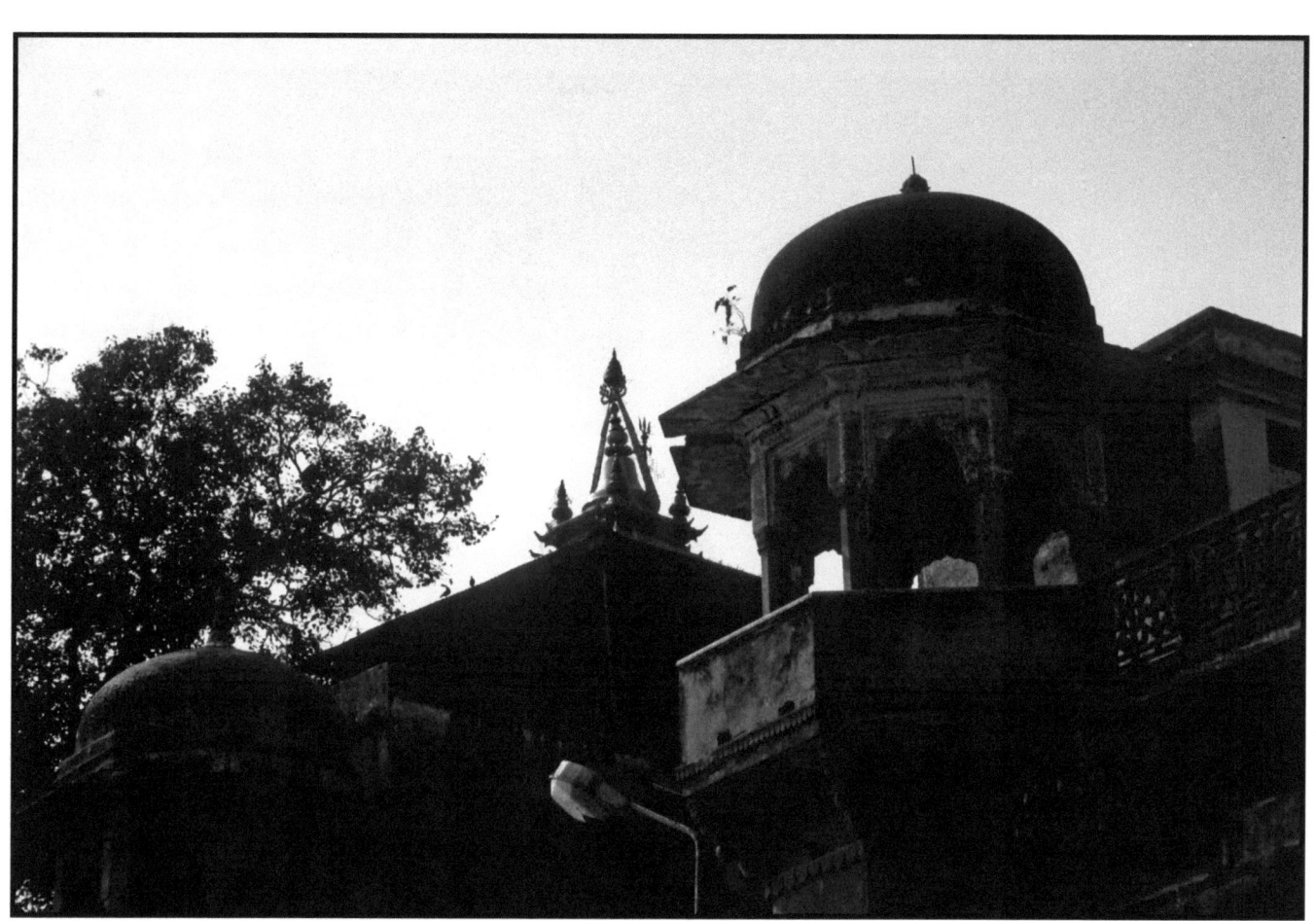

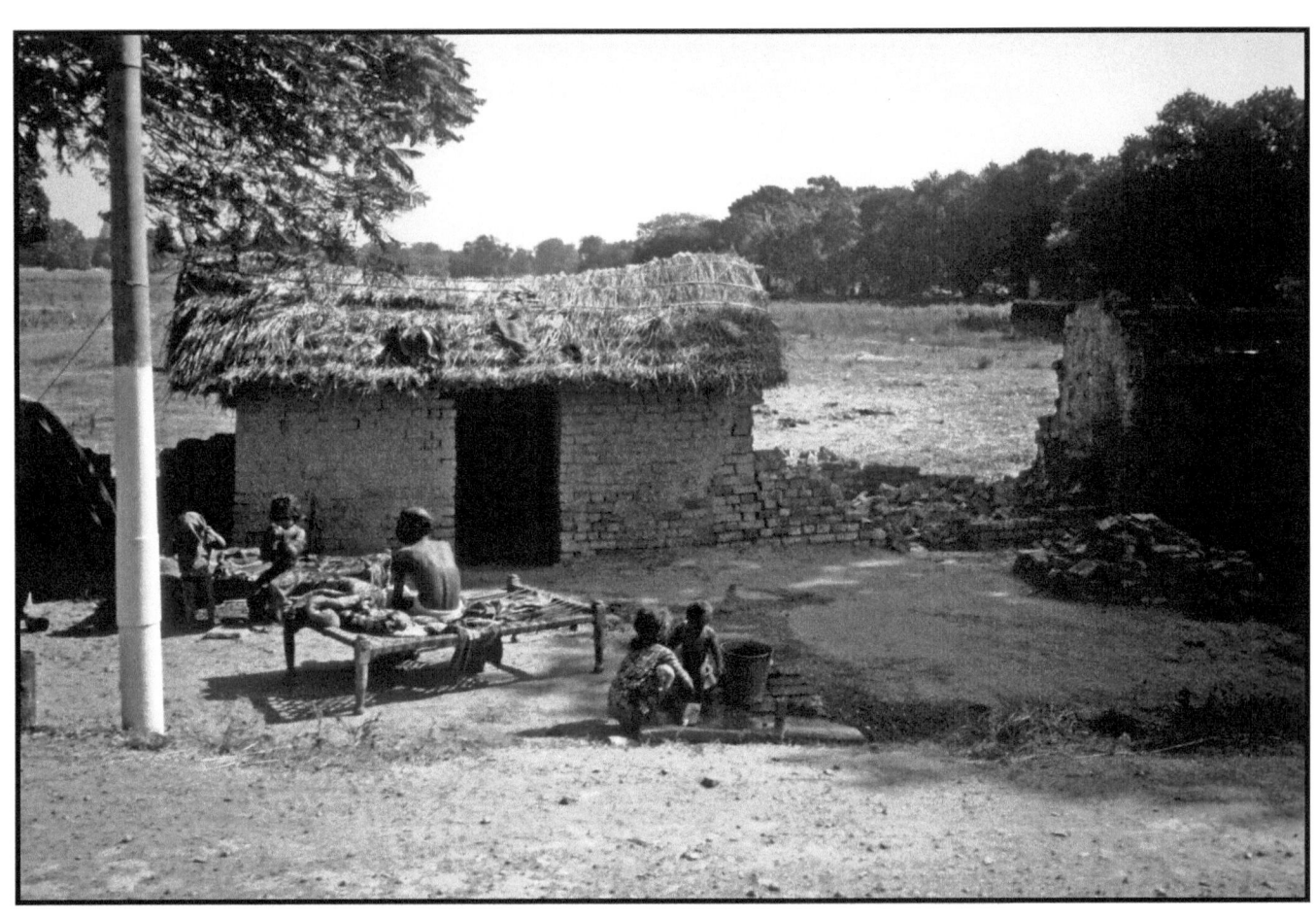

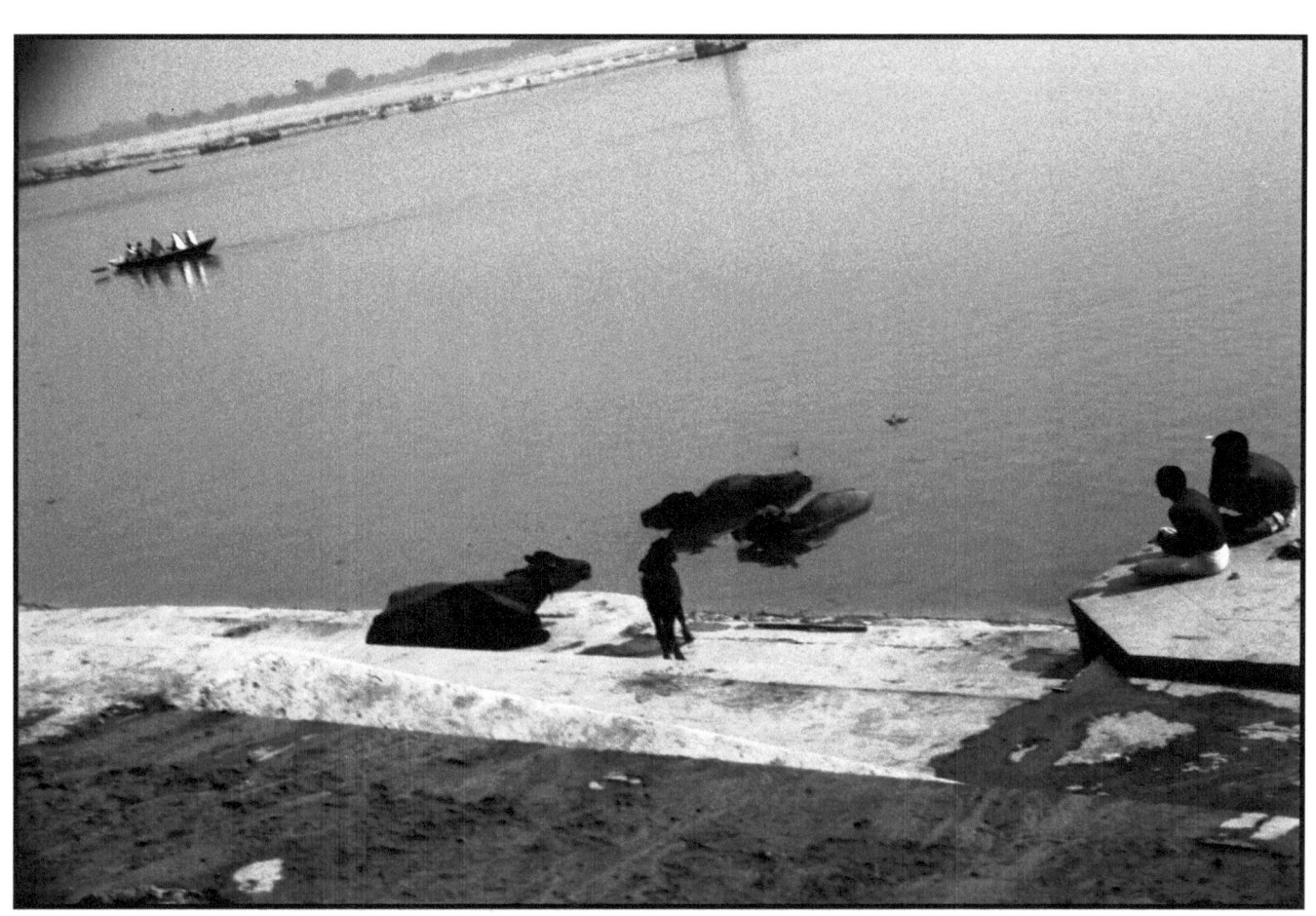

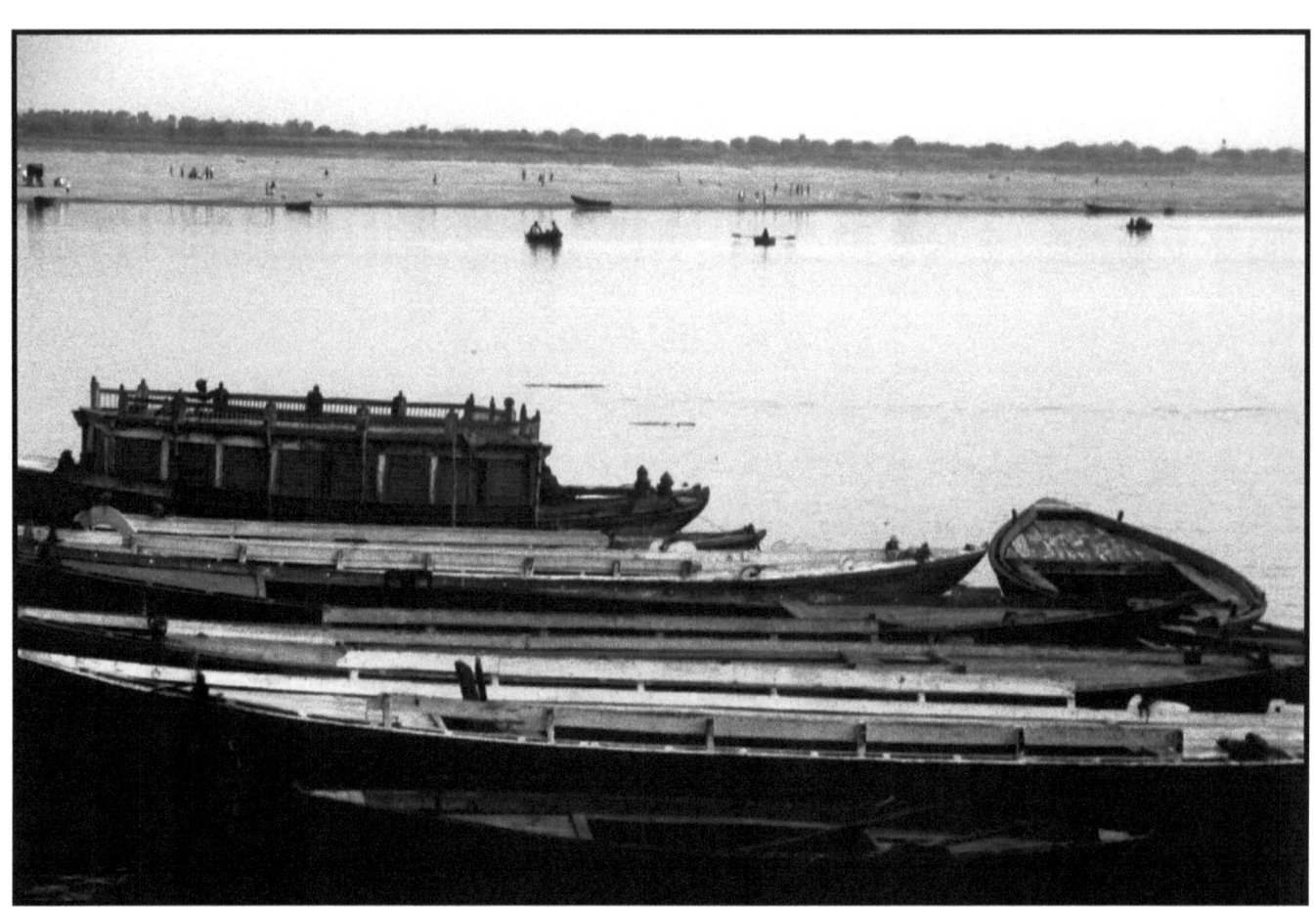

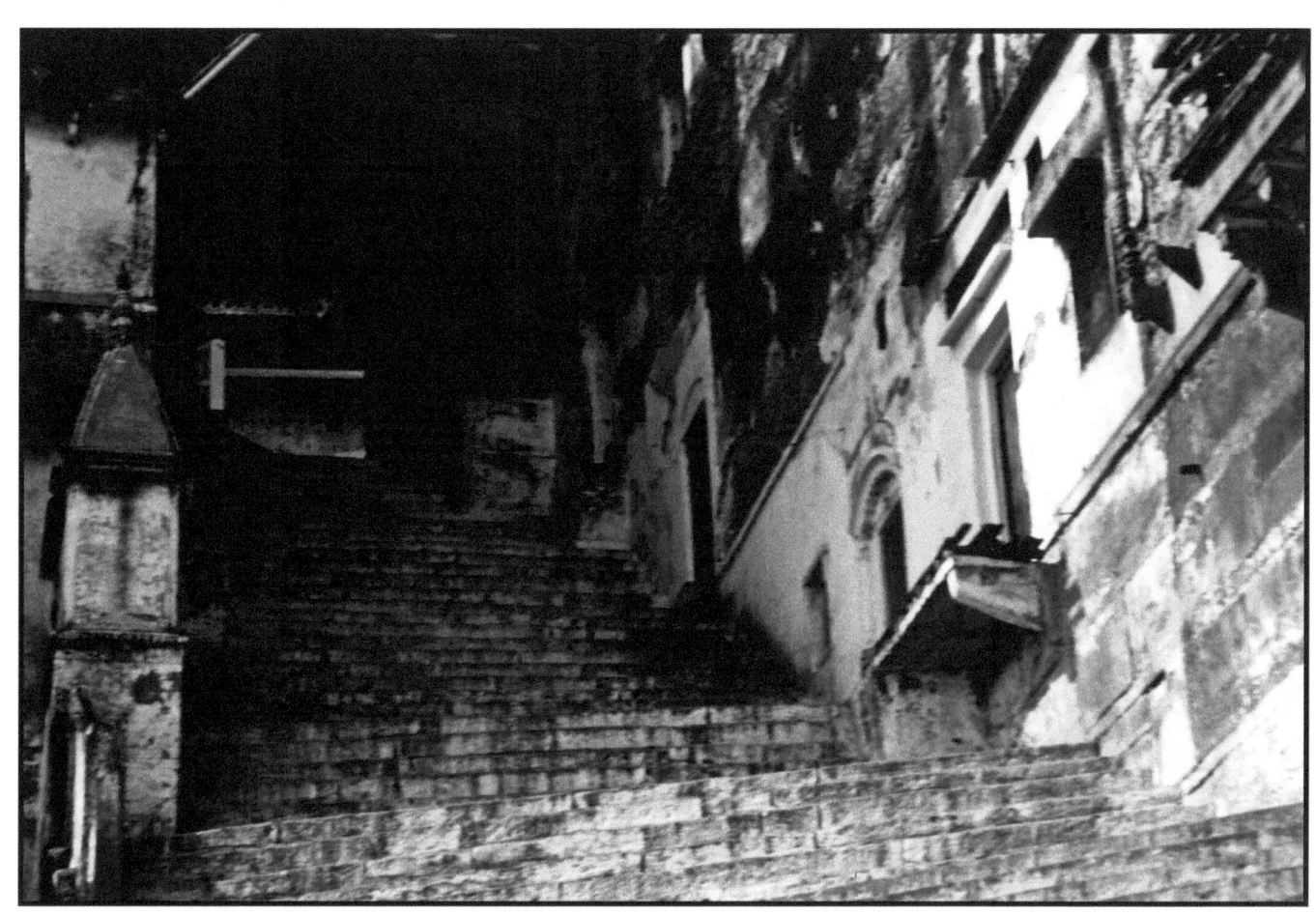

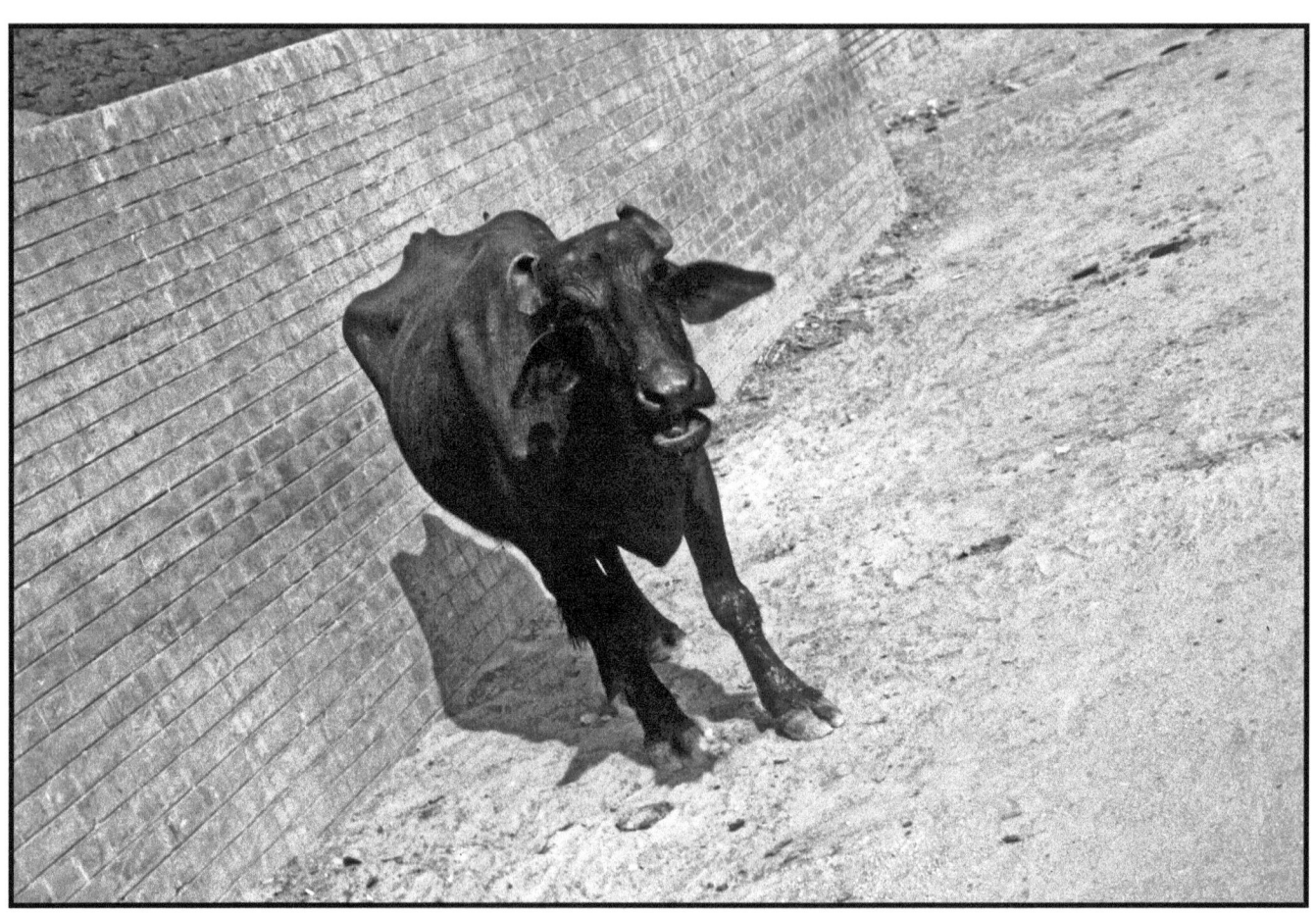

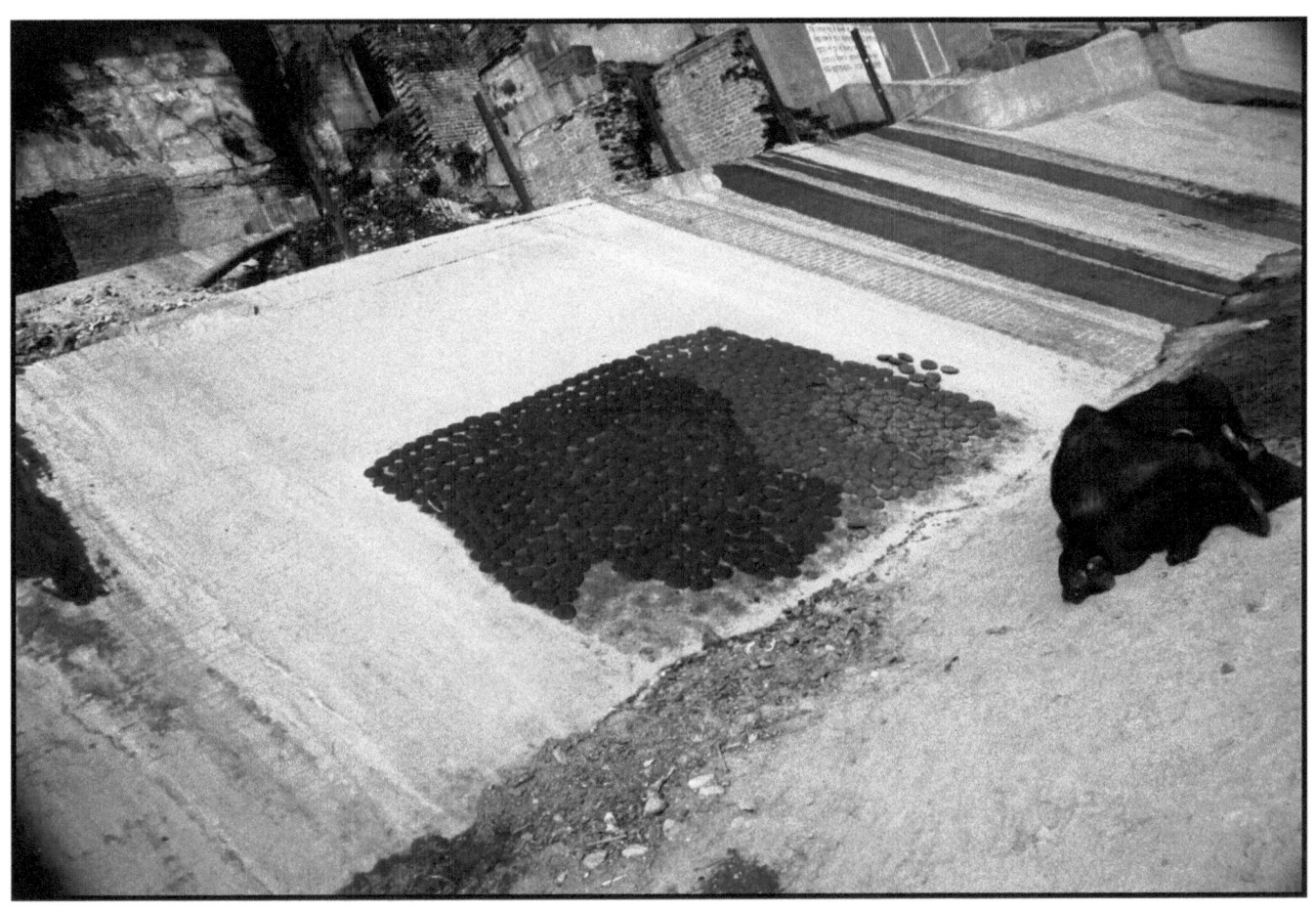

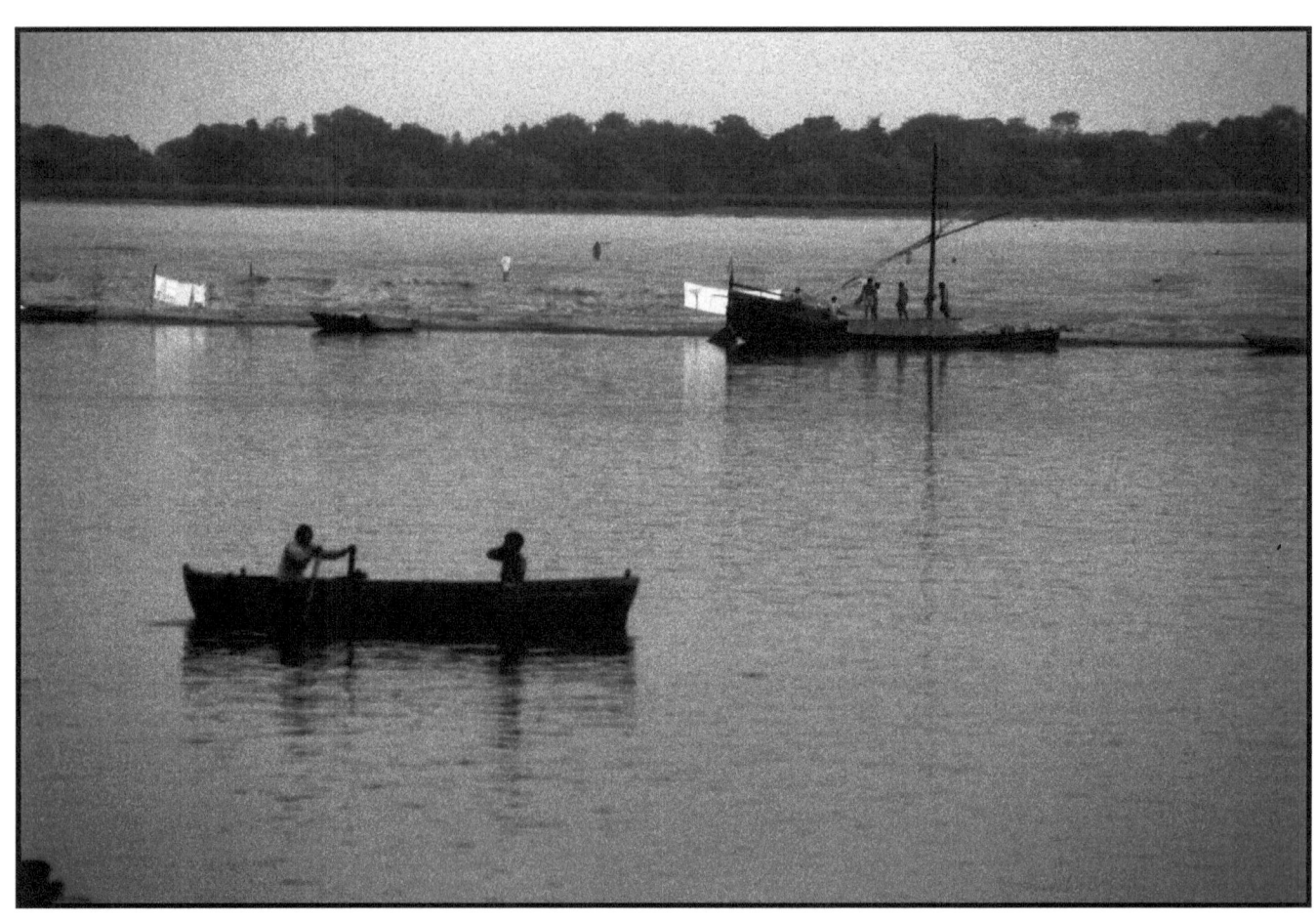

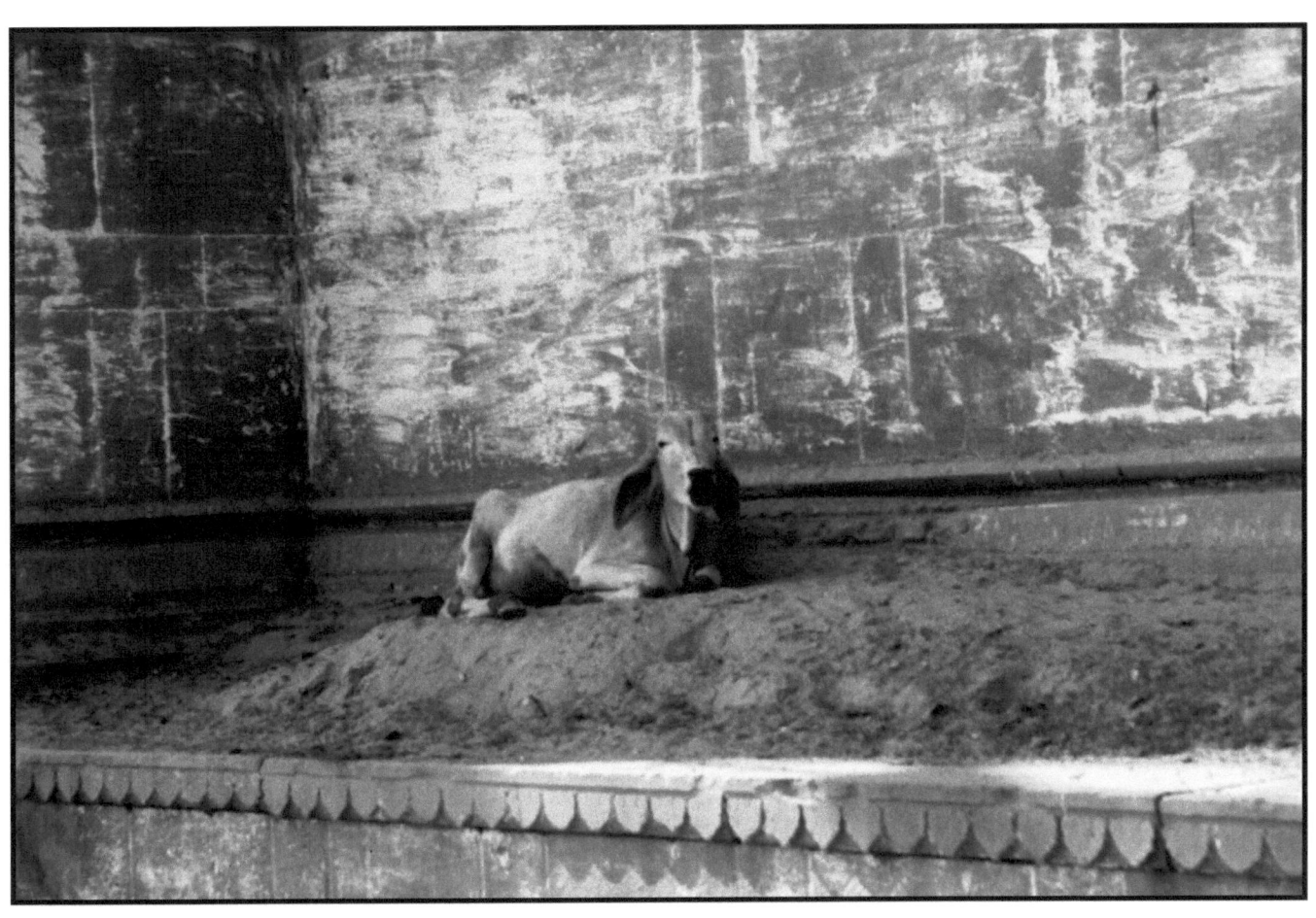

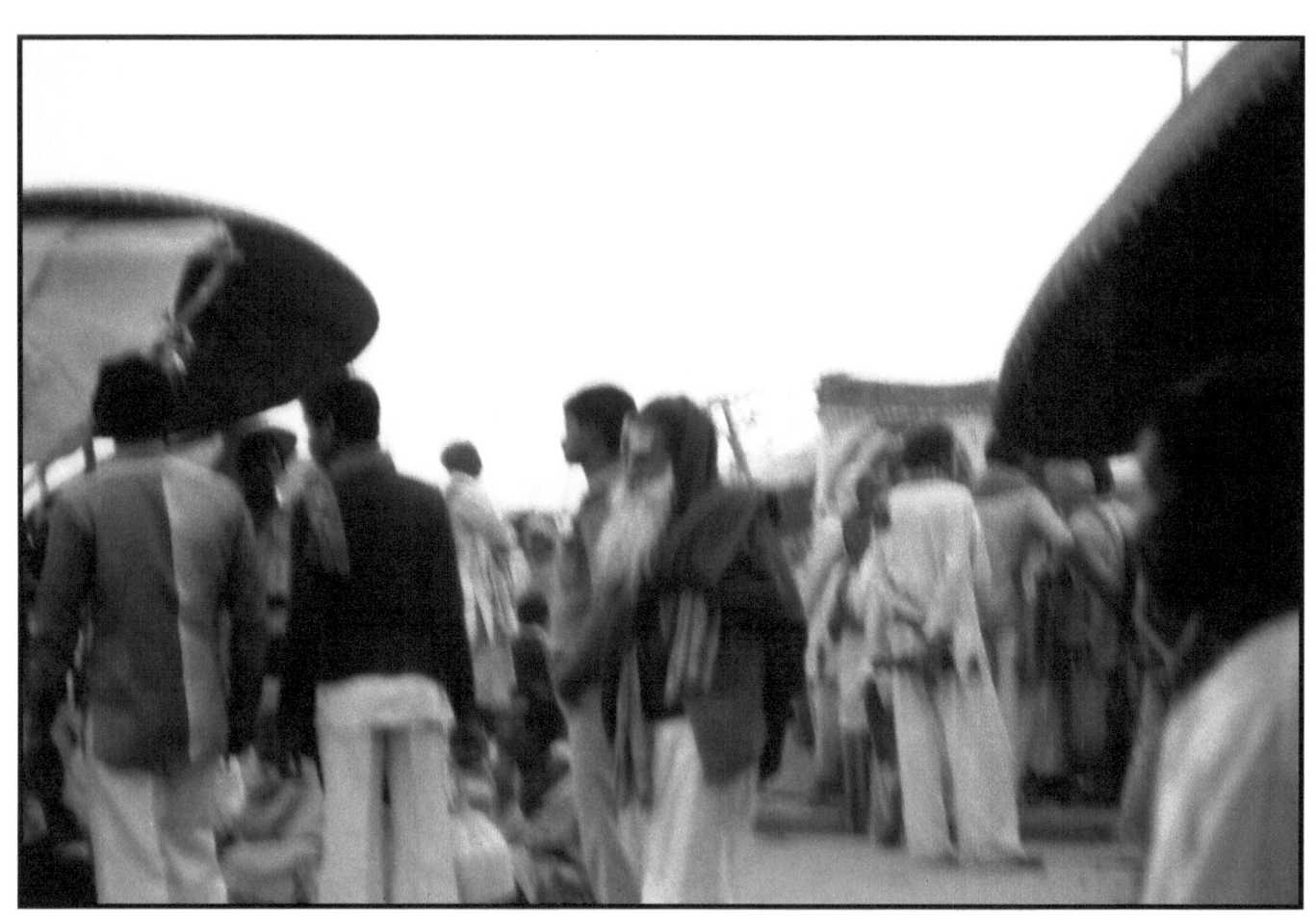

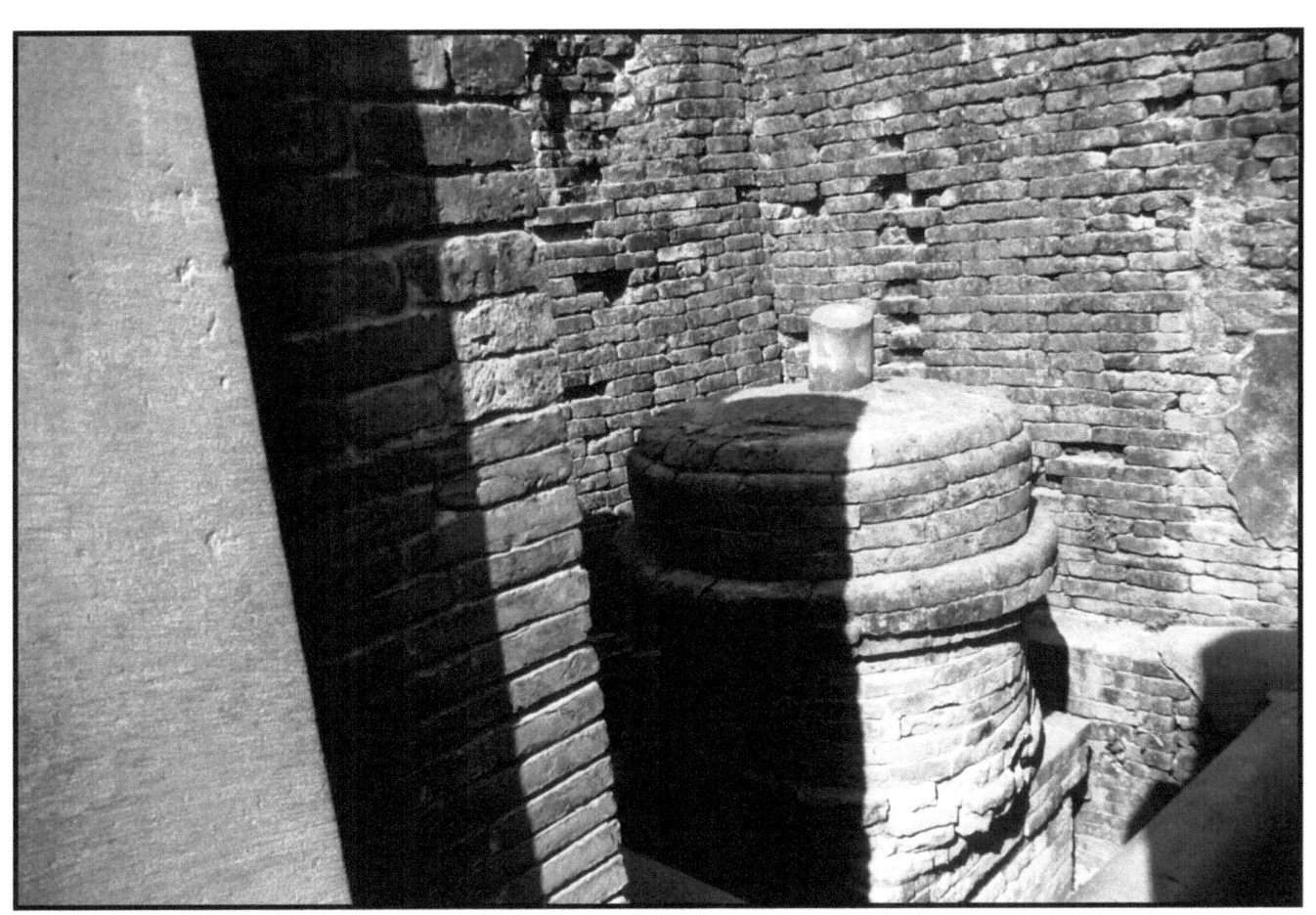

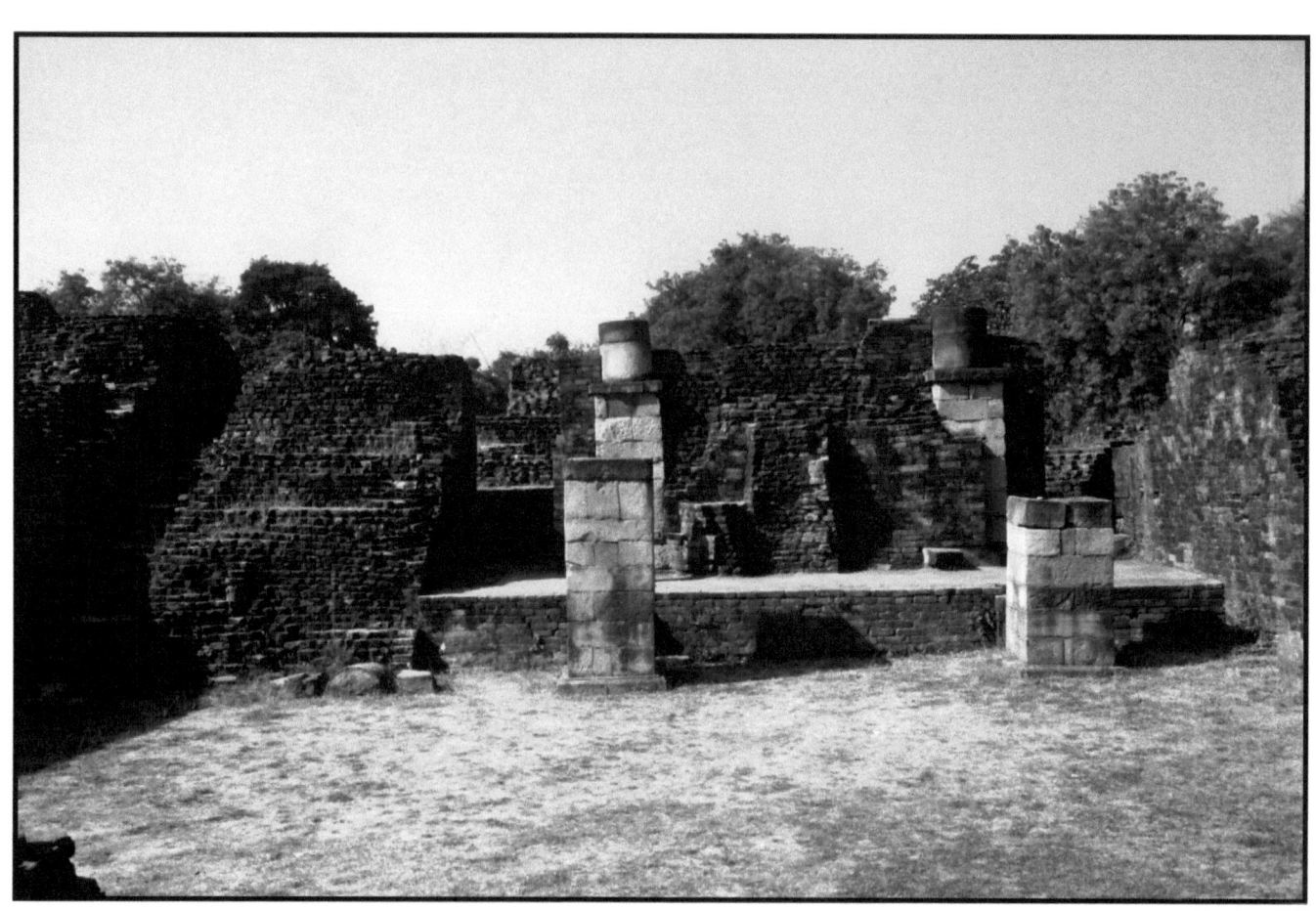

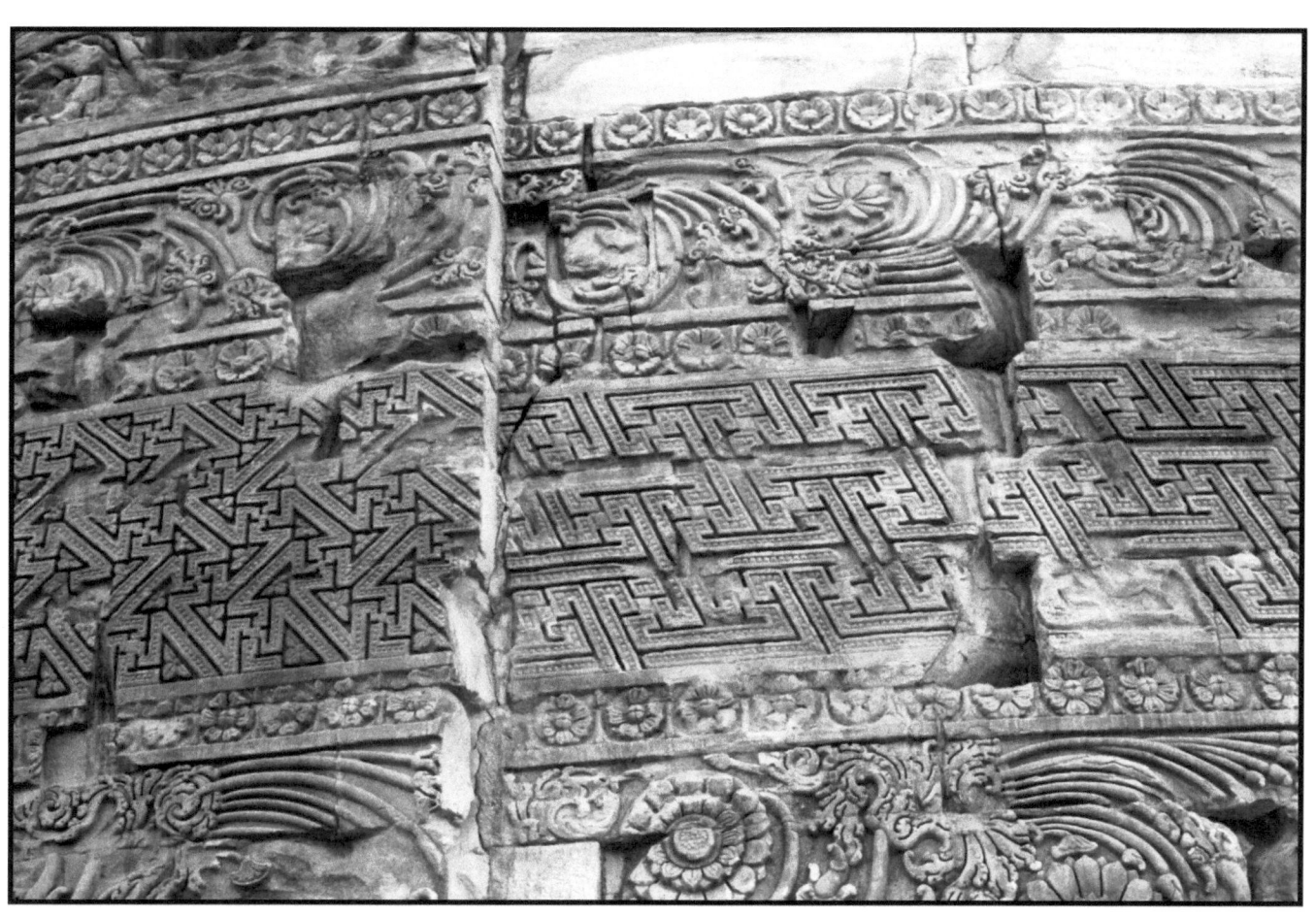

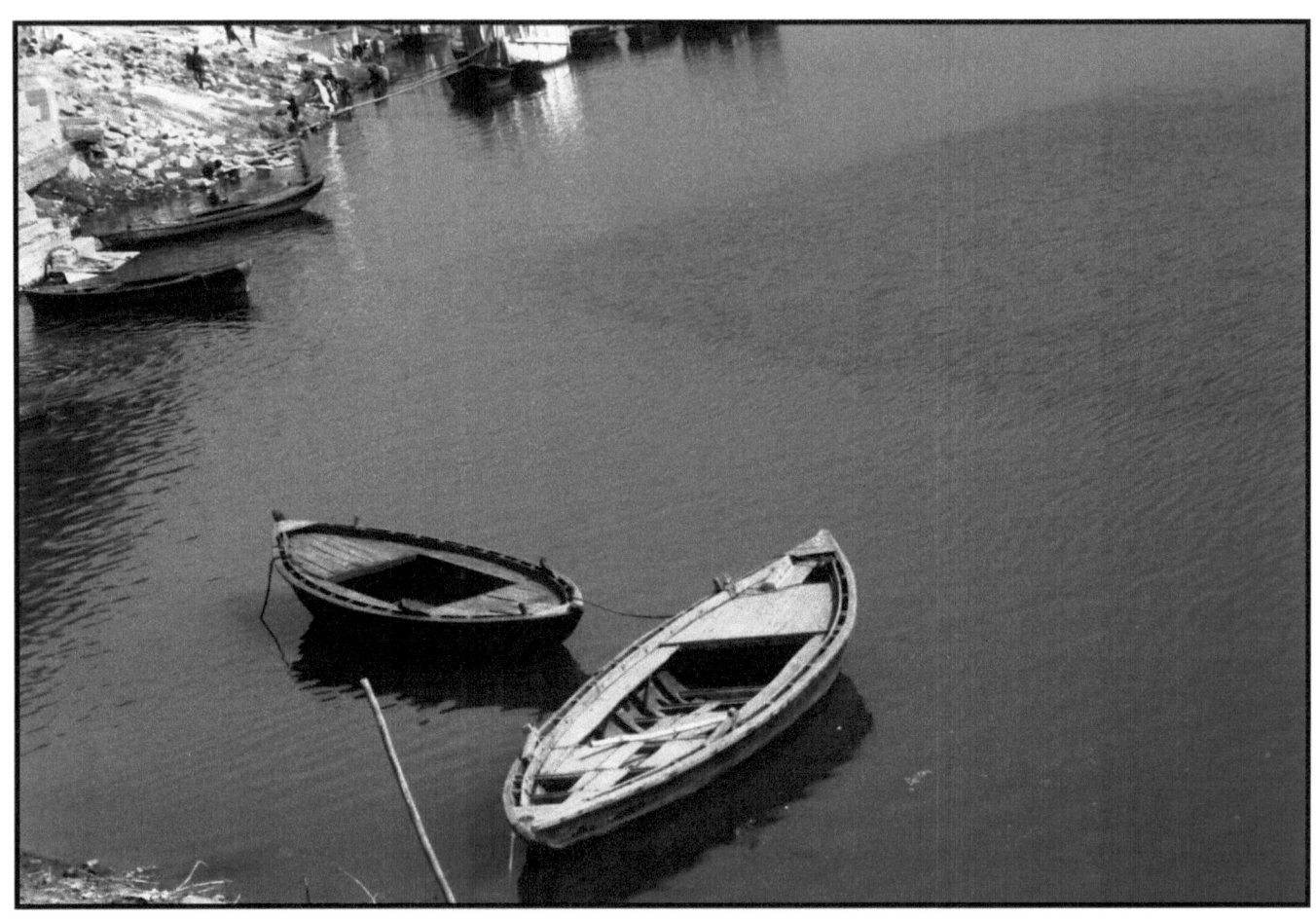

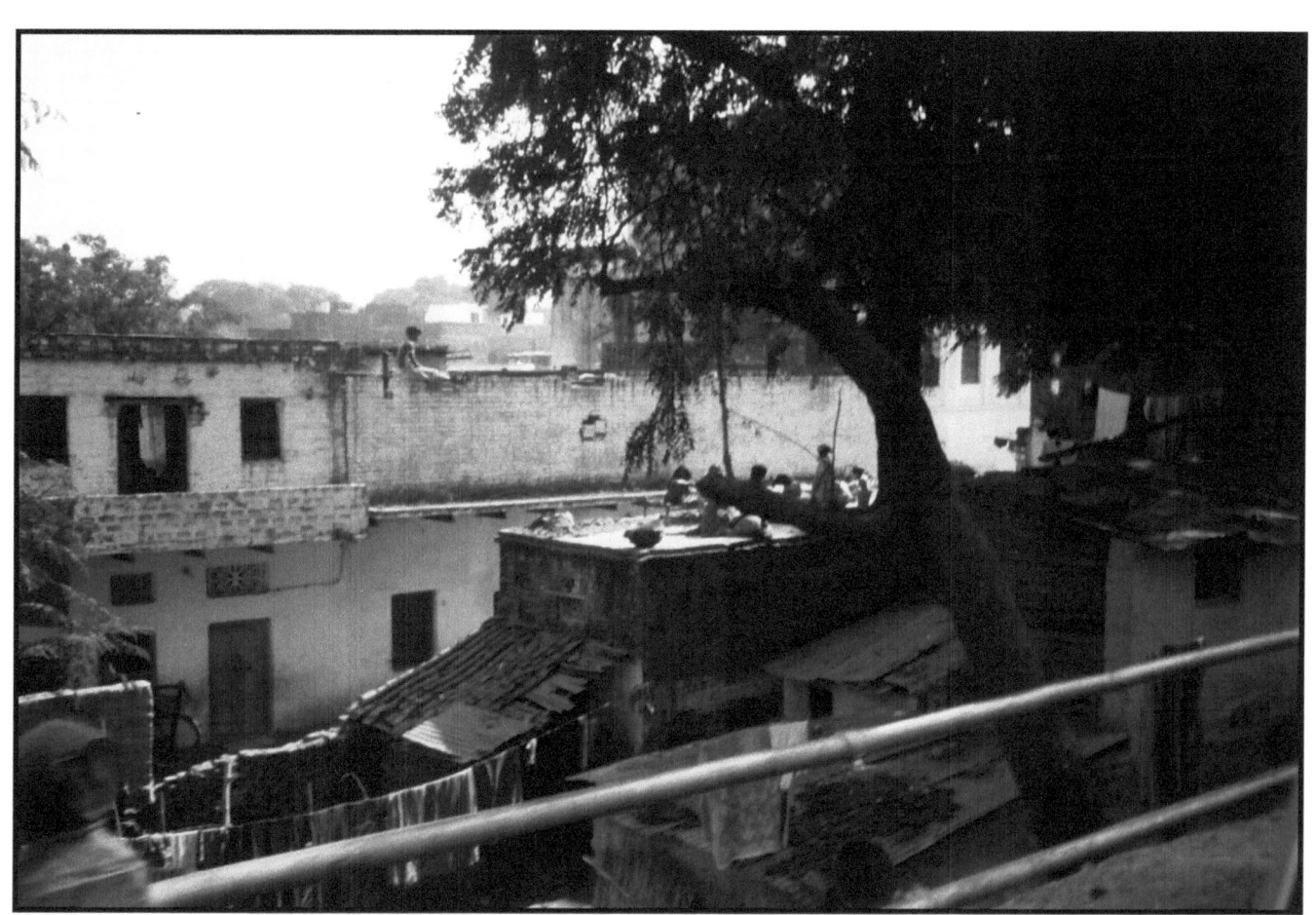

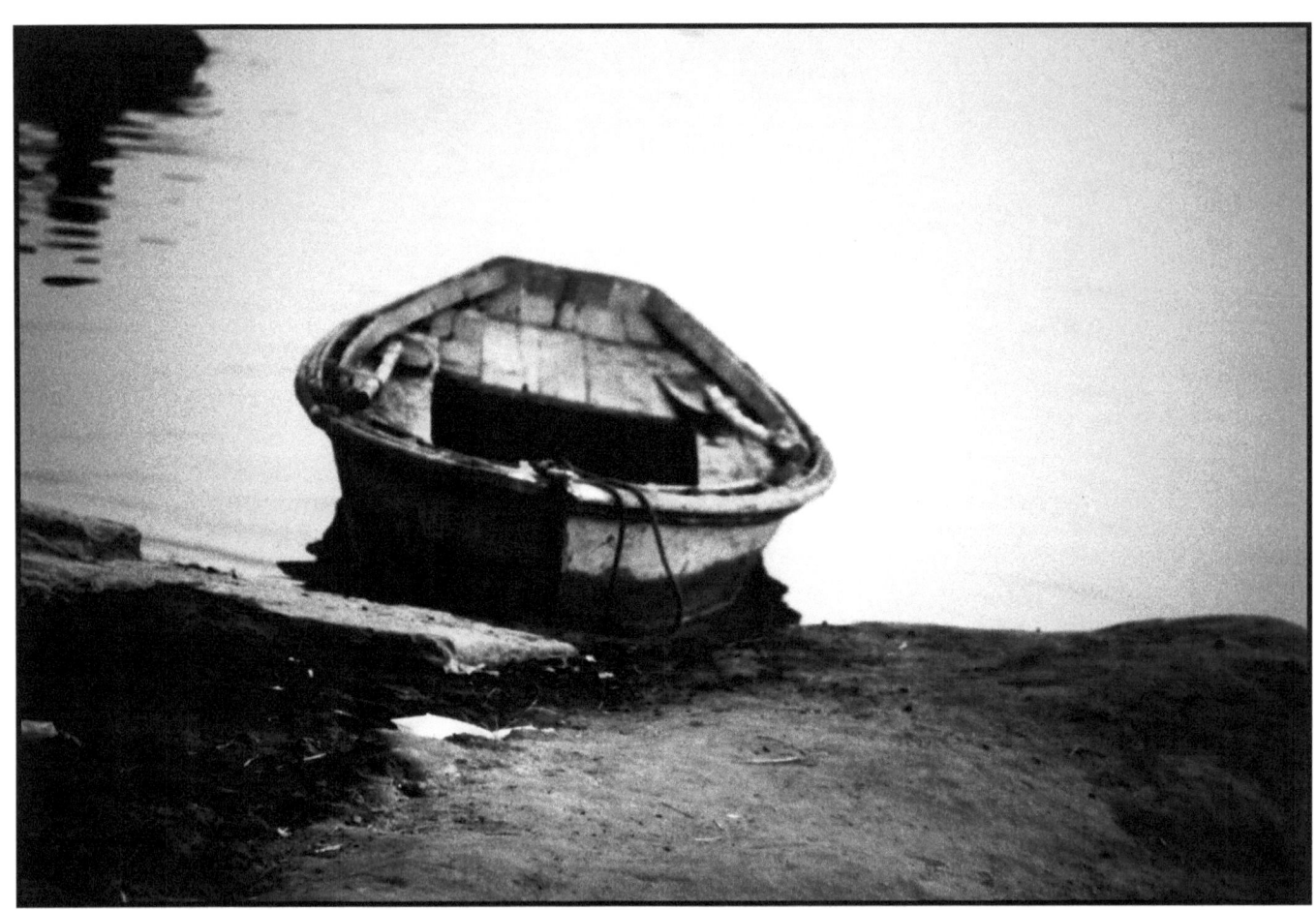

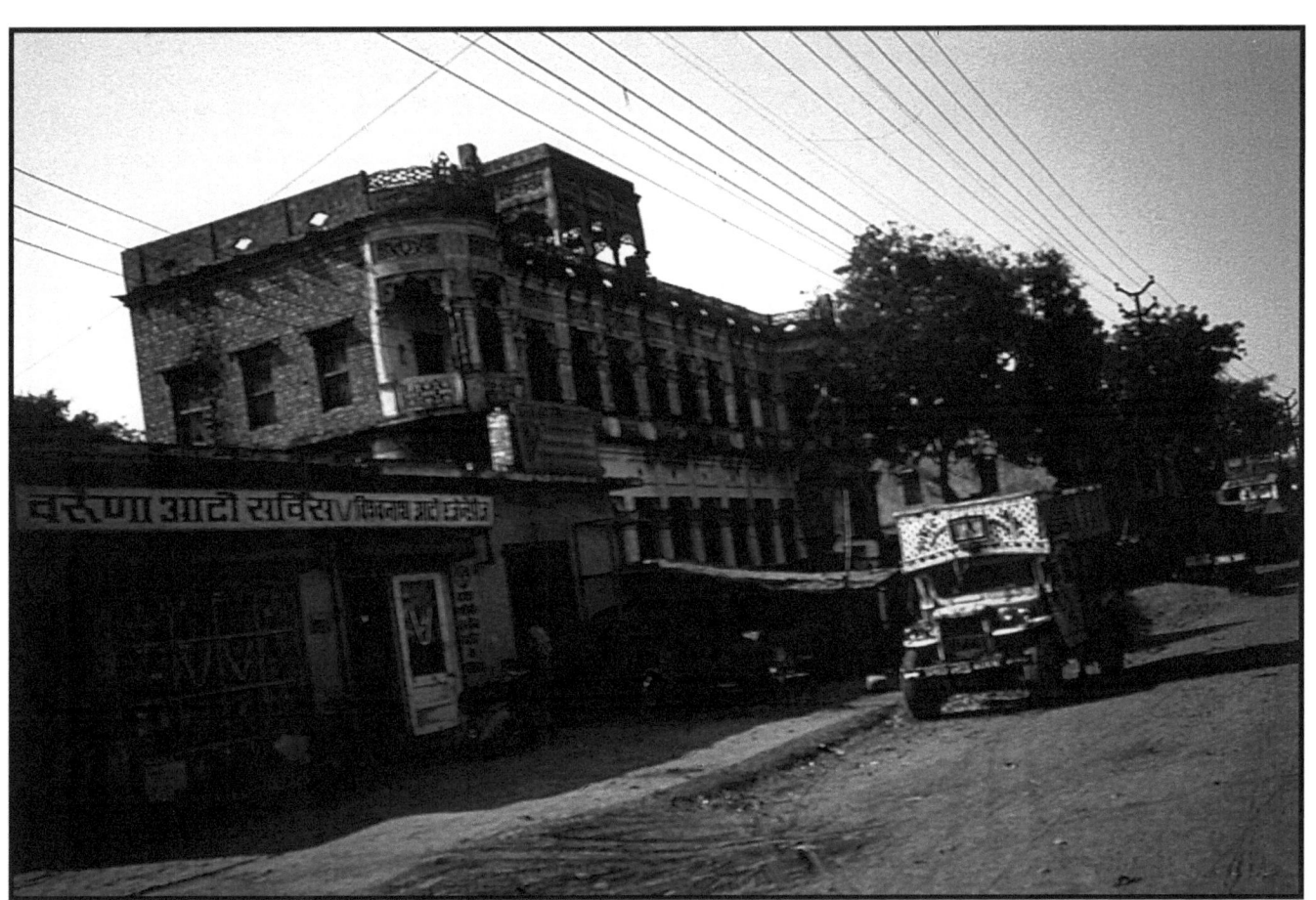

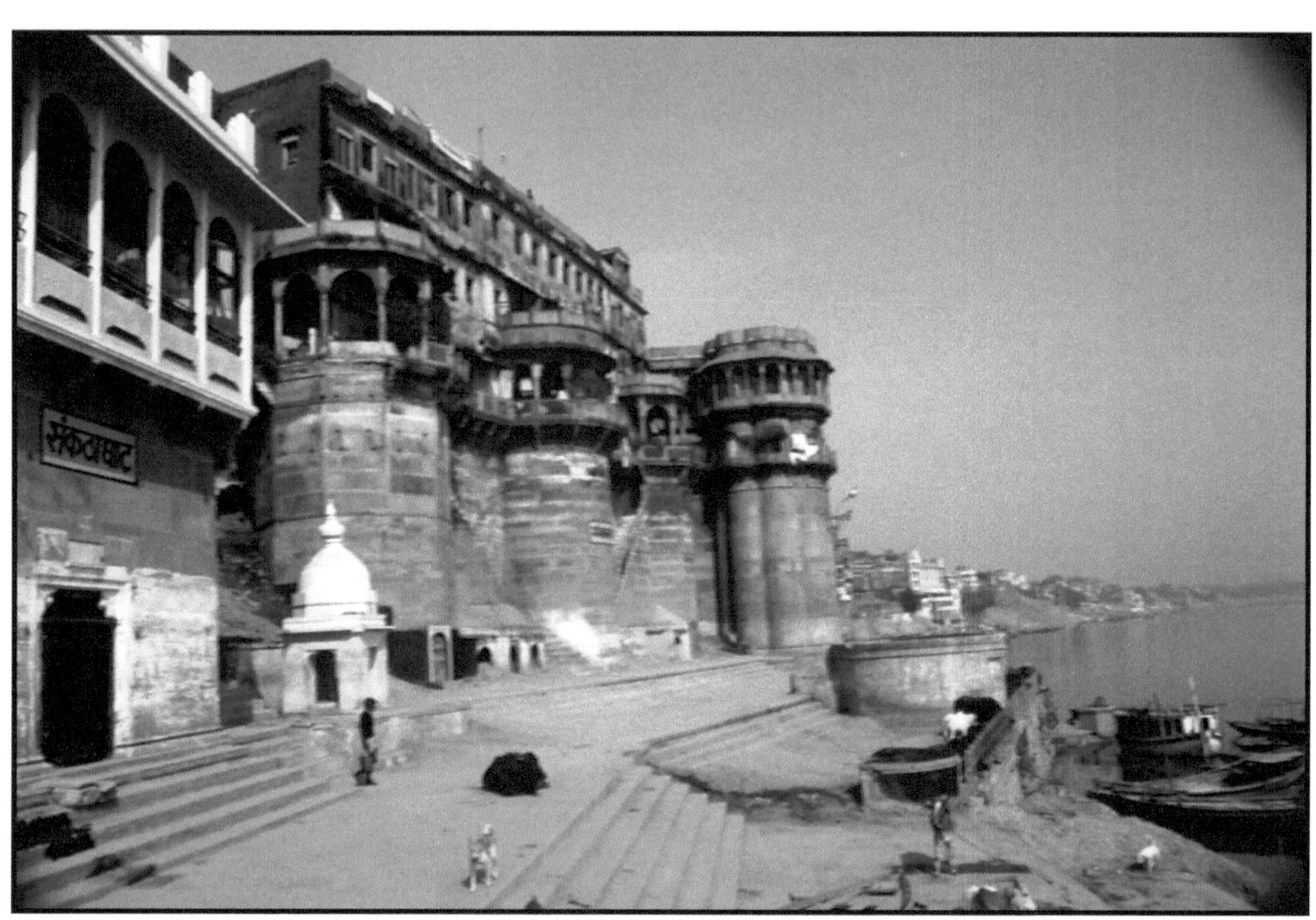

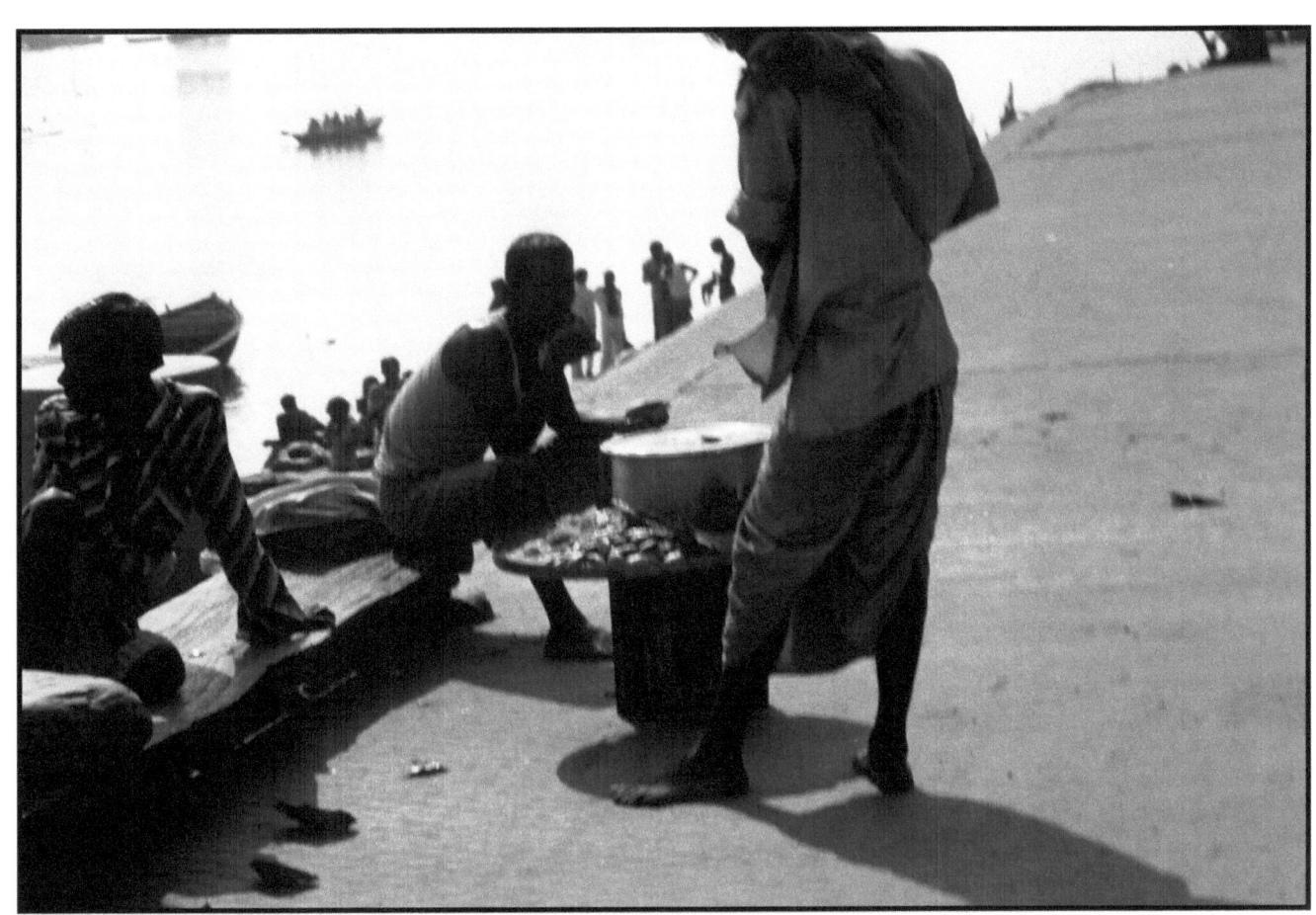

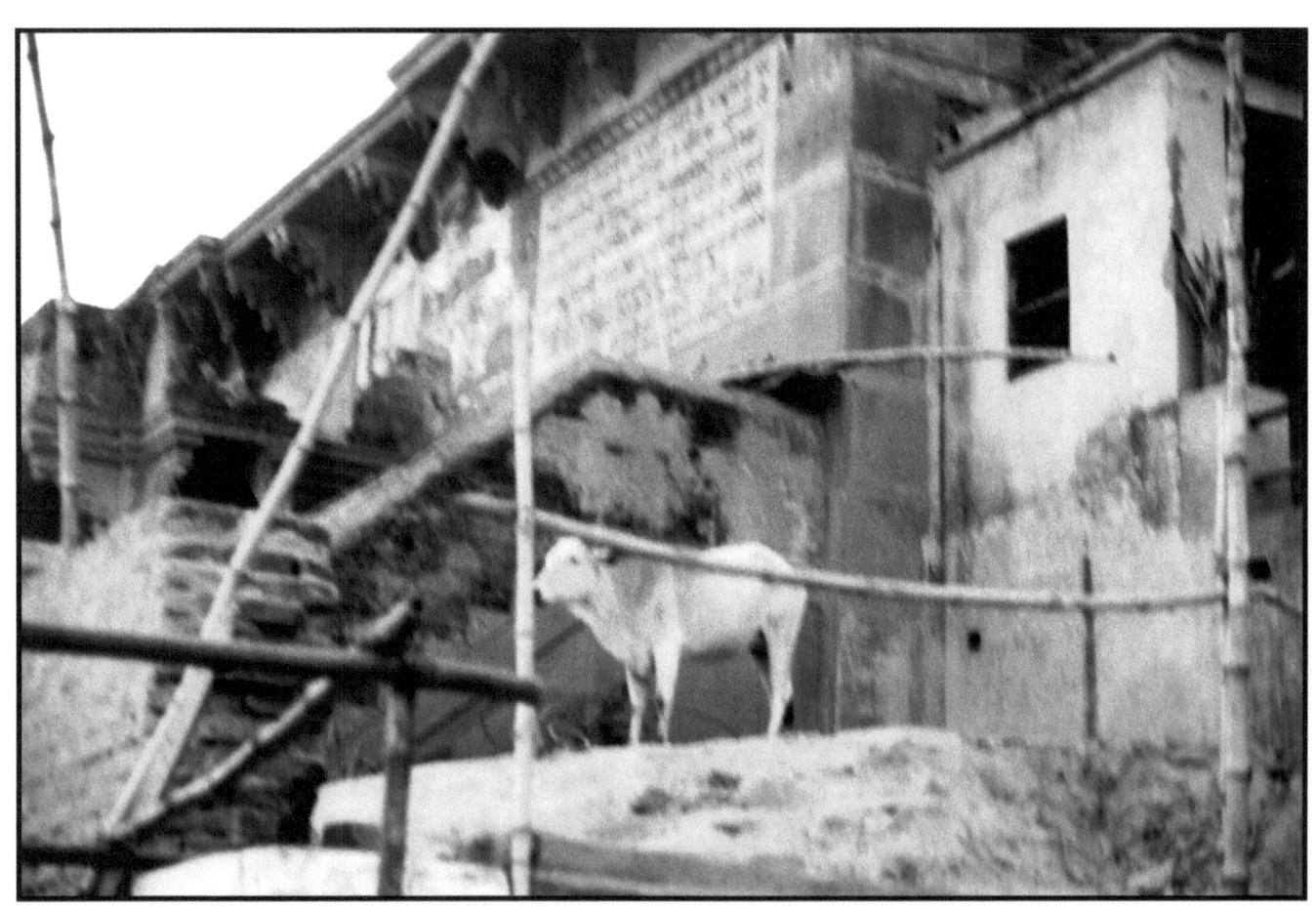

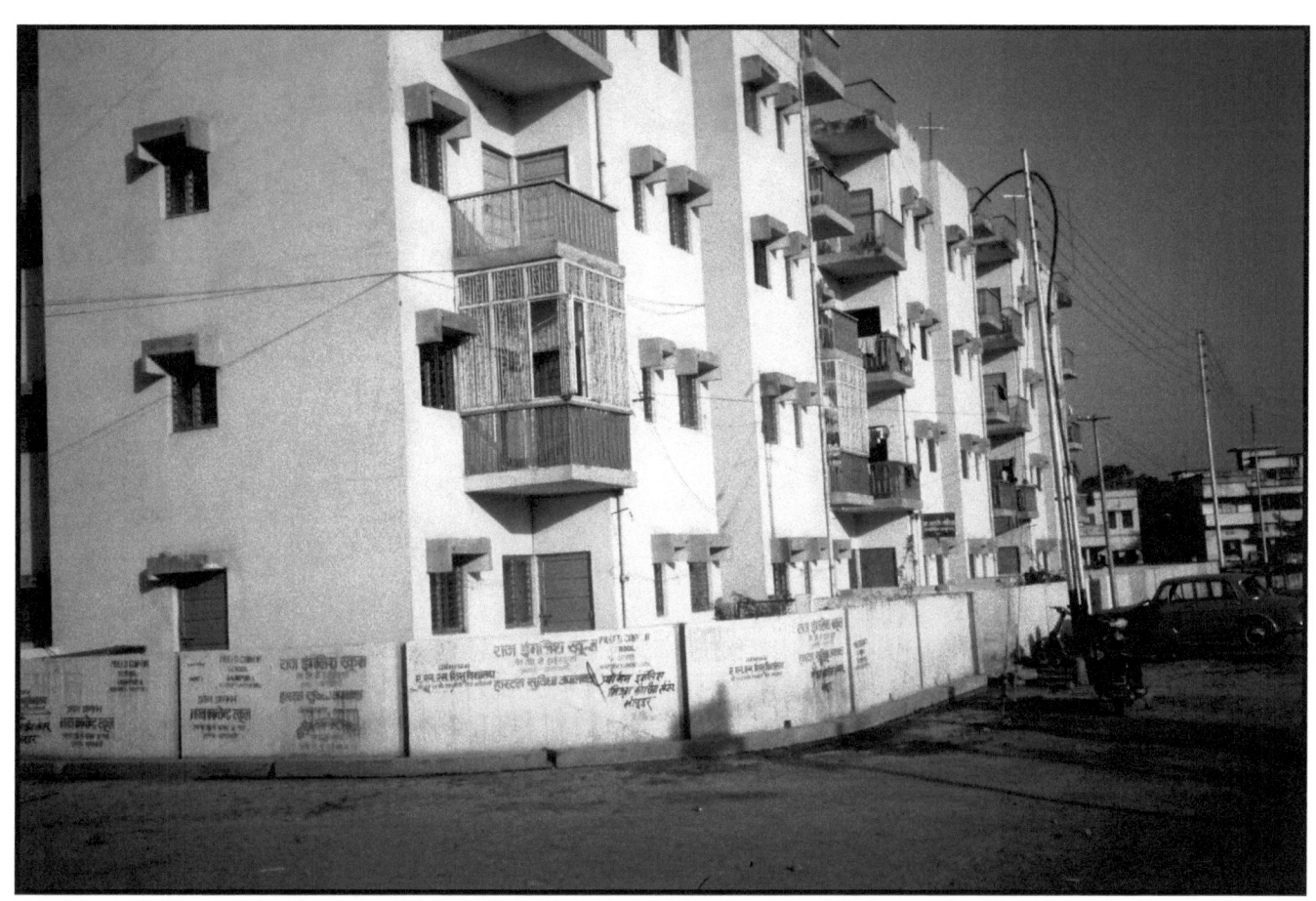

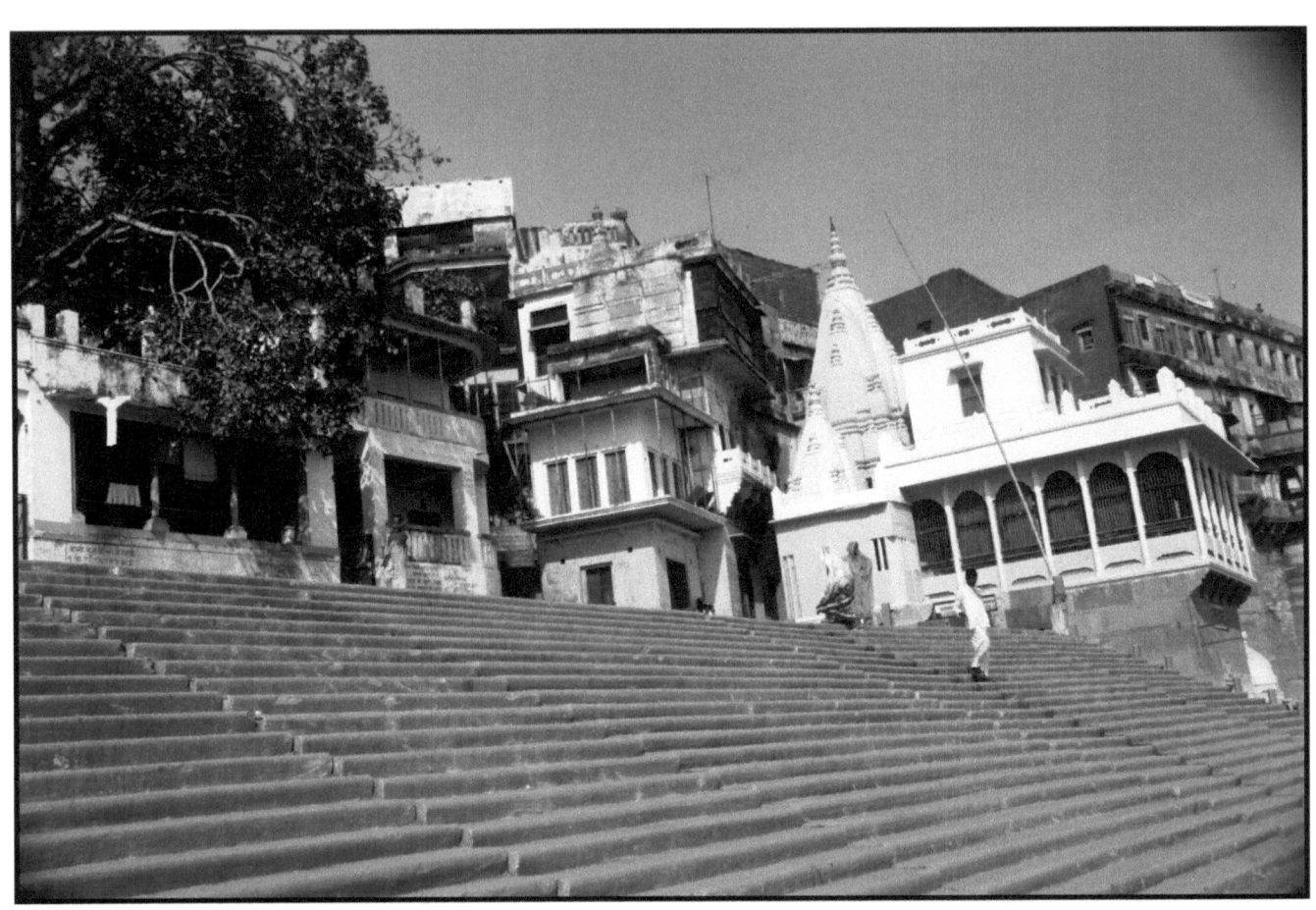

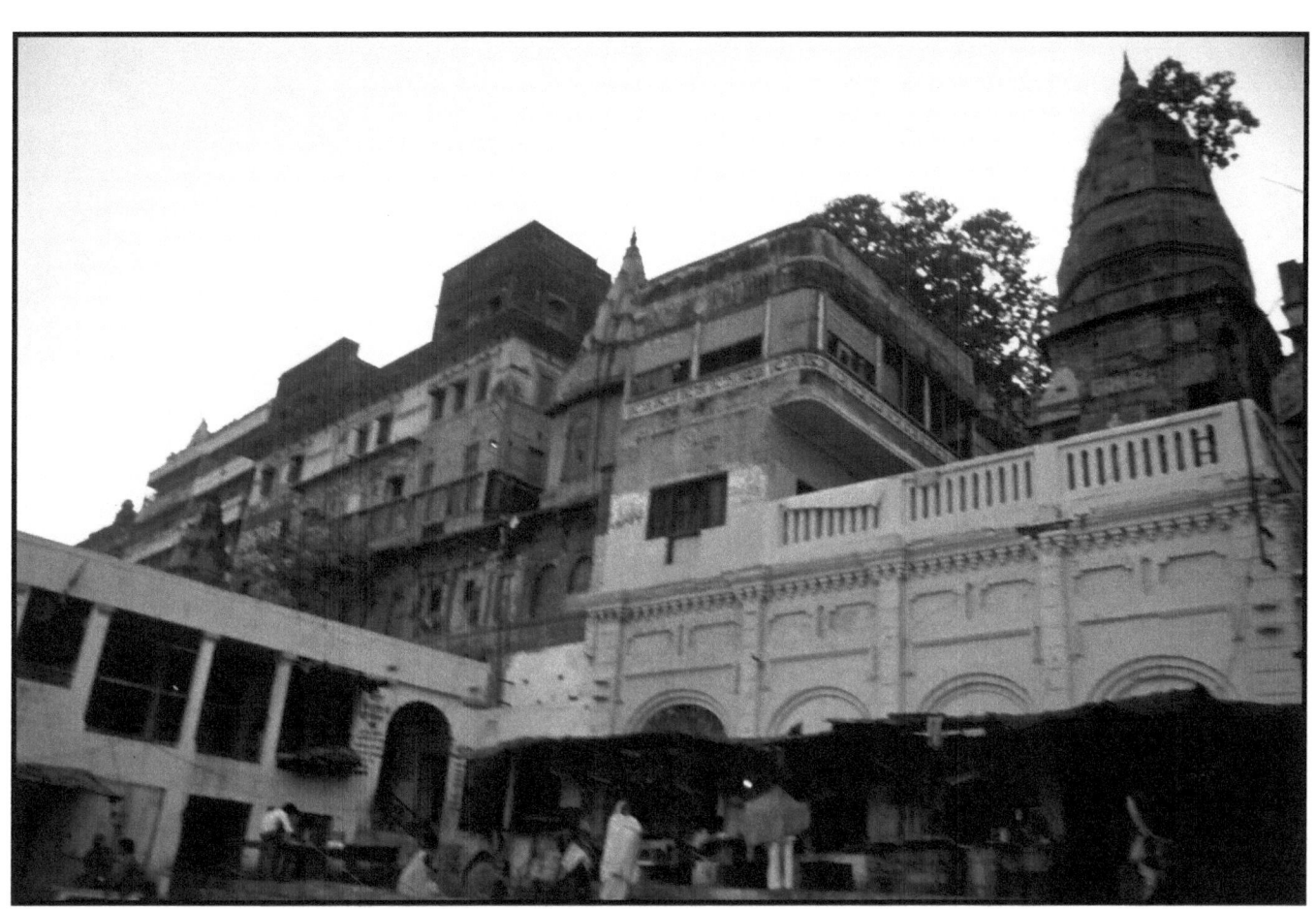

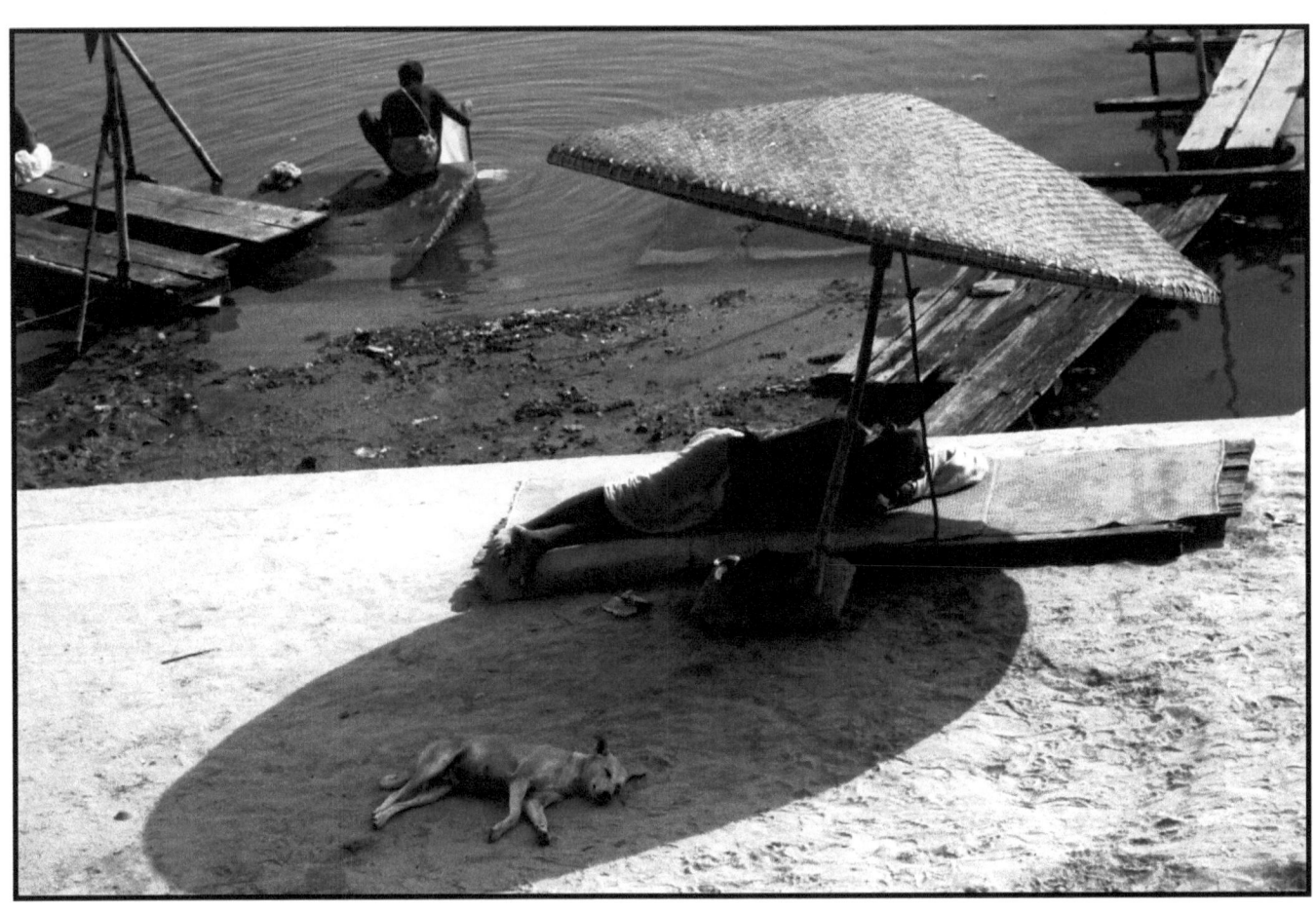

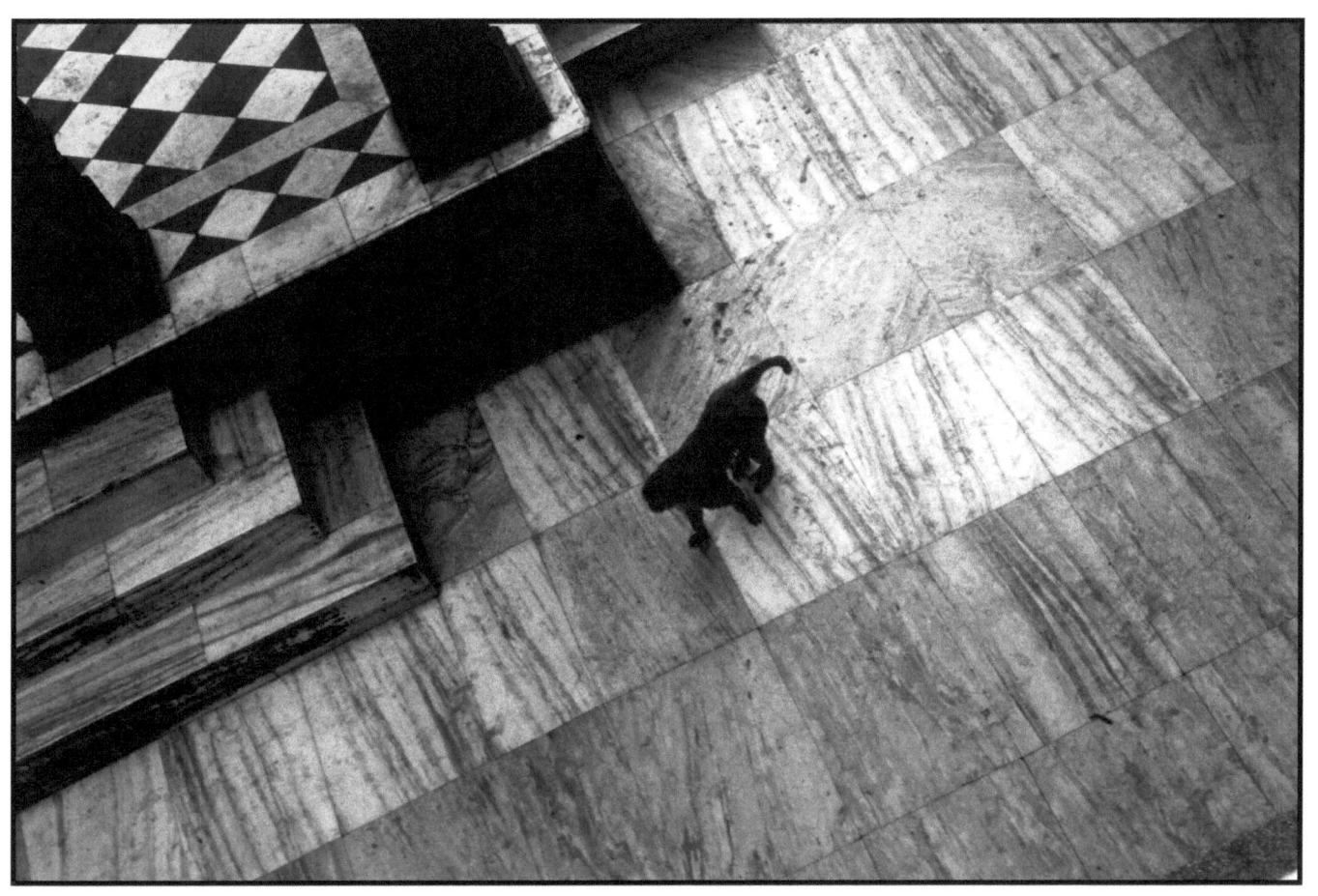

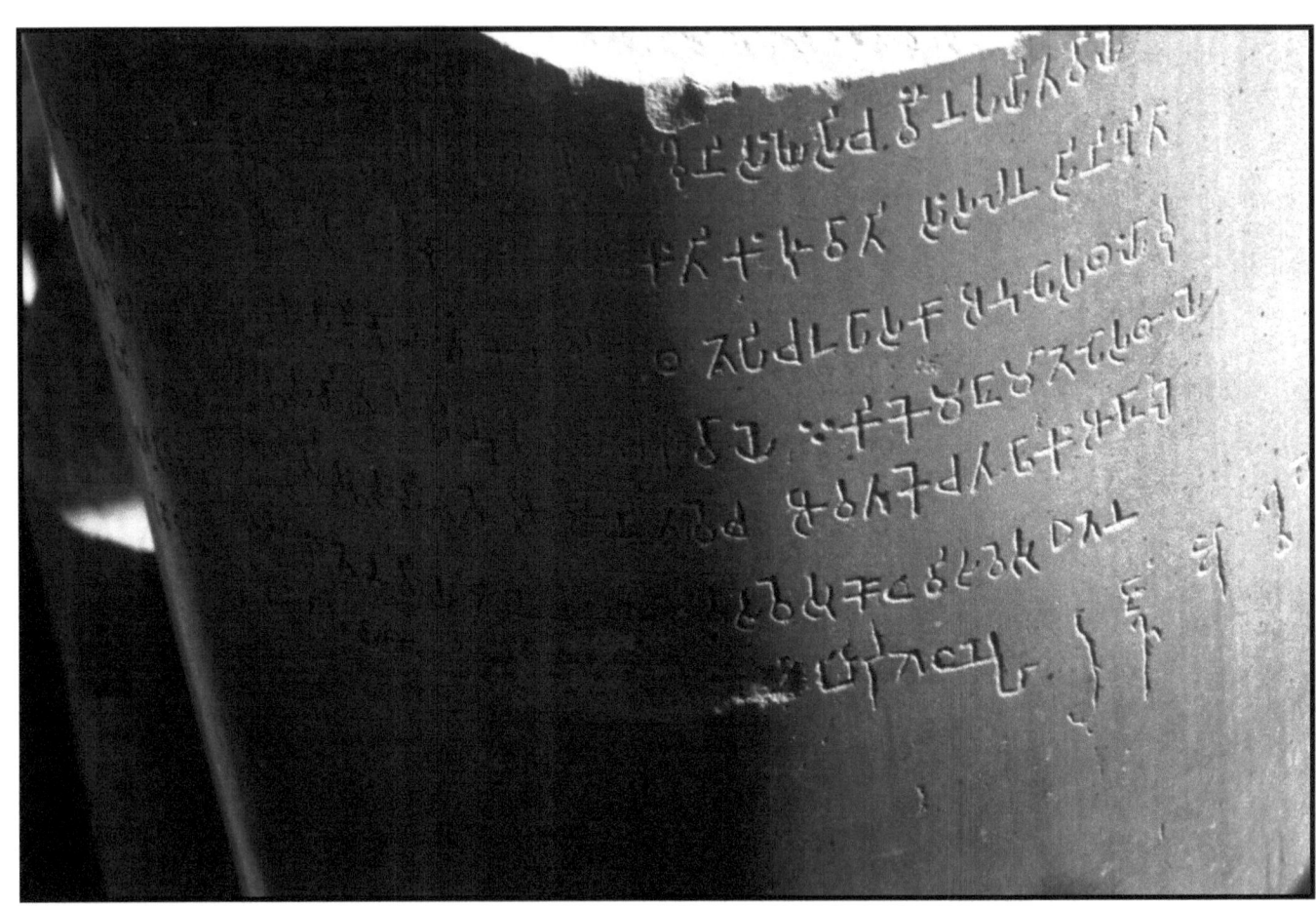

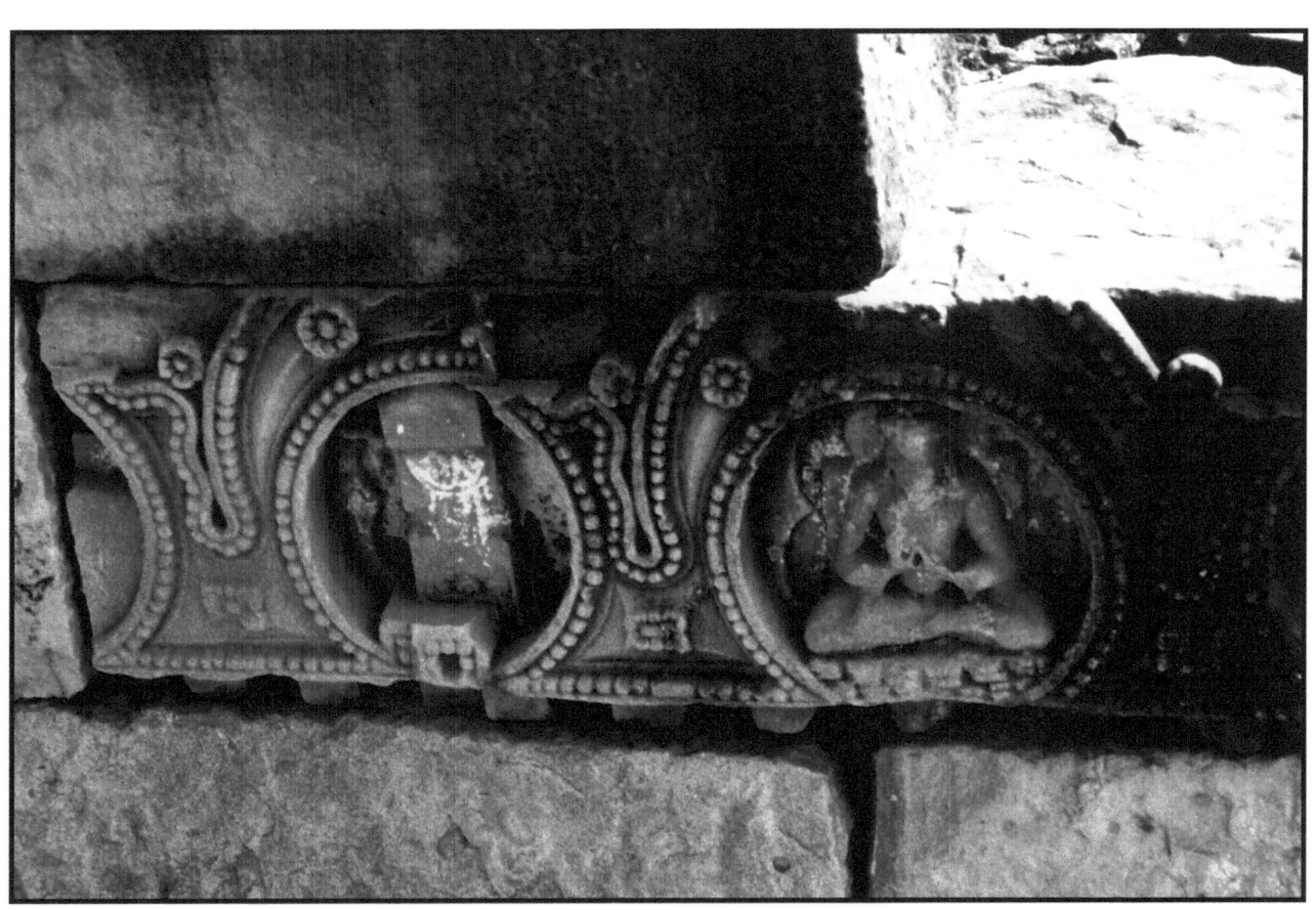

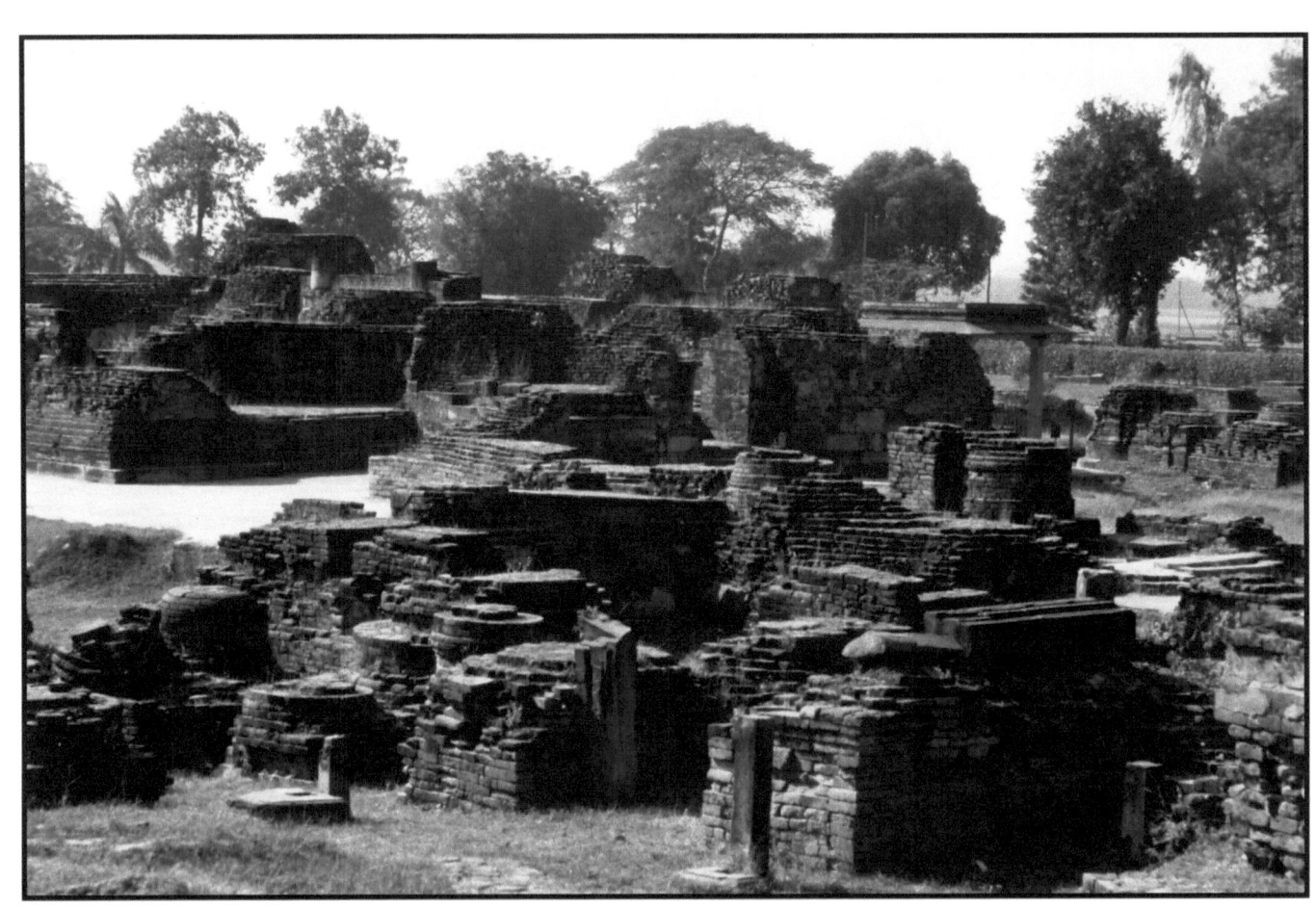

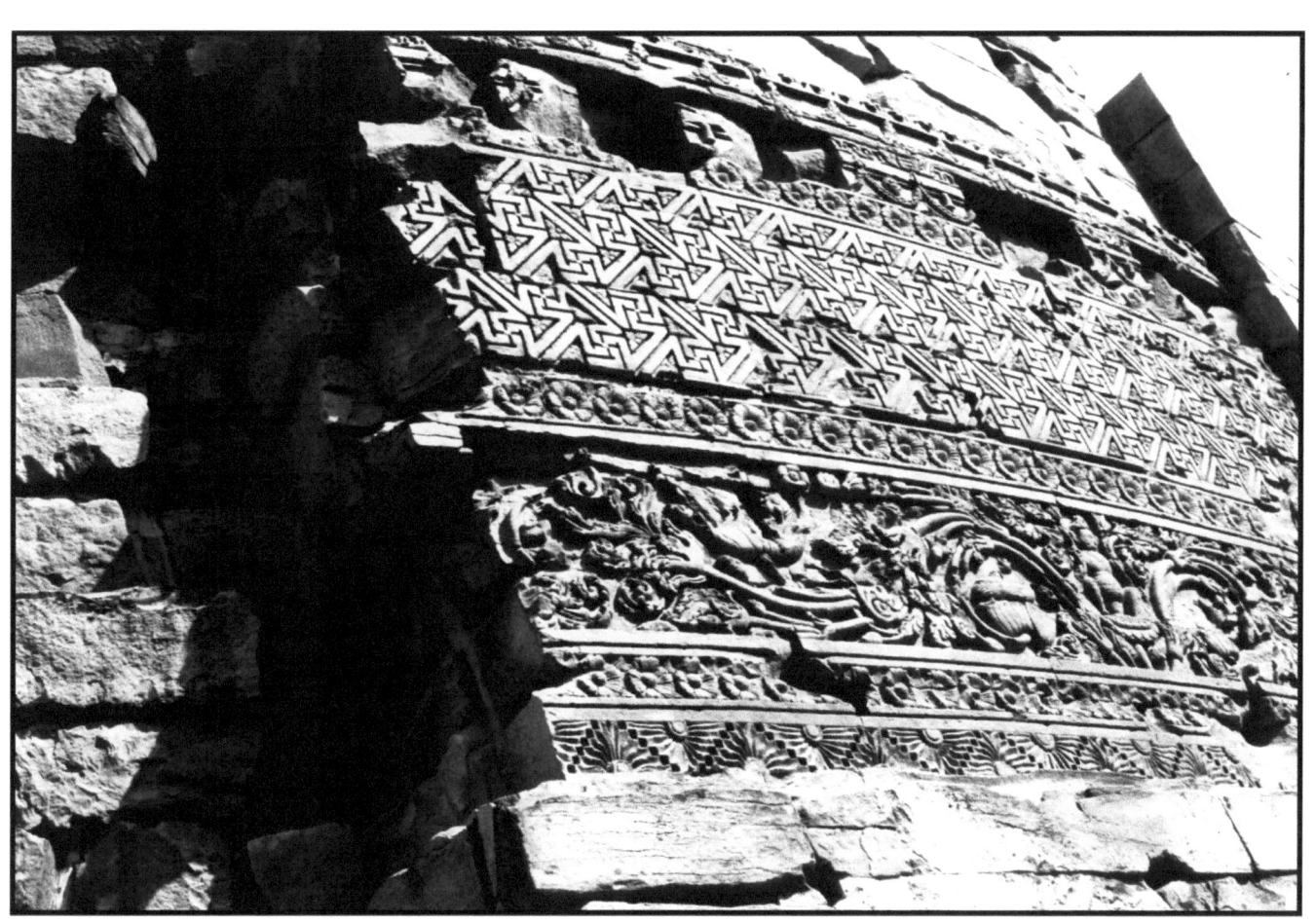

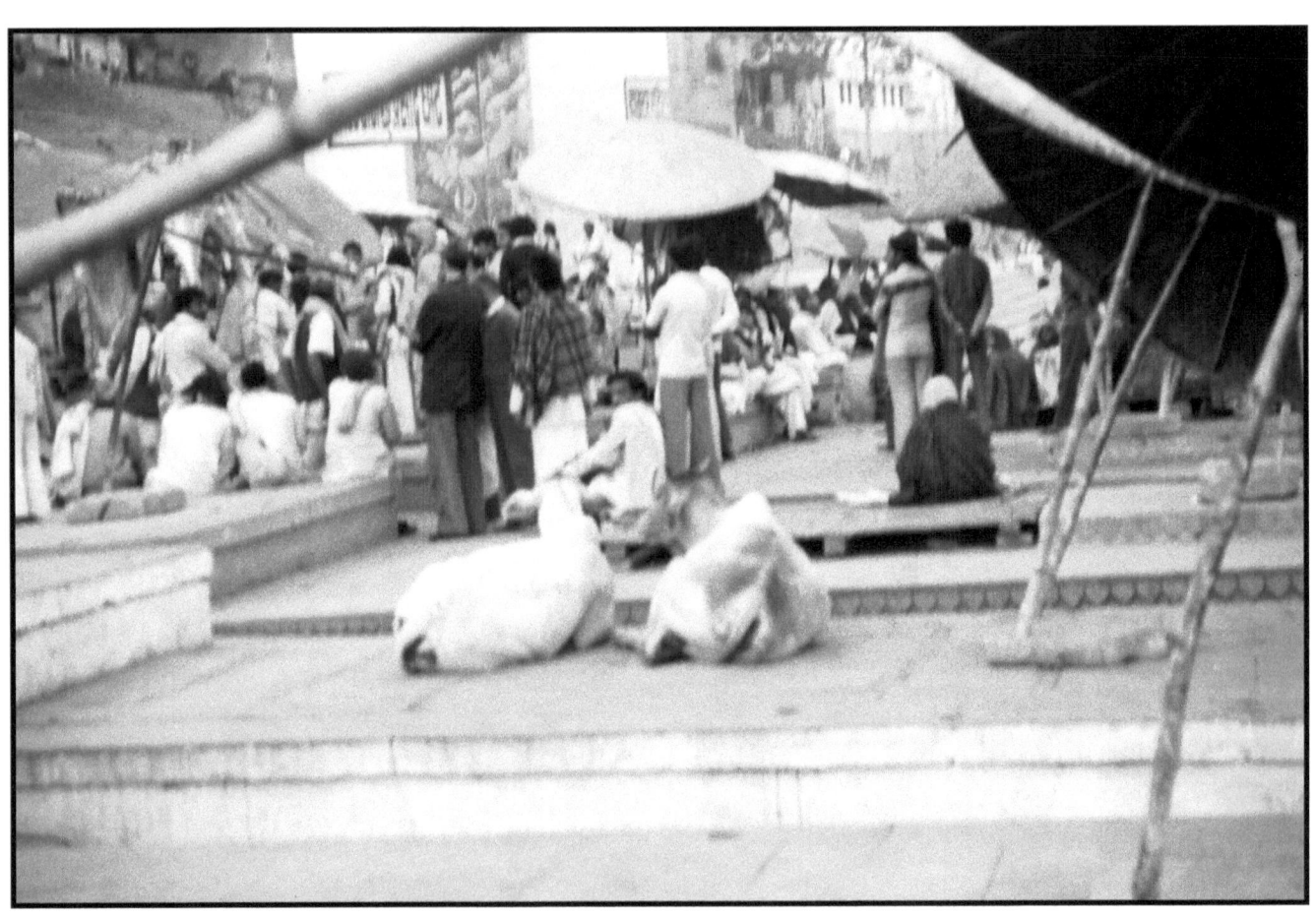

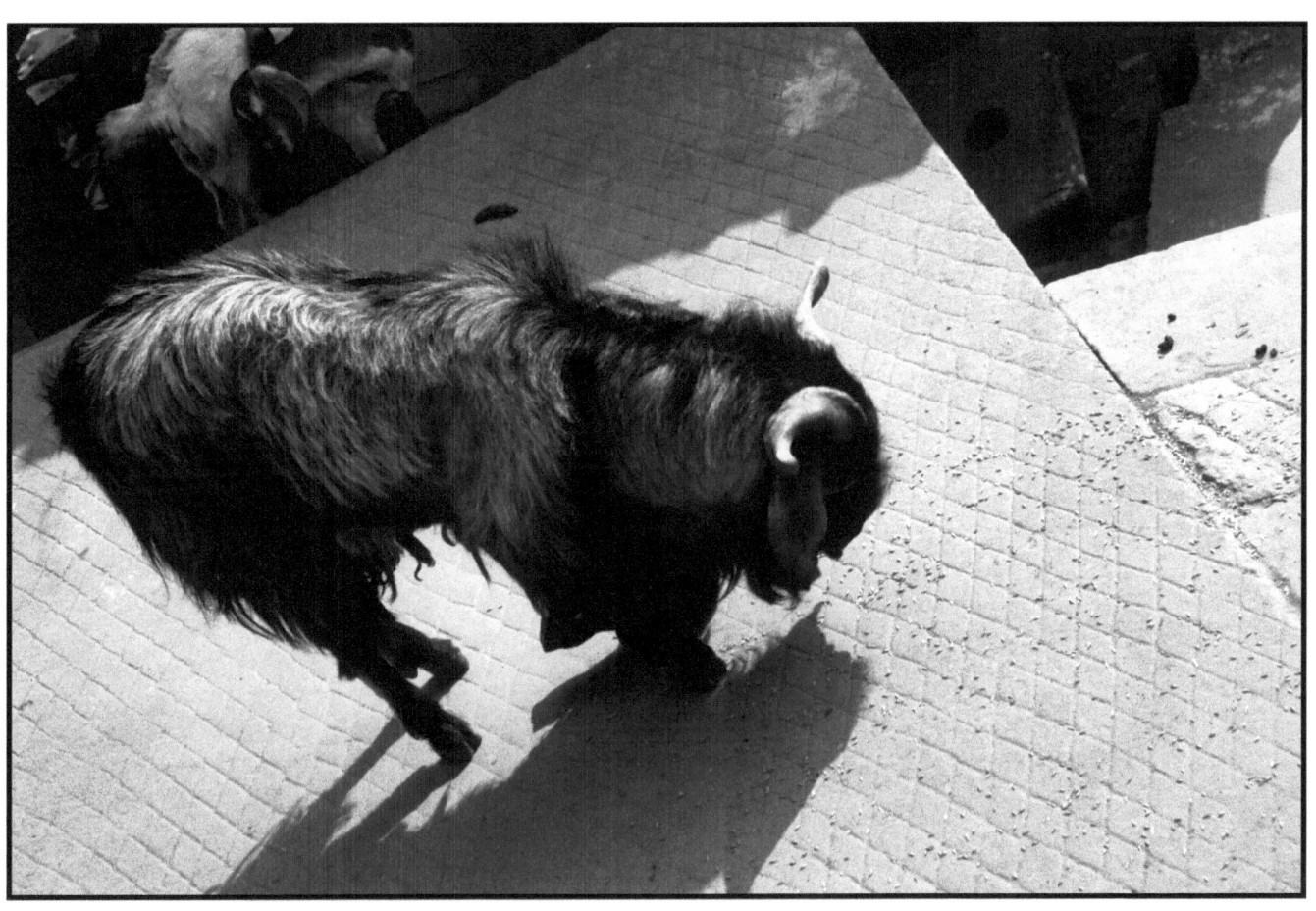

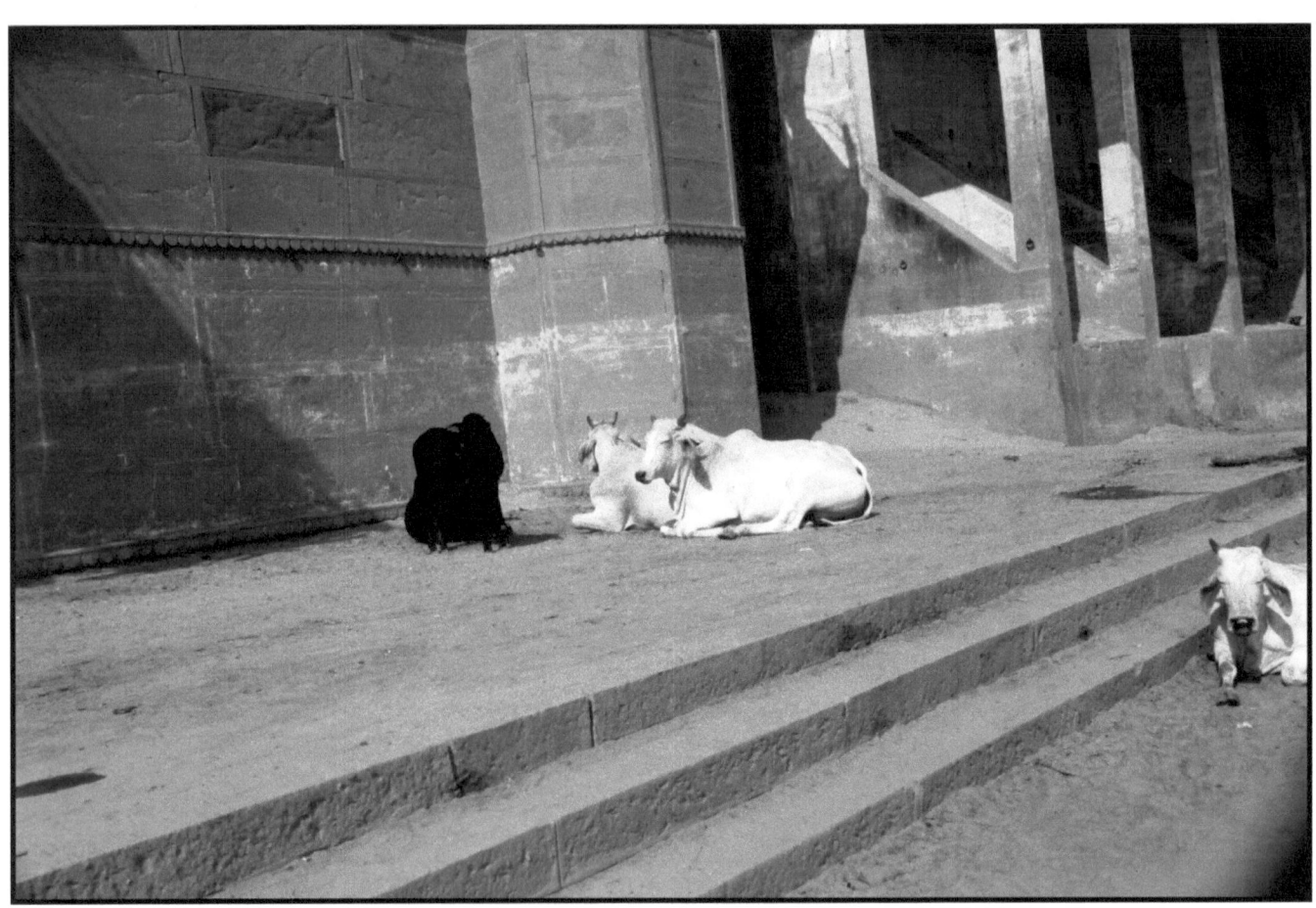

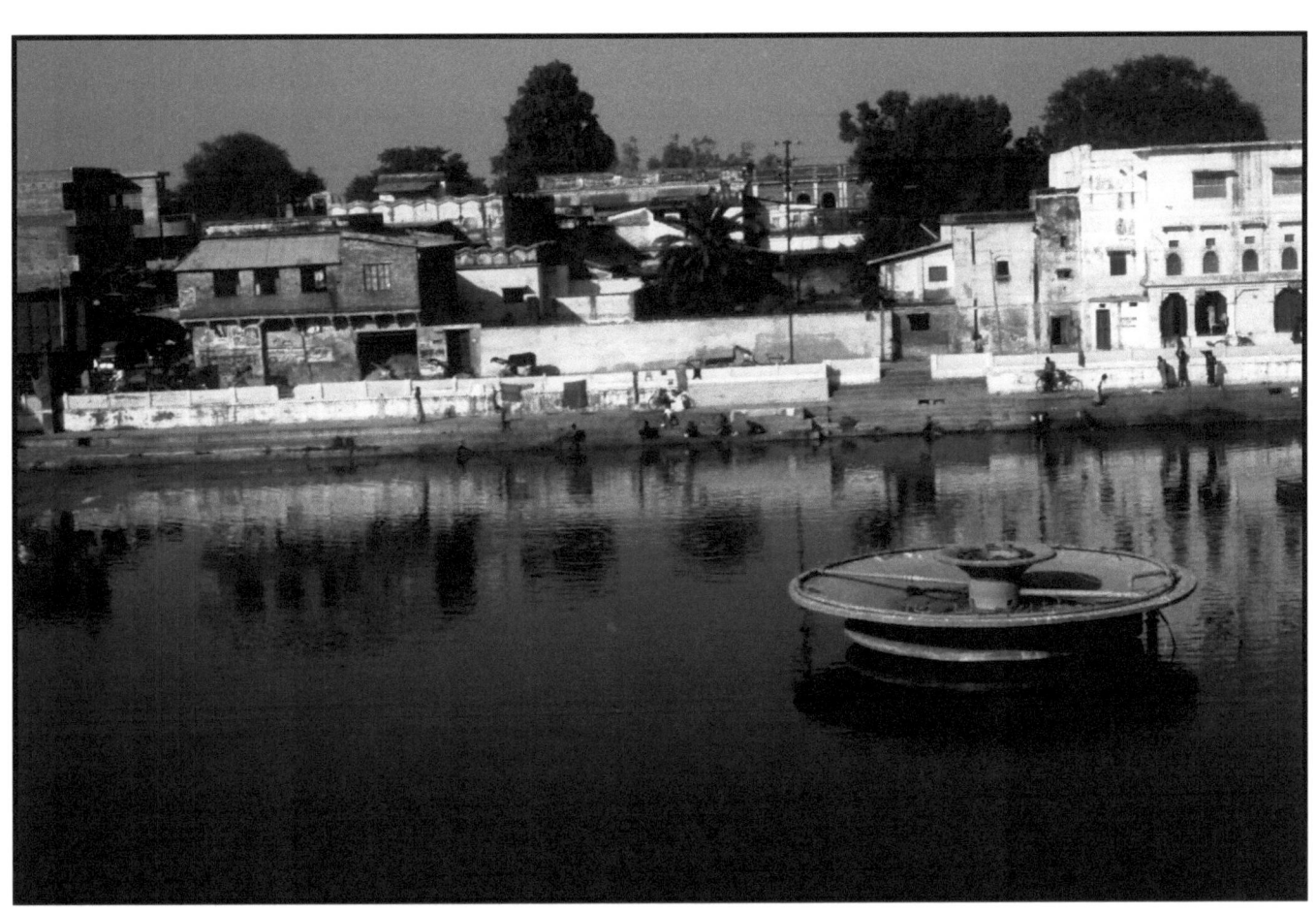

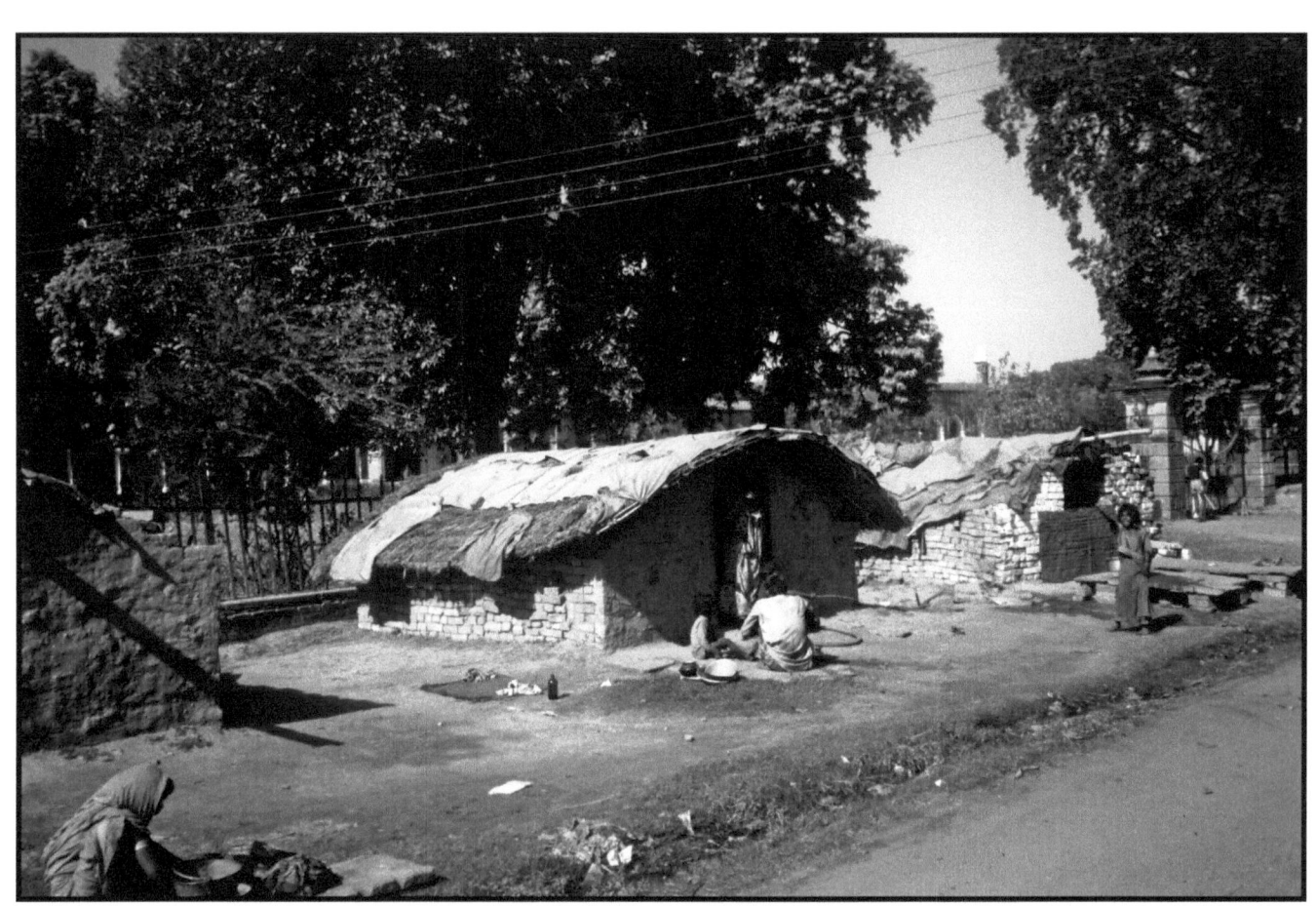

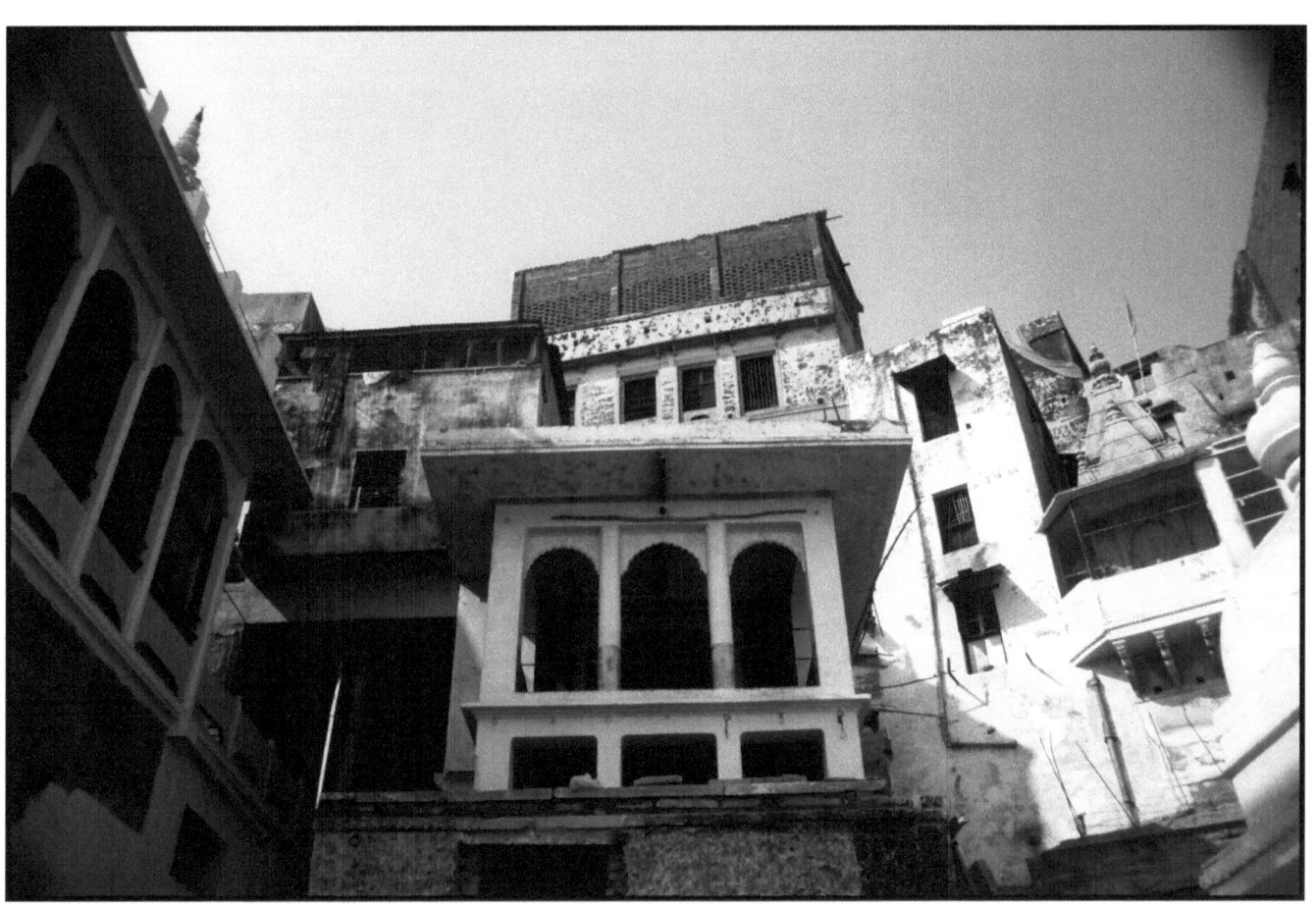

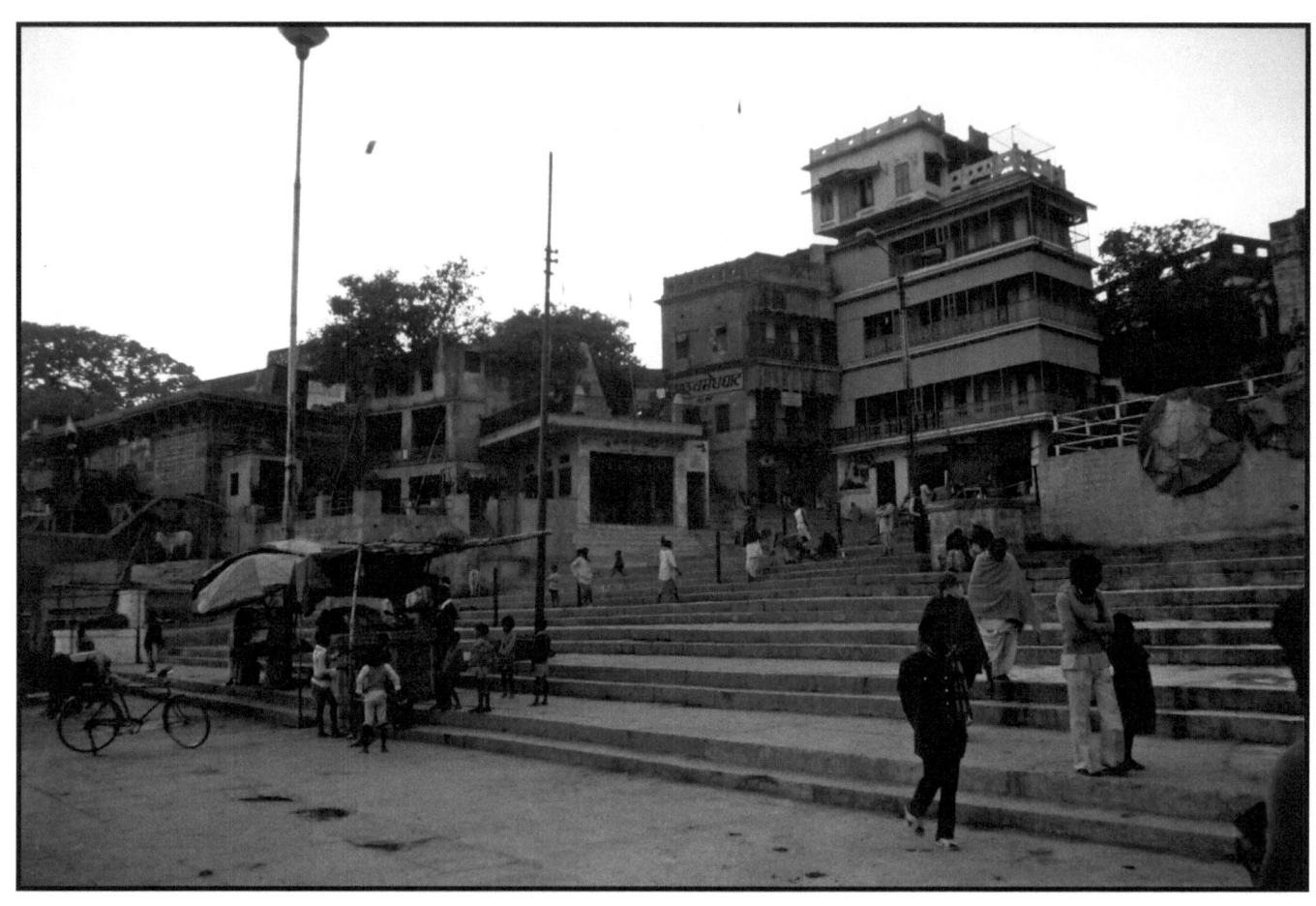

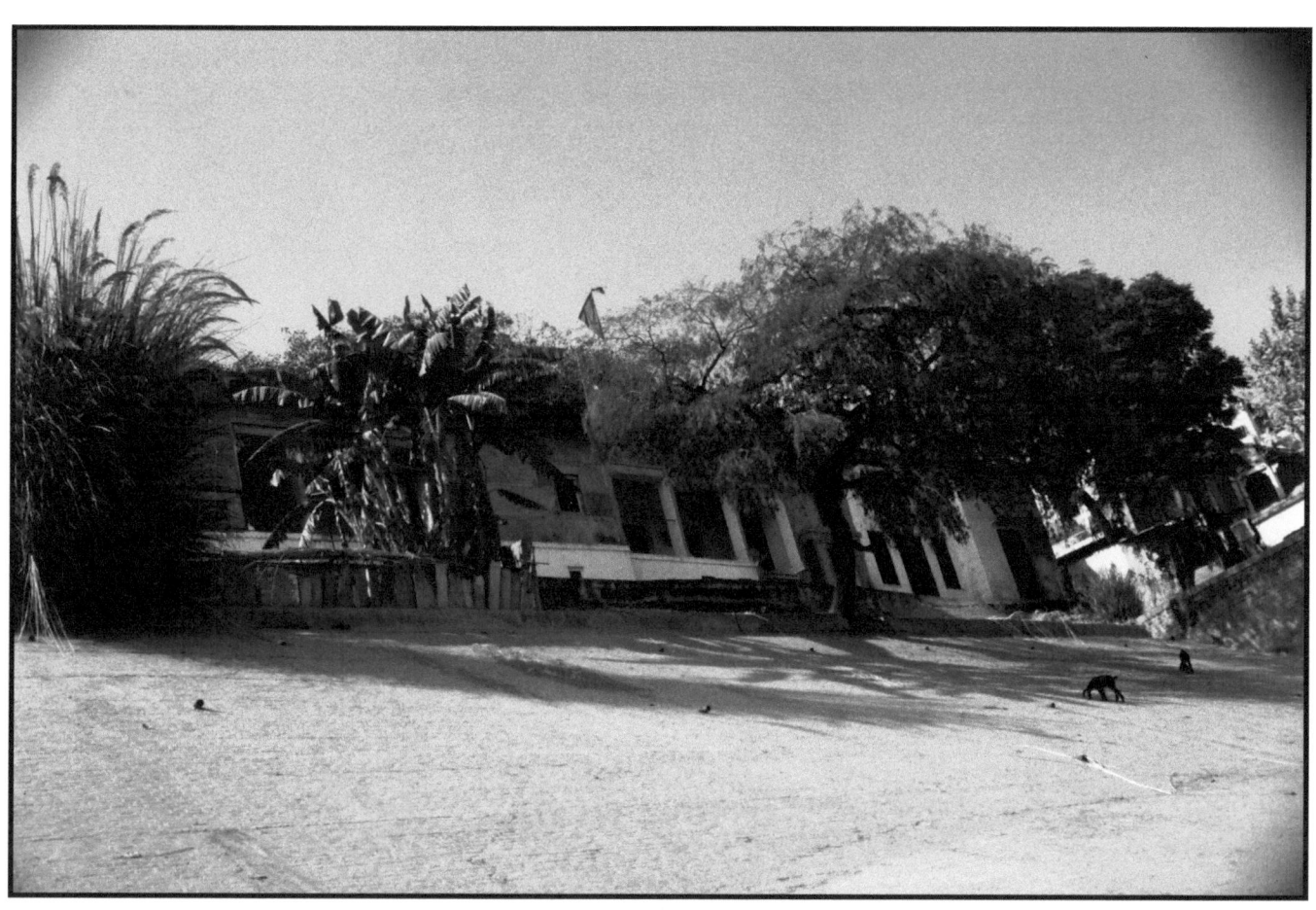

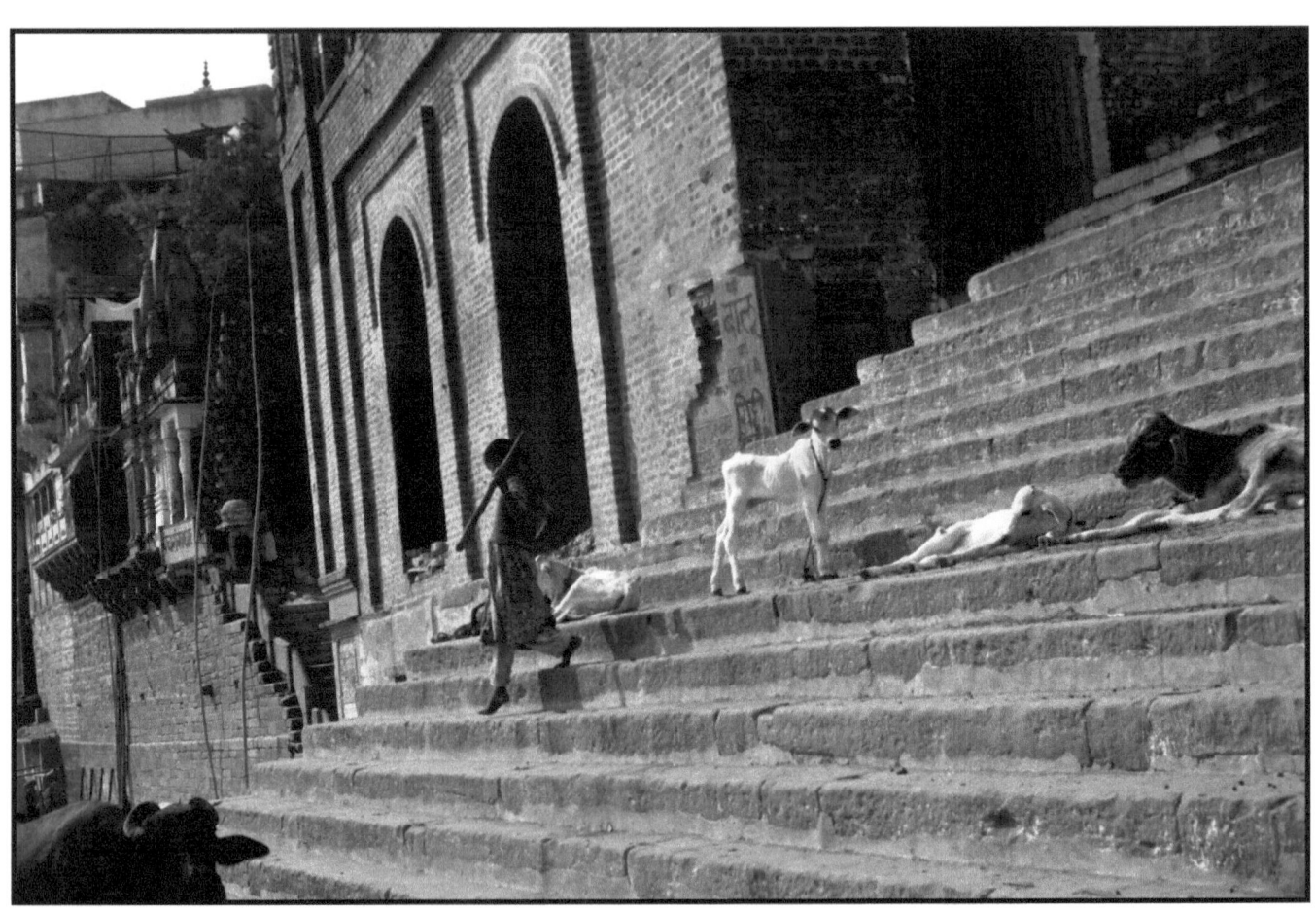

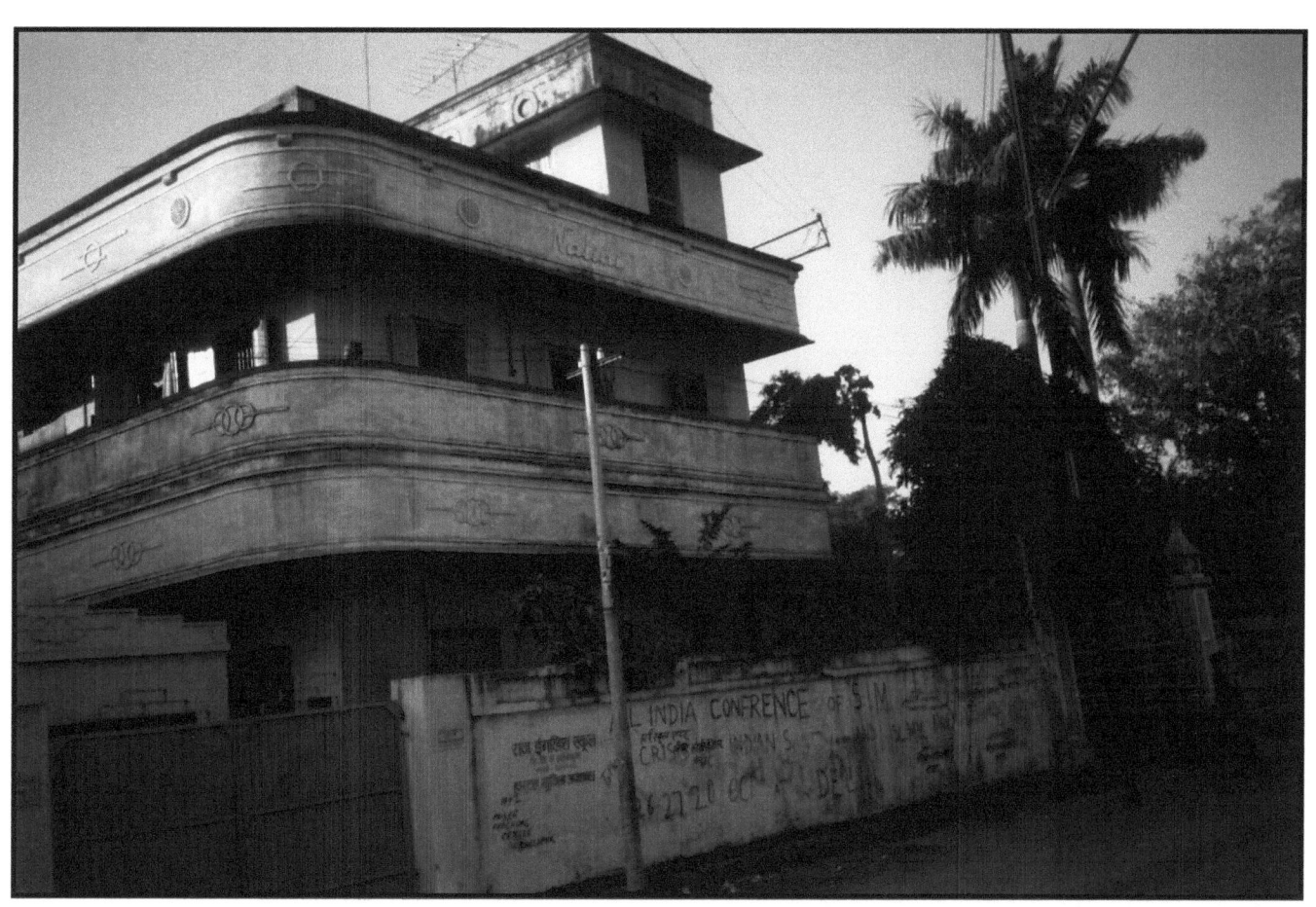

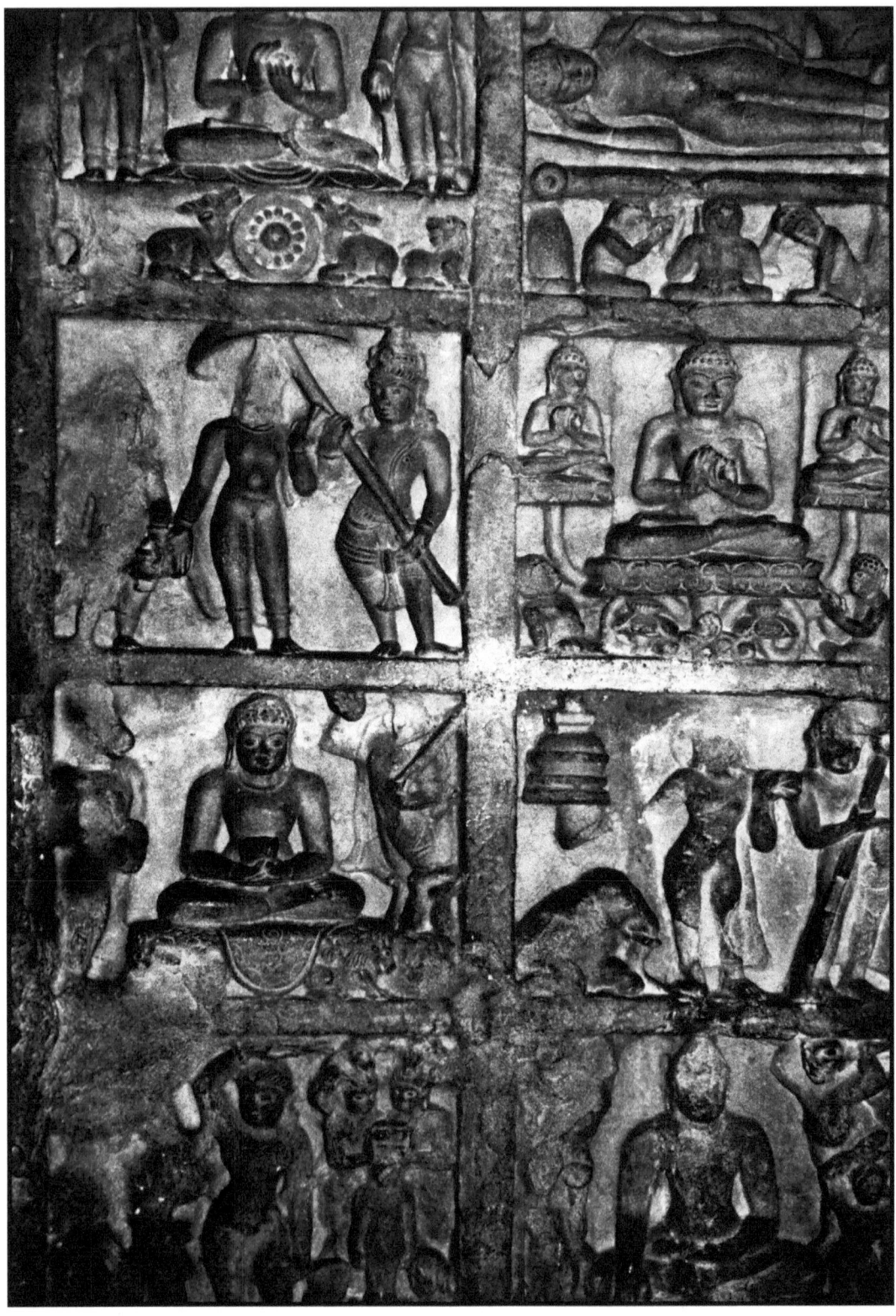

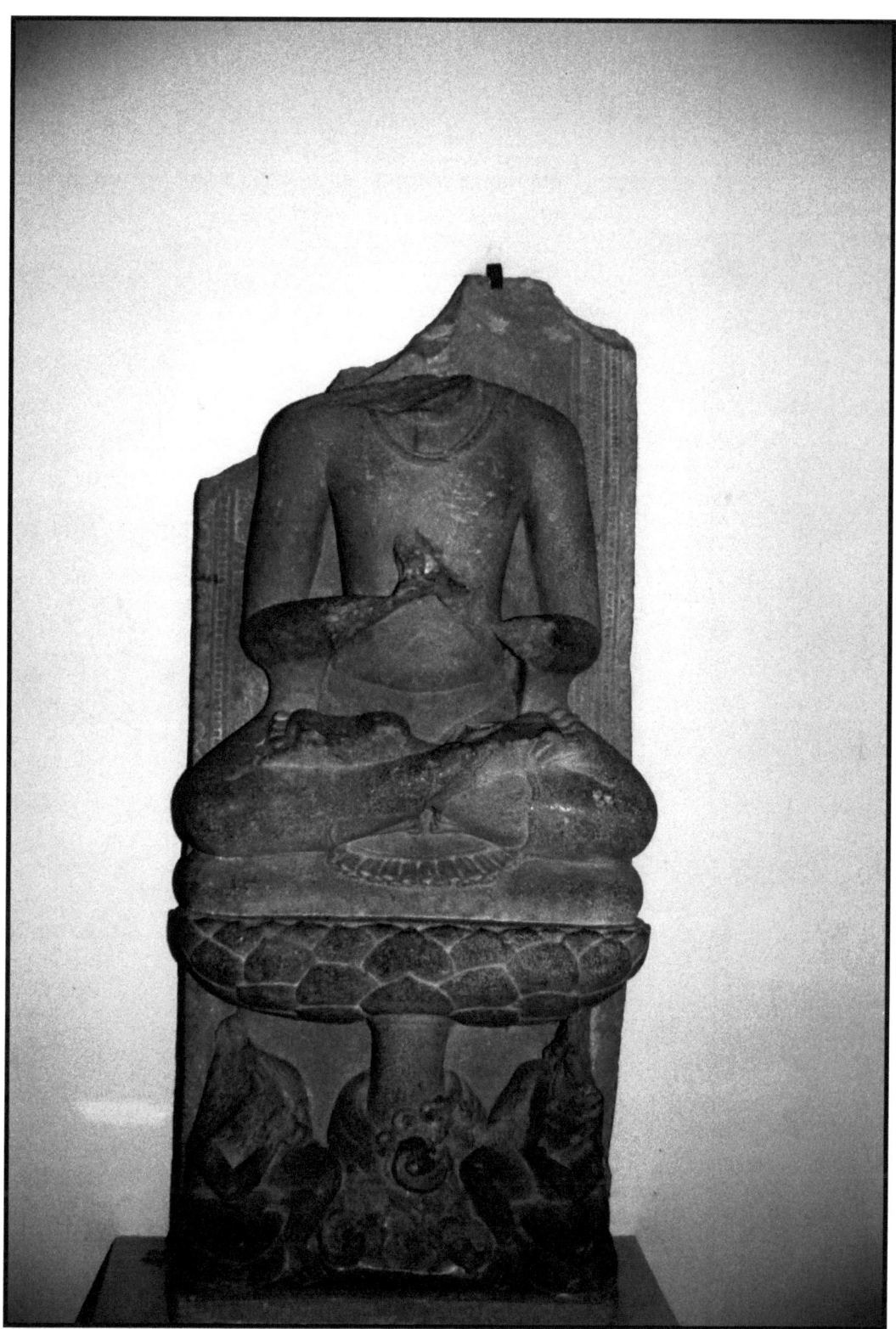

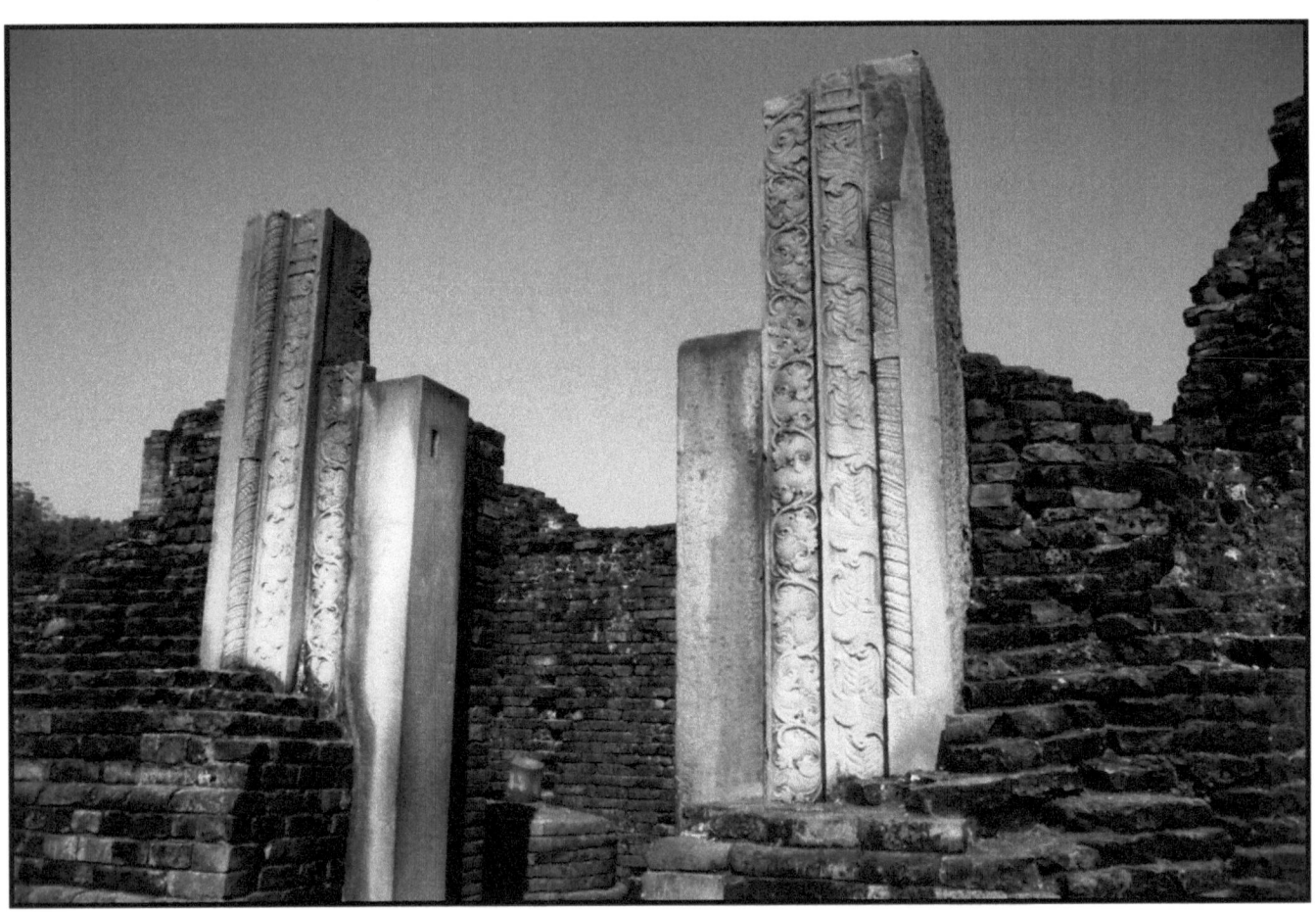

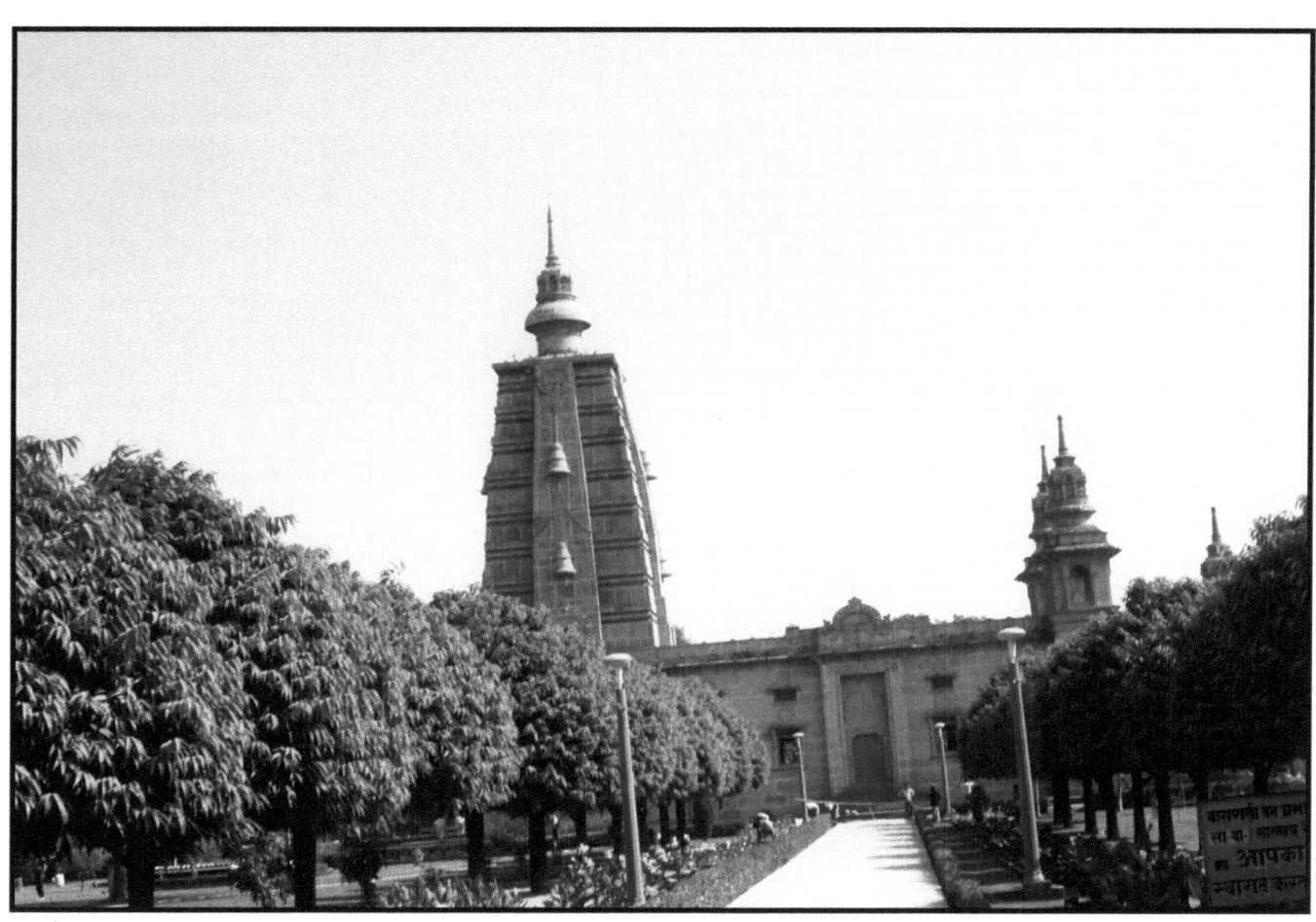

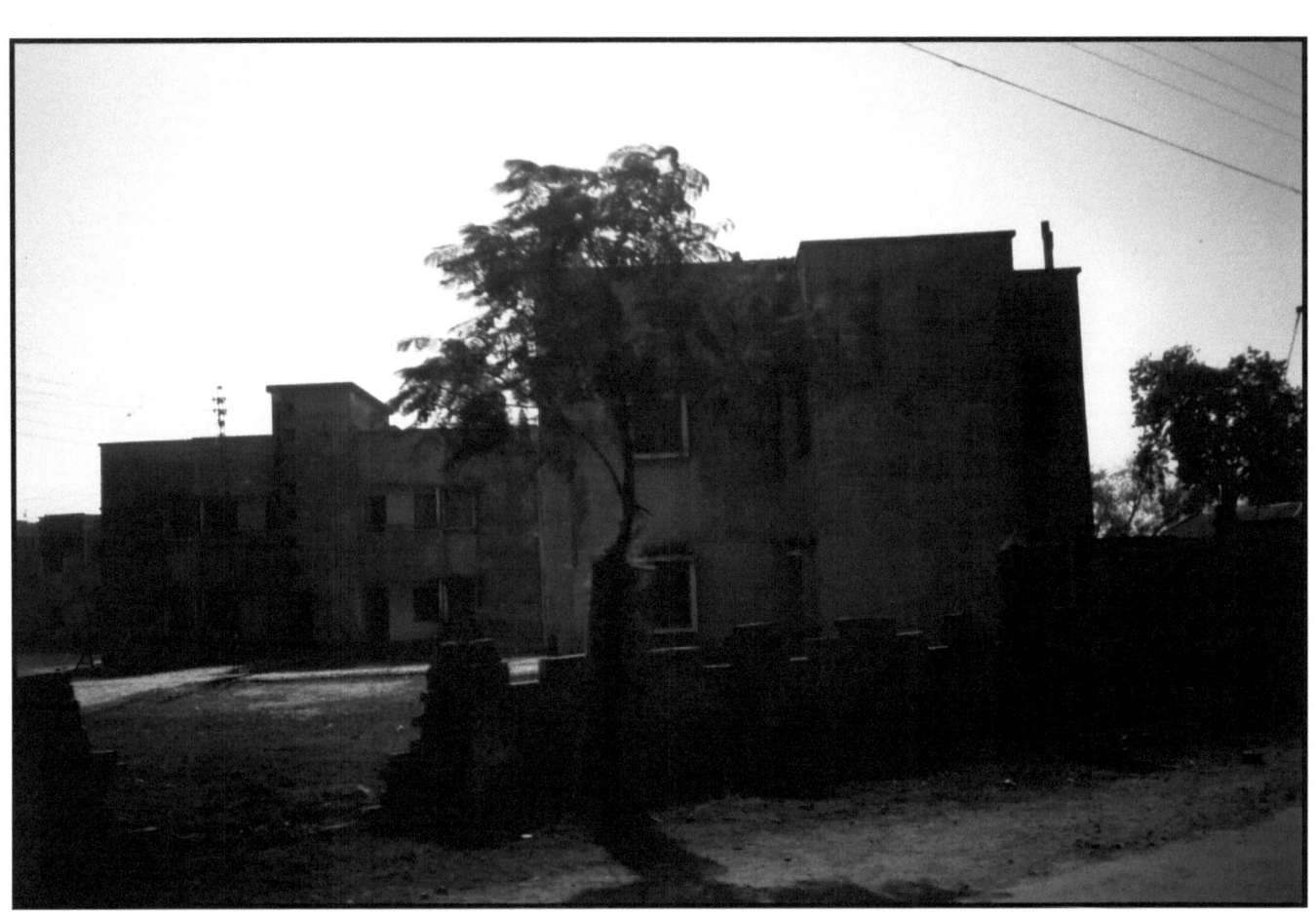

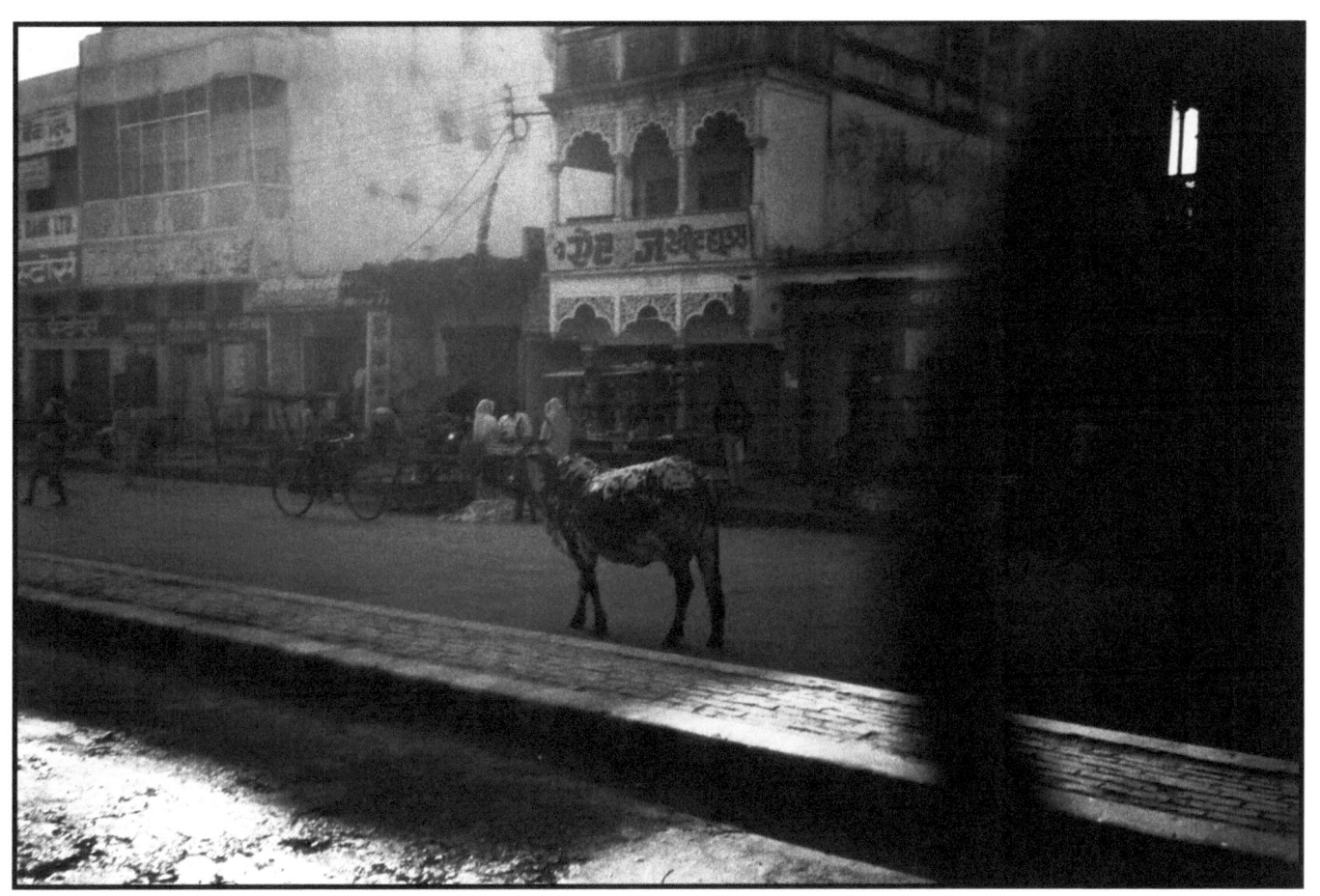

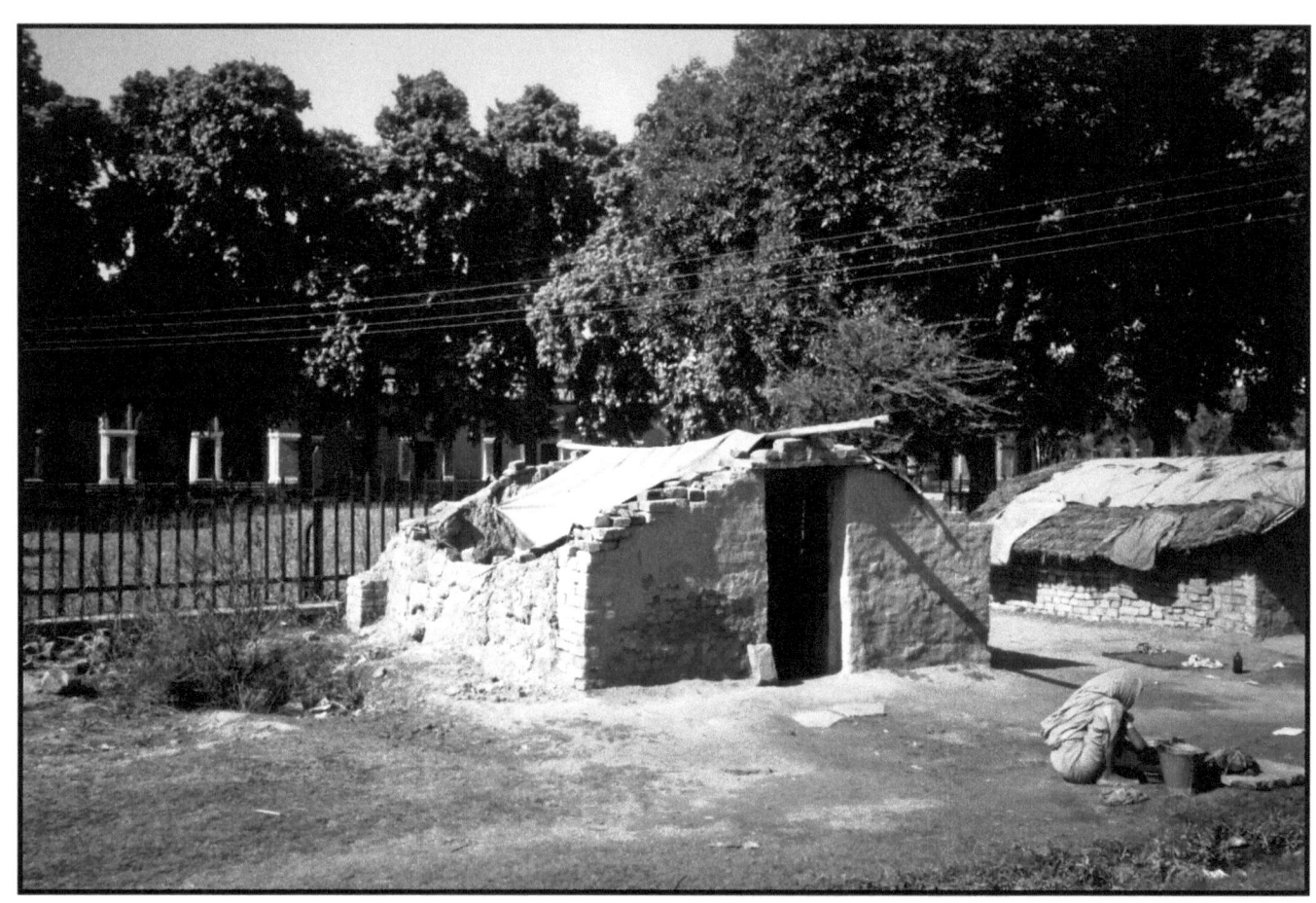

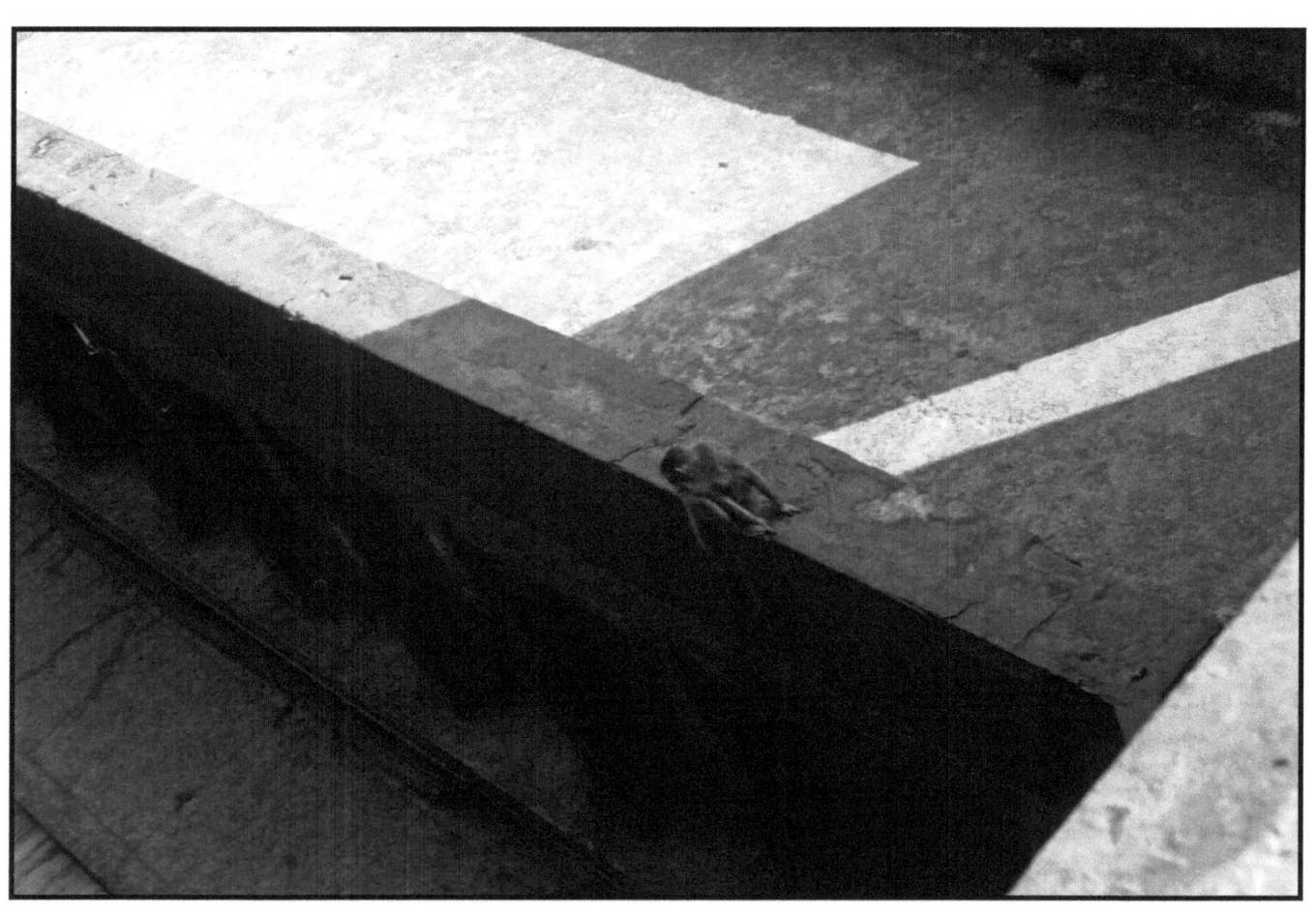

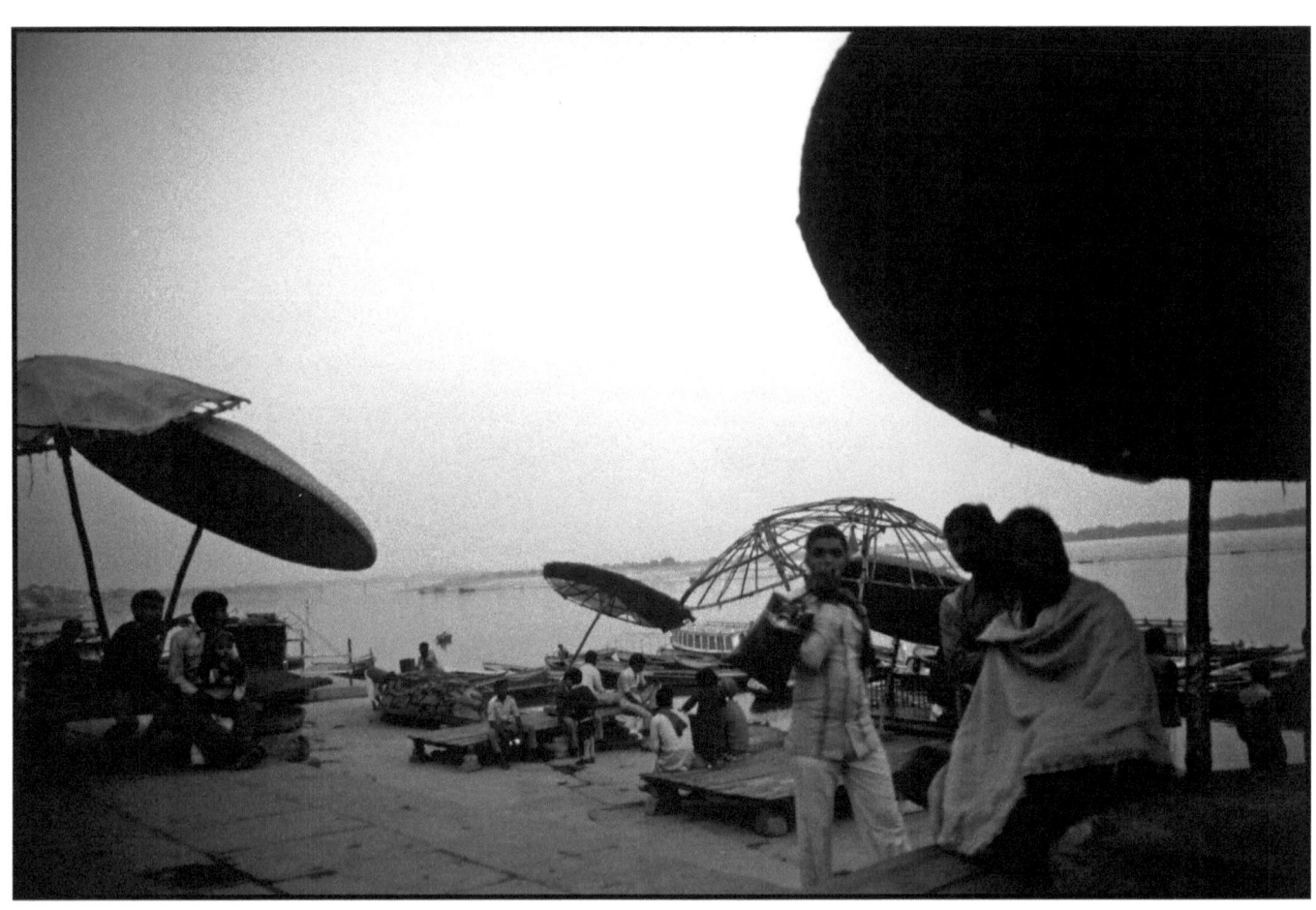

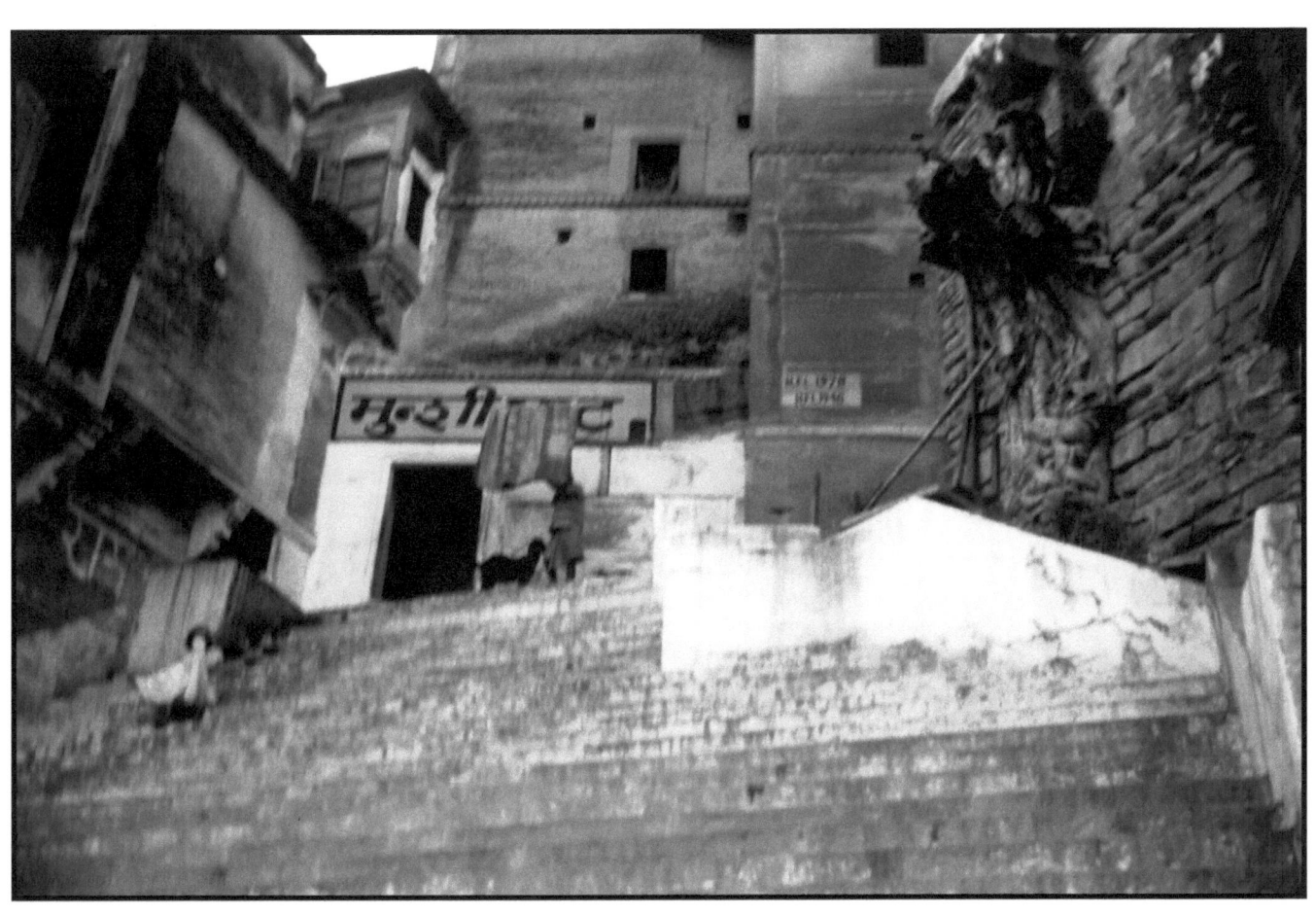

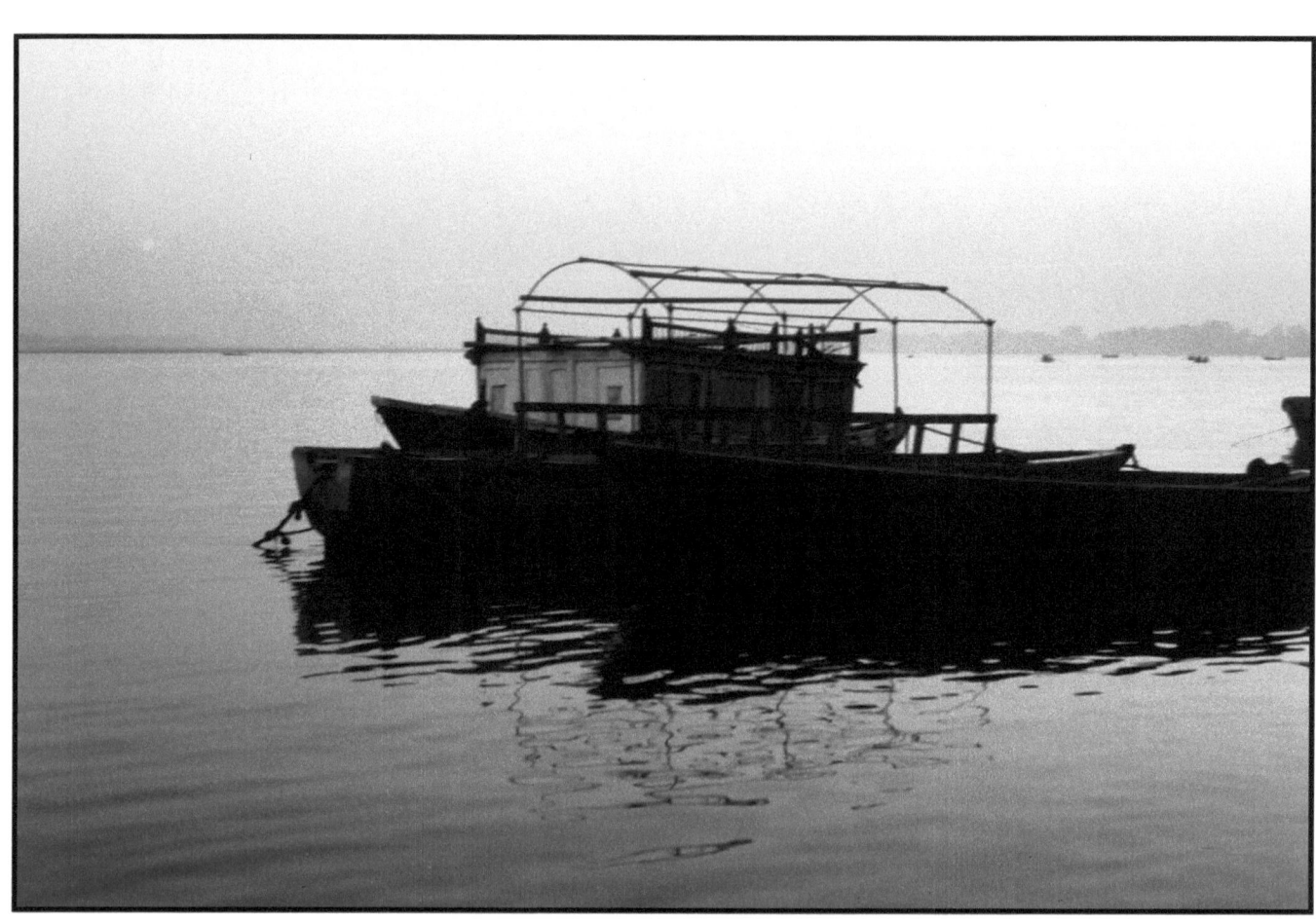

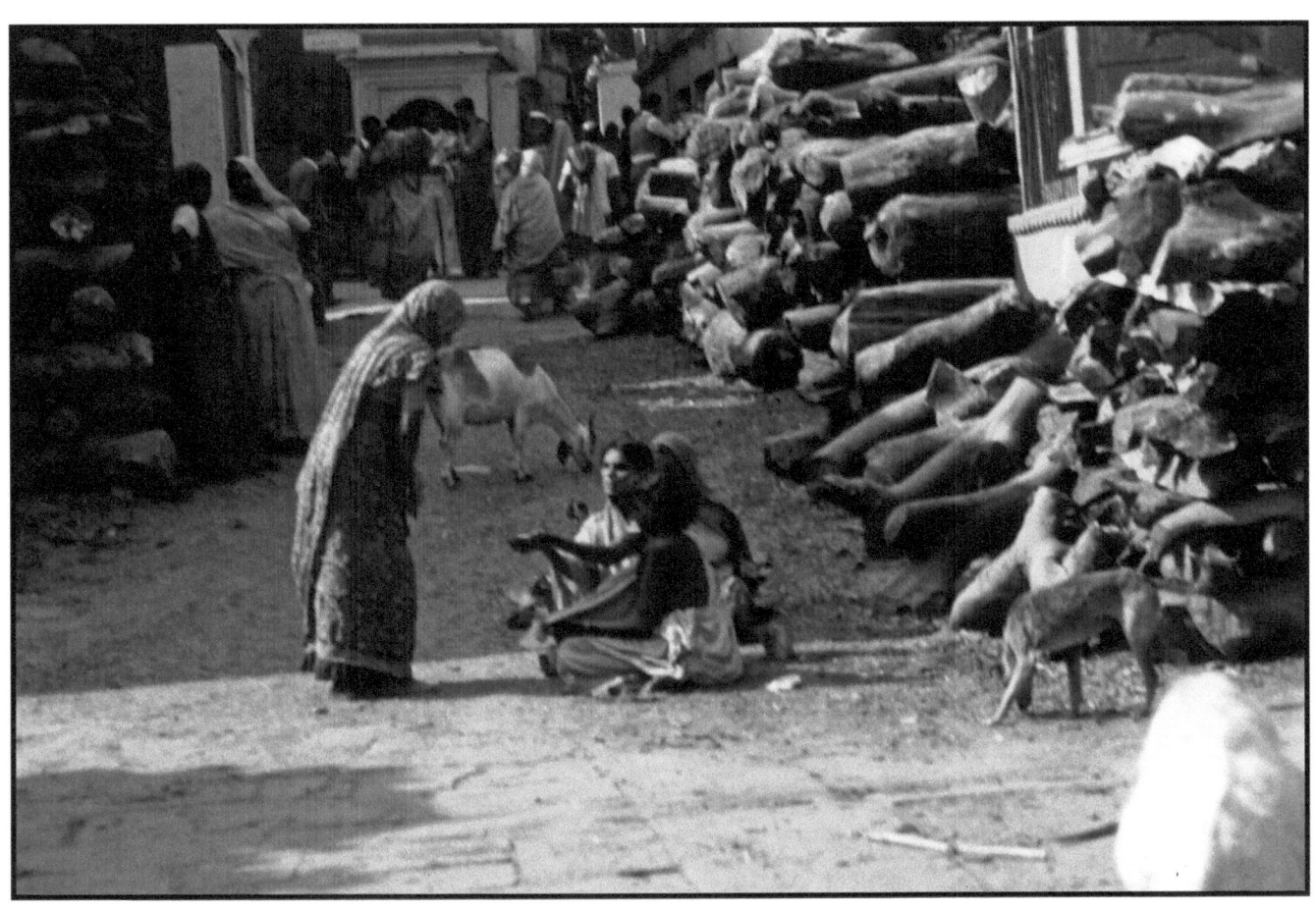

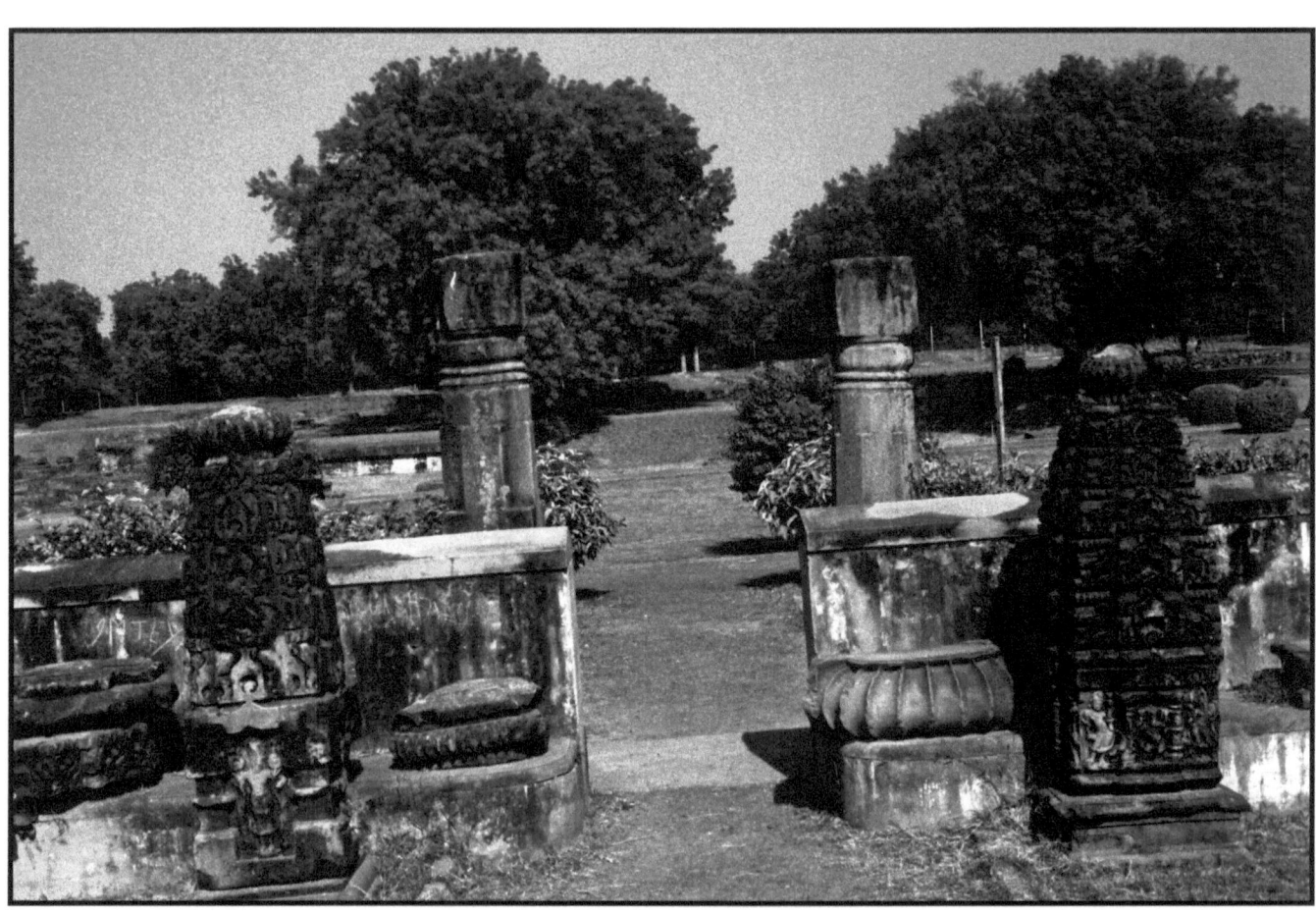

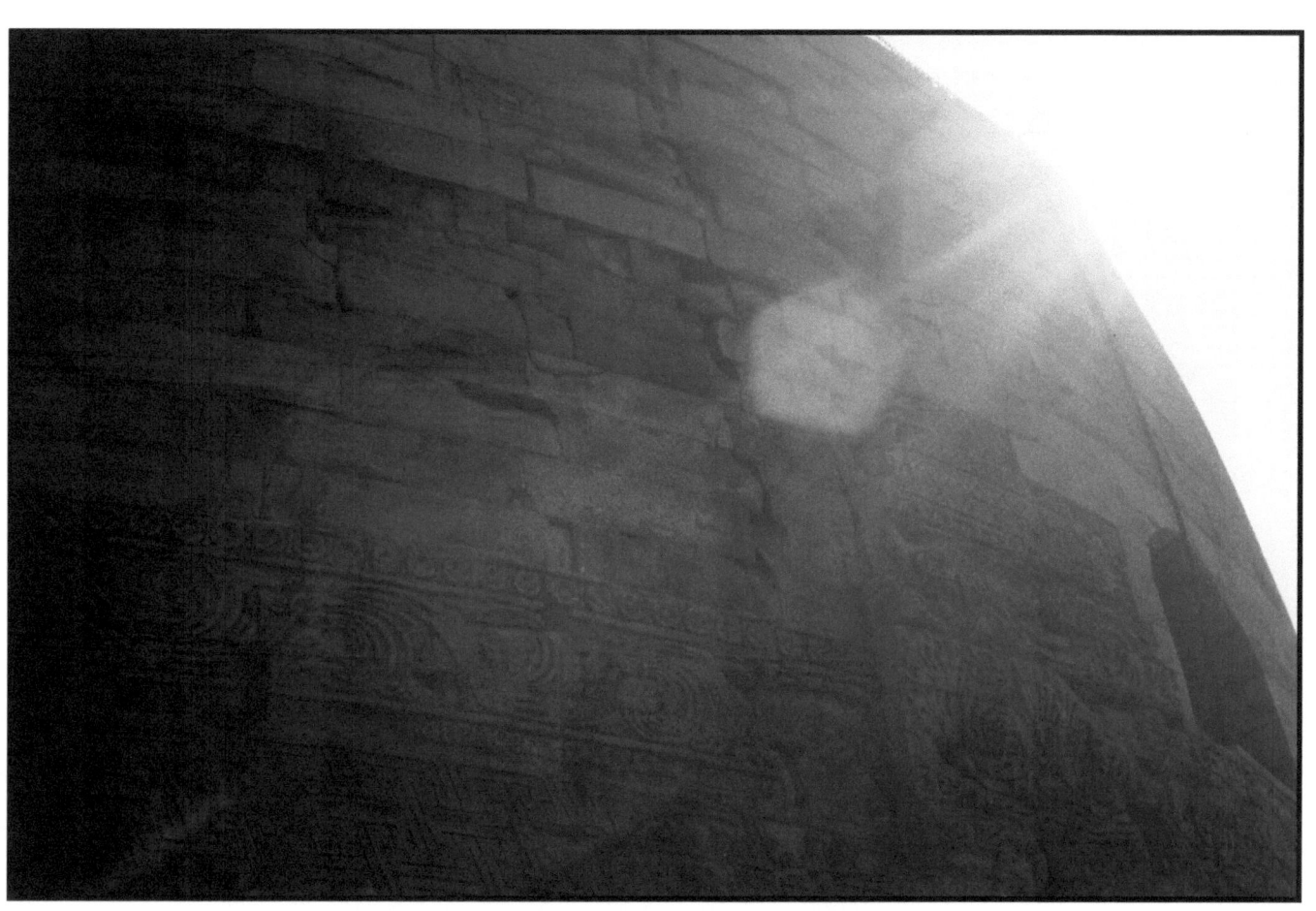

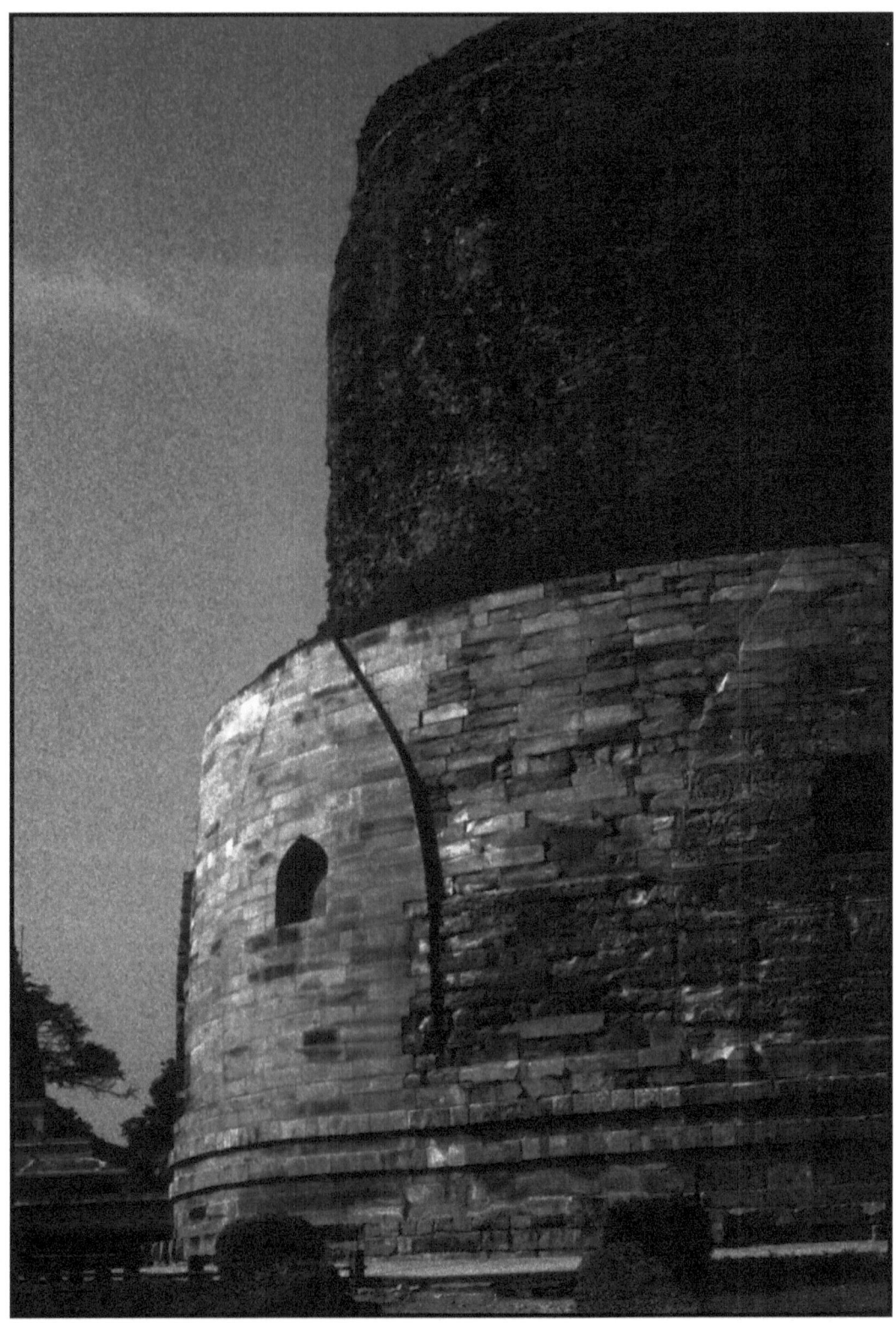

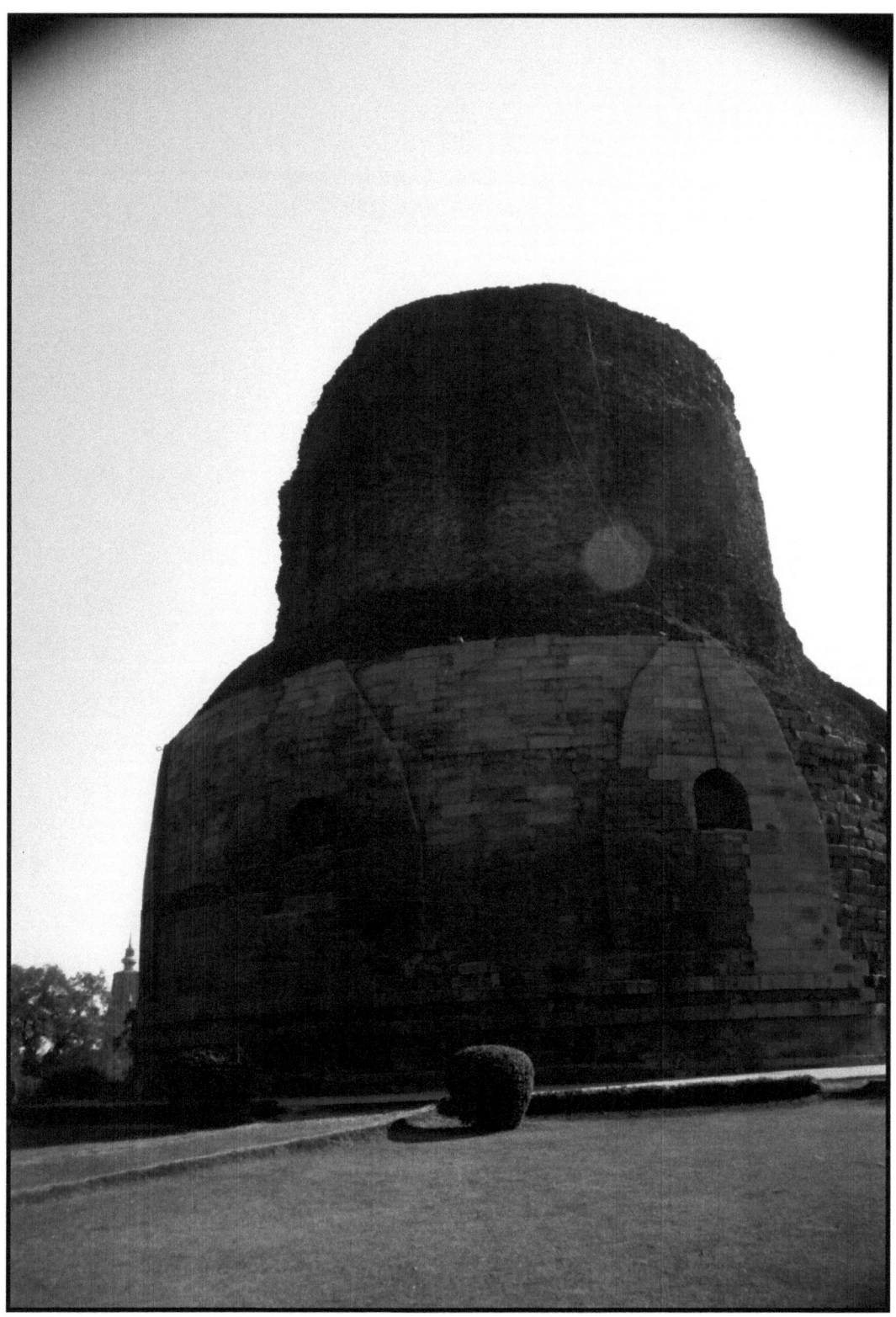

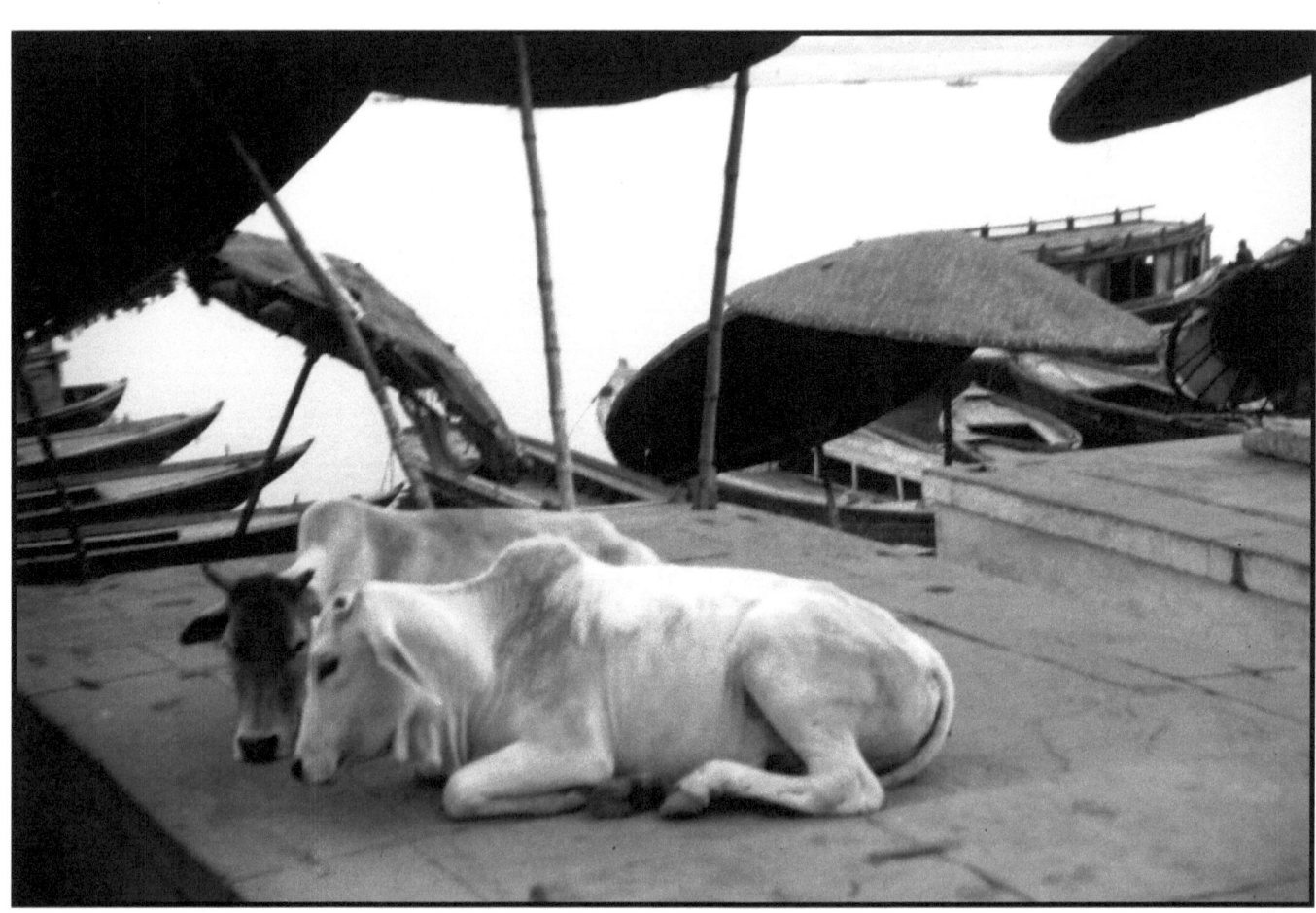

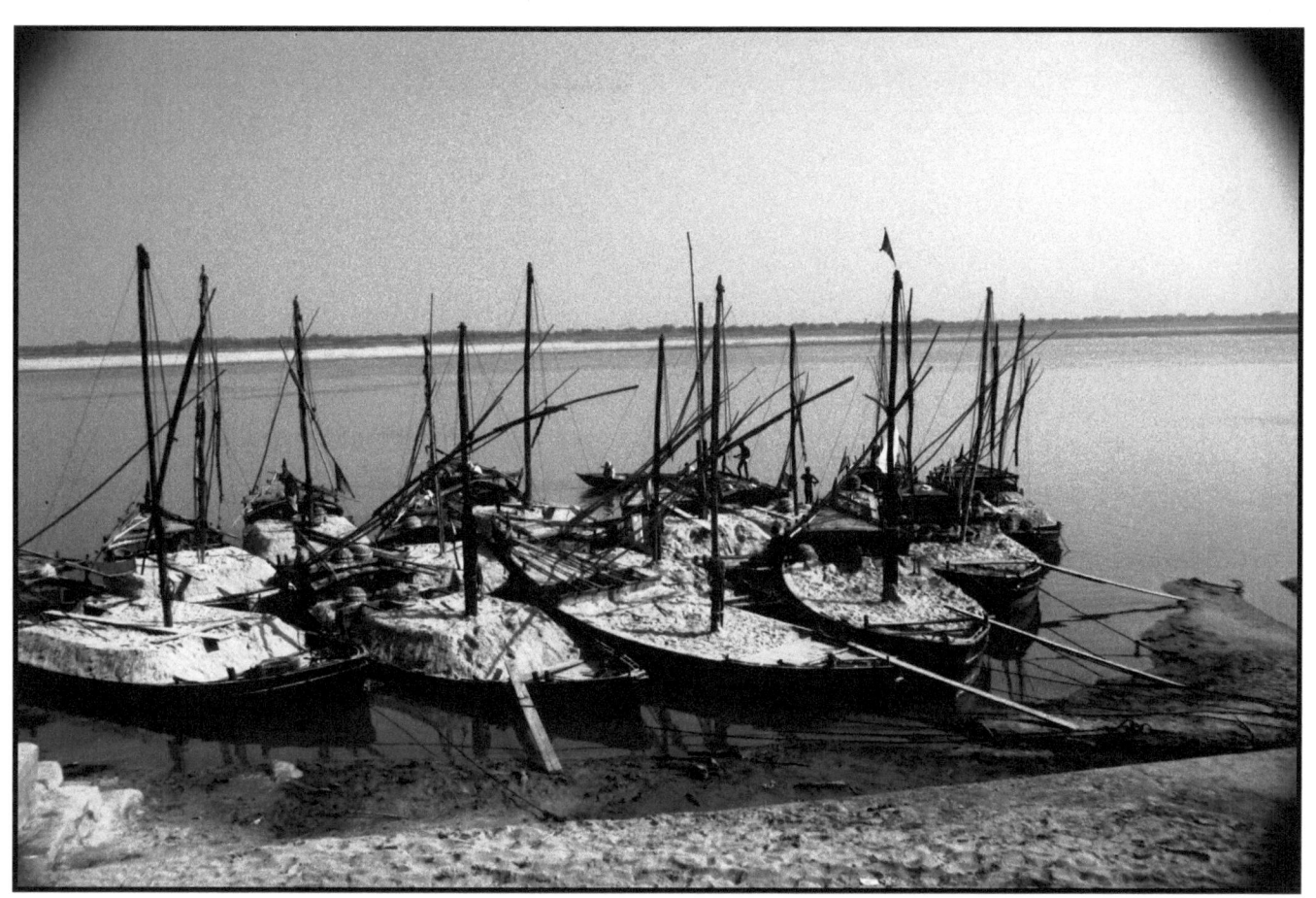

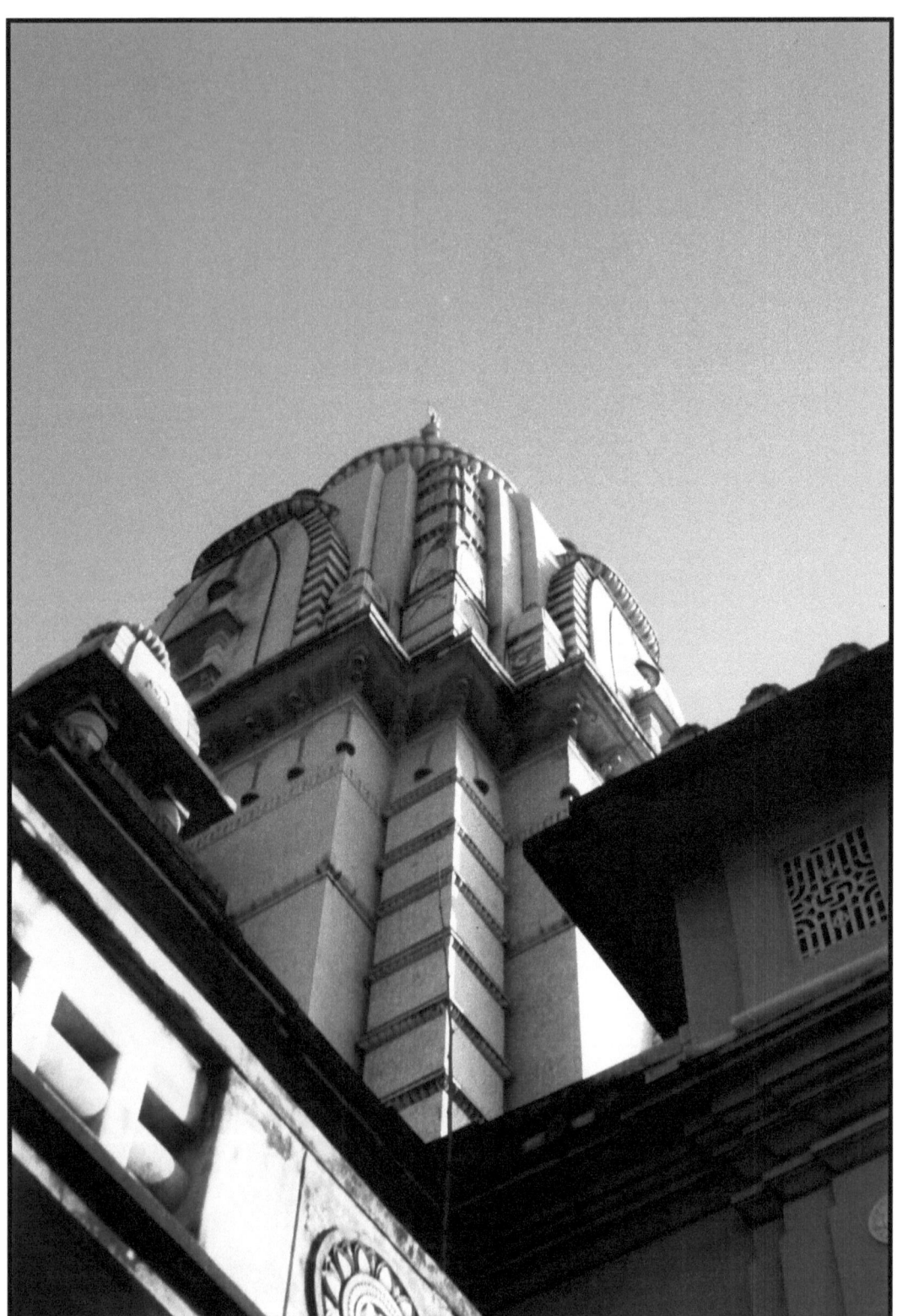

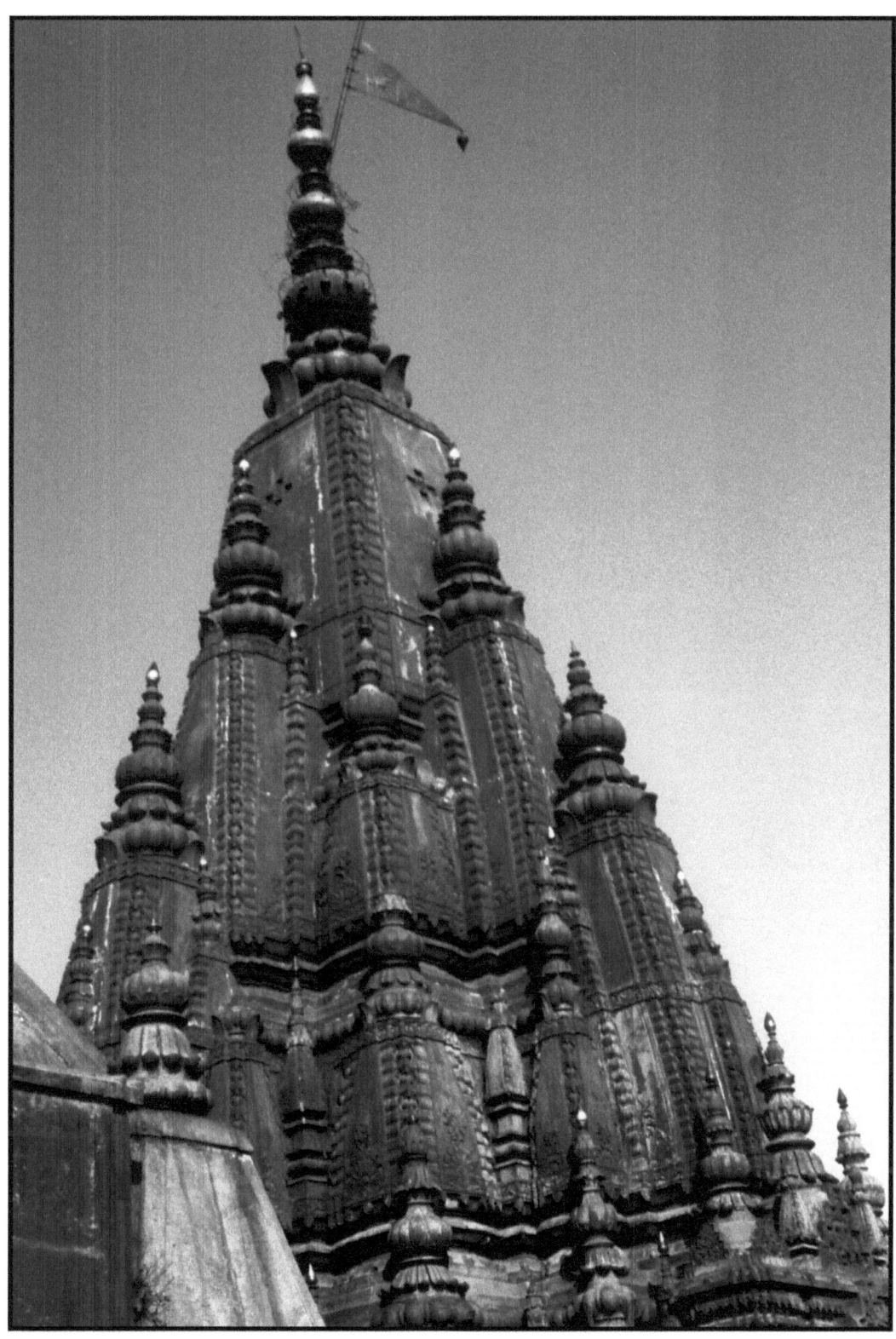

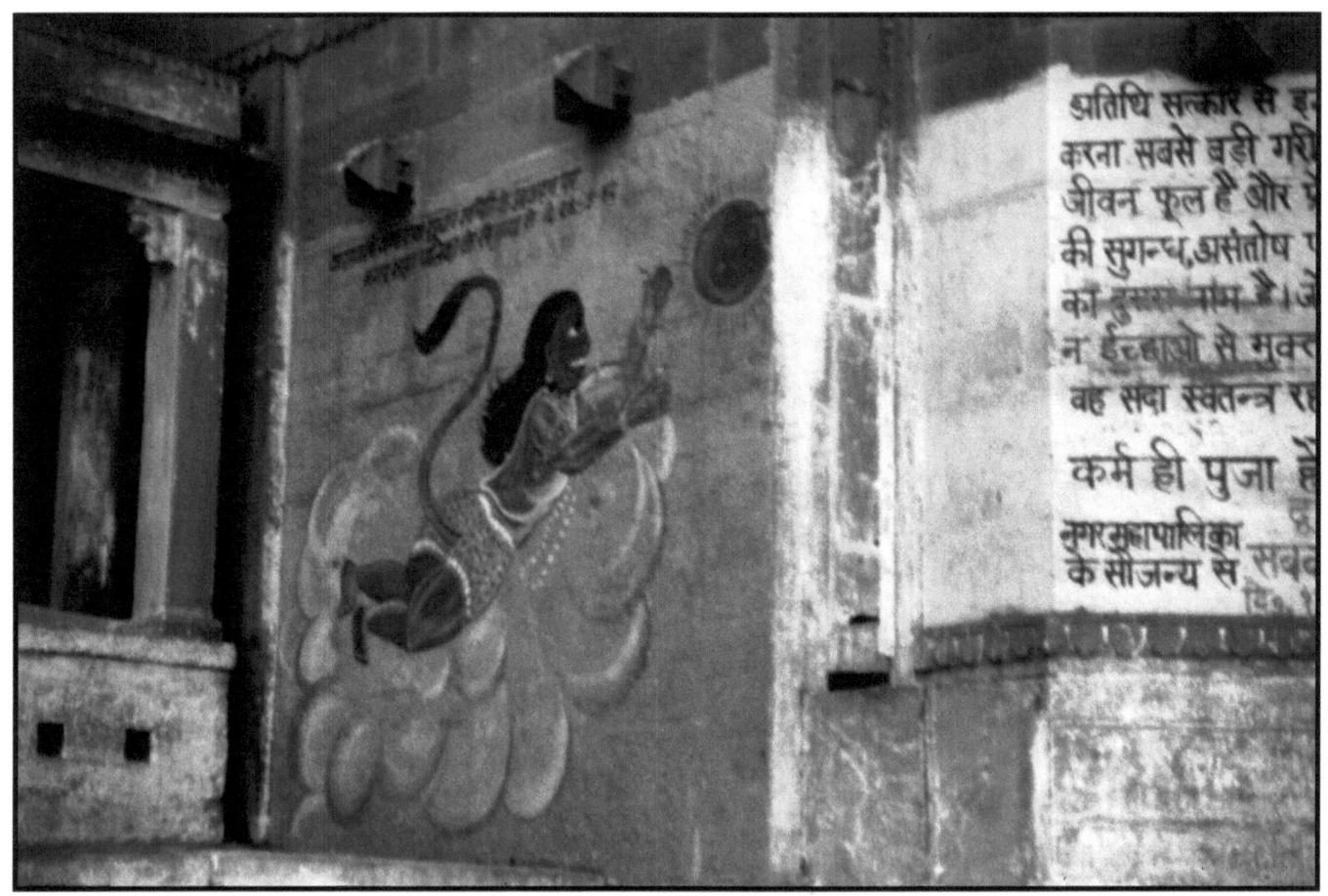

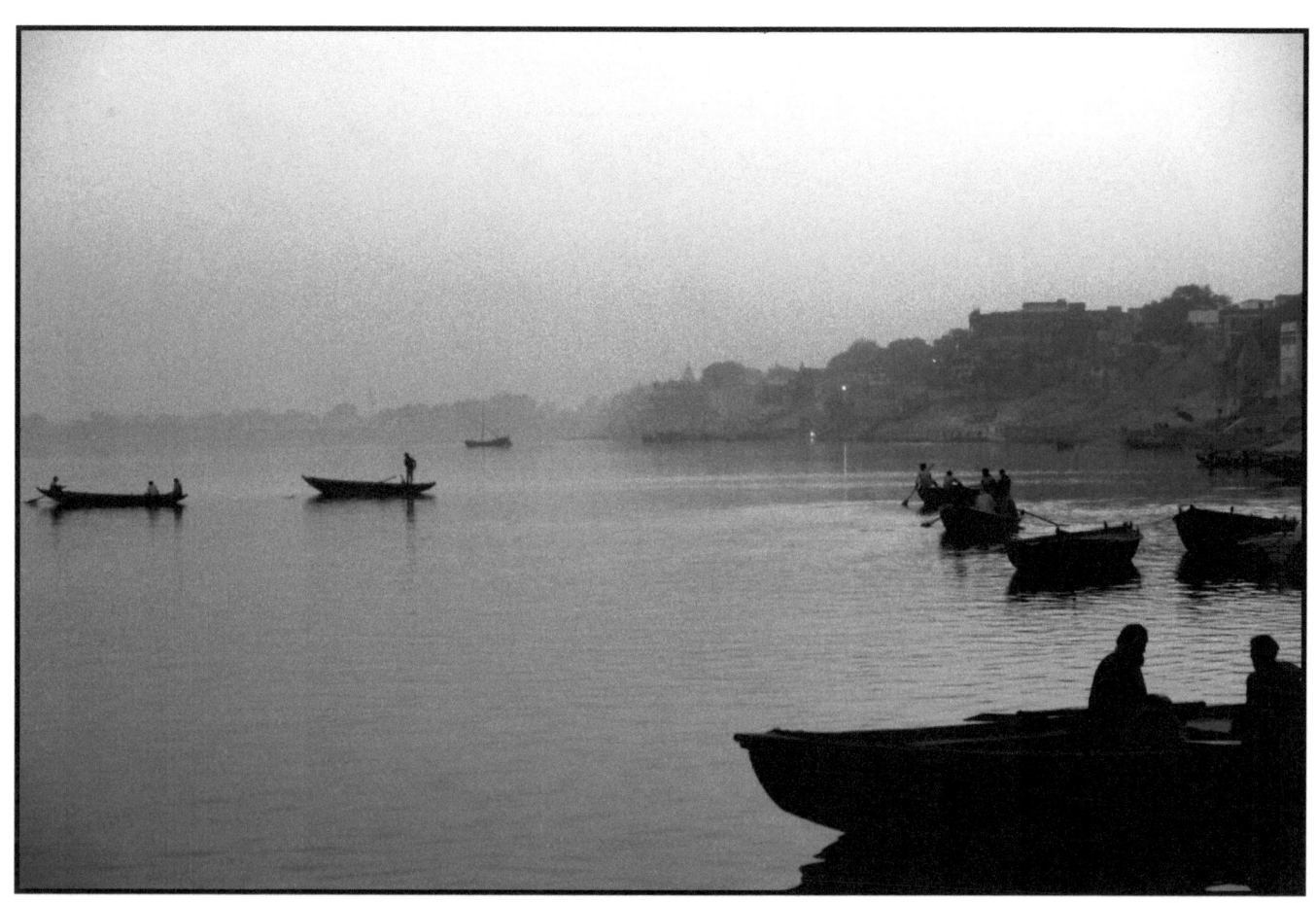

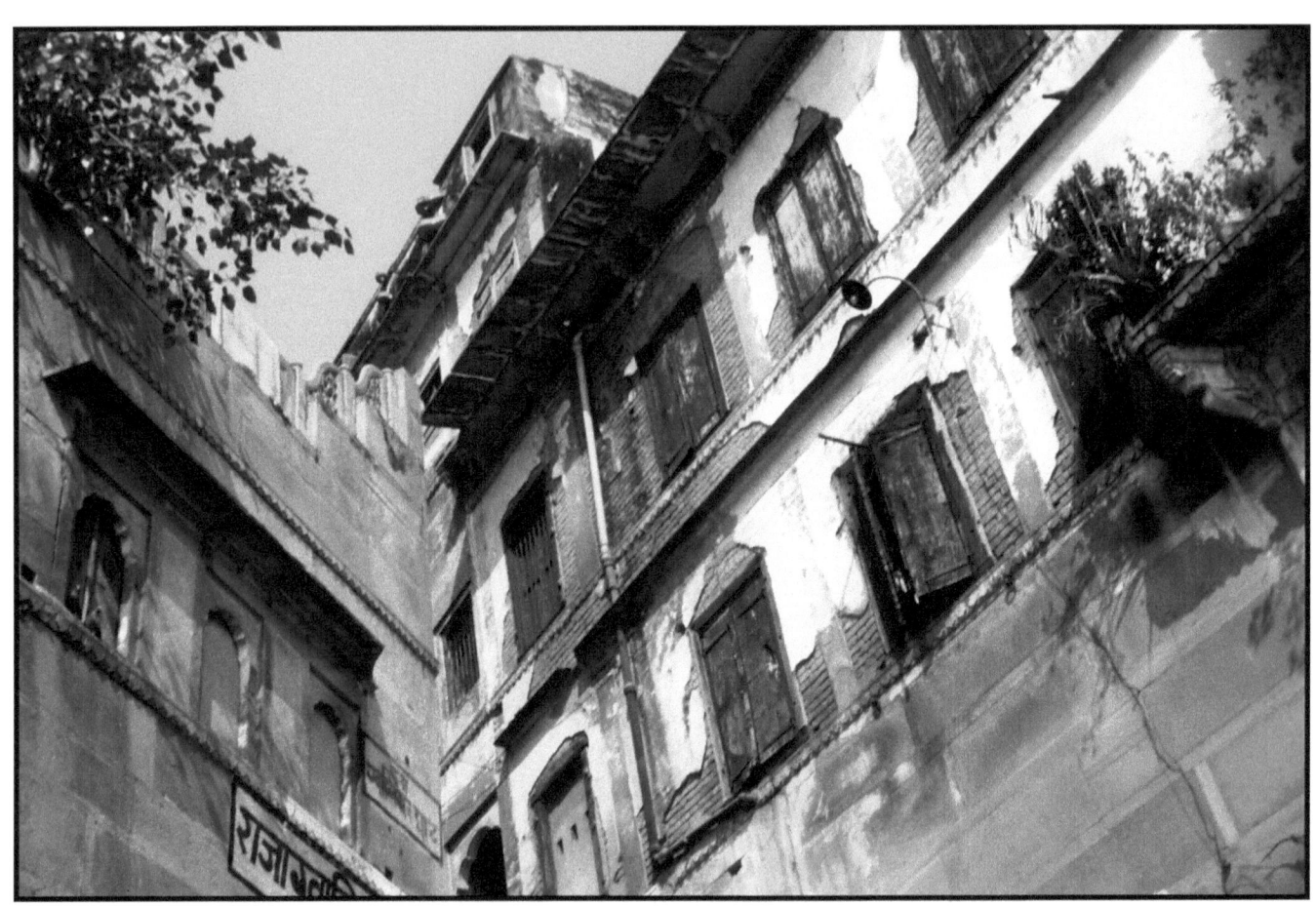

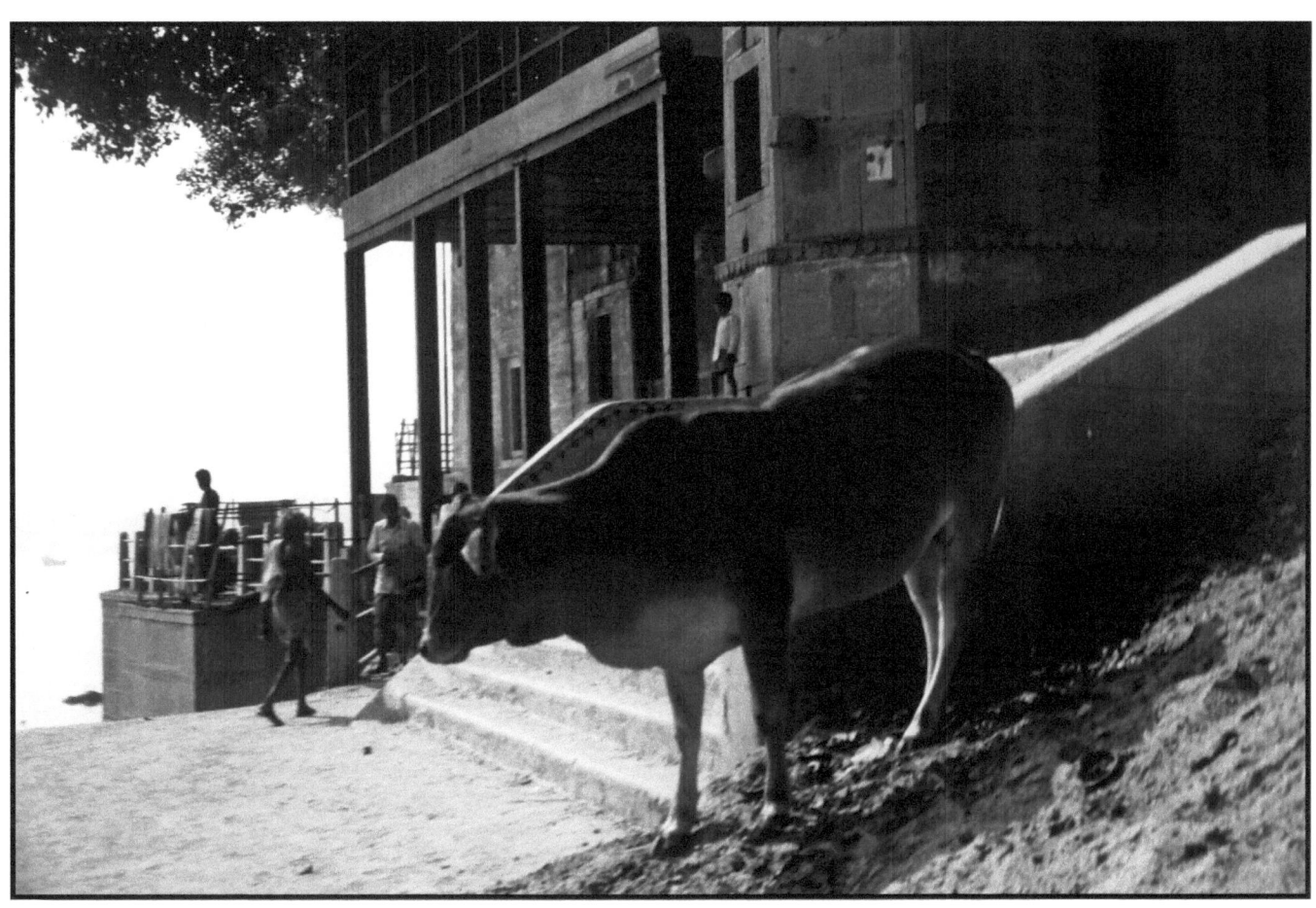

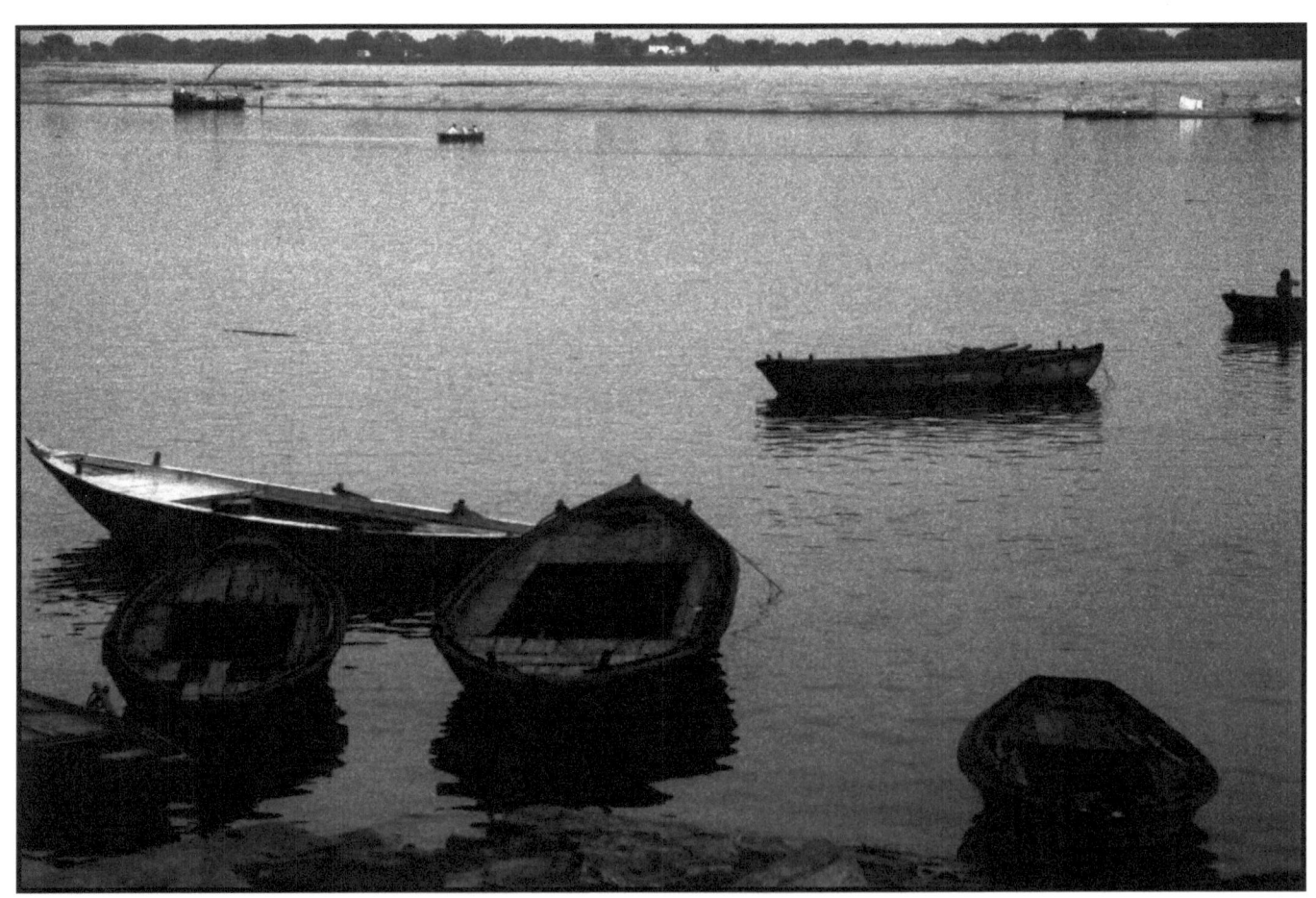

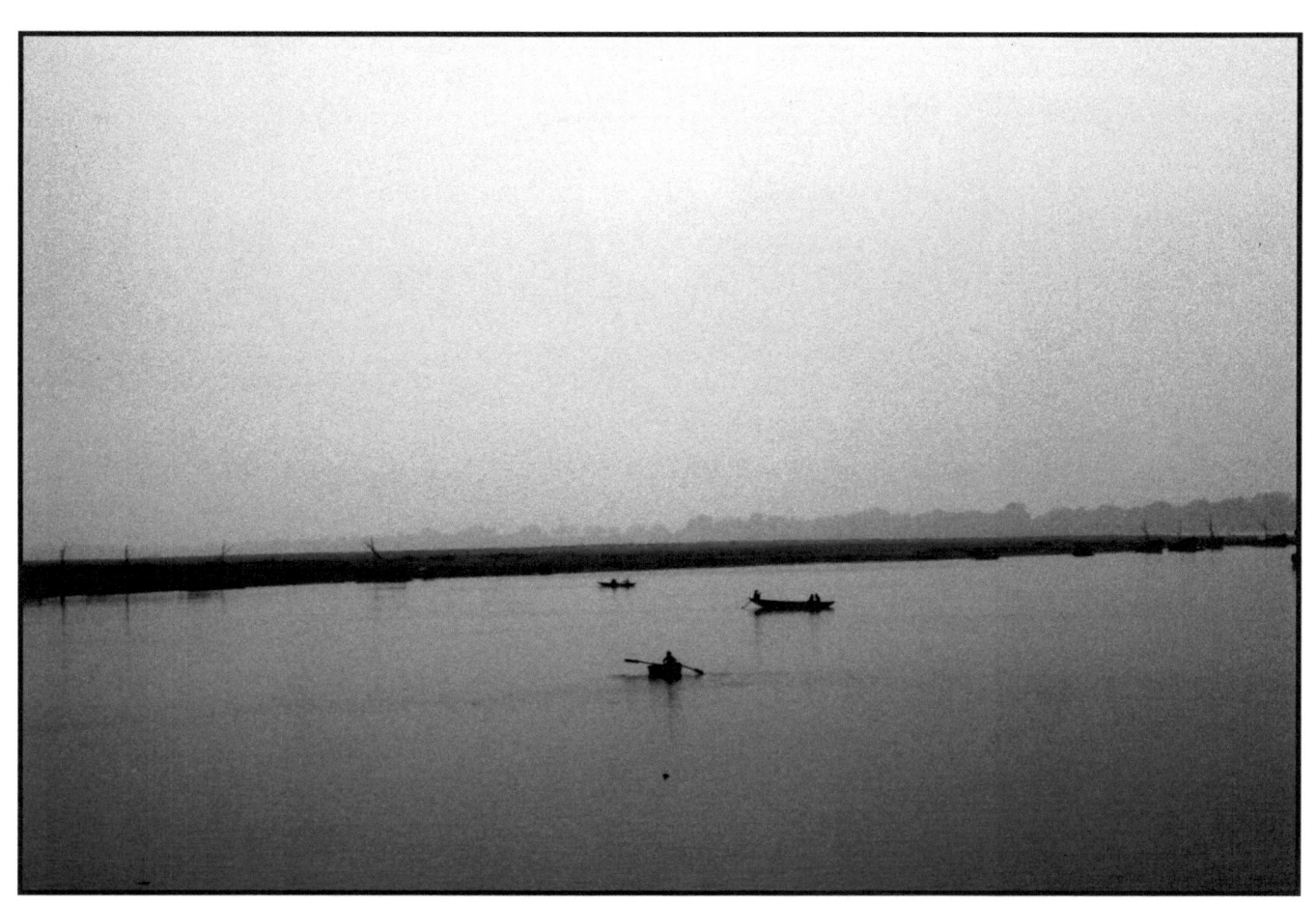

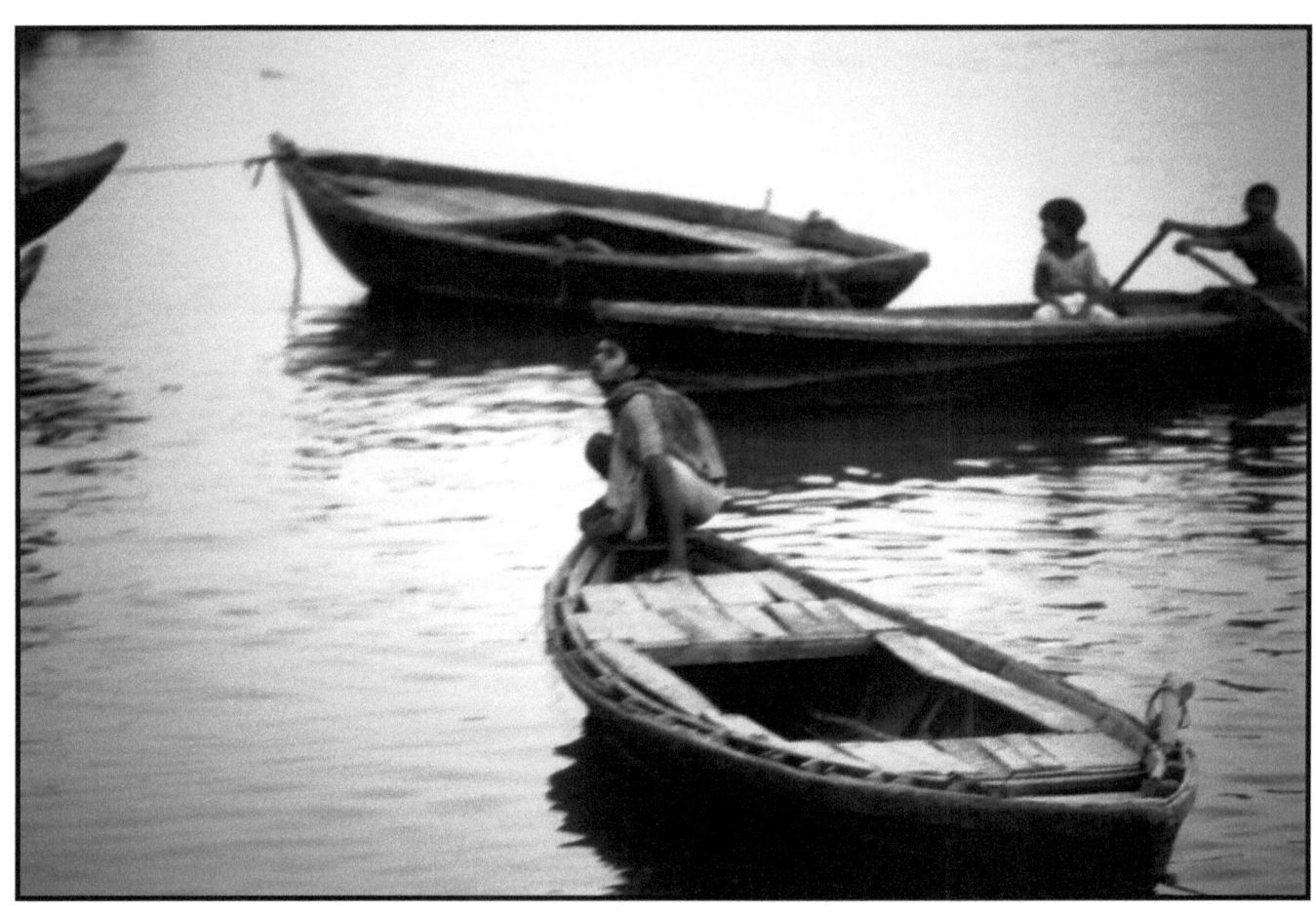

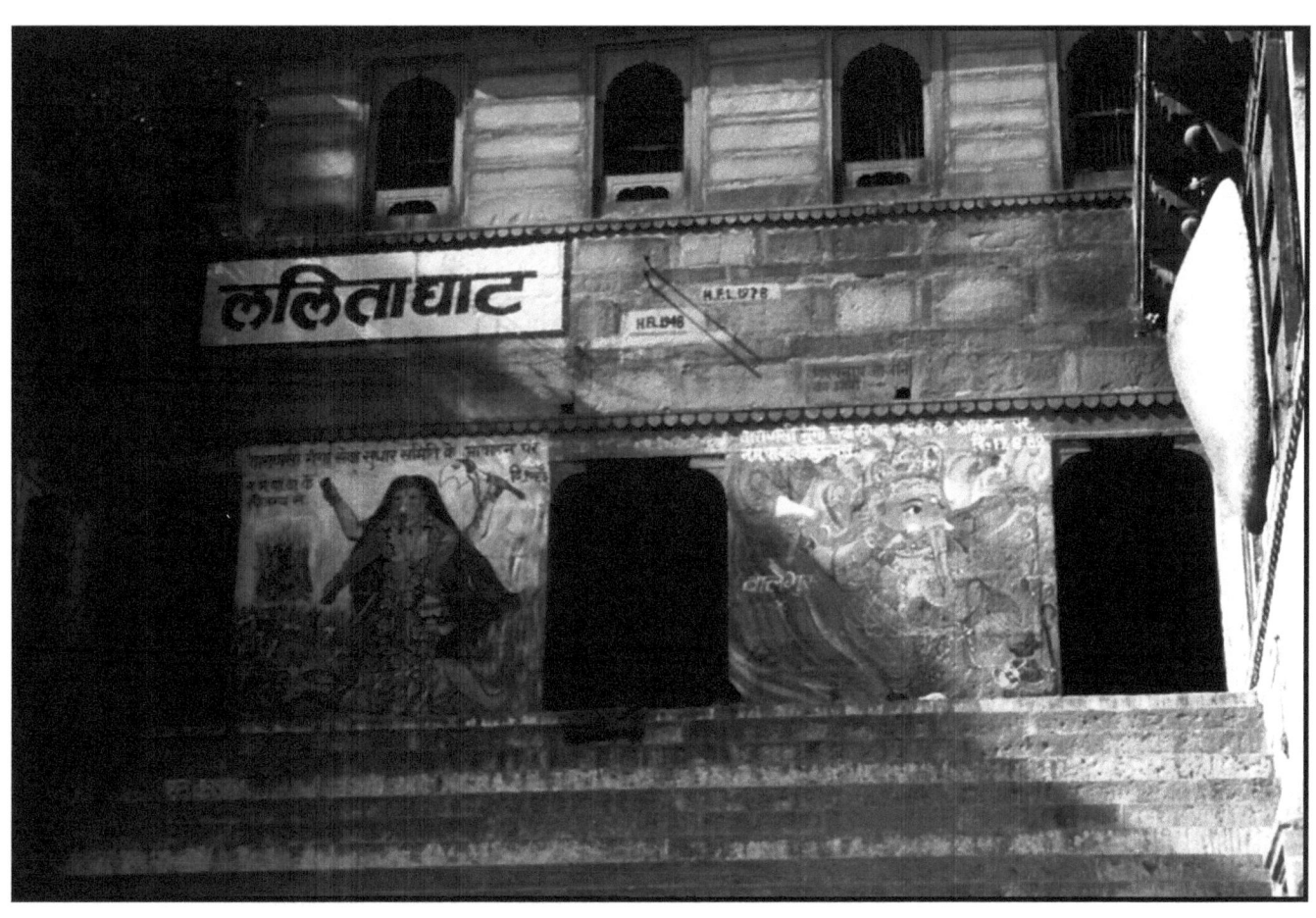

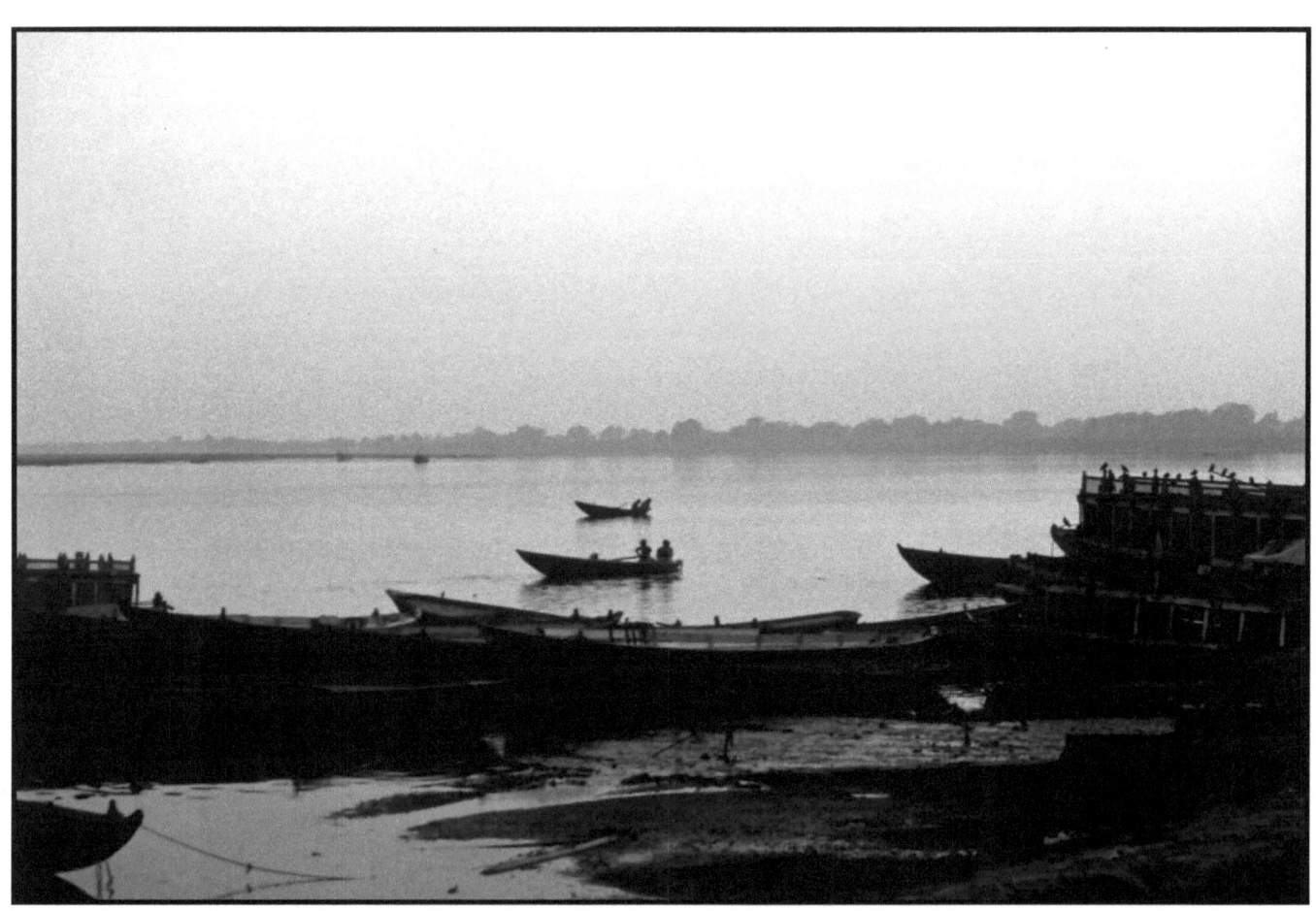

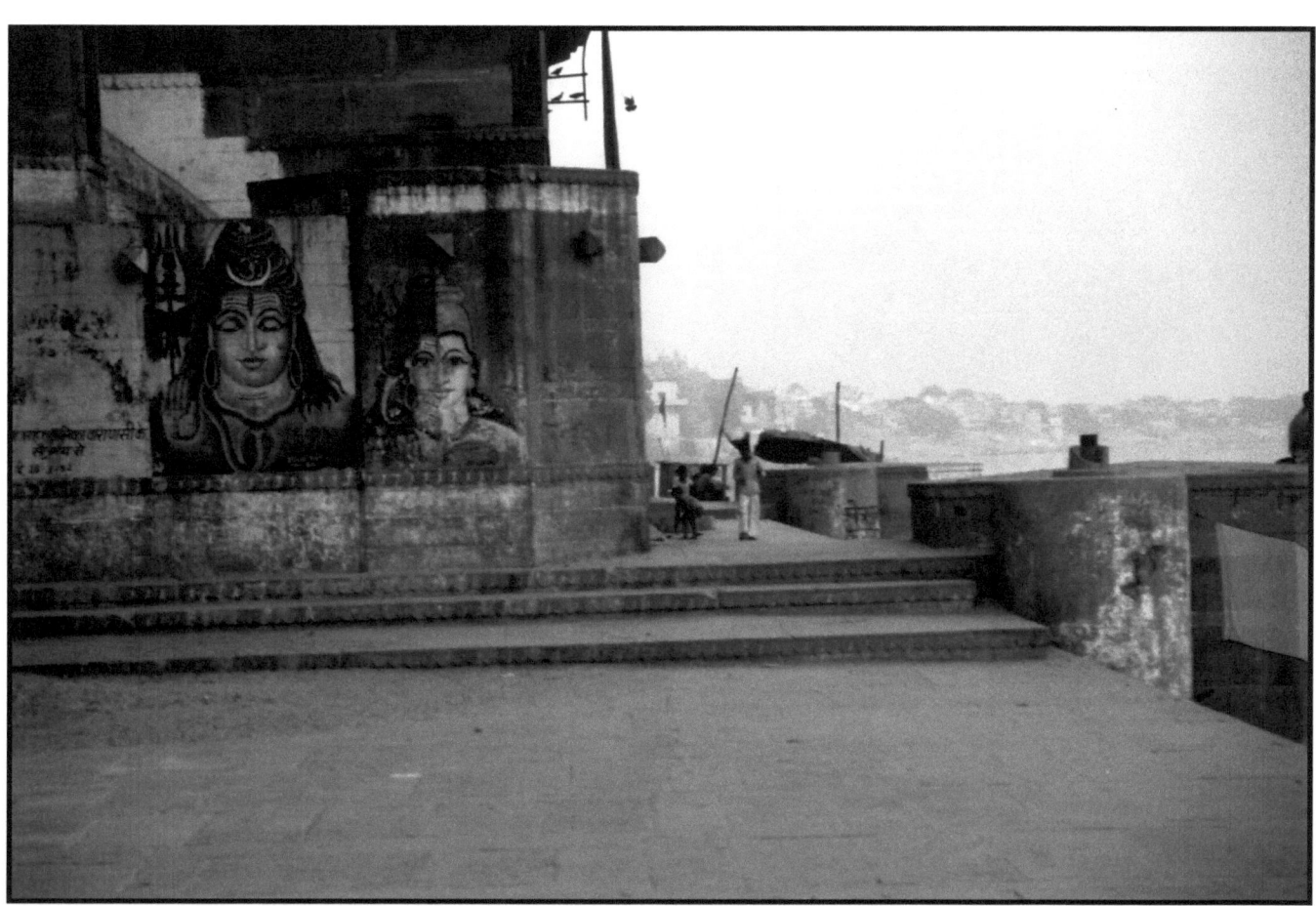

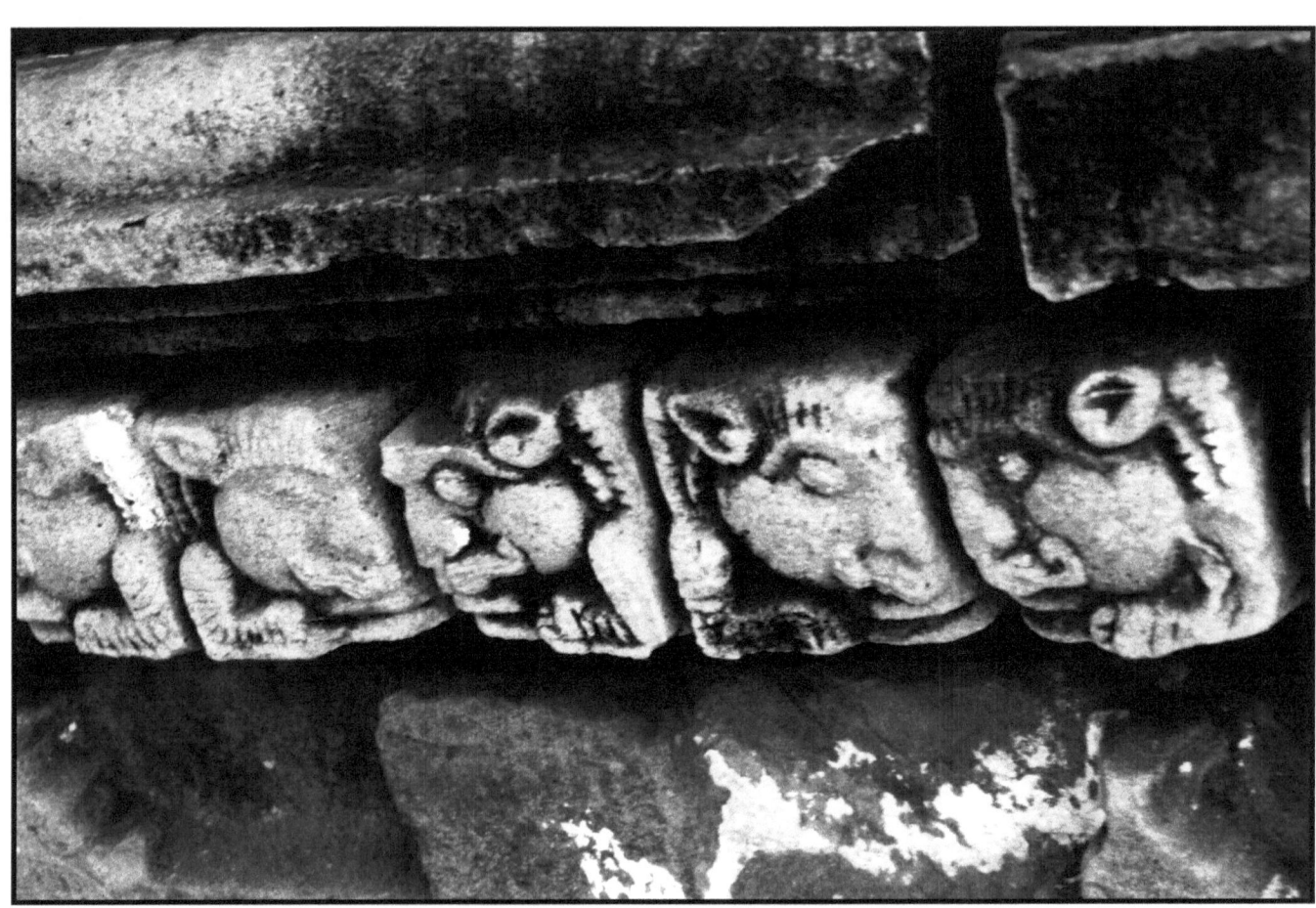

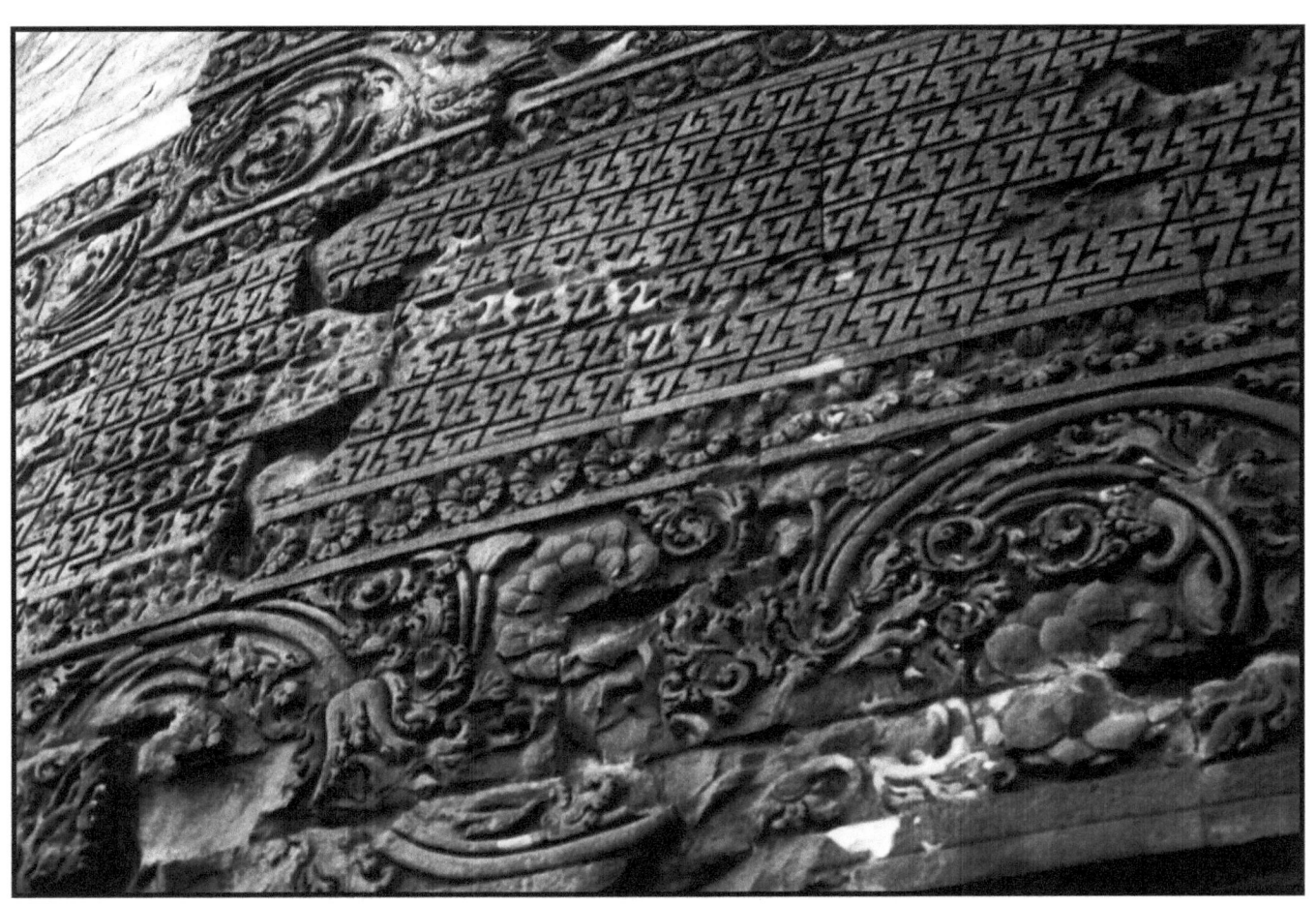

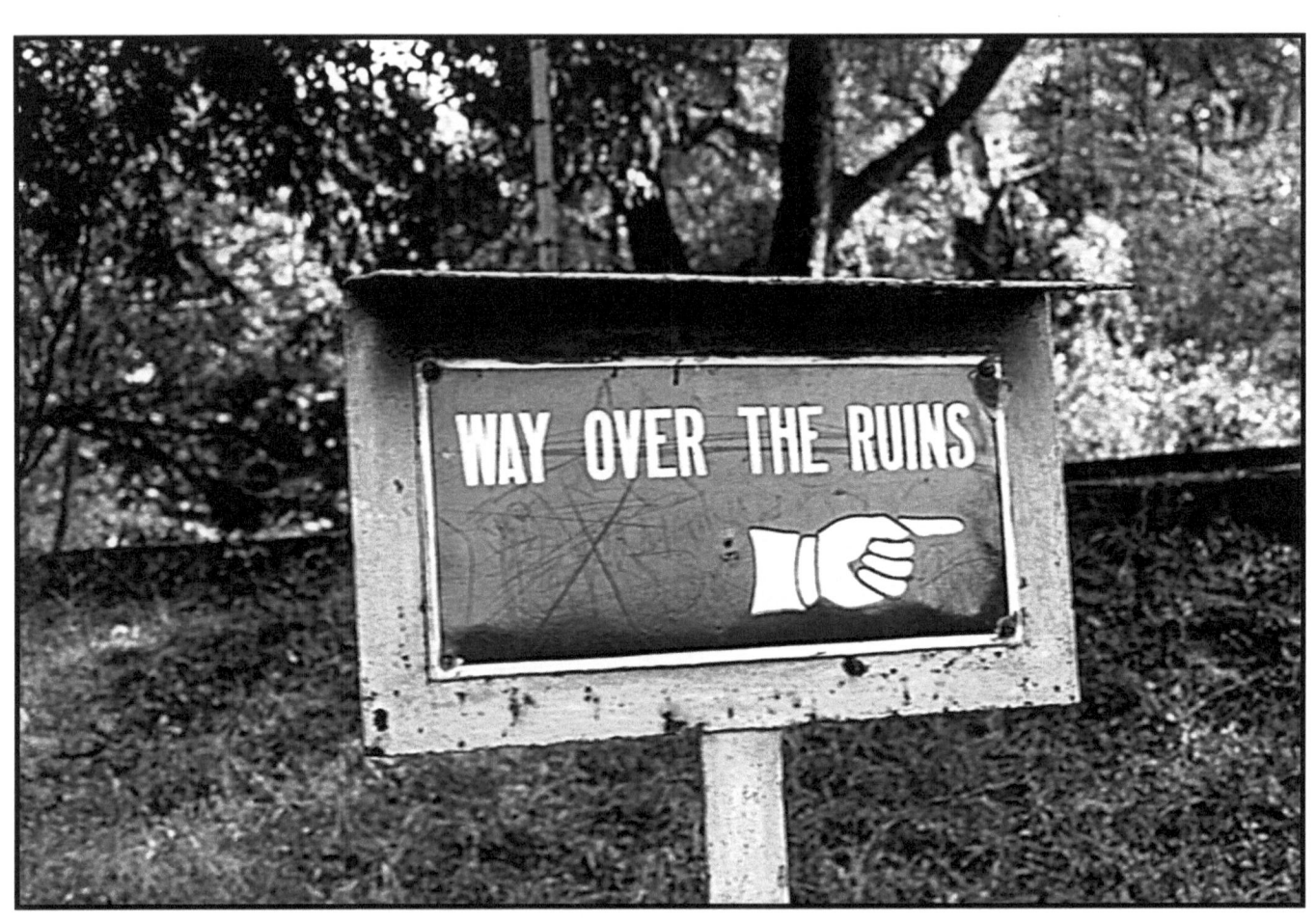

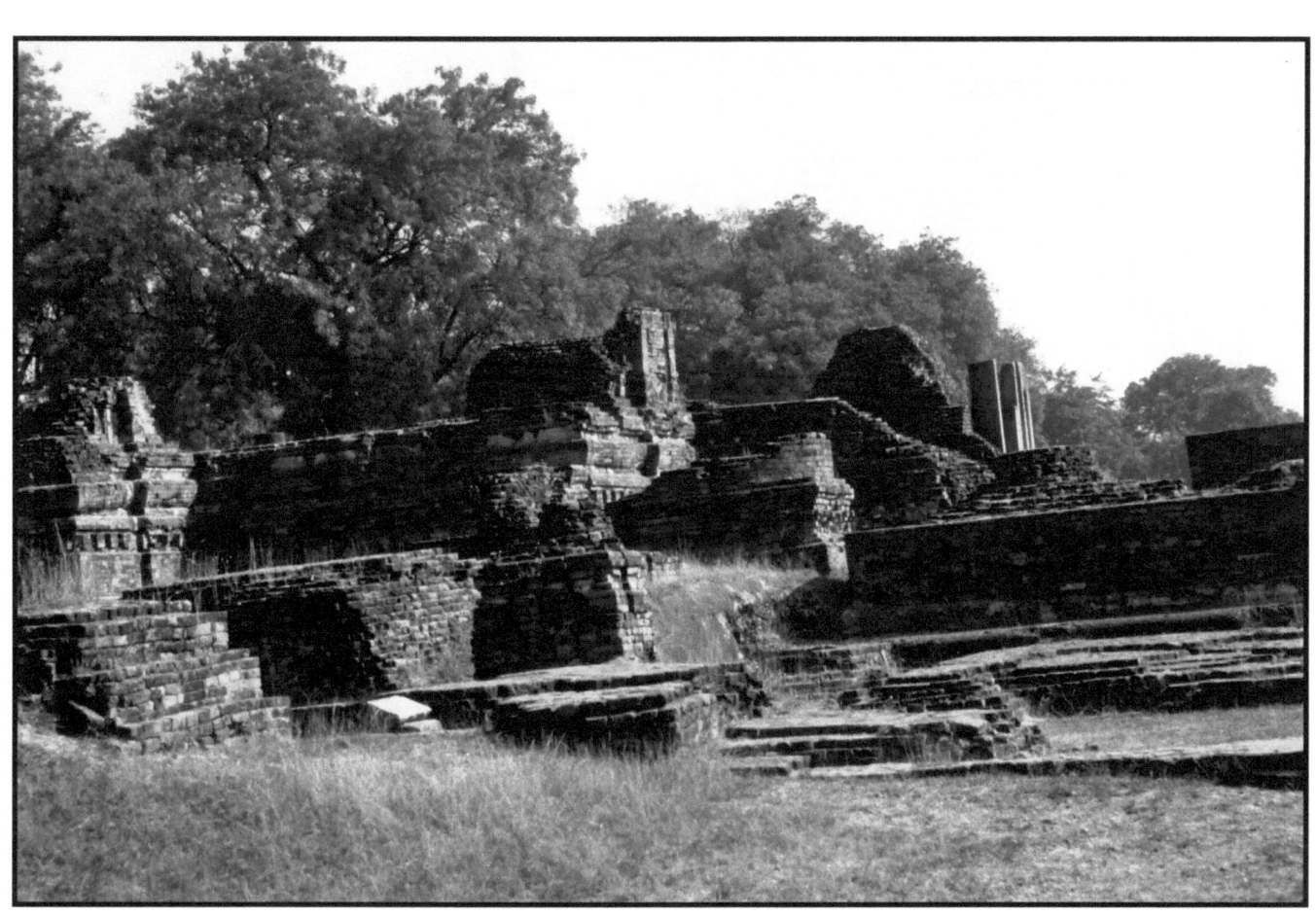

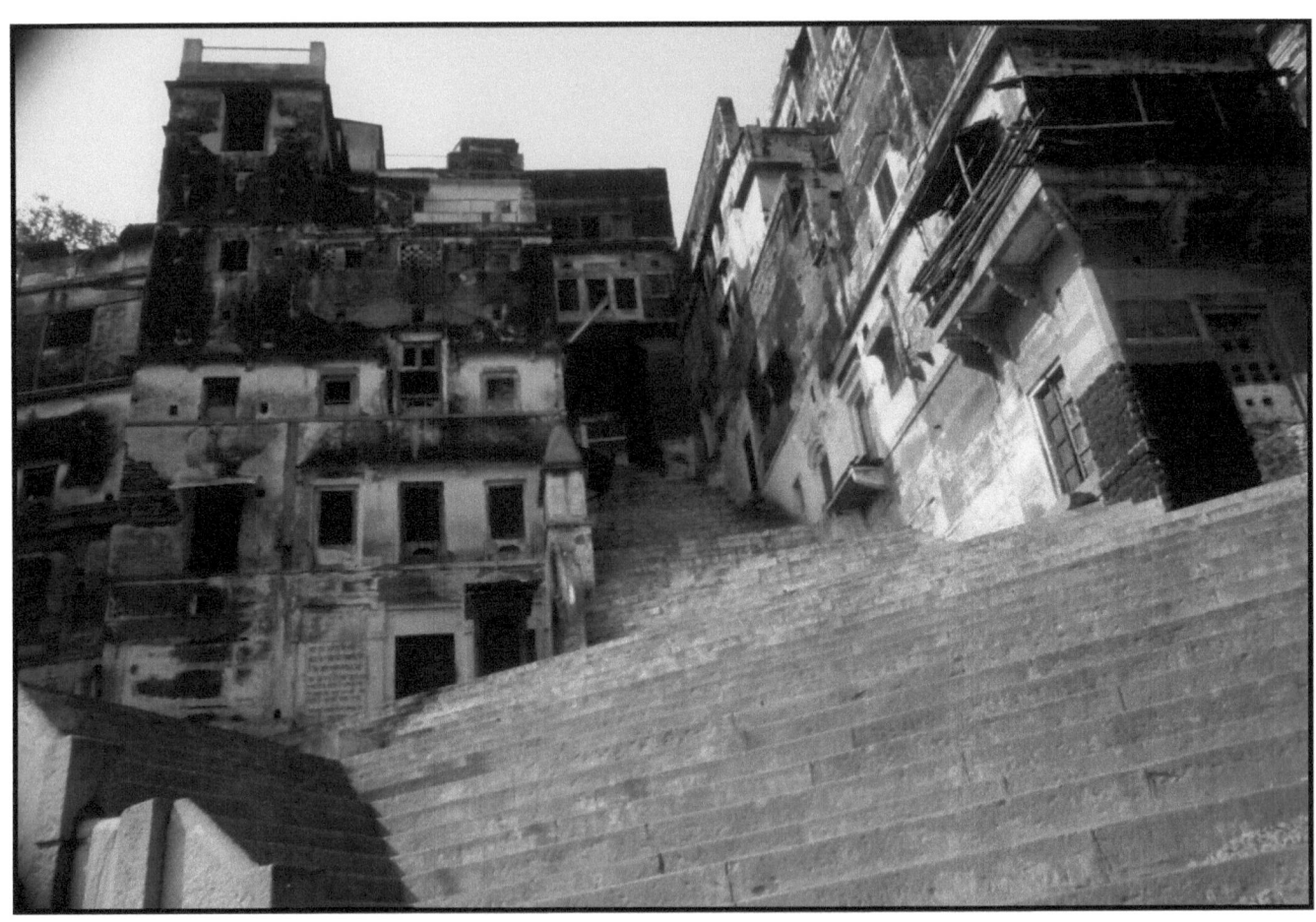

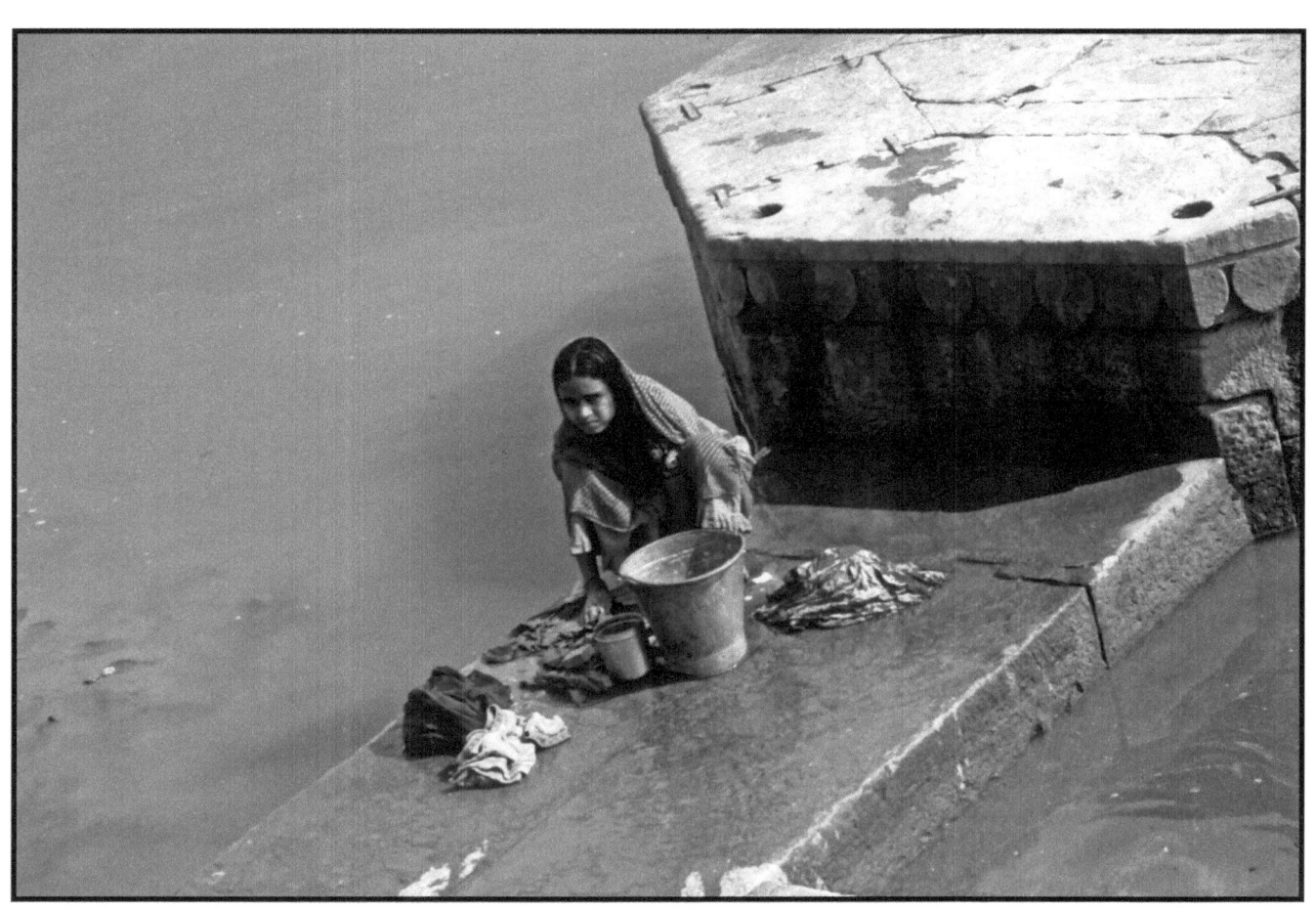

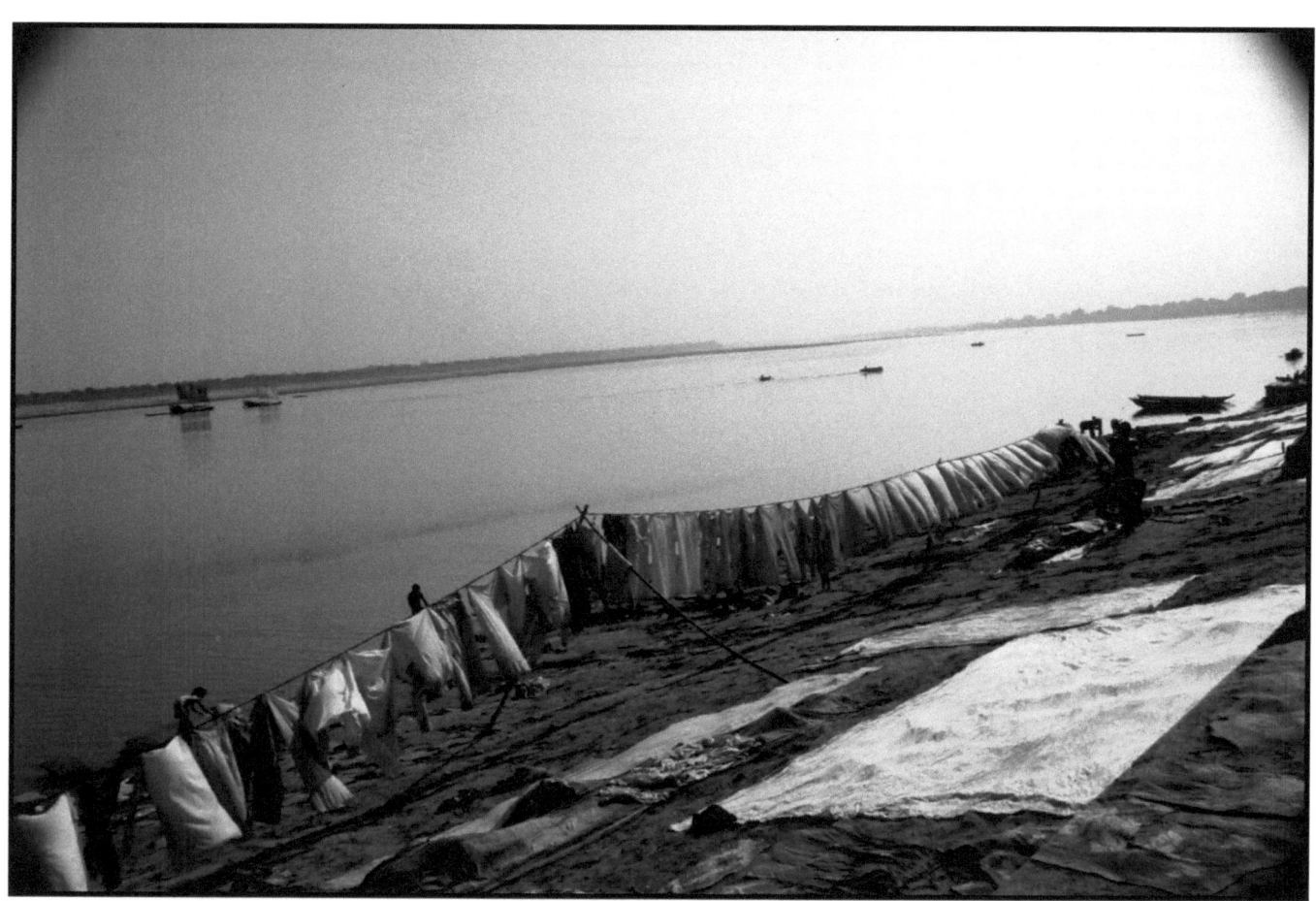

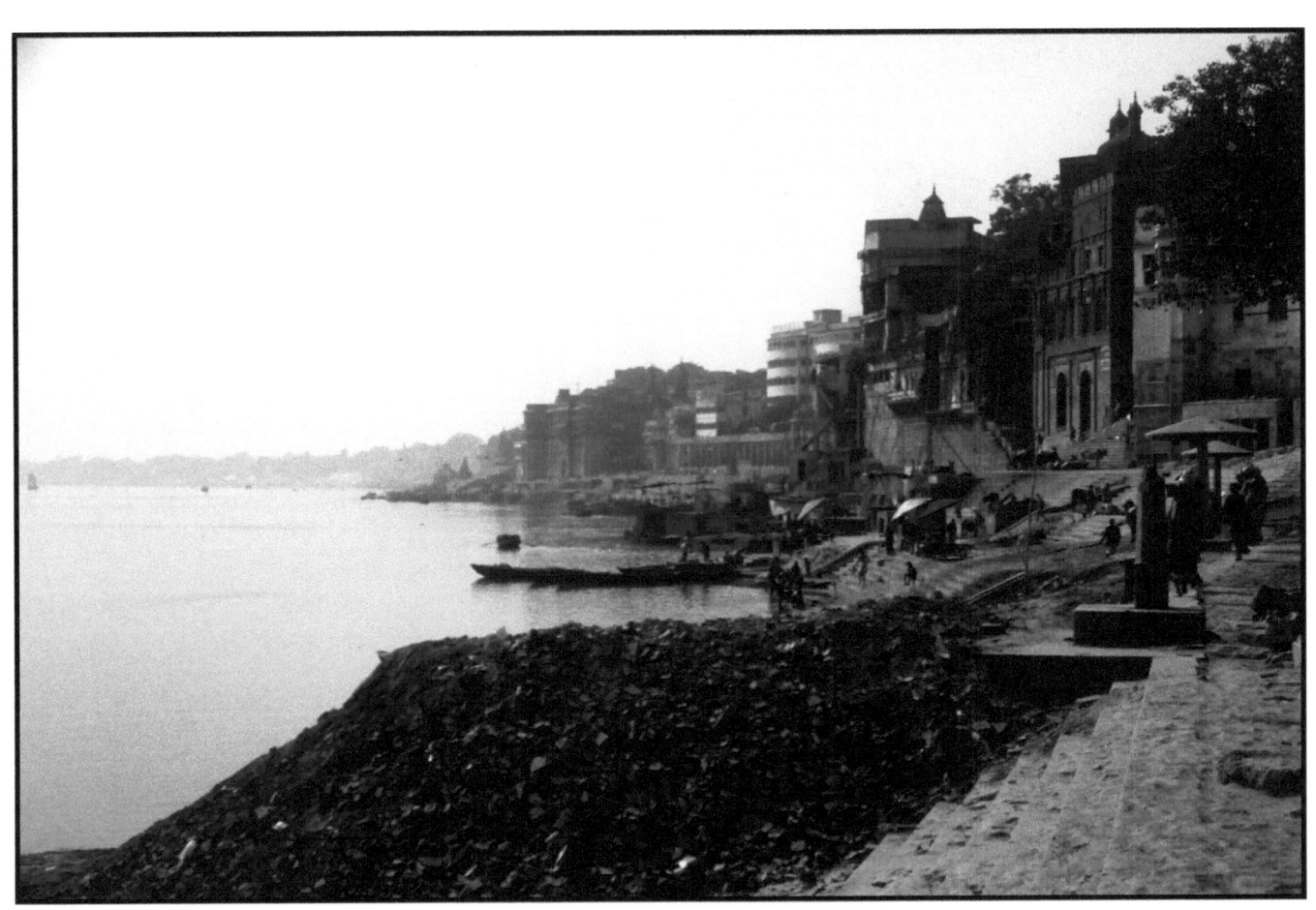

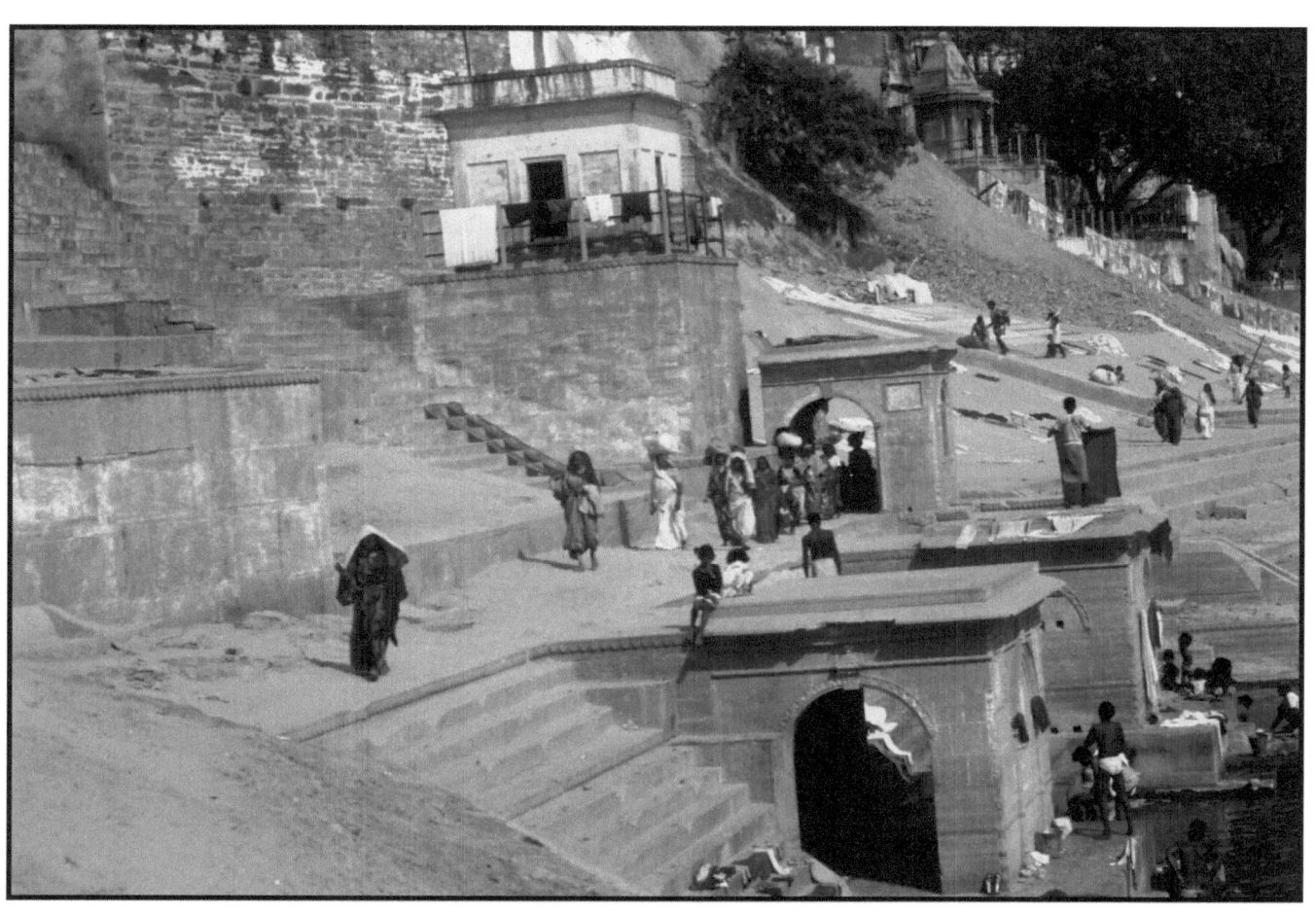

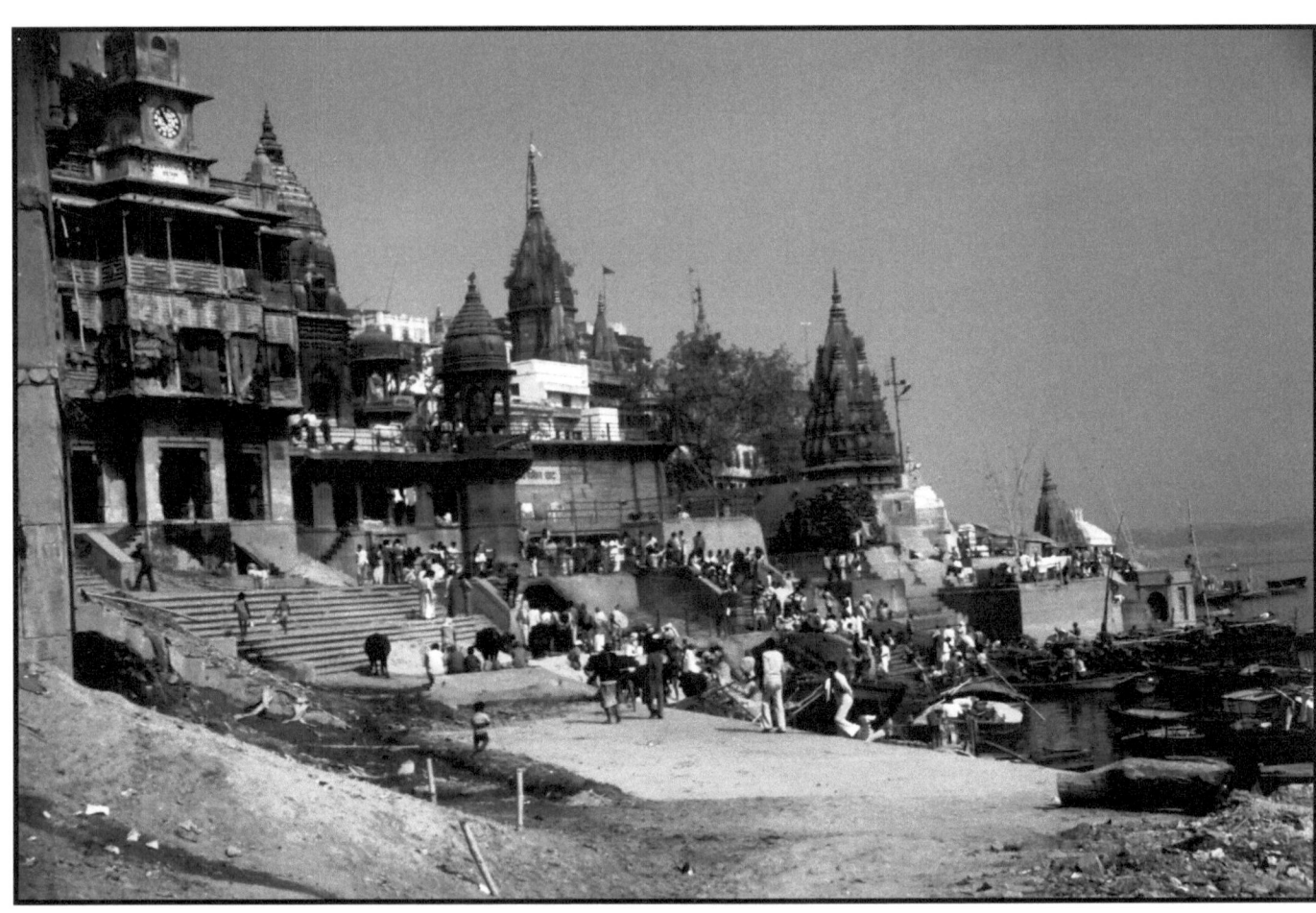

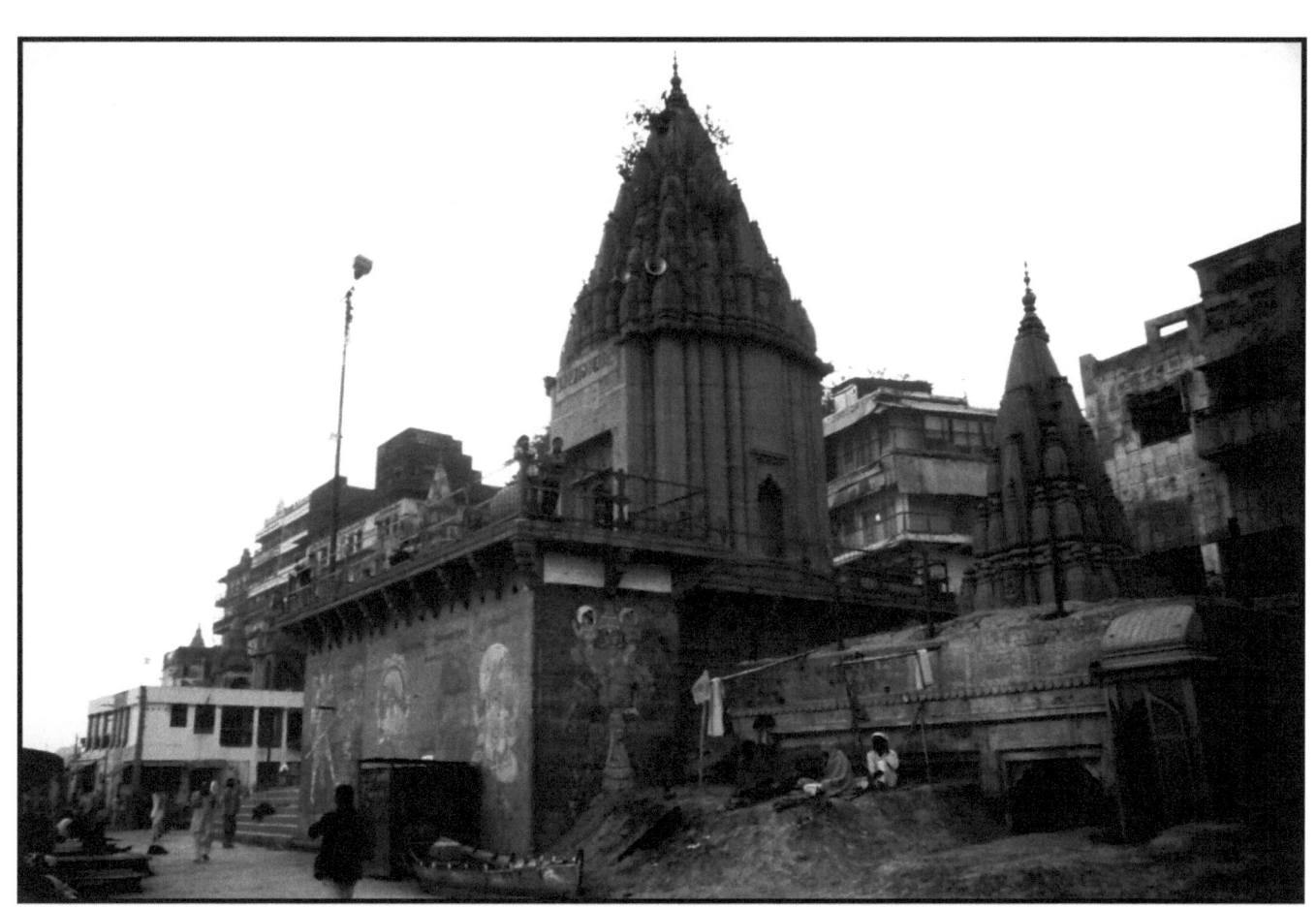

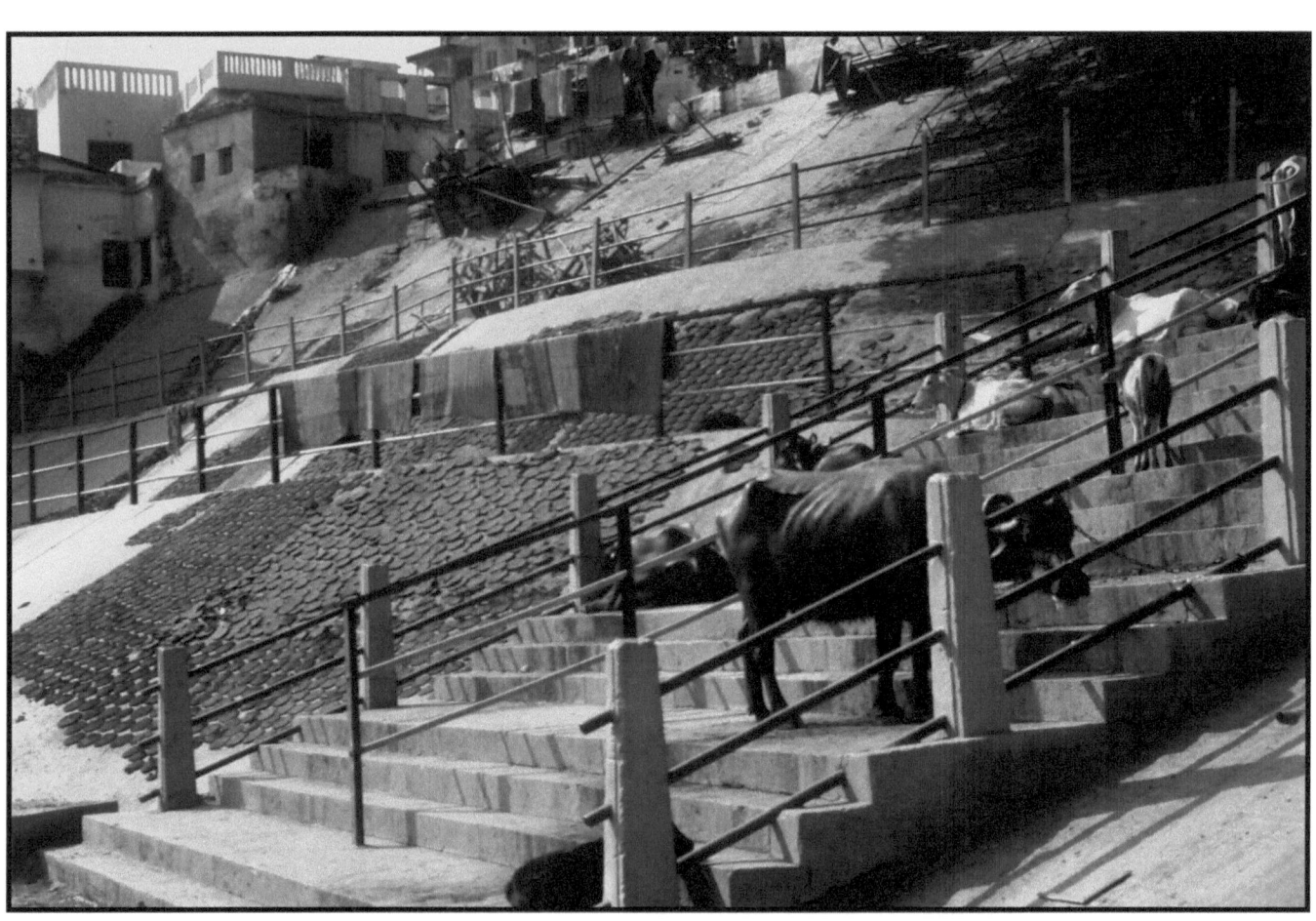

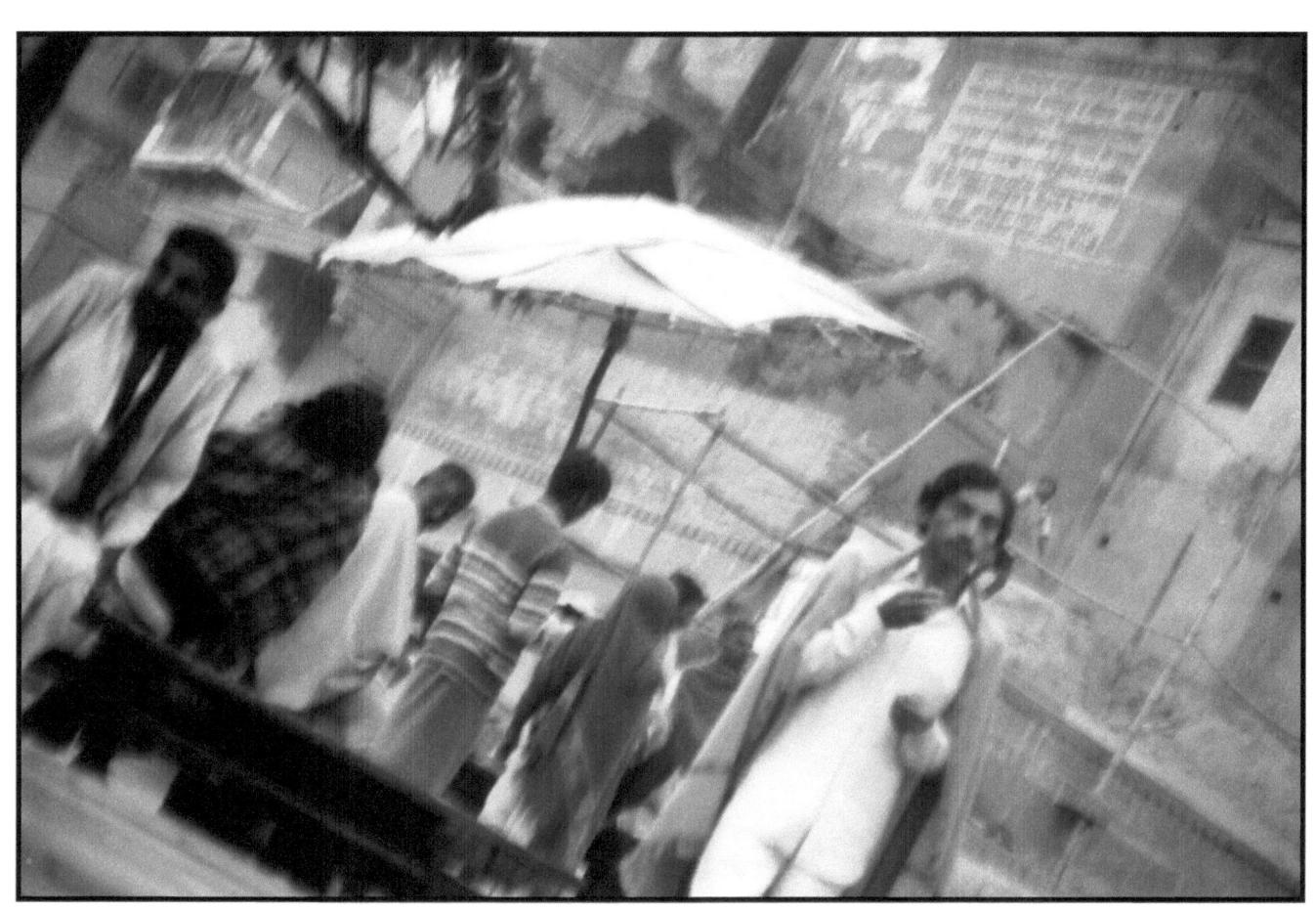

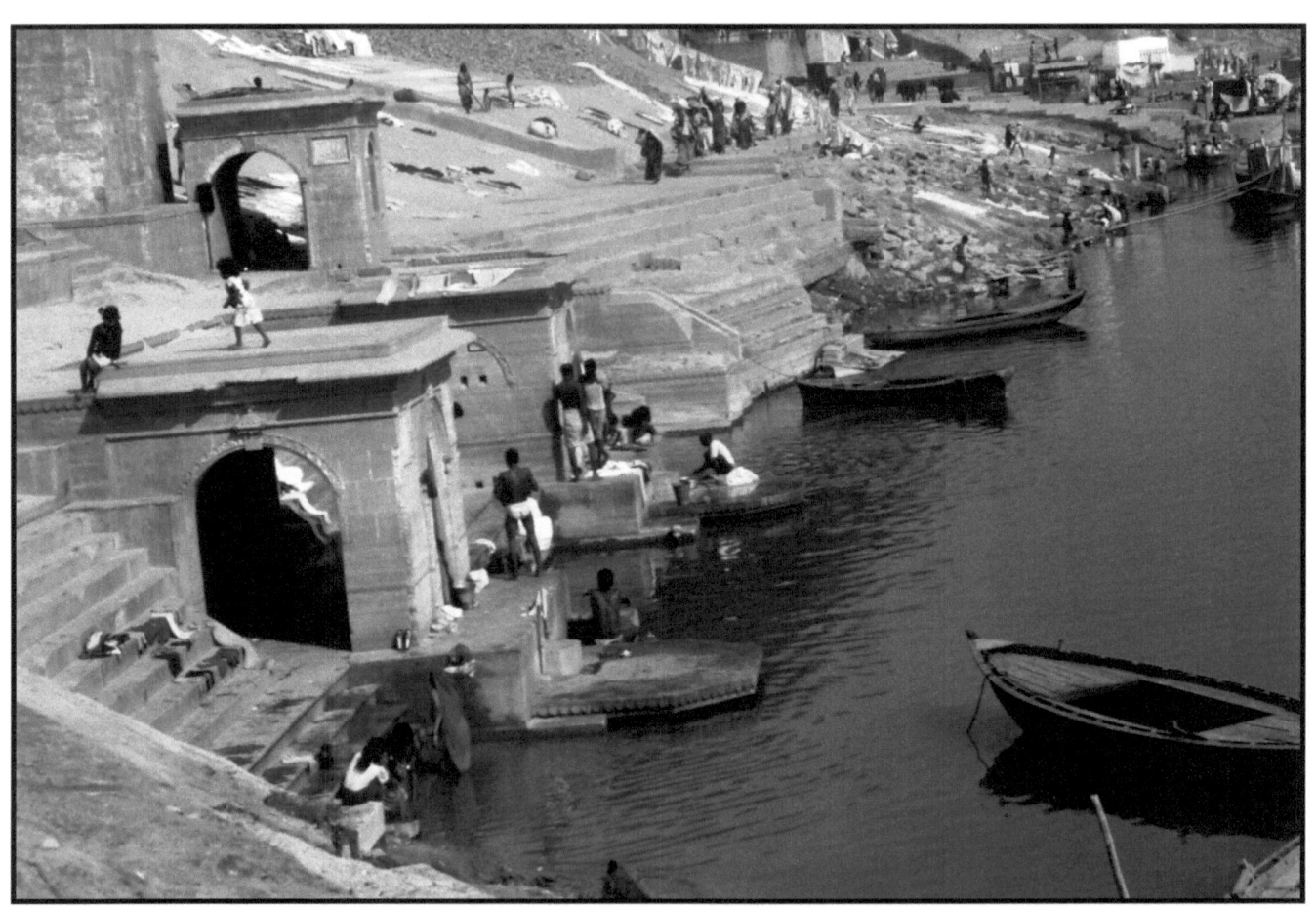

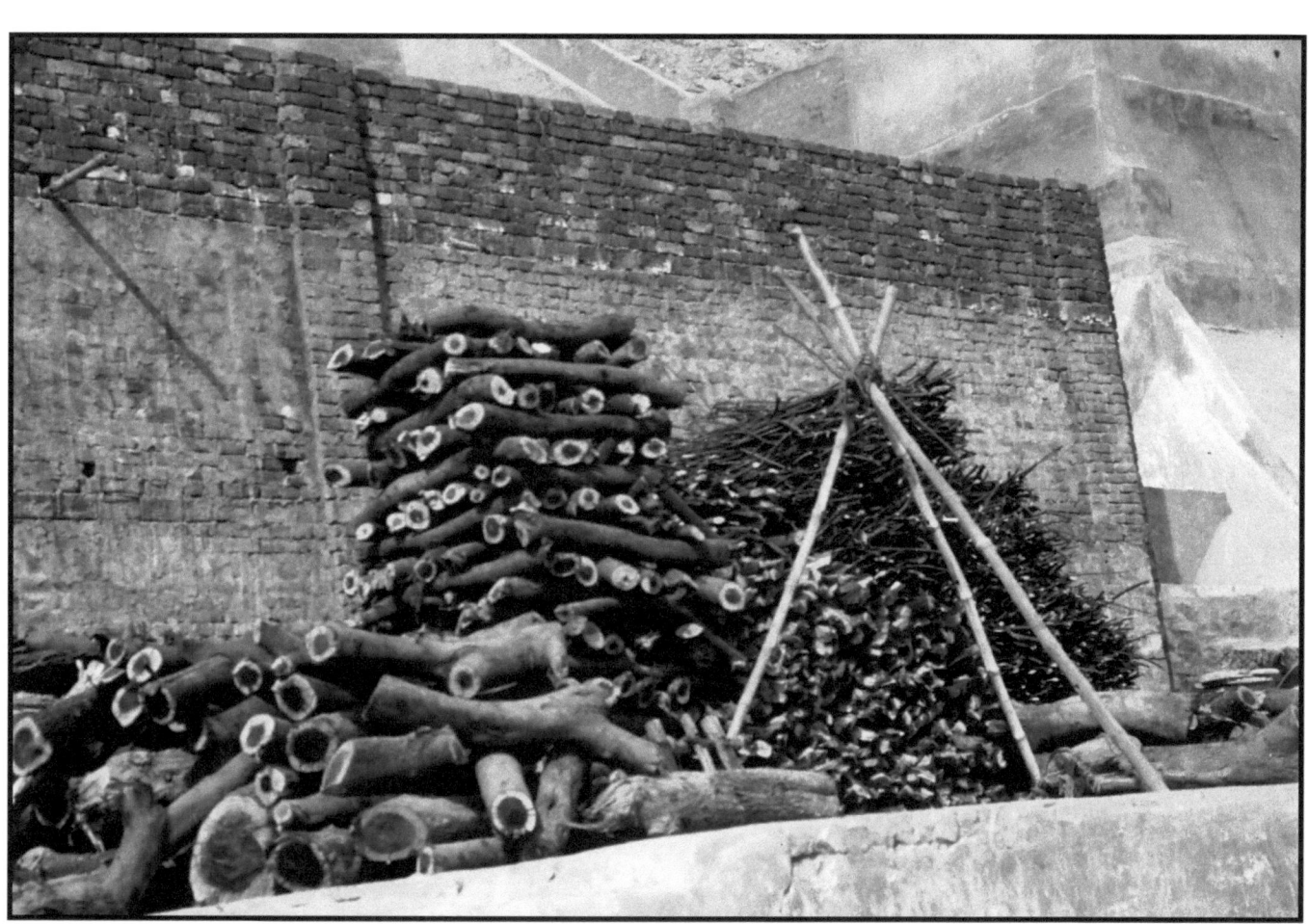

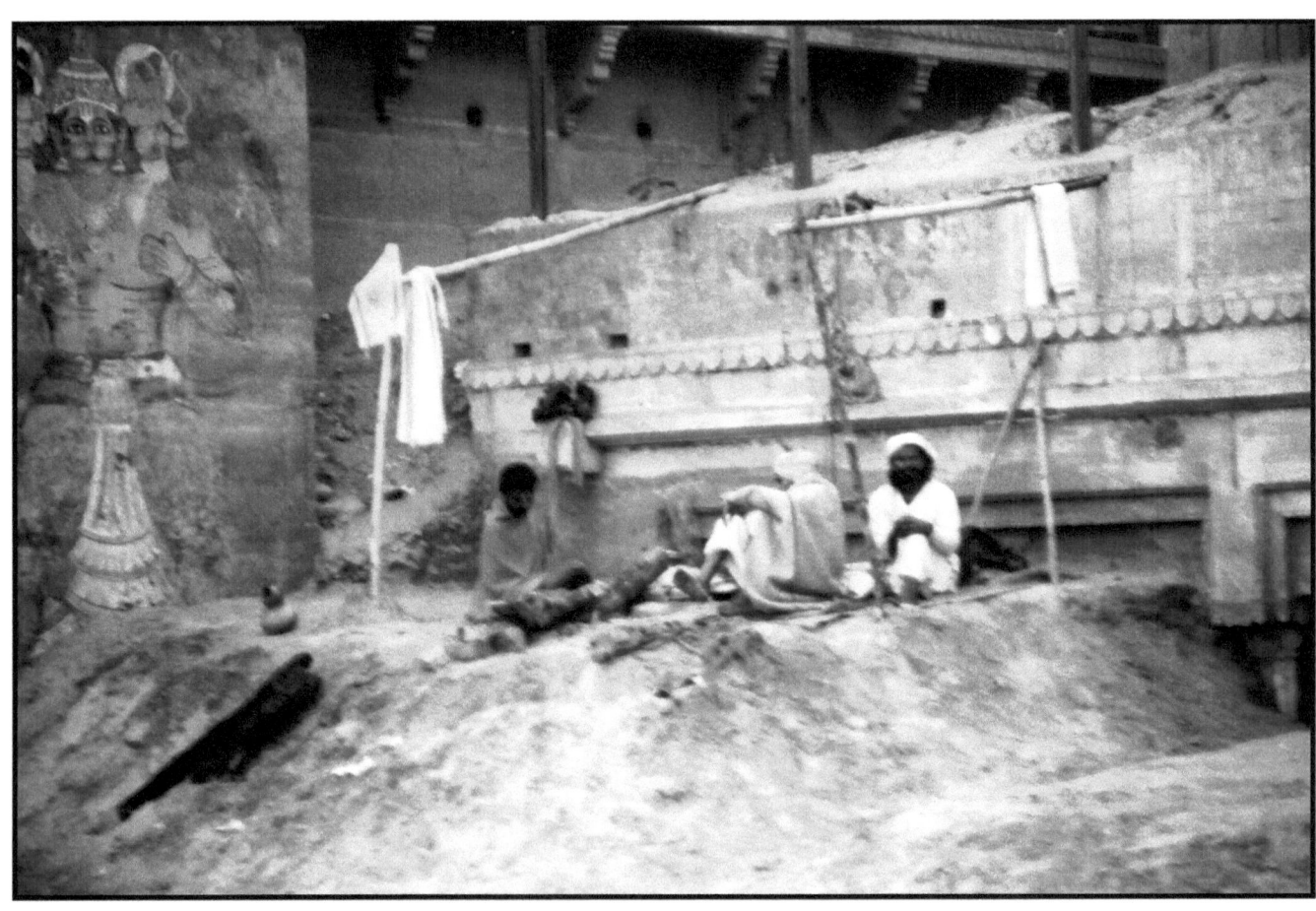

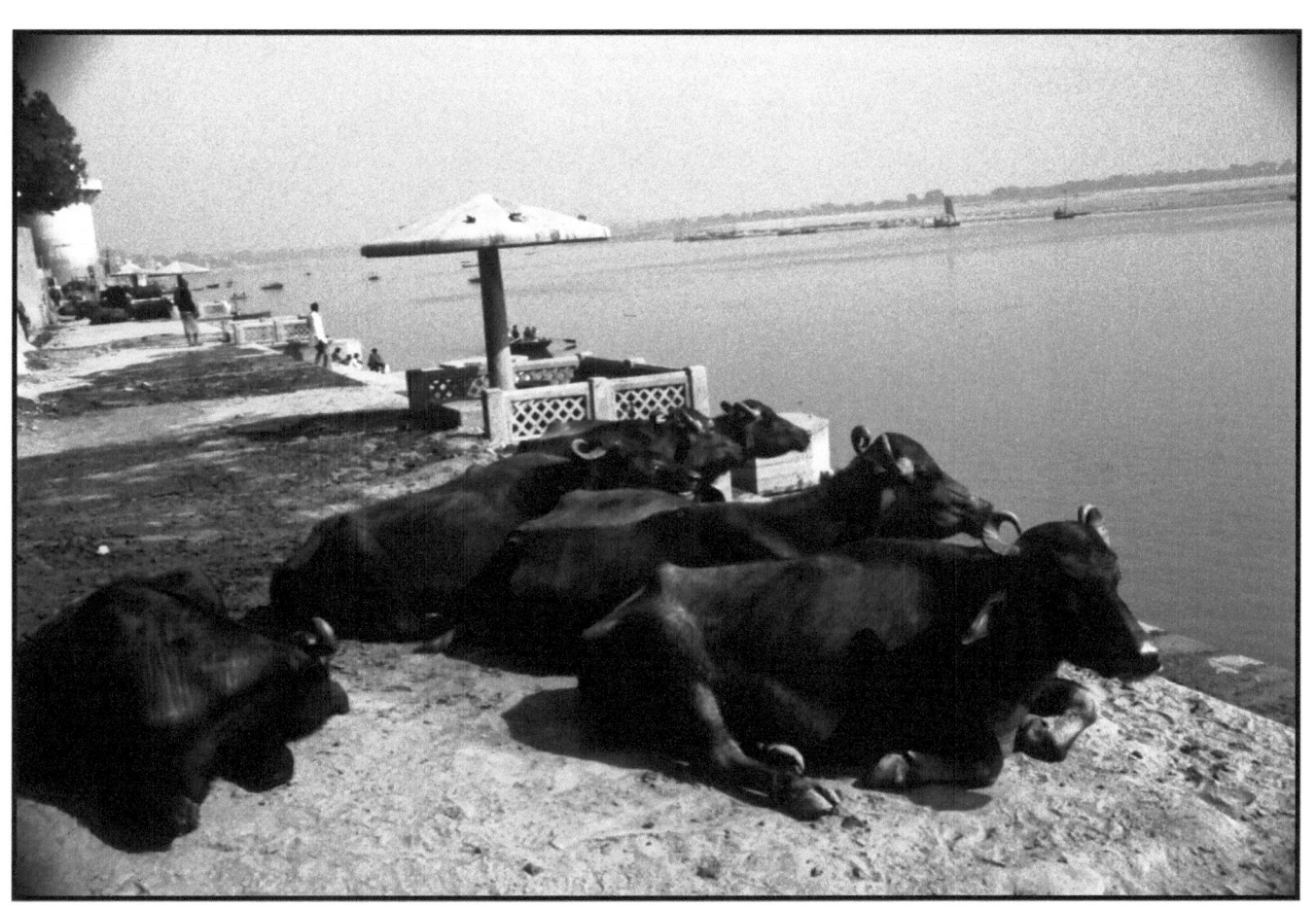

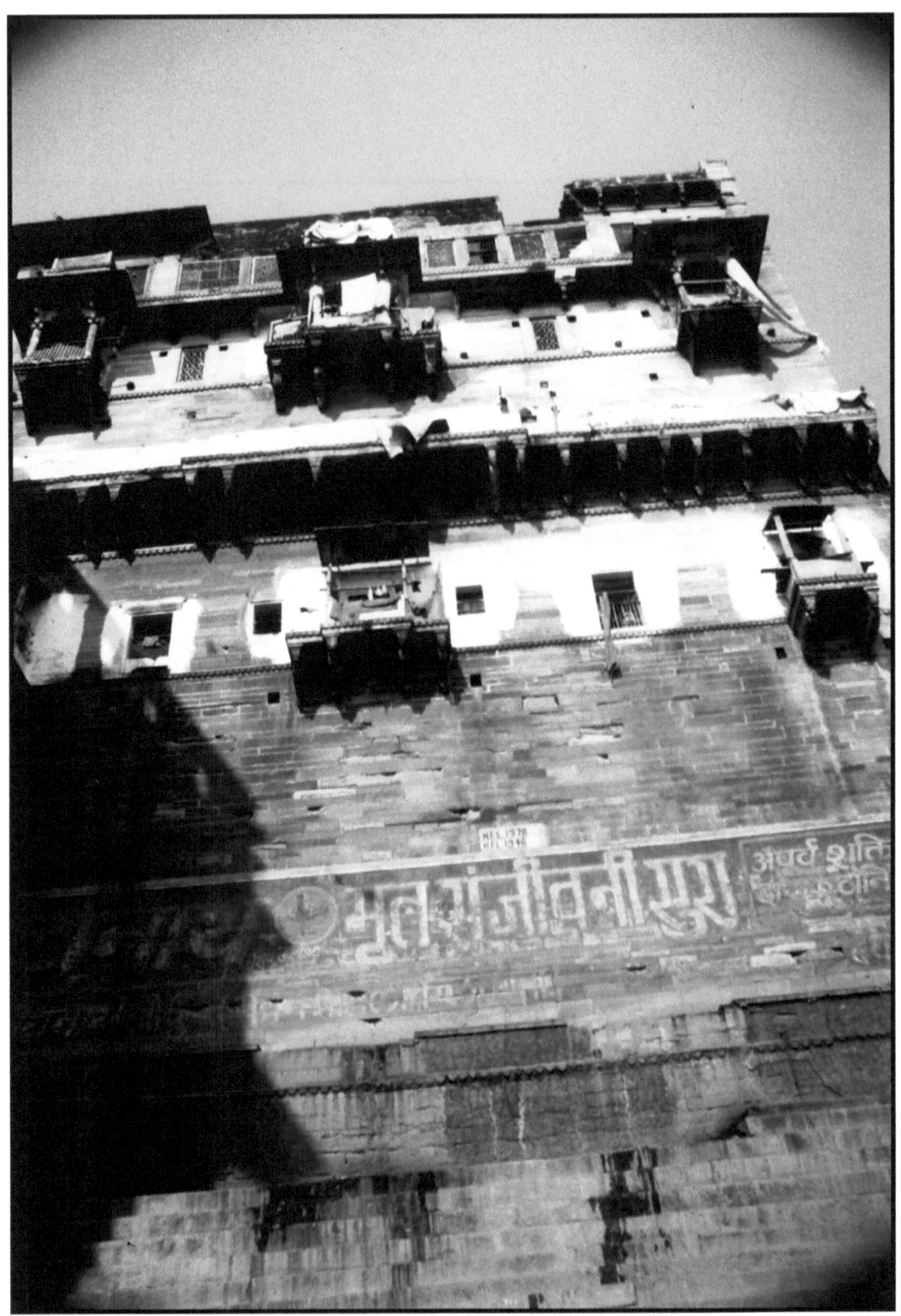

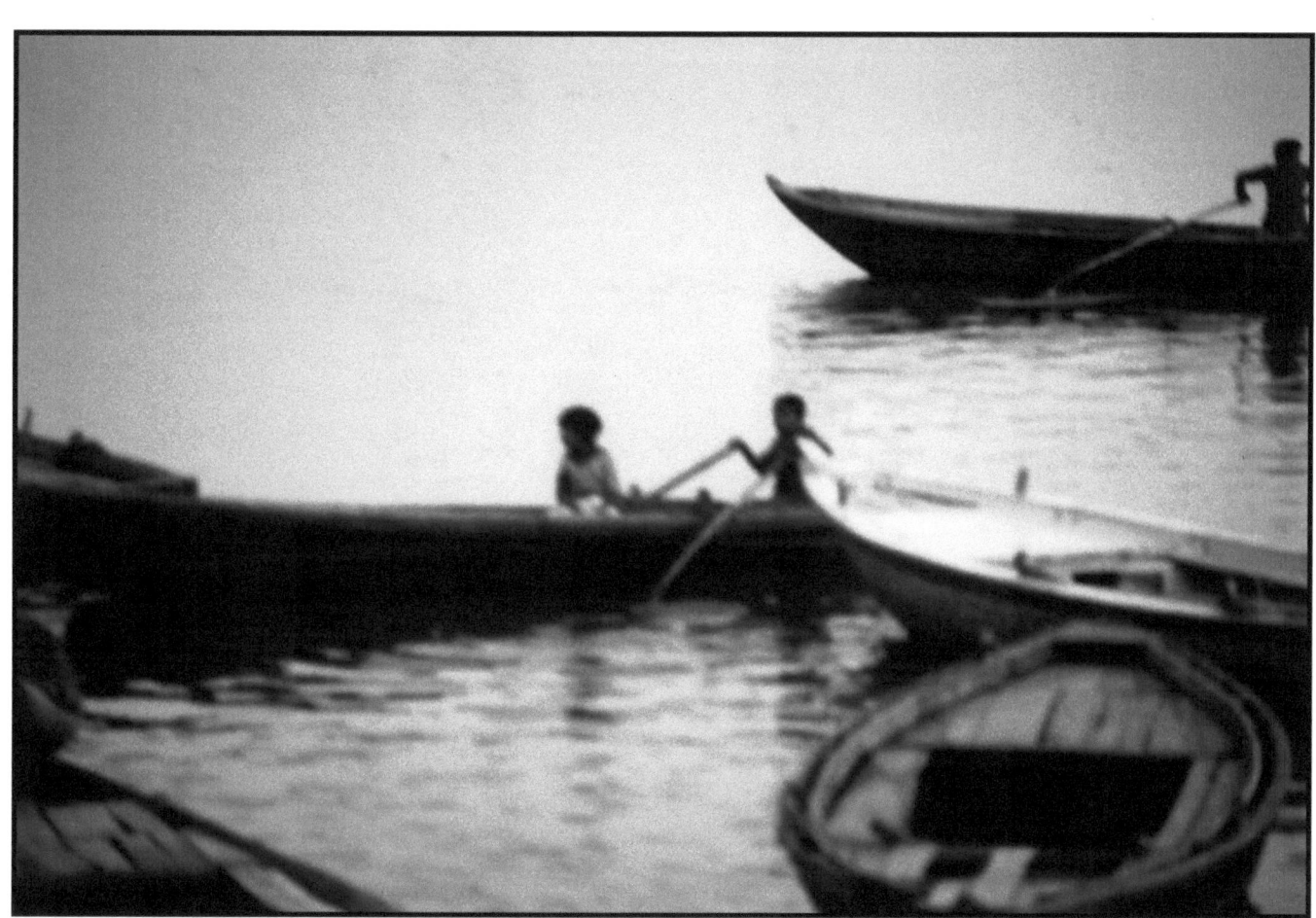

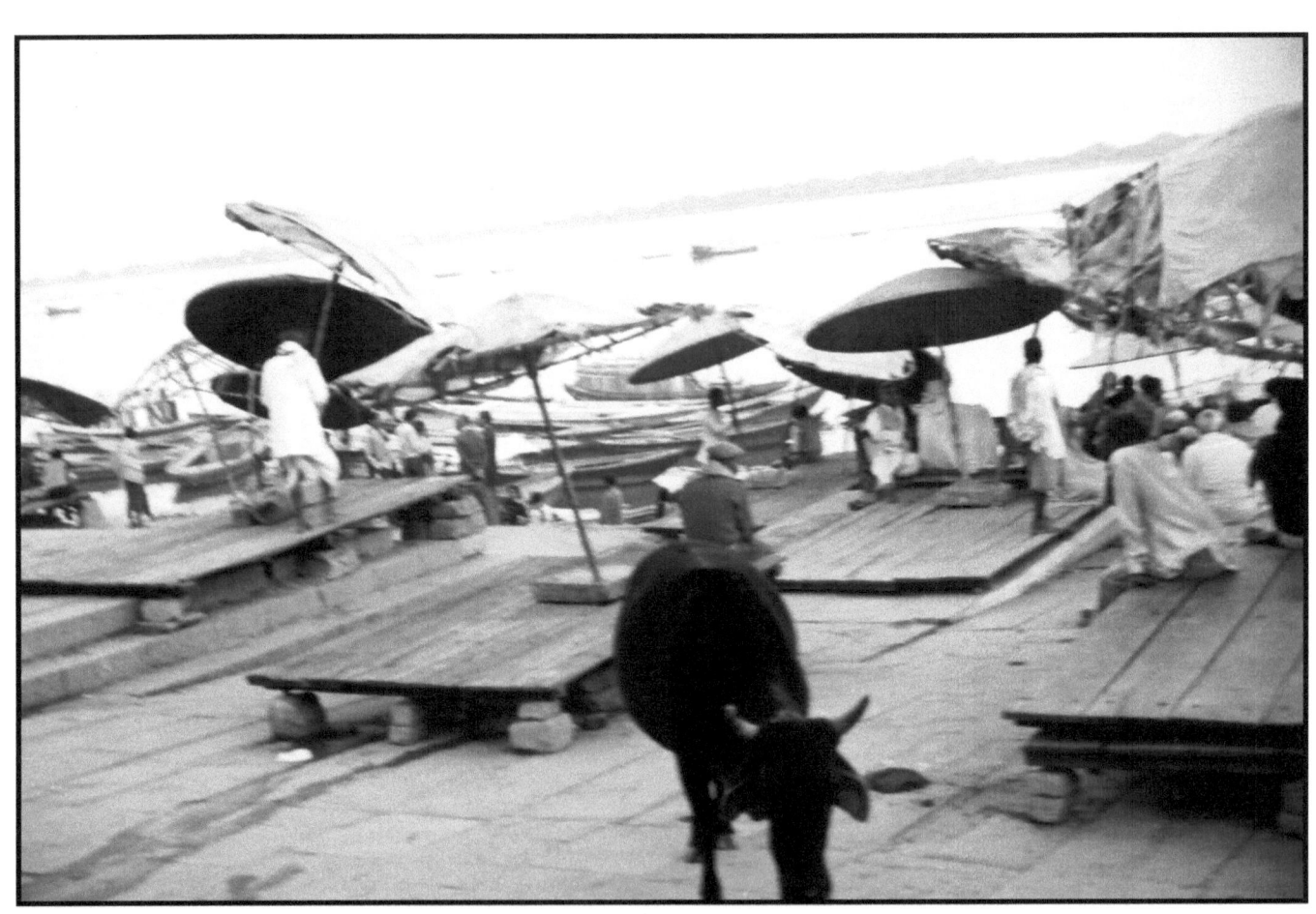

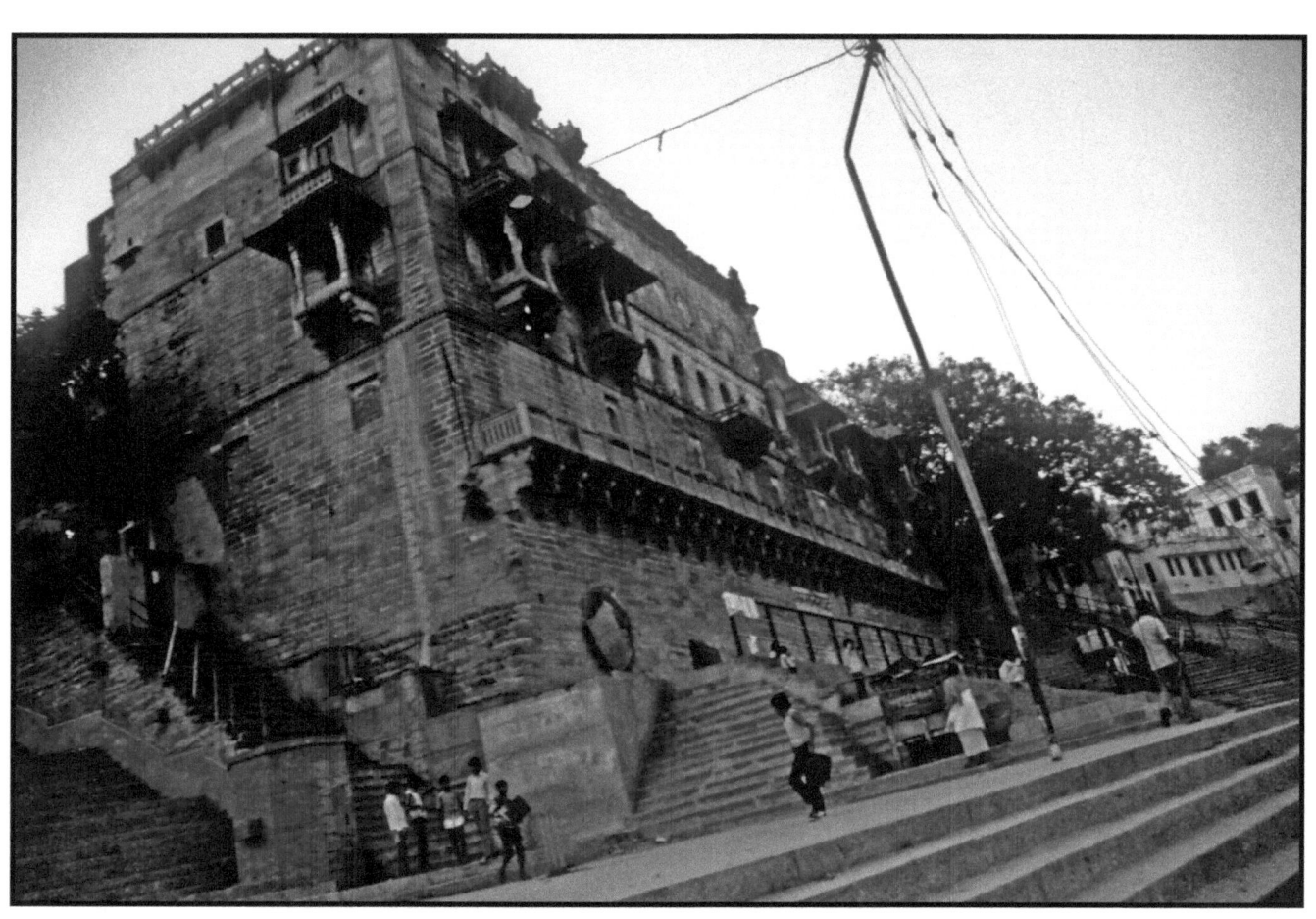

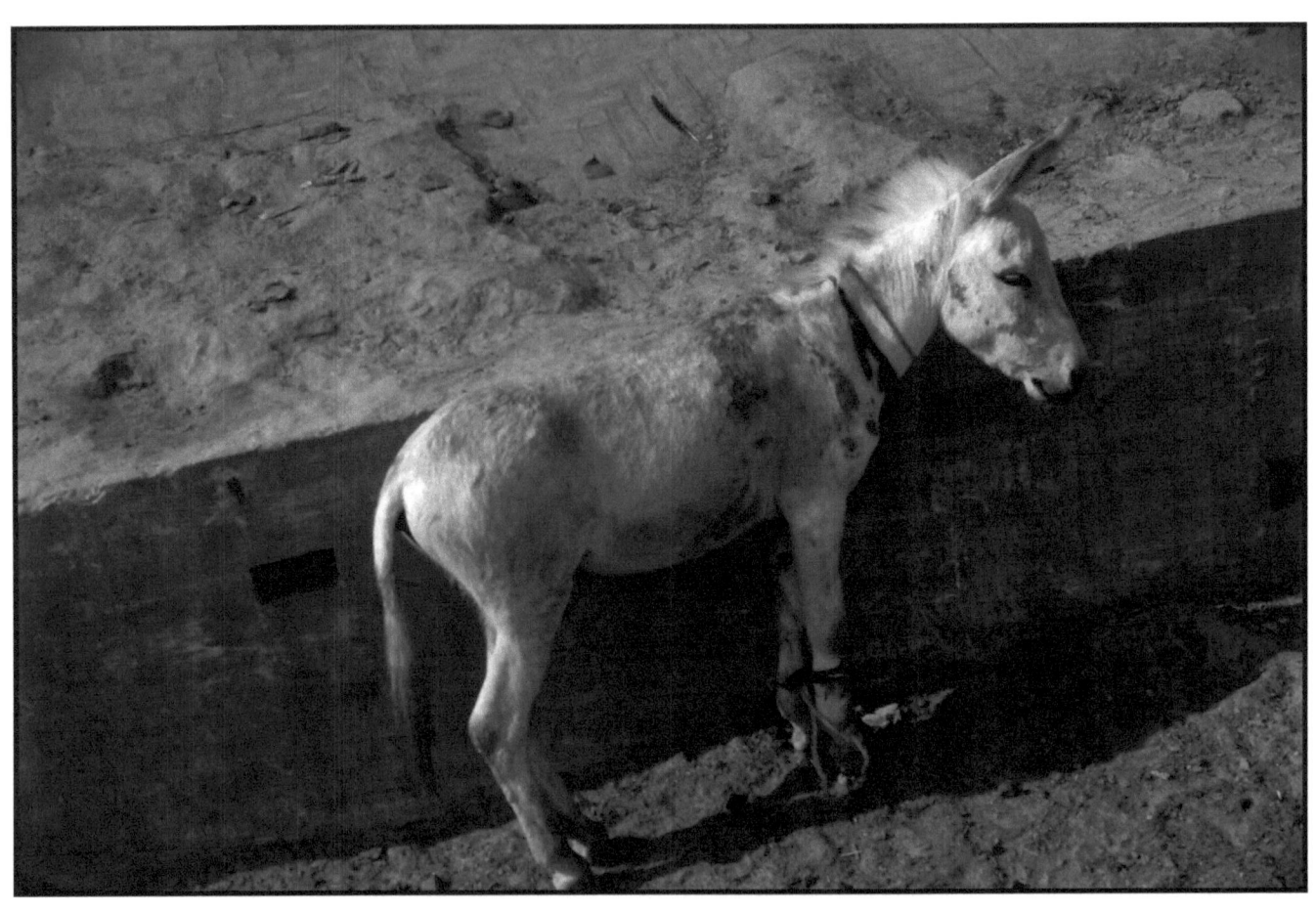

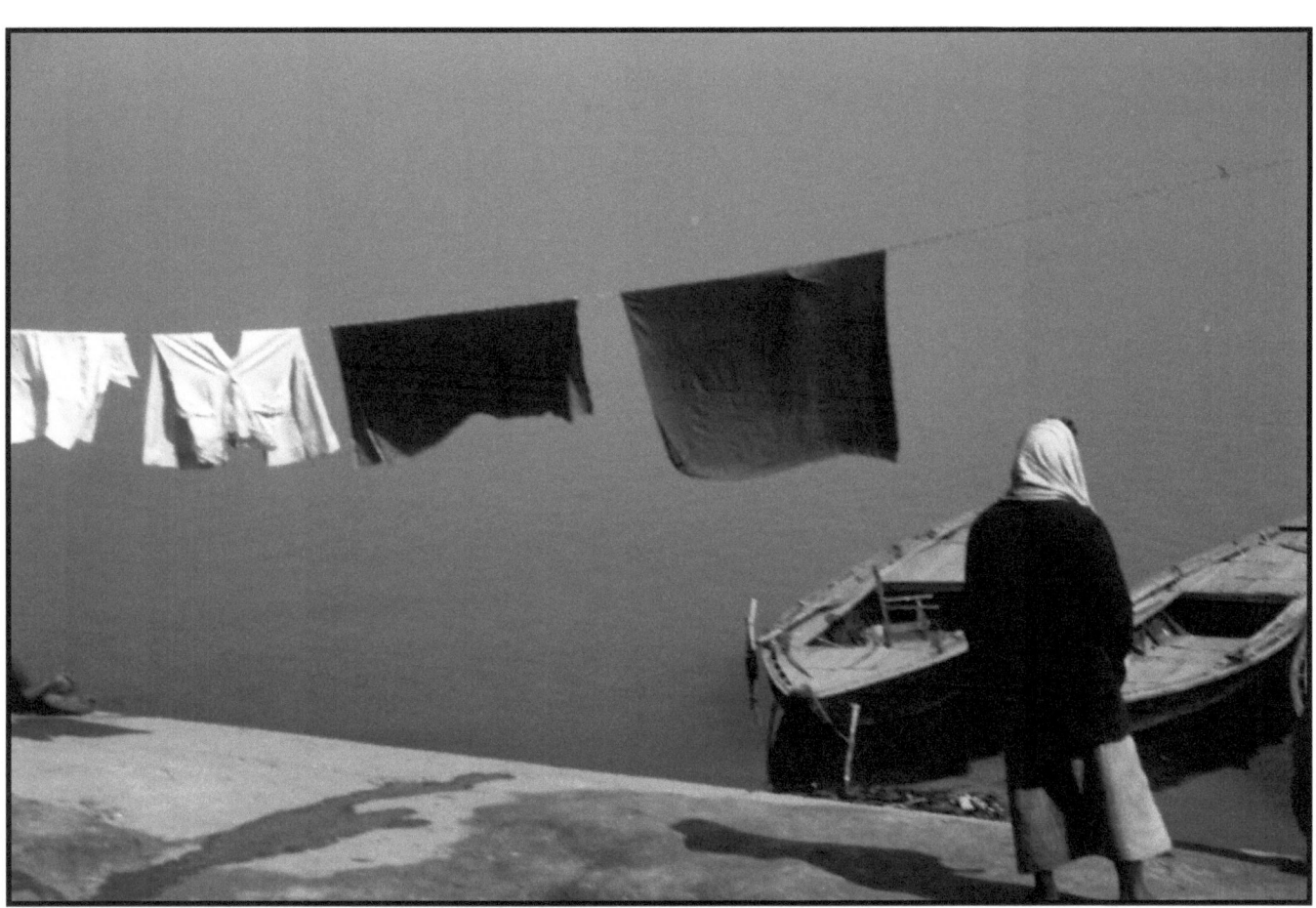

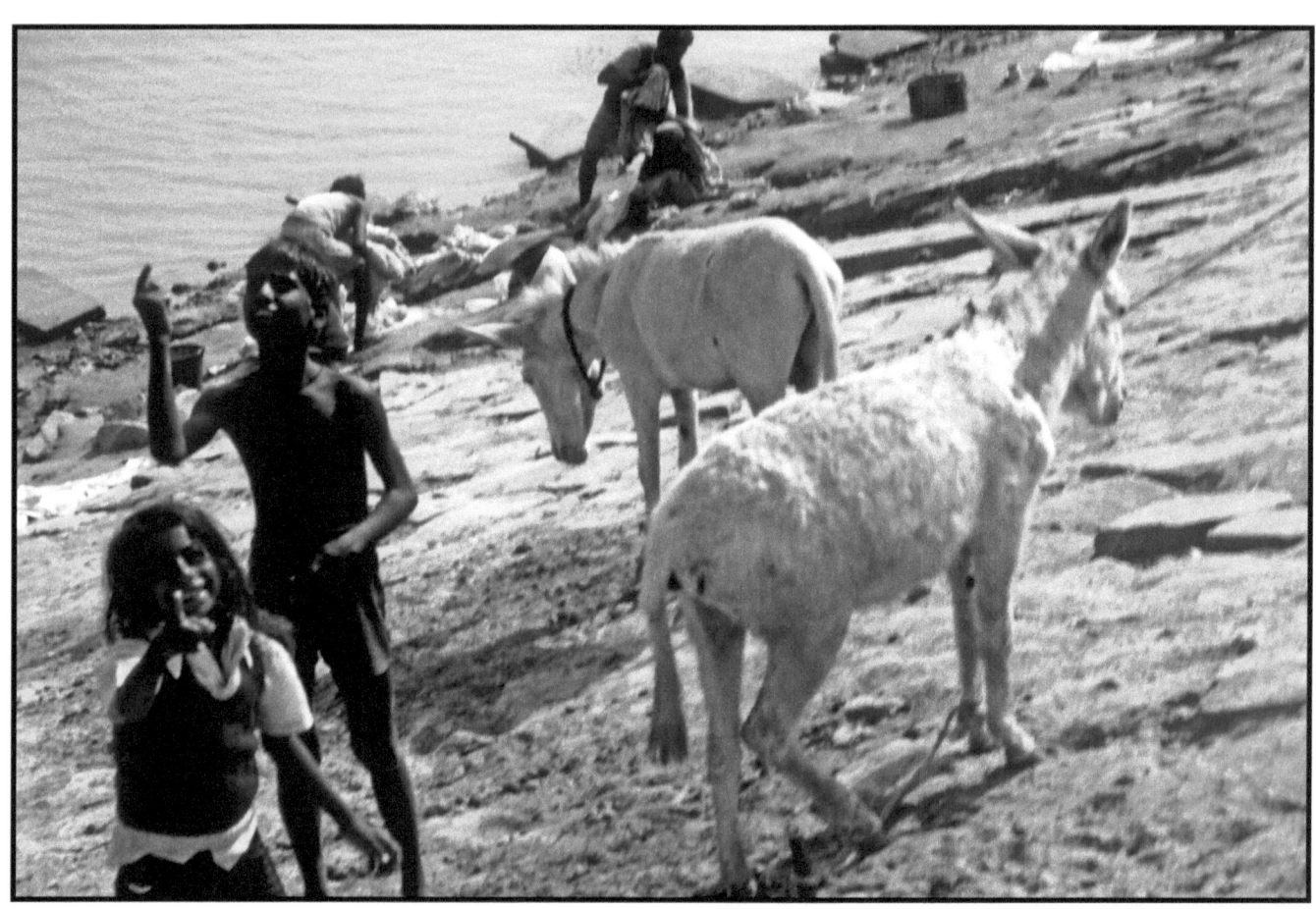

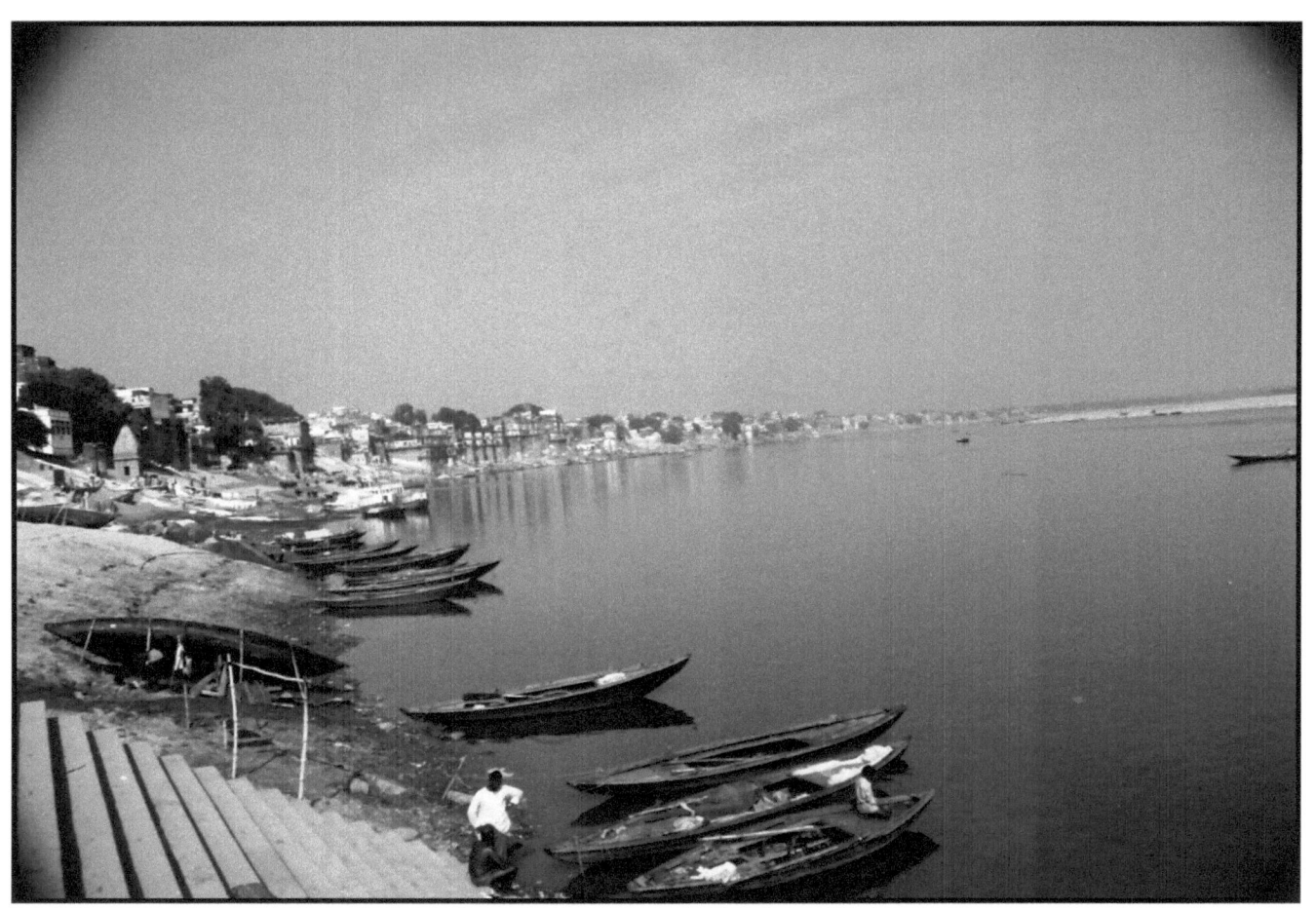

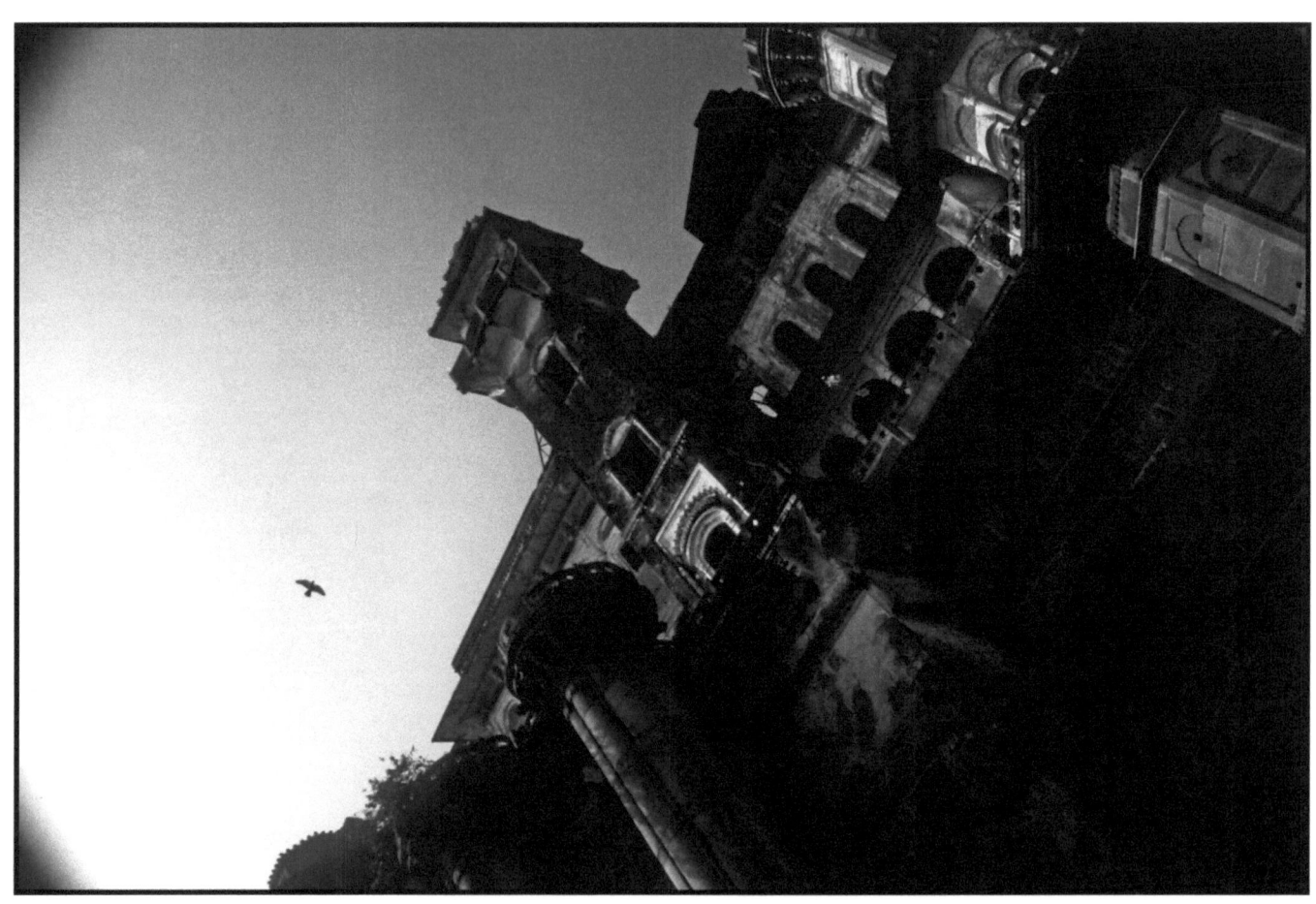

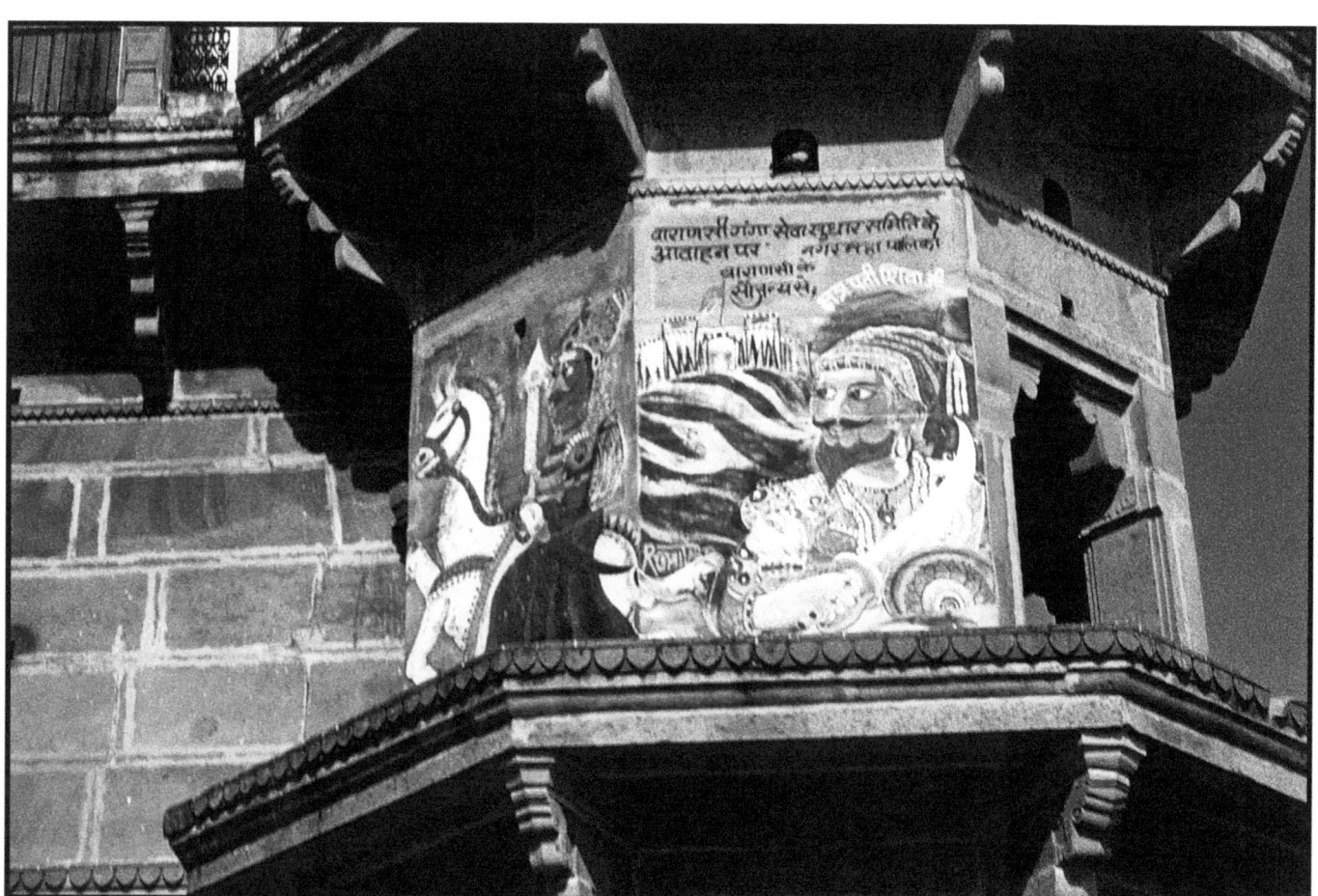

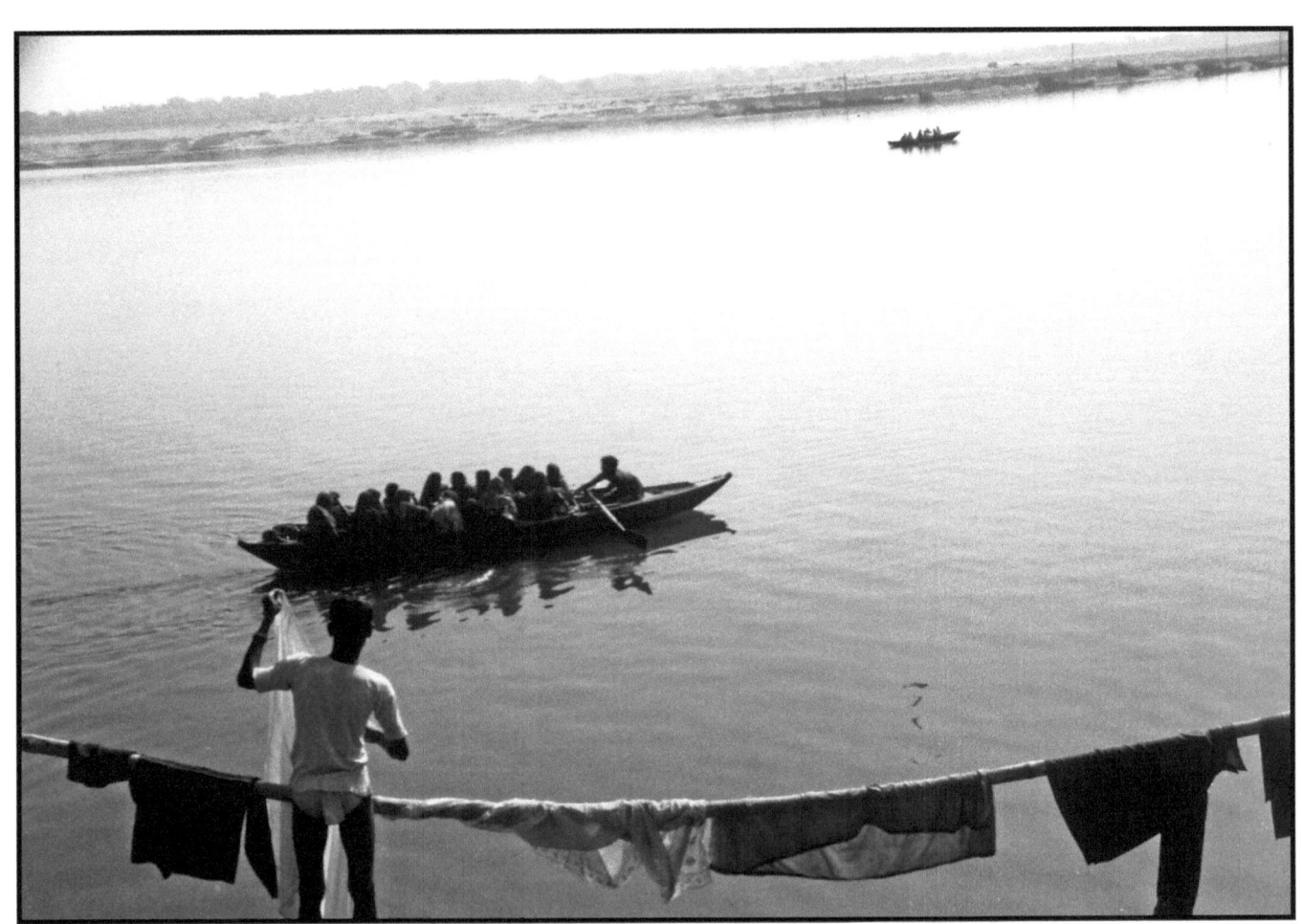

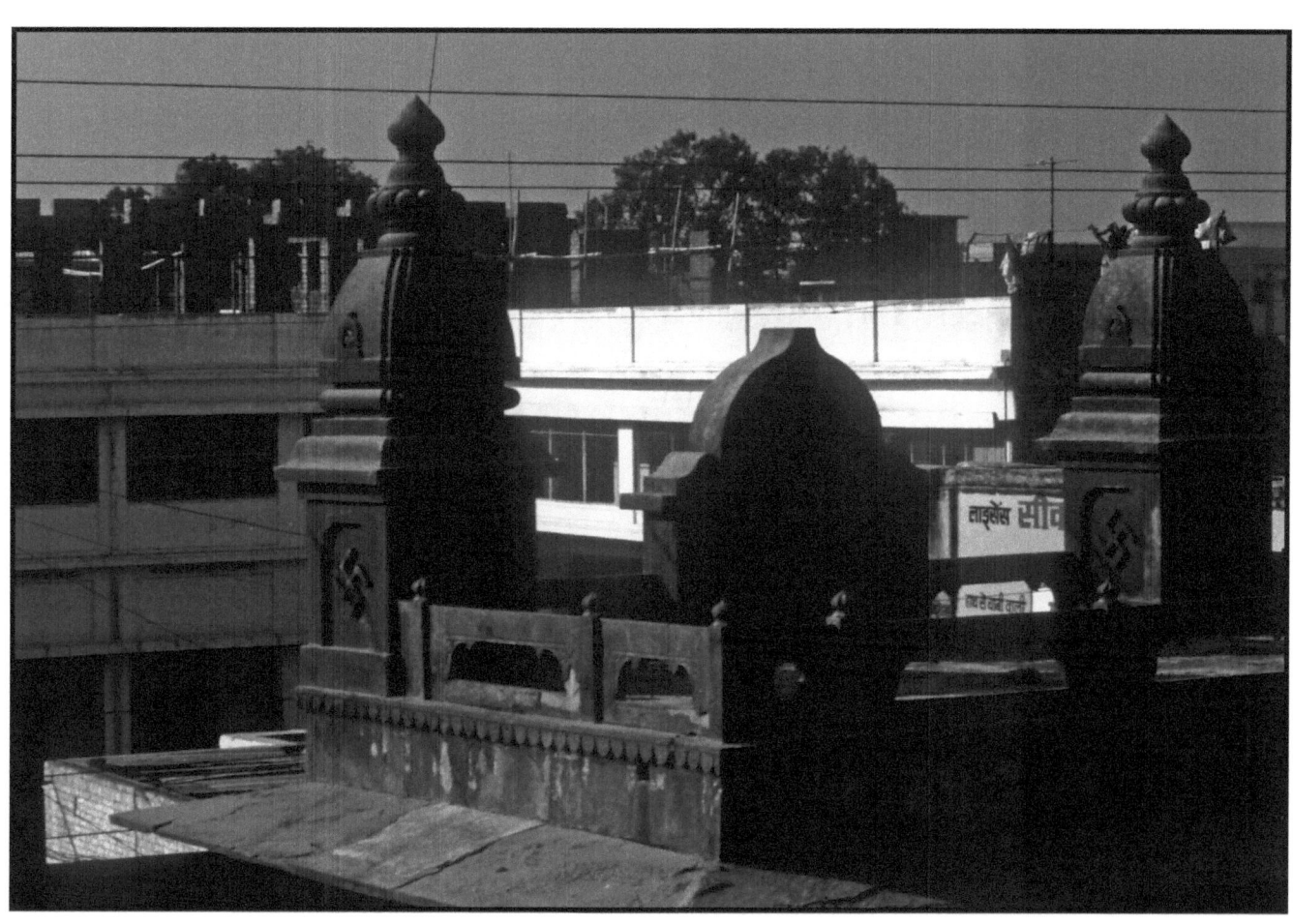

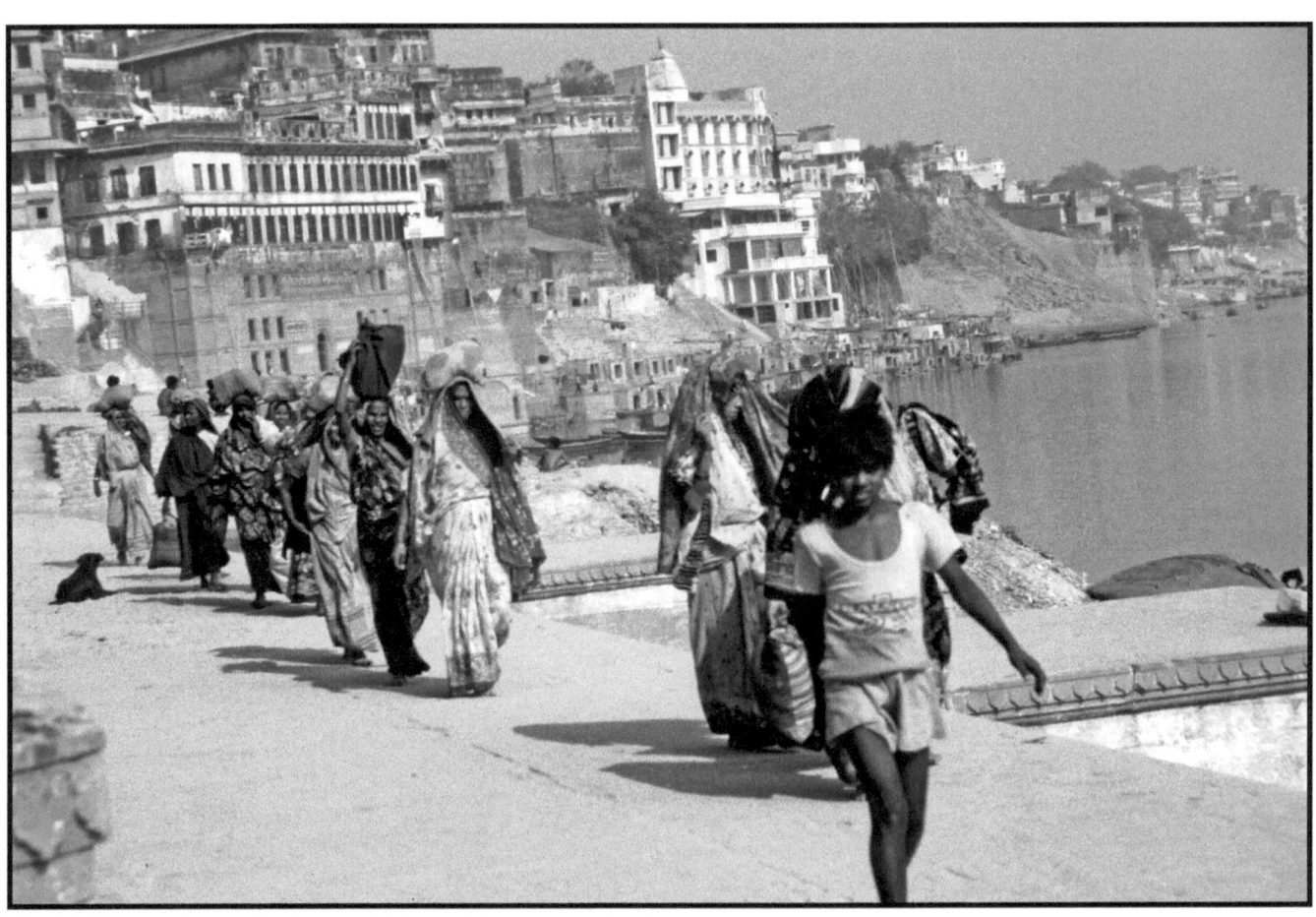

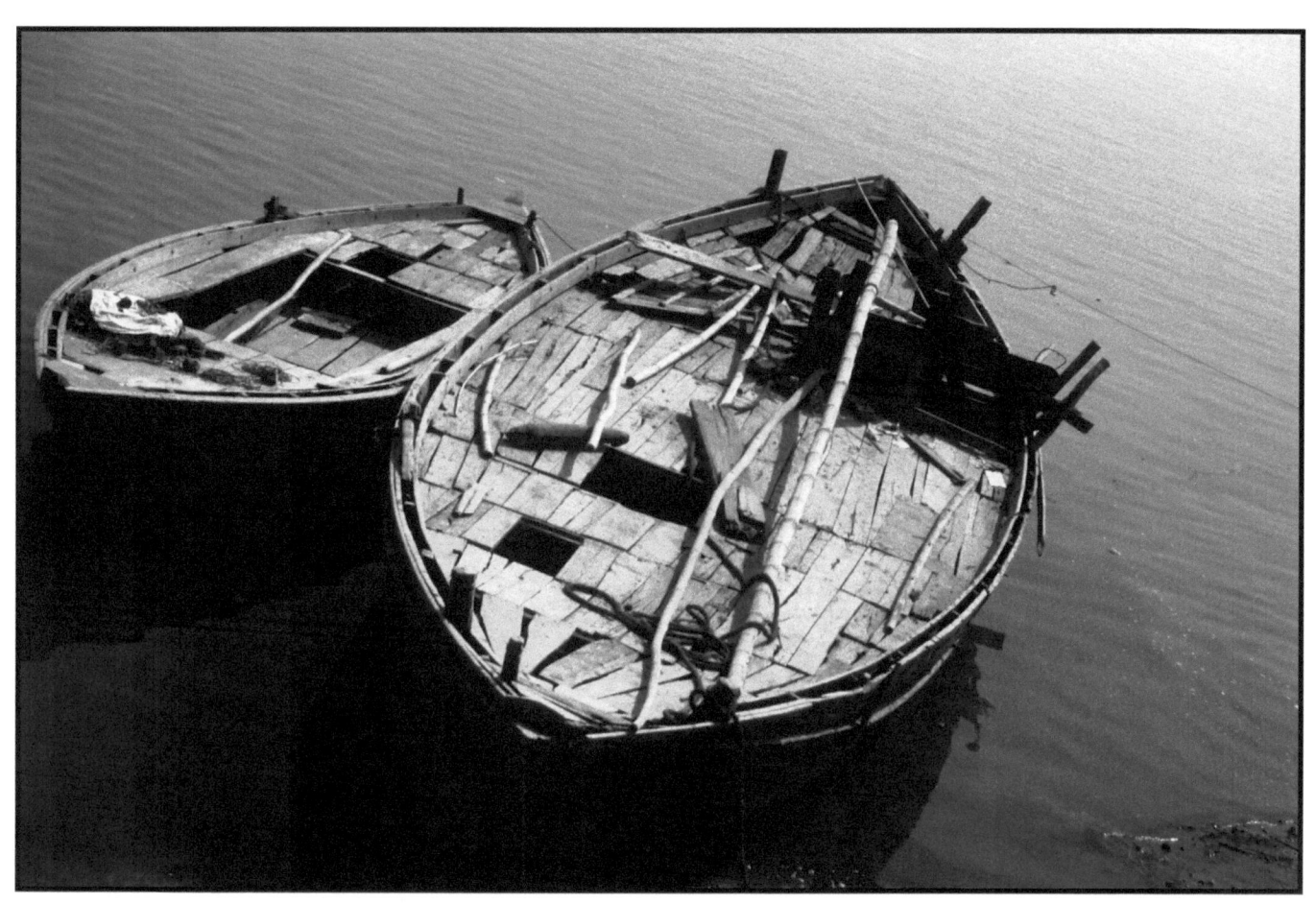

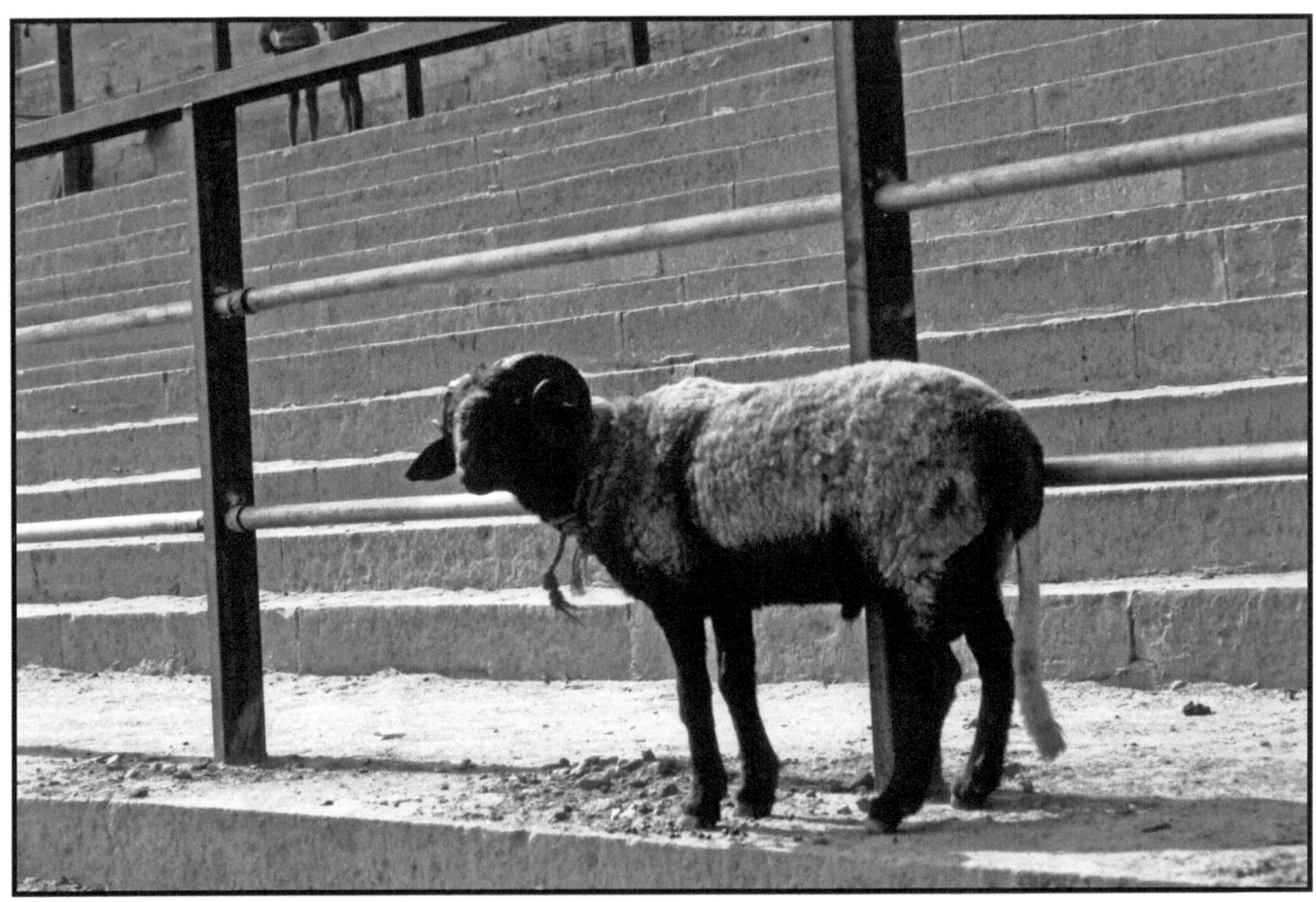

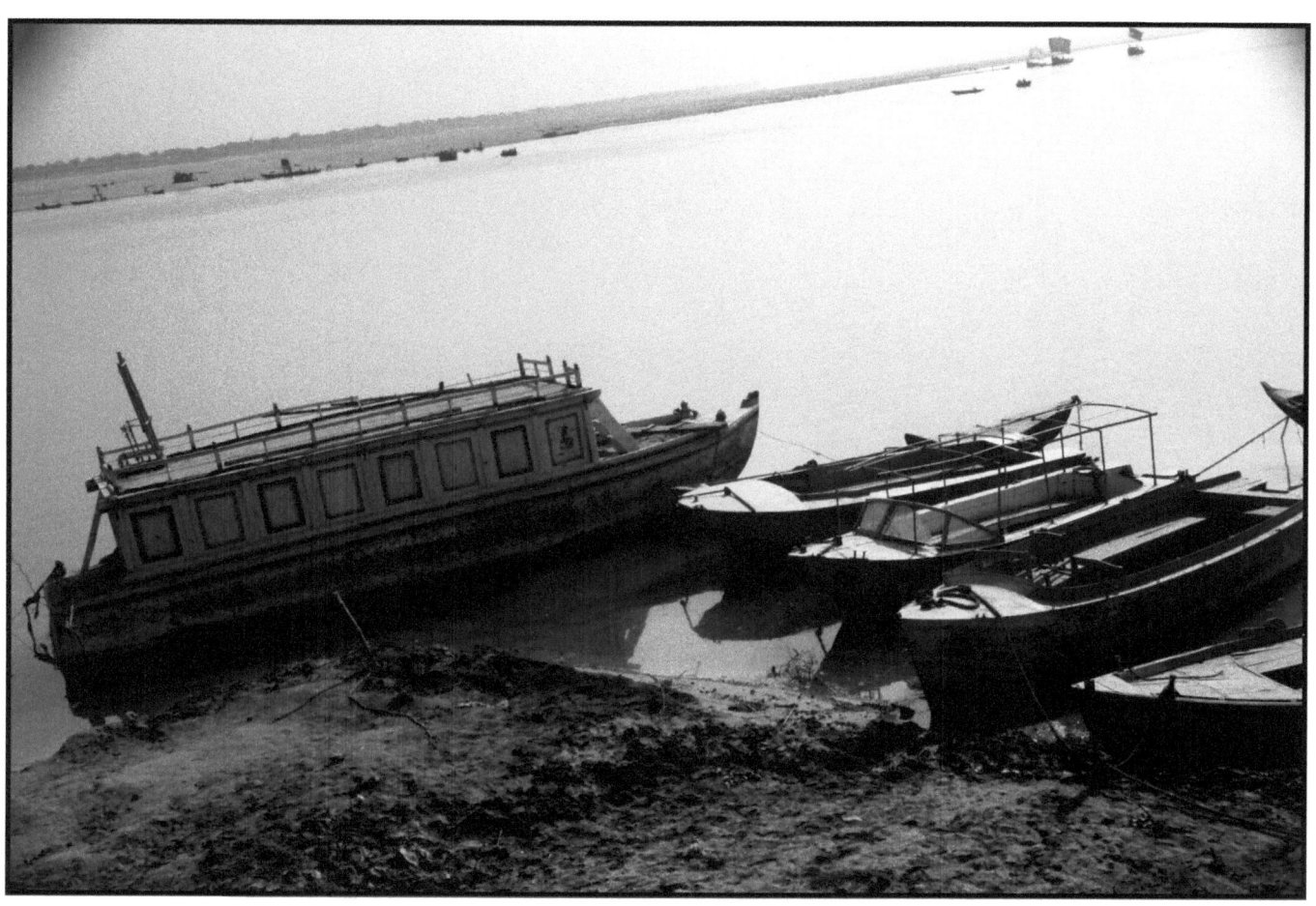

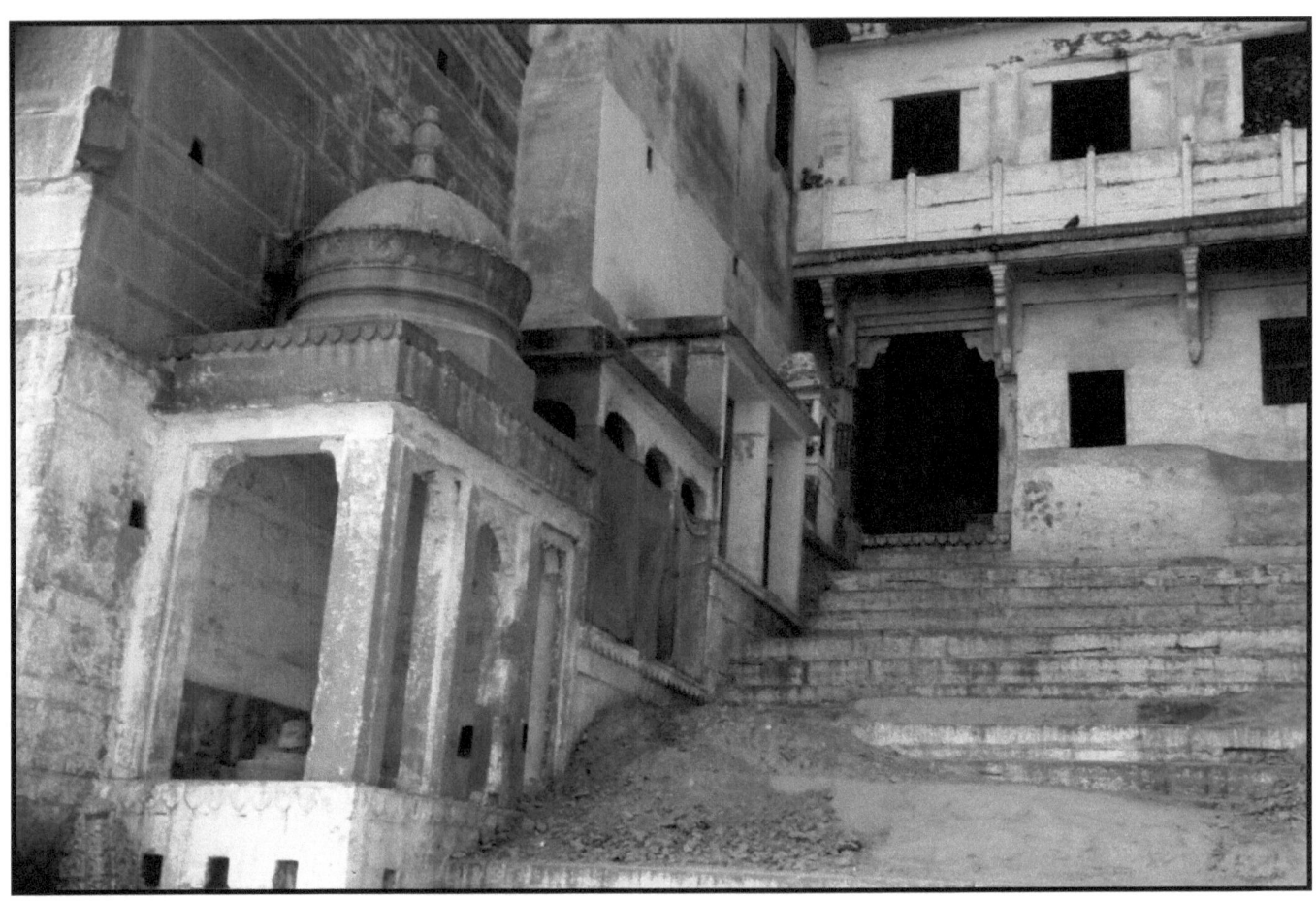

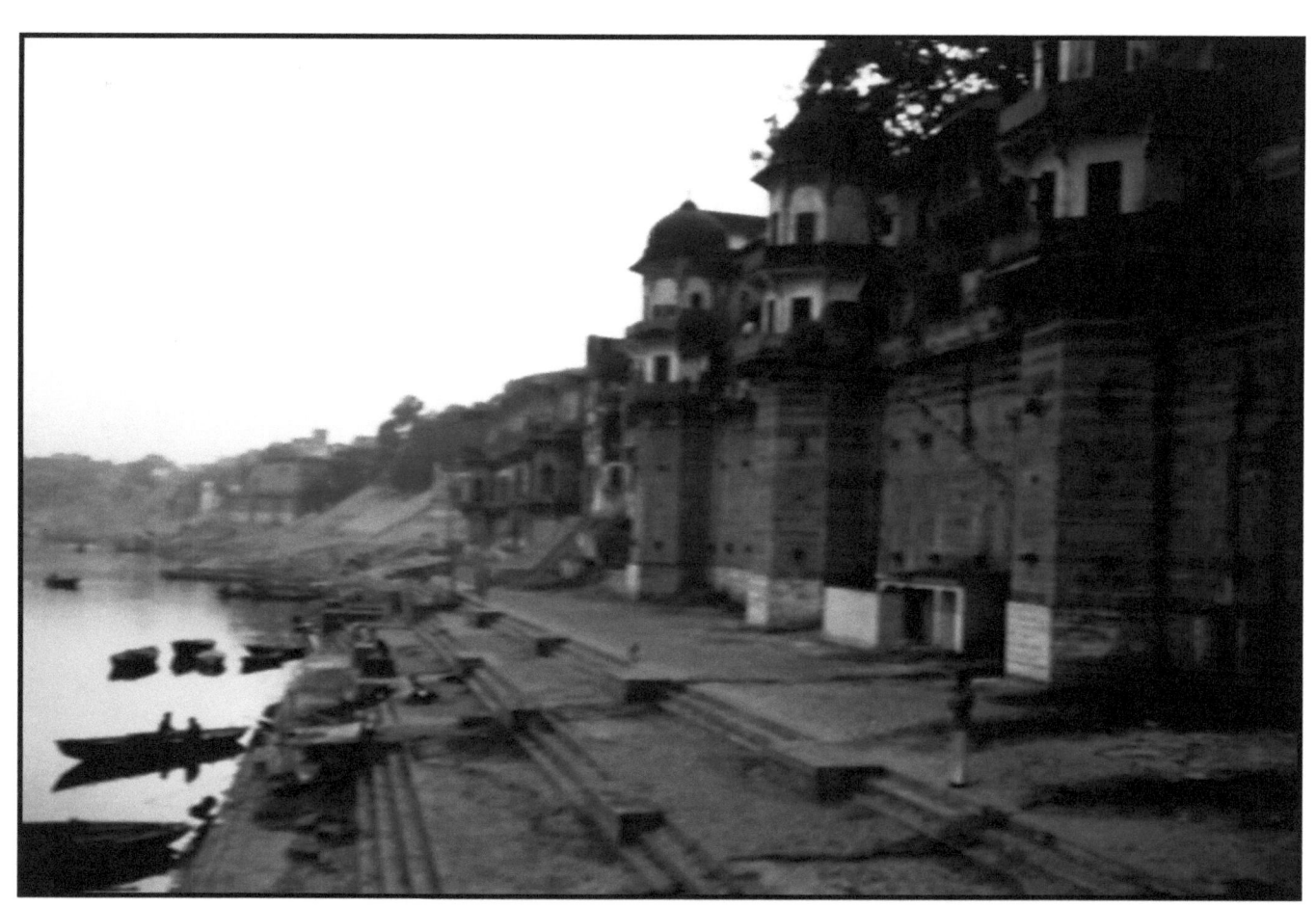

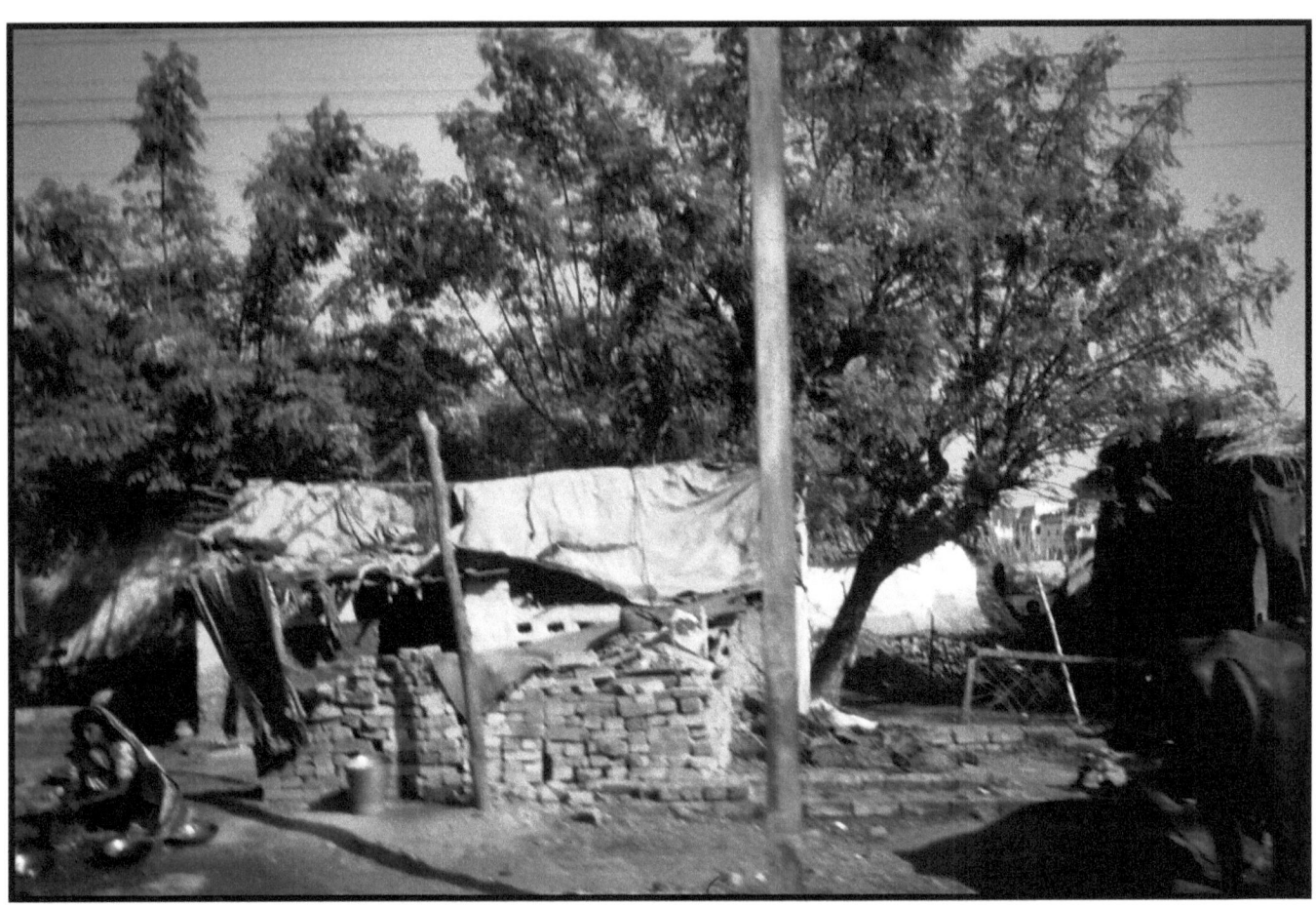

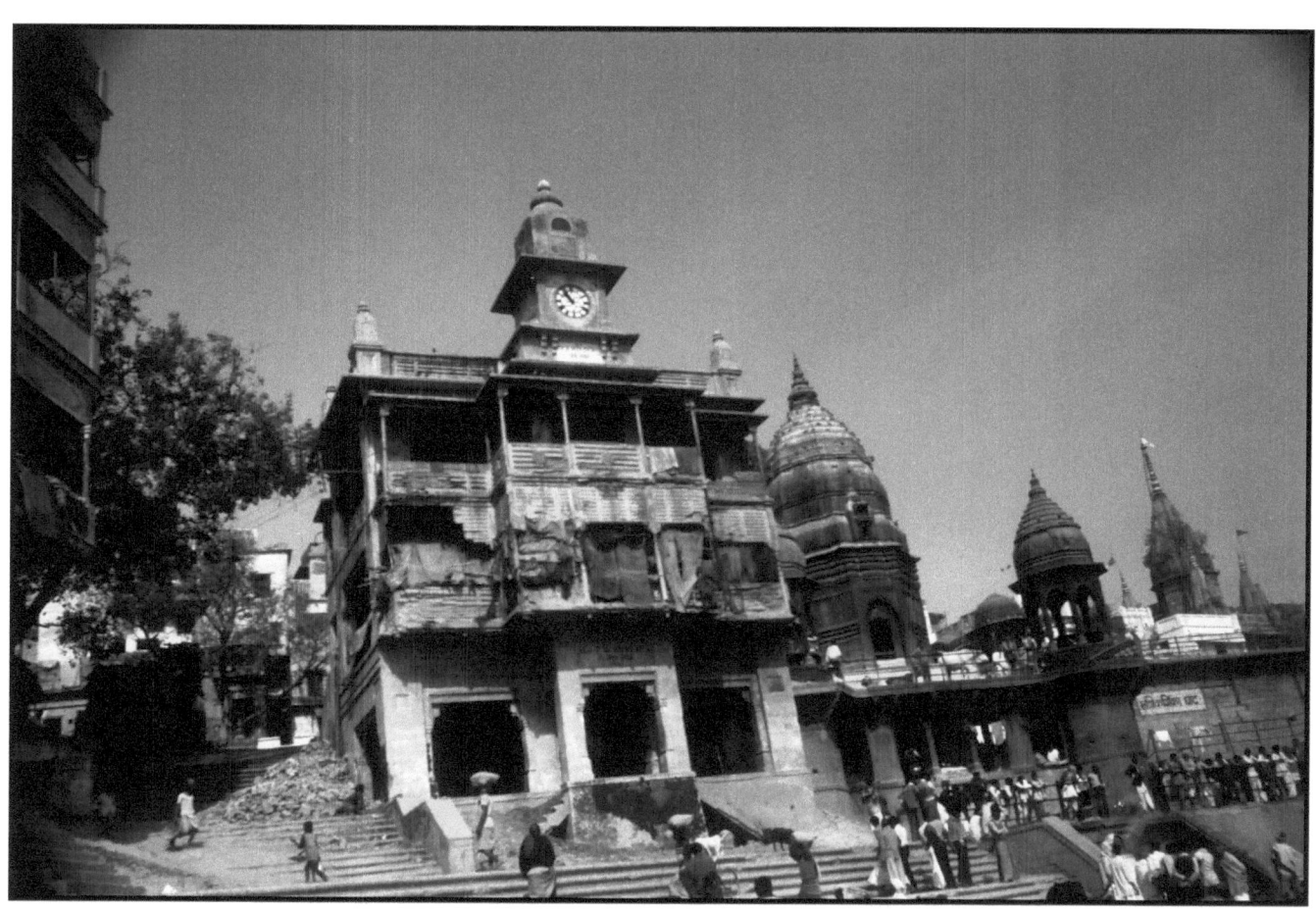